P9-EEU-042

Clashing Views
on Controversial
Social Issues

7th edition

Edited, Selected, and with Introductions by

Kurt Finsterbusch
University of Maryland

and

George McKenna
City College, City University of New York

The Dushkin Publishing Group, Inc.

To John, Alec, Ned, Laura, Maria, and Christopher, who must live these issues now and in the years ahead.

Copyright © 1992 by The Dushkin
Publishing Group, Inc., Guilford,
Connecticut 06437. All rights reserved. No
part of this book may be reproduced, stored,
or otherwise transmitted by any means—
mechanical, electronic, or otherwise—
without written permission from the
publisher.

Taking Sides ® is a registered trademark of
The Dushkin Publishing Group, Inc.

Library of Congress Catalog Card Number:
91–76395

Manufactured in the United States of America

Seventh Edition, First Printing
ISBN: 1–56134–060–X

 Printed on Recycled Paper

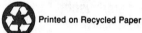

The Dushkin Publishing Group, Inc.
Sluice Dock, Guilford, CT 06437

Clashing Views
on Controversial
Social Issues

7th edition

PREFACE

The English word *fanatic* is derived from the Latin *fanum*, meaning temple. It refers to the kind of madmen often seen in the precincts of temples in ancient times, the kind presumed to be possessed by deities or demons. The term first came into English usage during the seventeenth century, when it was used to describe religious zealots. Soon after, its meaning was broadened to include a political and social context. We have come to associate the term *fanatic* with a person who acts as if his or her views were inspired, a person utterly incapable of appreciating opposing points of view. The nineteenth-century English novelist George Eliot put it precisely: "I call a man fanatical when . . . he . . . becomes unjust and unsympathetic to men who are out of his own track." A fanatic may hear, but is unable to listen. Confronted with those who disagree, a fanatic immediately vilifies opponents.

Most of us would avoid the company of fanatics, but who among us is not tempted to caricature opponents instead of listening to them? Who does not put certain topics off limits for discussion? Who does not grasp at euphemisms to avoid facing inconvenient facts? Who has not, in George Eliot's language, sometimes been "unjust and unsympathetic" to those on a different track? Who is not, at least in certain very sensitive areas, a *little* fanatical? The counterweight to fanaticism is open discussion. The difficult issues that trouble us as a society have at least two sides, and we lose as a society if we hear only one side. At the individual level, the answer to fanaticism is listening. And that is the underlying purpose of this book: to encourage its readers to listen to opposing points of view.

This book contains 40 selections presented in a pro and con format. A total of 20 different controversial social issues are debated. The sociologists, political scientists, economists, and social critics whose views are debated here make their cases vigorously. In order to effectively read each selection, analyze the points raised, debate the basic assumptions and values of each position, in other words, in order to think critically about what you are reading, you will first have to give each side a sympathetic hearing. John Stuart Mill, the nineteenth-century British philosopher, noted that the majority is not doing the minority a favor by listening to its views; it is doing *itself* a favor. By listening to contrasting points of view, we strengthen our own. In some cases we change our viewpoint completely. But in most cases, we either incorporate some elements of the opposing view—thus making our own richer—or else learn how to answer the objections to our viewpoint. Either way, we gain from the experience.

Organization of the book Each issue has an issue *introduction*, which sets the stage for the debate as it is argued in the YES and NO selections. Each issue concludes with a *postscript* that makes some final observations and points the way to other questions related to the issue. In reading the issue and forming your own opinions you should not feel confined to adopt one or the other of the positions presented. There are positions in between the given views or totally outside them, and the *suggestions for further reading* that appear in each issue postscript should help you find resources to continue your study of the subject. At the back of the book is a listing of all the *contributors to this volume*, which will give you information on the social scientists whose views are debated here.

Changes to this edition This new edition has been significantly updated. There are 11 completely new issues: *Does "Multiculturalism" Debase the Curriculum?* (Issue 1); *Has Individualism Become Excessive?* (Issue 3); *Is Feminism a Harmful Ideology?* (Issue 4); *Would a "Mommy Track" Benefit Employed Women?* (Issue 5); *Is Sexual Harassment a Pervasive Problem in America?* (Issue 6); *Should Traditional Families Be Preserved?* (Issue 7); *Is Black Self-Help the Solution to Racial Inequality?* (Issue 10); *Helping the Homeless: Do We Need More Government Regulation?* (Issue 12); *Does the Breakup of Communism Show the Success of Capitalism?* (Issue 15); *Does Population Growth Threaten Humanity?* (Issue 19); and *Is America's Socioeconomic System Breaking Down?* (Issue 20). Although Issue 4 is new, the NO reading has been retained from an issue that appeared in the previous edition because of its effectiveness. The YES reading in Issue 11 and the YES and NO readings in issues 13 and 14 have all been updated. The issues that were dropped from the previous edition were done so on the recommendation of professors who let us know what worked and what could be improved. In all, there are 26 new readings. Wherever appropriate, new introductions and postscripts have been provided.

A word to the instructor An *Instructor's Manual with Test Questions* (multiple-choice and essay) is available through the publisher. A general guidebook, called *Using Taking Sides in the Classroom*, which discusses methods and techniques for integrating the pro/con approach into any classroom setting, is also available.

Acknowledgments We received many helpful comments and suggestions from our friends and readers across the United States and Canada. Their suggestions have markedly enhanced the quality of this edition of *Taking Sides* and are reflected in the new issues and the updated selections.

Our thanks go to those who responded with suggestions for this edition:

Vicki Abt
Pennsylvania State University,
Ogontz

Donald F. Anspach
University of Southern Maine

Bret L. Billet
Wartburg College

Francis Boylston
Vanier College

Kris R. Clarkson
Southern Vermont College

Timothy Curry
Ohio State University

Richard Davin
Chaffey College

Gene Defelice
Purdue University, Calumet

Rich Feller
Colorado State University

Thomas J. Gerschick
University of Michigan

Susan L. Greenwood
University of Maine

Scott Grills
Camrose Lutheran University
   College

Charles L. Harper
Creighton University

Dee Wood Harper
Loyola University, New Orleans

Jean Humphreys
Dallas Baptist University

Robert Wm. Jolly, Jr.
Seton Hall University

Stan Knapp
Florida State University

Mehrdad Mashayekhi
St. Mary's College of Maryland

Jim A. Maynard
Georgia Southern University

Hugh Miller
University of Wisconsin, Green Bay

Cyndy Moniz
Plymouth State College

Louise Murray
Drew University

Patricia A. Murray
Salve Regina–The Newport College

Jack Niemonen
University of South Dakota

Albert Nissman
Rider College

Richard L. Ogmundson
University of Victoria

Robert G. Parr
Cedarville College

Fred L. Pincus
University of Maryland, Baltimore
   County

Lucille Pulitzer
State University of New York at
   Albany

Rebecca S. Riehm
Jefferson Community College

Kathleen Maurer Smith
Molloy College

Linda Stafford
University of Akron

Wendi J. Strickland
Georgia Southern University

Bahram Tavakolian
Denison University

Roger D. Thompson
University of Tennessee,
   Chattanooga

Carol A. Whitehurst
Humboldt State University

PREFACE

We also wish to acknowledge the encouragement and support given to this project over the years by Rick Connelly, president of The Dushkin Publishing Group, Inc. We are grateful as well to Mimi Egan, program manager for the Taking Sides series. Finally, we thank our families for their patience and understanding during the period in which we prepared this book.

Kurt Finsterbusch
College Park, MD

George McKenna
New York City

CONTENTS IN BRIEF

PART 1   **SOCIALIZATION AND VALUES**   1
Issue 1.   Does "Multiculturalism" Debase the Curriculum?   2
Issue 2.   Are Liberal Values Propagated by the News Media?   20
Issue 3.   Has Individualism Become Excessive?   36

PART 2   **SEX ROLES AND THE FAMILY**   57
Issue 4.   Is Feminism a Harmful Ideology?   58
Issue 5.   Would a "Mommy Track" Benefit Employed Women?   76
Issue 6.   Is Sexual Harrassment a Pervasive Problem in
              America?   90
Issue 7.   Should Traditional Families Be Preserved?   104

PART 3   **STRATIFICATION AND INEQUALITY**   121
Issue 8.   Is Economic Inequality Beneficial to Society?   122
Issue 9.   Does "Lower-Class" Culture Perpetuate Poverty?   148
Issue 10.   Is Black Self-Help the Solution to Racial Inequality?   164
Issue 11.   Is Affirmative Action Reverse Discrimination?   182
Issue 12.   Helping the Homeless: Do We Need More Government
              Regulation?   196

PART 4   **POLITICAL ECONOMY**   219
Issue 13.   Is Government Dominated by Big Business?   220
Issue 14.   Does Welfare Do More Harm Than Good?   246
Issue 15.   Does the Breakup of Communism Show the Success of
              Capitalism?   262

PART 5   **CRIME AND SOCIAL CONTROL**   279
Issue 16.   Is Street Crime More Harmful Than White-Collar
              Crime?   280
Issue 17.   Should Drugs Be Legalized?   298
Issue 18.   Is Incapacitation the Answer to the Crime Problem?   316

PART 6   **THE FUTURE: POPULATION/ENVIRONMENT/
              SOCIETY**   335
Issue 19.   Does Population Growth Threaten Humanity?   336
Issue 20.   Is America's Socioeconomic System Breaking Down?   354

CONTENTS

Preface   i

Introduction   xiv

PART 1   SOCIALIZATION AND VALUES   1

ISSUE 1. Does "Multiculturalism" Debase the Curriculum?   2

YES: Dinesh D'Souza, from "The Visigoths in Tweed," *Forbes*   4

NO: Troy Duster, from "They're Taking Over! and Other Myths About
Race on Campus," *Mother Jones*   12

Dinesh D'Souza, a research fellow at the American Enterprise Institute,
argues that poorly conceived attempts by many colleges to change their
curriculums by inserting minority and Third World studies have distorted
and politicized higher education in the United States. Professor of sociology
Troy Duster applauds the changes made by colleges and universities to
accommodate today's diverse student body.

ISSUE 2. Are Liberal Values Propagated by the News Media?   20

YES: William A. Rusher, from *The Coming Battle for the Media*   22

NO: Edward S. Herman and Noam Chomsky, from "Propaganda
Mill," *The Progressive*   28

William A. Rusher, a media analyst and former publisher of the *National
Review,* argues that the media are biased against conservatives and that news
coverage promotes liberal opinions. Professors Edward S. Herman and
Noam Chomsky critique the mass media from the perspective of the left and
find the media to be a "propaganda mill" in the service of the wealthy and
powerful.

ISSUE 3. Has Individualism Become Excessive?   36

YES: Robert N. Bellah et al., from *Habits of the Heart: Individualism
and Commitment in American Life*   38

NO: Henry Fairlie, from *The Spoiled Child of the Western World: The
Miscarriage of the American Idea in Our Time*   47

Sociologist Robert N. Bellah and his associates argue that the tendency of Americans has been to become absorbed in the self at the expense of transcendent values and the good of the community. British commentator Henry Fairlie suggests that the critics of "consumerism" fail to appreciate the extraordinary degree of freedom enjoyed by modern "mass man."

PART 2 SEX ROLES AND THE FAMILY   57

ISSUE 4. Is Feminism a Harmful Ideology?   58
YES: Michael Levin, from *Feminism and Freedom*   60
NO: Marilyn French, from *Beyond Power*   68

Professor of philosophy Michael Levin faults feminism for trying to impose an inappropriate equality on men and women that conflicts with basic biological differences between the sexes. Novelist and literary scholar Marilyn French advocates both equality between the sexes and the transformation of existing patriarchal structures to elevate feminine values to the same level as masculine values.

ISSUE 5. Would a "Mommy Track" Benefit Employed Women?   76
YES: Felice N. Schwartz, from "Management Women and the New Facts of Life," *Harvard Business Review*   78
NO: Barbara Ehrenreich and Deirdre English, from "Blowing the Whistle on the 'Mommy Track,' " *Ms.*   85

Felice N. Schwartz, president and founder of Catalyst, an organization that advises corporations on the development of women leaders, argues that some women are truly career minded and should be treated just as men are in terms of both demands and opportunities. However, for other women who are not so inclined, corporations should give them a less demanding path with fewer opportunities in order to facilitate their family lives. Journalists Barbara Ehrenreich and Deirdre English attack Schwartz's suggestion for a less demanding and less rewarding second path as unwarranted not only because Schwartz has no empirical evidence for her premises but also because her suggestion seems to be a justification for not treating women equally.

ISSUE 6. Is Sexual Harassment a Pervasive Problem in America?   90

YES: Catharine R. Stimpson, from "Over-Reaching: Sexual
Harassment and Education," *Initiatives*   92

NO: Gretchen Morgenson, from "May I Have the Pleasure," *National
Review*   97

Catharine R. Stimpson, graduate dean at Rutgers University, argues that
sexual harassment is a form of male domination in America and that the real
problem is not wrongful accusations of harassment but the refusal of the
wronged to file complaints. Gretchen Morgenson, senior editor of *Forbes*
magazine, argues that the notion of pervasive sexual harassment in the
workplace is largely the product of hype by an "anti-harassment industry"
and its supporters.

ISSUE 7. Should Traditional Families Be Preserved?   104

YES: David Popenoe, from "Breakup of the Family: Can We Reverse
the Trend?" *USA Today Magazine* (a publication of the Society for the
Advancement of Education)   106

NO: Judith Stacey, from *Brave New Families: Stories of Domestic
Upheaval in Late Twentieth Century America*   112

Sociologist David Popenoe decries the demise of the traditional nuclear
family, explains its causes, and recommends corrective actions. Sociologist
Judith Stacey argues that the falsely labeled traditional family with the wife
confined to the home is not an option for many women and is not the
preferred family practice for a majority of women.

PART 3   STRATIFICATION AND INEQUALITY   121

ISSUE 8. Is Economic Inequality Beneficial to Society?   122

YES: George Gilder, from *Wealth and Poverty*   124

NO: William Ryan, from *Equality*   136

Social critic George Gilder praises the American political economy that
provides so many incentives for people to get ahead and make money. He
maintains that the economy is dynamic and that all classes of people benefit.
Professor of psychology William Ryan contends that income inequalities in
America are excessive and immoral because they vastly exceed differences of
merit and result in tremendous hardships for the poor.

ISSUE 9. Does "Lower-Class" Culture Perpetuate Poverty?   **148**

YES: Edward Banfield, from *The Unheavenly City*   **150**

NO: William Ryan, from *Blaming the Victim*   **155**

Sociologist Edward Banfield suggests that it is the cultural outlook of the poor that tends to keep them in poverty. Professor of psychology William Ryan responds that attacking the culture of the poor is a form of "blaming the victims" for the conditions that surround them.

ISSUE 10. Is Black Self-Help the Solution to Racial Inequality?   **164**

YES: Glenn C. Loury, from "A Prescription for Black Progress," *The Christian Century*   **166**

NO: John E. Jacob, from "The Future of Black America," *Vital Speeches of the Day*   **173**

Professor of political economy Glenn C. Loury contends that government programs aimed at relieving black poverty often become job programs for middle-class professionals, and he argues that, historically, self-help has been the key to black progress. National Urban League president John E. Jacob argues that the notion of blacks pulling themselves out of poverty by their own bootstraps is a myth without basis in fact or in history.

ISSUE 11. Is Affirmative Action Reverse Discrimination?   **182**

YES: Shelby Steele, from *The Content of Our Character*   **184**

NO: Herman Schwartz, from "In Defense of Affirmative Action," *Dissent*   **189**

Associate professor of English Shelby Steele contends that instead of solving racial inequality problems, affirmative action mandates have generated racial discrimination in reverse. Professor of law Herman Schwartz argues that we must somehow undo the cruel consequences of racism that still plague our society and its victims.

ISSUE 12. Helping the Homeless: Do We Need More Government Regulation?   **196**

YES: Peter Dreier and Richard Appelbaum, from "American Nightmare: Homelessness," *Challenge*   **198**

NO: William Tucker, from "How Housing Regulations Cause
Homelessness," *The Public Interest*   **207**

Peter Dreier, a housing authority administrator, and sociologist Richard
Appelbaum explain homelessness as largely due to skyrocketing housing
prices and federal housing cuts. The solution to the housing crisis lies not in
freeing up the market but in implementing government programs, including
subsidies. Journalist William Tucker blames the housing crisis and homelessness in large part on government policies, particularly rent control.

PART 4   POLITICAL ECONOMY   **219**

ISSUE 13. Is Government Dominated by Big Business?   **220**
YES: Thomas Byrne Edsall, from *The New Politics of Inequality: How
Political Power Shapes Economic Policy*   **222**
NO: David Vogel, from *Fluctuating Fortunes: The Political Power of
Business in America*   **233**

Political reporter Thomas Byrne Edsall argues that the power of big business
is stronger than ever because of the increasing political sophistication of big
business coupled with the breakdown of political parties. Professor of
business administration David Vogel contends that the power of business
fluctuates with the times and is currently being kept in check by other forces
in U.S. society.

ISSUE 14. Does Welfare Do More Harm Than Good?   **246**
YES: Murray Weidenbaum, from "Beyond Handouts," *Across the
Board*   **248**
NO: Theodore R. Marmor, Jerry L. Mashaw, and Philip L. Harvey,
from *America's Misunderstood Welfare State: Persistent Myths,
Enduring Realities*   **253**

Economist Murray Weidenbaum argues that the extensive system of welfare
set up during the 1960s and early 1970s has mired the poor in dependency,
making their condition worse, not better. Social analysts Theodore R.
Marmor, Jerry L. Mashaw, and Philip L. Harvey contend that the American
welfare state has been widely misunderstood by its critics and that conservative "reforms" will only increase the misery of the poor.

ISSUE 15. Does the Breakup of Communism Show the Success of Capitalism?   262

YES: **Milton Friedman,** from "Four Steps to Freedom," *National Review*   264

NO: **Robert Pollin and Alexander Cockburn,** from "The World, the Free Market and the Left," *The Nation*   268

Economist Milton Friedman contends that the countries newly liberated from communist dictatorships can emerge from economic ruin by adopting laissez-faire capitalism. Economist Robert Pollin and Alexander Cockburn, columnist for *The Nation*, argue that the collapse of Soviet communism does not invalidate the role of socialist planning as an essential tool for broadening democracy and making the economy serve human needs.

PART 5 CRIME AND SOCIAL CONTROL   279

ISSUE 16. Is Street Crime More Harmful Than White-Collar Crime?   280

YES: **John J. DiIulio, Jr.,** from "The Impact of Inner-City Crime," *The Public Interest*   282

NO: **Jeffrey H. Reiman,** from *The Rich Get Richer and the Poor Get Prison*   288

Associate professor of politics and public affairs John J. DiIulio, Jr., analyzes the enormous harm done—especially to the urban poor and, by extension, to all of society—by street criminals and their activities. Professor of criminal justice Jeffrey H. Reiman suggests that the dangers visited on society by corporations and white-collar criminals are a great menace, and he reviews how some of those dangers threaten society.

ISSUE 17. Should Drugs Be Legalized?   298

YES: **Claudia Mills,** from "The War on Drugs: Is It Time to Surrender?" *QQ: Report from the Institute for Philosophy and Public Policy*   300

NO: **James Q. Wilson and John J. DiIulio, Jr.,** from "Crackdown," *The New Republic*   307

Claudia Mills, a writer and student of philosophy, concludes that the cost of fighting drugs—in financial and human terms—outweighs any benefits obtained from waging the battle against drugs, and she argues that they should therefore be legalized. Political scientists James Q. Wilson and John J. DiIulio, Jr., argue that drug legalization would vastly increase dangerous drug use and the social ills that are created by such usage.

ISSUE 18. Is Incapacitation the Answer to the Crime Problem?   316

YES: James Q. Wilson, from *Thinking About Crime*   318

NO: David L. Bazelon, from "Solving the Nightmare of Street Crime," *USA Today Magazine* (a publication of the Society for the Advancement of Education)   325

Criminologist and sociologist James Q. Wilson argues that imprisoning everyone convicted of a serious offense for several years would greatly reduce these crimes. He contends that incapacitation is the one policy that works. Judge David L. Bazelon discusses the moral and financial costs of the incapacitation approach and argues that society must attack the brutal social and economic conditions that are the root causes of street crime.

PART 6   THE FUTURE: POPULATION/ENVIRONMENT/ SOCIETY   335

ISSUE 19. Does Population Growth Threaten Humanity?   336

YES: Lester R. Brown, from "The New World Order," in Lester R. Brown et al., *State of the World 1991*   338

NO: Julian L. Simon, from "Population Growth Is Not Bad for Humanity," *National Forum: The Phi Kappa Phi Journal*   347

Lester R. Brown, president of the Worldwatch Institute, describes the major ways in which the environment is deteriorating due to economic and population growth. Professor of economics and business administration Julian L. Simon challenges the factual correctness of the negative effects of population growth that are cited by environmentalists.

ISSUE 20. Is America's Socioeconomic System Breaking Down?   354

YES: Werner Meyer-Larsen, from "America's Century Will End with a Whimper," *World Press Review*   356

NO: Herbert Stein, from "The U.S. Economy: A Visitors' Guide,"
The American Enterprise   **363**

Journalist Werner Meyer-Larsen describes the many problems of the American economy and society and concludes that the United States has declined considerably from its economic preeminence of three decades ago. Economist Herbert Stein puts America's economic problems in comparative perspective and concludes that the United States is still the richest country in the world and problems like the national debt are relatively small and quite manageable.

Contributors   **372**
Index   **378**

INTRODUCTION

Debating Social Issues
Kurt Finsterbusch
George McKenna

WHAT IS SOCIOLOGY?

"I have become a problem to myself," St. Augustine said. Put into a social and secular framework, St. Augustine's concern marks the starting point of sociology. We have become a problem to ourselves, and it is sociology that seeks to understand the problem and, perhaps, to find some solutions. The subject matter of sociology, then, is ourselves—people interacting with one another in groups.

Auguste Comte (1798–1857), the French mathematician and philosopher who is considered to be the father of sociology, had a vision of a well-run society based on social science knowledge. Sociologists (Comte coined the term) would discover the laws of social life and then determine how society should be structured and run. Society would not become perfect because some problems are intractable, but he believed that a society guided by scientists and other experts was the best possible society.

Unfortunately, Comte's vision was extremely naive. For most matters of state there is no one best way of structuring or doing things that sociologists can discover and recommend. Instead, sociologists debate more social issues than they resolve.

The purpose of sociology is to throw light on social issues and their relationship to the complex, confusing, and dynamic social world around us. It seeks to describe how society is organized and how individuals fit into it. But neither the organization of society nor the fit of individuals is perfect. Social disorganization is a fact of life—at least in modern, complex societies such as the one we live in. Here, perfect harmony continues to elude us, and "social problems" are endemic. The very institutions, laws, and policies that produce benefits also produce what sociologists call "unintended effects"— unintended and undesirable. The changes that please one sector of the society may displease another, or the changes that seem so indisputably healthy at first turn out to have a dark underside to them. The examples are endless. Modern urban life gives people privacy and freedom from snooping neighbors that the small town never afforded; yet, that very privacy seems to breed an uneasy sense of anonymity and loneliness. Or to take another example: Hierarchy is necessary for organizations to function efficiently, but hierarchy leads to the creation of a ruling elite. Flatten out the hierarchy, and you may achieve social equality—but at the price of confusion, incompetence, and low productivity.

This is not to say that all efforts to effect social change are ultimately futile and that the only sound view is the tragic one that concludes "nothing works." We can be realistic without falling into despair. In many respects, the human condition has improved over the centuries and has improved as a result of conscious social policies. But improvements are purchased at a price—not only a monetary price but one involving human discomfort and discontent. The job of policymakers is to balance the anticipated benefits against the probable costs.

It can never hurt policymakers to know more about the society in which they work or the social issues they confront. That, broadly speaking, is the purpose of sociology. It is what this book is about. This volume examines social issues that are central to the study of sociology.

SOCIALIZATION AND VALUES

A common value system is the major mechanism for integrating a society, so it is essential that young people understand the roots of their society's value system. But it is also important for young people to understand and appreciate other cultures, lest they fall into the kind of narrowness and ethnocentrism that prevents society from adapting to change. These are the concerns that underlie the debate in Issue 1, with Dinesh D'Souza arguing that "multicultural" studies, at least as they are envisaged by their promoters, are distorting and trivializing college curricula and Troy Duster insisting that multiculturalism is essential in today's world. Issue 2 switches to another socializing system, the media. The debate here is over whether or not the media, on average, are basically conservative, and teach compliance with the existing arrangements of society, or liberal, and act as social critics. William Rusher develops an argument from a right-wing viewpoint, while Edward Herman and Noam Chomsky debate this issue from a leftist perspective. Cultural values are also at issue in the debate over community versus the individual in contemporary America. Has American individualism, in the sense of self-seeking, become excessive lately? Or is American individualism a vital element of American self-respect? Robert Bellah et al. and Henry Fairlie debate the topic of individualism in Issue 3.

SEX ROLES AND THE FAMILY

An area of tremendous value change in the last several decades is sex roles and the family. Women in large numbers have rejected major aspects of their traditional sex roles and family roles while remaining strongly committed to much of the mother role and to many feminine characteristics. In fact, on these issues women are deeply divided. The ones who seek the most change identify themselves as feminists, and they have been in the forefront of the modern women's movement. Now a debate is raging as to whether or not the feminist cause really helps women. In Issue 4, Michael Levin attacks feminism as intellectually unsound and morally bankrupt. Feminist Marilyn French identifies positive changes that feminists have accomplished and many changes that are still needed. Issue 5 is more concrete. Would a "mommy track"—a special career track permitting working women with dependent children to spend more time with them in return for a slower pace of advancement—benefit women or set back their progress toward equality in the workplace? Felice Schwartz promotes this form of work arrangement, while Barbara Ehrenreich and Deirdre English consider it unfounded and dangerous to women's interests. Issue 6 is an issue that had been smoldering for years before it finally burst into the headlines with the Clarence Thomas–Anita Hill controversy in the fall of 1991. Is sexual harassment a pervasive problem in America? Catharine Stimpson says that it is (she discusses it in the area she knows best, academia), while Gretchen Morgenson suggests that the extent of genuine sexual harassment has been greatly exaggerated by self-serving interest groups. Issue 7 is another issue much debated by feminists and their critics: Should traditional families be preserved? David Popenoe is deeply concerned about the decline of the traditional family, while Judith Stacey thinks that such concern amounts to little more than nostalgia for a bygone era.

STRATIFICATION AND INEQUALITY

Issue 8 centers around a perennial sociological debate about whether or not economic inequality is beneficial (functional) to society. George Gilder claims that it is and William Ryan argues that inequalities should be greatly reduced. Closely related to this debate is the issue of why the poor are poor. The "culture of poverty" thesis maintains that most long-term poverty in America is the result of a culture that is all too common among the poor. The implication is that those who always seek immediate material gratification will not climb out of poverty, even if they are helped by welfare and social programs. Others see most of the poor as victims of adverse conditions; they ridicule the culture of poverty thesis as a way of "blaming the victim." Issue 9 offers a clear-cut exchange on this issue, with Edward Banfield saying yes to the question of whether or not "lower-class" culture perpetuates poverty and William Ryan saying no.

The next two issues deal with lively debates that have divided the African American community in recent years: black self-help and affirmative action. Glenn Loury, who rose from a Chicago ghetto and became a professor at Harvard's prestigious Kennedy School, argues in Issue 10 that blacks must learn to do more for themselves instead of always turning to government for help, while National Urban League president John Jacob claims that the "bootstrap" approach does not work "when you're talking to people who don't have boots." Then there is the controversy over affirmative action or racial quotas. Is equality promoted or undermined by such policies? Shelby Steele and Herman Schwartz take opposing sides on this question in Issue 11. The final issue under the topic of stratification deals with those closest to the bottom of American society: the homeless. What is the best way to help these people? In Issue 12, Peter Dreier and Richard Appelbaum argue that the American government must shift its national spending priorities and take housing out of the speculative market, while William Tucker sees the solution mainly at the local level and suggests that the government do away with rent control policies.

POLITICAL ECONOMY

Sociologists study not only the poor, the workers, and the victims of discrimination, but also those at the top of society—those who occupy what the late sociologist C. Wright Mills used to call "the command posts." The question is whether the "pluralist" model or the "power elite" model is the one that best fits the facts in America. Does a single power elite rule the United States or do many groups contend for power and influence so that the political process is accessible to all? In Issue 13, Thomas Byrne Edsall argues that the business elite have a dominating influence in government decisions and that no other group has nearly as much power, while David Vogel contends that the political power ebbs and flows with time and conditions (and is now in an ebb period).

The United States is a capitalist welfare state. The economy is based on private enterprise and the relatively free markets of capitalism. The state, however, is also committed to the welfare of those who are not provided for by the labor market. In Issue 14, Murray Weidenbaum claims that many welfare programs of the "Great Society" have mired people in dependency and should be abandoned, while Theodore Marmor, Jerry Mashaw, and Philip Harvey argue that the conservative case against welfare "dependency" is ill-founded and can only produce greater degradation among America's poor.

The final political economy issue examines the question of state intervention on a broader canvas. The issue, thrust upon us by the collapse of communism in the world, is whether or not socialism is a failed system that belongs in the dustbin of history. In Issue 15, Milton Friedman argues that it is, while Robert Pollin and Alexander Cockburn insist that it is capitalism, not socialism, that causes the most hardship for the peoples of the world.

CRIME AND SOCIAL CONTROL

Crime is interesting to sociologists because crimes are those activities that society makes illegal and will use force to stop. Why are some acts made illegal and others that may be more harmful not made illegal? Surveys indicate that concern about crime is extremely high in America. Is the fear of crime, however, rightly placed? Americans fear mainly street crime, but Jeffrey

Reiman argues in Issue 16 that corporate crimes cause far more death, harm, and financial loss to Americans than street crime. In contrast, John DiIulio points out the great harm done by street criminals, even to the point of social disintegration in some poor neighborhoods. Much of the harm that he describes is related to the illegal drug trade, which is having such bad consequences that some people are seriously talking about legalizing drugs in order to kill the illegal drug business. Claudia Mills argues this view in Issue 17, while James Wilson and John DiIulio argue that legalization would greatly expand the use of dangerous drugs and the personal tragedies and social costs resulting therefrom. Finally, we examine whether deterrence or tough sentencing of criminals will stop crime. The debate is whether the American society should focus on deterrence by meting out sentencing on a tougher and more uniform basis, or whether the emphasis should be on rehabilitating criminals and eliminating the social conditions that breed crime. These alternatives are explored in the debate between James Wilson and David Bazelon in Issue 18.

THE WORLD AND THE FUTURE

Many social commentators speculate on "the fate of the earth." The environmentalists have their own vision of apocalypse. They foresee the human race overshooting the carrying capacity of the globe. The resulting collapse could lead to the extinction of much of the human race and the end of free societies. Population growth and increasing per capita levels of consumption, say some experts, are leading us to this catastrophe. We examine an issue that has been much debated since the ecology movement began in the late 1960s. In Issue 19, Lester Brown and Julian Simon argue over whether or not the world is really threatened by overpopulation.

The last issue in this book deals with the future of America. Werner Meyer-Larsen, a German observer, has interviewed a number of Americans, and in Issue 20, he presents his conclusion that "the American century is dragging to a close, and not a single cry of triumph can be heard." One of those he apparently did not interview is Herbert Stein. His remarks on America's condition, particularly its financial condition, come close to being the "cry of triumph" that Meyer-Larsen finds absent in the America of the 1990s.

OBJECTIVITY AND SUBJECTIVITY

The topics presented in this book range far and wide—from sexual harassment to welfare to multicultural studies. What they all have in common is that they are at once subjective and objective issues. The point deserves some discussion.

When St. Augustine said "I have become a problem to myself," he was pondering the problem of how he could remember forgetfulness. If to forget means to obliterate from memory, how can forgetfulness be remembered? It was that riddle (which need not concern us here) that set him thinking about the vast difference between physical science and humanistic investigations. "For I am not now investigating the tracts of the heavens, or measuring the distance of the stars, or trying to discover how the earth hangs in space. I am investigating myself, my memory, my mind." The distinction is between the subjective, what is "in our heads," and the objective, that which is "out there." This is a valuable distinction, but it needs to be qualified. There is a third area, the public realm, that is partly subjective and partly objective. It consists of the actions and interactions of human beings and leads to all sorts of objective happenings; yet the subjective obviously plays a role in what happens. People act on what they believe and think and feel, and their minds, in turn, are influenced by the public environment.

At its best, sociology attempts to hold together both the objective and the subjective without allowing either to overwhelm the other.

CONCLUSION

Writing in the 1950s, a period in some ways like our own, the sociologist C. Wright Mills said that Americans know a lot about their "troubles," but they cannot make the connections between seemingly personal concerns and the concerns of others in the world. If they could only learn to make those connections, they could turn their concerns into *issues*. An issue transcends the realm of the personal. According to Mills, "An issue is a public matter: some value cherished by publics is felt to be threatened. Often there is a debate about what the value really is and what it is that really threatens it."

It is not primarily personal troubles but social issues that we have tried to present in this book. The variety of topics in it can be taken as an invitation to discover what Mills called "the sociological imagination." This imagination, said Mills, "is the capacity to shift from one perspective to another—from the political to the psychological; from examination of a single family to comparative assessment of the national budgets of the world. . . . It is the capacity to range from the most impersonal and remote transformations to the most intimate features of the human self—and to see the relations between the two." This book, with a range of issues well suited to the sociological imagination, is intended to enlarge that capacity.

Richard Pawlikowski/DPG

PART 1

Socialization and Values

Sociologists recognize that a society's view of what is acceptable, or worthy, or moral, is subject to change as that society's culture evolves. The values of a society—and the social skills needed for an individual to function within that society's framework of values—can be inculcated in many ways. For example, is the study of cultures other than one's own valuable to students, or does an emphasis on multicultural studies detract from the traditional college curriculum? What role do the news media play in transmitting values, particularly political values? Are they advocates of one political view or another? What are the effects of individualism on society? Have people in America become too individualistic? These are some of the questions sociologists face in a dynamic, rapidly changing, highly industrialized society.

Does "Multiculturalism" Debase the
    Curriculum?

Are Liberal Values Propagated by the
    News Media?

Has Individualism Become Excessive?

1

ISSUE 1

Does "Multiculturalism" Debase the Curriculum?

YES: Dinesh D'Souza, from "The Visigoths in Tweed," *Forbes* (April 1, 1991)

NO: Troy Duster, from "They're Taking Over! and Other Myths About Race on Campus," *Mother Jones* (September/October 1991)

ISSUE SUMMARY

YES: Dinesh D'Souza, a research fellow at the American Enterprise Institute, argues that poorly conceived attempts by many colleges to change their curriculums by inserting minority and Third World studies have distorted and politicized higher education in the United States.
NO: Professor of sociology Troy Duster applauds the changes made by colleges and universities to accommodate today's diverse student body.

The issue of multiculturalism—what it means, what its role should be in the educational curriculum, and whether it is good or bad for the nation's youth—is of interest to sociologists because schools are one of the key agents of socialization. The courses that are taught in schools and colleges impart to society's young people the skills and values that society regards as important or essential for functioning in that society.

Multiculturalism has sparked a major controversy, especially on America's campuses. To proponents it represents a long-overdue effort to bring greater diversity into a curriculum dominated by Western white male studies. To critics it stands for the dilution and corruption of liberal arts by ideologues. Neither side seems to take much trouble to define terms. Does *multiculturalism* mean simply adding to the traditional liberal arts reading lists some authors and books outside the traditional bounds? Or is it something more involved, such as a deliberate policy of assigning books that attack Western culture, or the requirement that all students take special Third World courses, or the establishment of entire curricula in black studies? There are apples and oranges here, not to mention peaches, plums, and whatever, so the debate can get confusing.

It might help to look at this issue from a historical perspective. Thirty years ago, in the early 1960s, the usual liberal arts curriculum in the United States included courses on the classics of Western culture, plus European and American history, philosophy, and politics. It was rare for any student to read any classics of Asian or Indian literature, and there were virtually no courses—certainly no required ones—on the Third World. A few women authors, such as Jane Austen, might be assigned in literature courses, but no women's studies courses were available. Perhaps not so coincidentally, about two-thirds of the students, and a much larger majority of the faculty, were male, and, at a time when only 3 percent of American blacks completed college, the percentage of racial minorities on campus was almost infinitesimal.

Changes started in the late sixties, gathering momentum over the next two decades. Increasing numbers of blacks began entering college, and so did other racial minorities as changing immigration laws brought more Third World immigrants to U.S. shores. Women, seeing new career opportunities or simply wanting more education, also began entering college in record numbers. Colleges and universities helped to augment these numbers by establishing outreach and affirmative action programs for those student populations that were formerly underrepresented. In terms of demographics alone, then, there was bound to come a time when awkward questions would be asked about the appropriateness of Western Civilization courses for the new student body.

In addition to the civil rights and women's movements, another catalyst was at work in the late sixties: the Vietnam War. As the decade came to a close, the United States found itself bogged down in a bloody war that, to many, particularly on leading campuses in the United States, seemed to be morally atrocious. Serious questions were raised about the legitimacy not only of the war but of the United States and its moral underpinnings. Social critic Susan Sontag wrote in 1969 that American culture was "inorganic, dead, coercive, authoritarian," and full of "dehumanized individuals" and "heartless bureaucrats of death and empty affluence." Indeed, Sontag suggested, the entire culture of the West was sick: the white race "is the cancer of human history." Views such as these, not at all uncommon in the late sixties, struck a chord among many of the younger academics—under-graduates, graduate assistants, and junior professors. Today, many of those former students occupy leadership positions in the universities; they are tenured professors, department chairpersons, deans, provosts, even college presidents. Though most have probably moderated their views, the spirit of the late sixties left a deep imprint on the American university, making it more receptive than ever to demands for a liberal arts curriculum less focused on Western culture.

Multiculturalism has thus come into its own. Variants of it are being tried out in colleges and high schools across the United States. These experiments range from modest revisions of the traditional curriculum, to the establishment of full-scale curricula that systematically denigrate all things white and Western. In the following selections, Dinesh D'Souza (himself an immigrant from India) expresses worry about the way Third World studies, feminism, and black nationalism manifest themselves on U.S. campuses. Troy Duster argues that such fears are based upon myths, not facts.

3

YES   Dinesh D'Souza

THE VISIGOTHS IN TWEED

"I am a male WASP who attended and succeeded at Choate (preparatory) School, Yale College, Yale Law School and Princeton Graduate School. Slowly but surely, however, my lifelong habit of looking, listening, feeling and thinking as honestly as possible has led me to see that white, male-dominated, western European culture is the most destructive phenomenon in the known history of the planet.

"[This Western culture] is deeply hateful of life and committed to death; therefore, it is moving rapidly toward the destruction of itself and most other life forms on earth. And truly it deserves to die. . . . We have to face our own individual and collective responsibility for what is happening—our greed, brutality, indifference, militarism, racism, sexism, blindness. . . . Meanwhile, everything we have put into motion continues to endanger us more every day."

This bizarre outpouring, so reminiscent of the "confessions" from victims of Stalin's show trials, appeared in a letter to *Mother Jones* magazine and was written by a graduate of some of our finest schools. But the truth is that the speaker's anguish came not from any balanced assessment but as a consequence of exposure to the propaganda of the new barbarians who have captured the humanities, law and social science departments of so many of our universities. It should come as no surprise that many sensitive young Americans reject the system that has nurtured them. At Duke University, according to the *Wall Street Journal*, professor Frank Lentricchia in his English course shows the movie *The Godfather* to teach his students that organized crime is "a metaphor for American business as usual."

Yes, a student can still get an excellent education—among the best in the world—in computer technology and the hard sciences at American universities. But liberal arts students, including those attending Ivy League schools, are very likely to be exposed to an attempted brainwashing that deprecates Western learning and exalts a neo-Marxist ideology promoted in the name of multiculturalism. Even students who choose hard sciences must often take required courses in the humanities, where they are almost certain to be inundated with an anti-Western, anticapitalist view of the world.

From Dinesh D'Souza, "The Visigoths in Tweed," *Forbes* (April 1, 1991), pp. 81-84, 86. Adapted from Dinesh D'Souza, *Illiberal Education: The Politics of Race and Sex on Campus* (Vintage Books, 1991). Copyright © 1991 by Forbes, Inc. Reprinted by permission of *Forbes* magazine.

4

Each year American society invests $160 billion in higher education, more per student than any nation in the world except Denmark. A full 45% of this money comes from the federal, state and local governments. No one can say we are starving higher education. But what are we getting for our money, at least so far as the liberal arts are concerned?

A fair question? It might seem so, but in university circles it is considered impolite because it presumes that higher education must be accountable to the society that supports it. Many academics think of universities as intellectual enclaves, insulated from the vulgar capitalism of the larger culture.

Yet, since the academics constantly ask for more money, it seems hardly unreasonable to ask what they are doing with it. Honest answers are rarely forthcoming. The general public sometimes gets a whiff of what is going on—as when Stanford alters its core curriculum in the classics of Western civilization—but it knows very little of the systematic and comprehensive change sweeping higher education.

An academic and cultural revolution has overtaken most of our 3,535 colleges and universities. It's a revolution to which most Americans have paid little attention. It is a revolution imposed upon the students by a university elite, not one voted upon or even discussed by the society at large. It amounts, according to University of Wisconsin-Madison Chancellor Donna Shalala, to "a basic transformation of American higher education in the name of multiculturalism and diversity."

The central thrust of this "basic transformation" involves replacing traditional core curriculums—consisting of the great works of Western culture—with curriculums flavored by minority, female and Third World authors.

Here's a sample of the viewpoint represented by the new curriculum. Becky Thompson, a sociology and women's studies professor, in a teaching manual distributed by the American Sociological Association, writes: "I begin my course with the basic feminist principle that in a racist, classist and sexist society we have all swallowed oppressive ways of being, whether intentionally or not. Specifically, this means that it is not open to debate whether a white student is racist or a male student is sexist. He/she simply is."

Professors at several colleges who have resisted these regnant dogmas about race and gender have found themselves the object of denunciation and even university sanctions. Donald Kagan, dean of Yale College, says: "I was a student during the days of Joseph McCarthy, and there is less freedom now than there was then."

As in the McCarthy period, a particular group of activists has cowed the authorities and bent them to its will. After activists forcibly occupied his office, President Lattie Coor of the University of Vermont explained how he came to sign a 16-point agreement establishing, among other things, minority faculty hiring quotas. "When it became clear that the minority students with whom I had been discussing these issues wished to pursue negotiations *in the context of occupied offices* . . . I agreed to enter negotiations." As frequently happens in such cases, Coor's "negotiations" ended in a rapid capitulation by the university authorities.

At Harvard, historian Stephan Thernstrom was harangued by student activists and accused of insensitivity and bigotry. What was his crime? His course included a reading from the journals of slave owners, and his textbook gave a reasonable definition of affirmative action as "preferential treatment" for minorities. At the University of Michigan, renowned demographer Reynolds Farley was assailed in the college press for criticizing the excesses of Marcus Garvey and Malcolm X; yet the administration did not publicly come to his defense.

University leaders argue that the revolution suggested by these examples is necessary because young Americans must be taught to live in and govern a multiracial and multicultural society. Immigration from Asia and Latin America, combined with relatively high minority birth rates, is changing the complexion of America. Consequently, in the words of University of Michigan President James Duderstadt, universities must "create a model of how a more diverse and pluralistic community can work for our society."

No controversy, of course, about benign goals such as pluralism or diversity, but there is plenty of controversy about how these goals are being pursued. Although there is no longer a Western core curriculum at Mount Holyoke or Dartmouth, students at those schools must take a course in non-Western or Third World culture. Berkeley and the University of Wisconsin now insist that every undergraduate enroll in ethnic studies, making this virtually the only compulsory course at those schools.

If American students were truly exposed to the richest elements of other cultures, this could be a broadening and useful experience. A study of Chinese philosophers such as Confucius or Mencius would enrich students' understanding of how different peoples order their lives, thus giving a greater sense of pur-

pose to their own. Most likely, a taste of Indian poetry such as Rabindranath Tagore's *Gitanjali* would increase the interest of materially minded young people in the domain of the spirit. An introduction to Middle Eastern history would prepare the leaders of tomorrow to deal with the mounting challenge of Islamic culture. It would profit students to study the rise of capitalism in the Far East.

But the claims of the academic multiculturalists are largely phony. They pay little attention to the Asian or Latin American classics. Rather, the non-Western or multicultural curriculum reflects a different agenda. At Stanford, for example, Homer, Plato, Dante, Machiavelli and Locke are increasingly scarce. But often their replacements are not non-Western classics. Instead the students are offered exotic topics such as popular religion and healing in Peru, Rastafarian poetry and Andean music.

What do students learn about the world from the books they are required to read under the new multicultural rubric? At Stanford one of the non-Western works assigned is *I, Rigoberta Menchu*, subtitled "An Indian Woman in Guatemala."

The book is hardly a non-Western classic. Published in 1983, *I, Rigoberta Menchu* is the story of a young woman who is said to be a representative voice of the indigenous peasantry. Representative of Guatemalan Indian culture? In fact Rigoberta met the Venezuelan feminist to whom she narrates this story at a socialist conference in Paris, where, presumably, very few of the Third World's poor travel. Moreover, Rigoberta's political consciousness includes the adoption of such politically correct causes as feminism, homosexual rights, socialism and Marxism. By the middle of the book she is discoursing on "bourgeois youths" and

"Molotov cocktails," not the usual terminology of Indian peasants. One chapter is titled "Rigoberta Renounces Marriage and Motherhood," a norm that her tribe could not have adopted and survived.

If Rigoberta does not represent the convictions and aspirations of Guatemalan peasants, what is the source of her importance and appeal? The answer is that Rigoberta seems to provide independent Third World corroboration for Western left-wing passions and prejudices. She is a mouthpiece for a sophisticated neo-Marxist critique of Western society, all the more powerful because it seems to issue not from some embittered American academic but from a Third World native. For professors nourished on the political activism of the late 1960s and early 1970s, texts such as *I, Rigoberta Menchu* offer a welcome opportunity to attack capitalism and Western society in general in the name of teaching students about the developing world.

We learn in the introduction of *I, Rigoberta Menchu* that Rigoberta is a quadruple victim. As a person of color, she has suffered racism. As a woman, she has endured sexism. She lives in South America, which is—of course—a victim of North American colonialism. She is also an Indian, victimized by Latino culture within Latin America.

One of the most widely used textbooks in so-called multicultural courses is *Multi-Cultural Literacy*, published by Graywolf Press in St. Paul, Minn. The book ignores the *Analects* of Confucius, the *Tale of Genji*, the Upanishads and Vedas, the Koran and Islamic commentaries. It also ignores such brilliant contemporary authors as Jorge Luis Borges, V. S. Naipaul, Octavio Paz, Naguib Mahfouz and Wole Soyinka. Instead it offers 13 essays of protest, including Michele Wallace's autobiographical "Invisibility Blues" and Paula Gunn Allen's "Who Is Your Mother? The Red Roots of White Feminism."

One student I spoke with at Duke University said he would not study *Paradise Lost* because John Milton was a Eurocentric white male sexist. At the University of Michigan, a young black woman who had converted to Islam refused to believe that the prophet Muhammad owned slaves and practiced polygamy. She said she had taken courses on cultural diversity and the courses hadn't taught her that.

One of the highlights of this debate on the American campus was a passionate statement delivered a few years ago by Stanford undergraduate William King, president of the Black Student Union, who argued the benefits of the new multicultural curriculum before the faculty senate of the university. Under the old system, he said, "I was never taught . . . the fact that Socrates, Herodotus, Pythagoras and Solon studied in Egypt and acknowledged that much of their knowledge of astronomy, geometry, medicine and building came from the African civilization in and around Egypt. [I was never taught] that the Hippocratic Oath acknowledges the Greeks' 'father of medicine,' Imhotep, a black Egyptian pharaoh whom they called Aesculapius. . . . I was never informed when it was found that the 'very dark and woolly haired Moors in Spain preserved, expanded and reintroduced the classical knowledge that the Greeks had collected, which led to the 'renaissance.' . . . I read the Bible without knowing Saint Augustine looked black like me, that the Ten Commandments were almost direct copies from the 147 Negative Confessions of Egyptian initiates. . . . I didn't learn Toussaint L'Ouverture's defeat of Napoleon in Haiti directly influenced the French Revolution, or that the Iroquois Indians in America had a representative democracy which served as a model for the American system."

This statement drew wild applause and was widely quoted. The only trouble is that much of it is untrue. There is no evidence that Socrates, Pythagoras, Herodotus and Solon studied in Egypt, although Herodotus may have traveled there. Saint Augustine was born in North Africa, but his skin color is unknown, and in any case he could not have been mentioned in the Bible; he was born over 350 years after Christ. Viewing King's speech at my request, Bernard Lewis, an expert on Islamic and Middle Eastern culture at Princeton, described it as "a few scraps of truth amidst a great deal of nonsense."

Why does multicultural education, in practice, gravitate toward such myths and half-truths? To find out why, it is necessary to explore the complex web of connections that the academic revolution generates among admissions policies, life on campus and the curriculum.

American universities typically begin with the premise that in a democratic and increasingly diverse society the composition of their classes should reflect the ethnic distribution of the general population. Many schools officially seek "proportional representation," in which the percentage of applicants admitted from various racial groups roughly approximates the ratio of those groups in society at large.

Thus universities routinely admit black, Hispanic and American Indian candidates over better-qualified white and Asian American applicants. As a result of zealously pursued affirmative action programs, many selective colleges admit minority students who find it extremely difficult to meet demanding academic standards and to compete with the rest of the class. This fact is reflected in the dropout rates of blacks and Hispanics, which are more than 50% higher than those of whites and Asians. At Berkeley a study of students admitted on a preferential basis between 1978 and 1982 concluded that nearly 70% failed to graduate within five years.

For affirmative action students who stay on campus, a common strategy of dealing with the pressures of university life is to enroll in a distinctive minority organization. Among such organizations at Cornell University are Lesbian, Gay & Bisexual Coalition; La Asociacion Latina; National Society of Black Engineers; Society of Minority Hoteliers; Black Students United; and Simba Washanga.

Although the university brochures at Cornell and elsewhere continue to praise integration and close interaction among students from different backgrounds, the policies practiced at these schools actually encourage segregation. Stanford, for example, has "ethnic theme houses" such as the African house called Ujaama. And President Donald Kennedy has said that one of his educational objectives is to "support and strengthen ethnic theme houses." Such houses make it easier for some minority students to feel comfortable but help to create a kind of academic apartheid.

The University of Pennsylvania has funded a black yearbook, even though only 6% of the student body is black and all other groups appeared in the general yearbook. Vassar, Dartmouth and the University of Illinois have allowed separate graduation activities and ceremonies for minority students. California State University at Sacramento has just established an official "college within a college" for blacks.

Overt racism is relatively rare at most campuses, yet minorities are told that bigotry operates in subtle forms such as baleful looks, uncorrected stereotypes and "institutional racism"—defined as the underrepresentation of blacks and Hispanics among university trustees, administrators and faculty.

Other groups such as feminists and homosexuals typically get into the game, claiming their own varieties of victim status. As Harvard political scientist Harvey Mansfield bluntly puts it, "White students must admit their guilt so that minority students do not have to admit their incapacity."

Even though universities regularly accede to the political demands of victim groups, their appeasement gestures do not help black and Hispanic students get a genuine liberal arts education. They do the opposite, giving the apologists of the new academic orthodoxy a convenient excuse when students admitted on a preferential basis fail to meet academic standards. At this point student activists and administrators often blame the curriculum. They argue that it reflects a "white male perspective" that systematically depreciates the views and achievements of other cultures, minorities, women and homosexuals.

With this argument, many minority students can now explain why they had such a hard time with Milton in the English department, Publius in political science and Heisenberg in physics. Those men reflected white male aesthetics, philosophy and science. Obviously, nonwhite students would fare much better if the university created more black or Latino or Third World courses, the argument goes. This epiphany leads to a spate of demands: Abolish the Western classics, establish new departments such as Afro-American Studies and Women's Studies, hire minority faculty to offer distinctive black and Hispanic "perspectives."

Multicultural or non-Western education on campus frequently glamorizes Third World cultures and omits inconvenient facts about them. In fact, several non-Western cultures are caste-based or tribal, and often disregard norms of racial equality. In many of them feminism is virtually nonexistent, as indicated by such practices as dowries, widow-burning and genital mutilation; and homosexuality is sometimes regarded as a crime or mental disorder requiring punishment. These nasty aspects of the non-Western cultures are rarely mentioned in the new courses. Indeed, Bernard Lewis of Princeton argues that while slavery and the subjugation of women have been practiced by all known civilizations, the West at least has an active and effective movement for the abolition of such evils.

Who is behind this academic revolution, this contrived multiculturalism? The new curriculum directly serves the purposes of a newly ascendant generation of young professors, weaned in the protest culture of the late 1960s and early 1970s. In a frank comment, Jay Parini, who teaches English at Middlebury College, writes, "After the Vietnam War, a lot of us didn't just crawl back into our library cubicles. We stepped into academic positions. . . . Now we have tenure, and the work of reshaping the university has begun in earnest."

The goal that Parini and others like him pursue is the transformation of the college classroom from a place of learning to a laboratory of indoctrination for social change. Not long ago most colleges required that students learn the basics of the physical sciences and mathematics, the rudiments of economics and finance, and the fundamental principles of American history and government. Studies by the National Endowment for the Humanities show that this coherence has disappeared from the curriculum. As a result, most universities are now graduating students who are scientifically and culturally impoverished, if not illiterate.

At the University of Pennsylvania, Houston Baker, one of the most prominent black academics in the country, denounces reading and writing as oppressive technologies and celebrates such examples of oral culture as the rap group N.W.A. (Niggers With Attitudes). One of the group's songs is about the desirability of killing policemen. Alison Jaggar, who teaches women's studies at the University of Colorado, denounces the traditional nuclear family as a "cornerstone of women's oppression" and anticipates scientific advances enabling men to carry fetuses in their bodies so that child-bearing responsibilities can be shared between the sexes. Duke professor Eve Sedgwick's scholarship is devoted to unmasking what she terms the heterosexual bias in Western culture, a project that she pursues through papers such as "Jane Austen and the Masturbating Girl" and "How To Bring Your Kids Up Gay."

Confronted by racial tension and balkanization on campus, university leaders usually announce that, because of a resurgence of bigotry, "more needs to be done." They press for redoubled preferential recruitment of minority students and faculty, funding for a new Third World or Afro-American center, mandatory sensitivity education for whites, and so on. The more the university leaders give in to the demands of minority activists, the more they encourage the very racism they are supposed to be fighting. Surveys indicate that most young people today hold fairly liberal attitudes toward race, evident in their strong support for the civil rights agenda and for interracial dating. However, these liberal attitudes are sorely tried by the demands of the new orthodoxy: Many undergraduates are beginning to rebel against what they perceive as a culture of preferential treatment and double standards actively fostered by university policies.

Can there be a successful rolling back of this revolution, or at least of its excesses? One piece of good news is that blatant forms of racial preference are having an increasingly tough time in the courts, and this has implications for university admissions policies. The Department of Education is more vigilant than it used to be in investigating charges of discrimination against whites and Asian Americans. With help from Washington director Morton Halperin, the American Civil Liberties Union has taken a strong stand against campus censorship. Popular magazines such as *Newsweek* and *New York* have poked fun at "politically correct" speech. At Tufts University, undergraduates embarrassed the administration into backing down on censorship by putting up taped boundaries designating areas of the university to be "free speech zones," "limited speech zones" and "Twilight Zones."

Even some scholars on the political left are now speaking out against such dogmatism and excess. Eugene Genovese, a Marxist historian and one of the nation's most respected scholars of slavery, argues that "too often we find that education has given way to indoctrination. Good scholars are intimidated into silence, and the only diversity that obtains is a diversity of radical positions." More and more professors from across the political spectrum are resisting the politicization and lowering of standards. At Duke, for example, 60 professors, led by political scientist James David Barber, a liberal Democrat, have repudiated the extremism of the victims' revolution. To that end they have joined the National Association of Scholars, a Princeton, N.J.-based group devoted to fairness, excellence and rational debate in universities.

But these scholars need help. Resistance on campus to the academic revolution is outgunned and sorely needs outside reinforcements. Parents, alumni, corporations, foundations and state legislators are generally not aware that they can be very effective in promoting reform. The best way to encourage reform is to communicate in no uncertain terms to university leadership and, if necessary, to use financial incentives to assure your voice is heard. University leaders do their best to keep outsiders from meddling or even finding out what exactly is going on behind the tall gates, but there is little doubt that they would pay keen attention to the views of the donors on whom they depend. By threatening to suspend donations if universities continue harmful policies, friends of liberal learning can do a lot. In the case of state-funded schools, citizens and parents can pressure elected representatives to ask questions and demand more accountability from the taxpayer-supported academics.

The illiberal revolution can be reversed only if the people who foot the bills stop being passive observers. Don't just write a check to your alma mater; that's an abrogation of responsibility. Keep abreast of what is going on and don't be afraid to raise your voice and even to close your wallet in protest. Our Western, free-market culture need not provide the rope to hang itself.

NO

Troy Duster

THEY'RE TAKING OVER! AND OTHER MYTHS ABOUT RACE ON CAMPUS

The University of California at Berkeley has been my permanent academic home since 1969, when I was appointed to the tenured faculty in the Department of Sociology. At the time, I was one of only 6 blacks on a faculty of 1,350, and the most junior. In those early years, it was not uncommon for students, white and black, to come to my office, look dead at me, and ask, "Is Professor Duster here?"

The question, which turned me into a living Invisible Man, reflected the depth of racial problems in U.S. higher education, even at its most progressive university. Years of fury and tumult followed. And for over two decades now, I've been thinking about race and higher education—both as my area of professional study, and because of the realities that have shaped my personal life here. A few months ago, I went to the retirement party of one of my original black colleagues, who caught me off guard by saying that I was now the senior African American on the faculty. From this vantage point, I have a story to tell about the remarkable transformation of Berkeley's undergraduate student population. Because Berkeley, once again, is at the center of a raging national controversy—this time over the issue of "multiculturalism" and what its enemies call "political correctness"—a storm that I believe to be, at bottom, about the shifting sands of racial privilege. It is also about the future of American education: what happens in Berkeley, one of the nation's largest public universities and the bellwether of social change and innovation in academia, will affect all of us.

In January 1989, Berkeley's chancellor commissioned me and the Institute for the Study of Social Change to prepare a report on multiculturalism on campus. Our research team intensively interviewed hundreds of students over an eighteen-month period—-first in single-ethnic groups with an interviewer of the same background, then in mixed groups. We asked them what kind of environment they'd hoped to find upon arriving on campus, and what they actually encountered. Who were their friends, where and how powerfully were racial tensions felt, what did they think of other ethnic

From Troy Duster, "They're Taking Over! and Other Myths About Race on Campus," *Mother Jones* (September/October 1991). Copyright © 1991 by the Foundation for National Progress. Reprinted by permission of *Mother Jones* magazine.

groups, of affirmative action? We asked them about their frustrations and their positive experiences around racial and ethnic issues, and what they would do to change things. We developed a rich and complicated portrait of campus culture at Berkeley, drawn directly from the students who make it up. It isn't an easy picture to draw, nor to compress into a headline. And it certainly isn't the side of the story that ideologues like Dinesh D'Souza and his imitators have focused on. What the study, and my own experience, tell me, is that multiculturalism's critics are selling students short by propagating five key myths.

MYTH 1. TERRIBLE "TRIBALISM"

Multiculturalism is tearing the campus apart.
Self-segregation. Balkanization. School days claustrophobically lived out in ethnic enclaves. That's how Berkeley's and other campuses are often portrayed these days, as intellectual and cultural disaster zones racked by racial conflict.

Very rarely is there any mention of the forces that push students into familiar groups. Long before there were African-American theme houses, even before World War II, on-campus Catholic and Jewish societies helped those "minority" students survive; the Hillel and Newman Foundations supported students navigating through hostile WASP territory. Today, I almost never read that this phenomenon might also benefit African-American or Latino students. As many students told us, those who otherwise would feel alienated on a supercompetitive campus are getting together and finding support, creating a common comfort zone, making it easier to succeed.

In 1968, the Berkeley campus was primarily white. The student body was 2.8 percent black, 1.3 percent Chicano/Latino, and the massive Asian immigration of the 1970s had yet to occur. Only twenty-three years later, half the Berkeley student body is made up of people of color. Inevitably, with such a dramatic social transformation, there is tension and sometimes even open conflict over resources, turf, and "ownership" of the place.

Back in the 1950s, students either turned the campus radio station on or off. In the late 1980s, different ethnic groups fought over what kind of music it should play during prime time: salsa, rap, country, or heavy metal? (This same issue surfaced during the gulf war, when Latino troops demanded more salsa on Armed Forces Radio.)

Conflict is expected, perhaps even healthy, in a social situation where people have different interests and compete for scarce resources. Few of California's "feeder" high schools are racially integrated, so it's not surprising that students experience shock and tension when they arrive at their first experience of multiculturalism. But it may be a more realistic preparation for life's later turns.

Berkeley, of course, is no more a racial utopia than any other place in this divided and racially wounded country. Nonetheless, what strikes this sociologist as remarkable is how well and relatively peaceably it works.

MYTH 2. DIVERSITY MEANS DUMBER

Multiculturalism is diluting our standards.
Nowadays we hear that the academy is in deep trouble because multicultural ad-

missions policies let in students who are less capable. Actually, by the measures the critics themselves tend to use, SAT scores and grade point averages, the typical Berkeley student is now far more competent, far more eligible, far more prepared than when this was an all-white university in 1950. Of the more than 21,300 students who applied in 1989, over 5,800 had straight-A averages—and all were competing for only 3,500 spots in the freshman class.

As recently as 1980, only 8,000 students *total* applied to Berkeley. In 1988, about 7,500 Asians alone applied. Such demographic facts can't help but heighten racial awareness on campus. Many more thousands of students wanting the relatively scarce Berkeley diploma create increasingly ferocious competition at the same-sized admissions gate.

Back in the 1960s, when the campus was mainly white, almost every eligible student who applied to Berkeley was admitted. So in a framework of plenty, people could afford to be gracious, and say that civil rights, even affirmative action, were good ideas. When the United States changed its immigration laws in the 1970s, well-qualified candidates with families from China, Hong Kong, and Korea swelled the pool of applicants. Suddenly, not everyone who was eligible could get in. Today, Berkeley is 30 percent Asian, and that means that white students who are not getting in are feeling the crunch from the "top" (students with higher GPAs and SATs) and from the "bottom" (students admitted through music, athletic ability, affirmative action, and other eligibility allowances). The media, so far, has chosen to emphasize the beleaguered white student who has to adjust to affirmative action. Isn't it a shame, stories imply, that these students are feeling uncomfortable in an environment that used to be *their* university?

It isn't theirs anymore. Since the demographics of this state are changing at a rapidly accelerating rate—by 2000, whites will account for only 52 percent of California's population—shouldn't the university population and curriculum reflect more of this new reality? Meanwhile, the quality of student at Berkeley is only getting better.

MYTH 3. AFFIRMATIVE IS NEGATIVE

Getting rid of affirmative action and other special admissions programs would improve the university.

In the 1960s, there was so little diversity on campus that white students experienced other cultures voluntarily, on their own terms, like choosing ethnic cuisine on the night you're in the mood for it. Now there's no way to avoid it, and that leads to the big question on campus: *Why are you here?* Some white students have told us in their interviews how unfair they think a policy is that permits students with lower GPAs and SATs to be here.

Black and Chicano students know the rap. What they never hear, even from university officials, is strong morally, historically, and politically informed language that justifies affirmative action. Most of the black and Chicano students we interviewed were themselves unclear on why affirmative action exists.

It exists because, over the past two hundred years, blacks and Latinos have had a difficult time entering higher education, and that legacy hasn't gone away. The median family income of white Berkeley students is approximately $70,000 a year, and for blacks it is $38,000 a year. The gap isn't closing; the economic barriers that restrict minority access to college aren't disappearing.

But Americans' cultural memory lasts about five years, so the idea that affirmative action exists to redress past grievances doesn't resonate with today's students—of all colors. The notion that black people have a past of slavery and discrimination, that this is a fact of American history, is buried so deep in the consciousness of most students that it doesn't surface. The right wing says that if you bring that fact to the fore and teach it, that's called Oppression Studies, or "political correctness," and by telling people of color they should feel good about themselves, you're making white people feel bad about themselves.

There is a different way to argue for affirmative action, which hits home with even historical amnesiacs. That is to remind students that the future will reward those who master the art of coming together across ethnic, cultural, and racial lines. Suddenly, affirmative-action admissions are not a debt payment that lets in students who "don't deserve to be here," but rather a way of enriching the student culture—and career hopes. Just ask Xerox or other corporations that promote executives who have proven their ability to "manage diversity."

A lot of white students are already intuitively on board. When we asked graduating students what they regretted about their time on campus, many told us, in effect "I wish I had spent more time availing myself of the potential of Berkeley's diversity." The smartest among them also see that in a globalized economy, Berkeley's multiculturalism can make them better leaders.

MYTH 4. GOOD OLD "MERITOCRACY"

GPA + SAT = MIT
I've already said that using critics' own yardsticks, GPAs and SATs, Berkeley's student body is more qualified than ever. To those who, in the interest of "preserving meritocracy," would admit every student solely on GPA and SAT, I say: Get real. There are over 1,200 high schools in California. To assume a 3.7 means the same in each is nonsensical. Even within the same school, one 3.7 student may have taken advanced elective physics and chemistry while another 3.7 was piled up via Mickey Mouse courses. And yet by laying such emphasis on GPA, we've encouraged students to convert a bureaucratic convenience into a moral right.

What we know about SAT scores is that they correlate almost perfectly with zip-code and economic status. It's no secret that expensive cram courses can boost your score hundreds of points. Obviously there should be other routes into the university. And in allowing them, Berkeley reflects the historical norm, not some new "politically correct" departure.

Before 1955, GPA and SAT were not used as the sole basis for admissions. Elite universities like Yale and Princeton have regularly tinkered with their entrance criteria in order to bring in students from different parts of the country. And such institutions have a different kind of affirmative action for one group: children of alumni who, in 1988, entered Harvard in greater numbers than did those admitted via affirmative action.

Yet the only time we scream "Unfair!" as a nation is when the beneficiaries are people of color. We never screamed when it came to privilege for people of privilege. Arguments for "meritocracy" are usually on behalf of privilege, one more time.

MYTH 5. FIRE-BREATHING FACULTY

Radical professors are setting the campus political agenda.
Late in the 1950s, U.S. universities exploded in size, and new faculty arrived in droves. Thirty years later, they are in their sixties and still around. They haven't changed, but their students sure have. And that inevitably creates another source of tension on campus.

Today at multicultural Berkeley, 88.6 percent of the professors are white, and 83.9 percent are men. Given its 1960s reputation, the faculty should be a hotbed of radicalism, but by any sort of criteria, finding a leftist on the Berkeley faculty is like searching for a needle in a haystack. In a sociology department of thirty members, there is only one self-described Marxist. The political-science department is profoundly conservative. Berkeley reflects the findings of a recent poll of 35,478 professors at 392 institutions nationwide, conducted by the Higher Education Research Institute at UCLA: only 4.9 percent of all college instructors rate themselves "far left," while the vast majority, 94.8 percent, call themselves "liberal" (36.8 percent), "moderate" (40.2 percent), or "conservative" (17.8 percent).

Some of my colleagues, left and right, have a knee-jerk ideological position on the topics discussed here, and a few are heavy-handed in their "political correctness." Also, there have always been many eighteen-to-twenty-year-olds who are strident and angrily simplistic in their rhetoric. But it insults those who are agitating for change on campus simply to say they've been programmed with "PC" ideas by a cadre of leftist academics.

BEYOND THE MYTHS— A REALITY CHECK

Berkeley students have a chance that students at the far more white University of California at Santa Barbara don't have—they're rubbing up against difference all the time. Many of them told us they came here specifically for that reason, though some graduated with stereotypes intact, or disappointed that they weren't leaving with a better sense of other cultures. How can we make diversity a constructive experience? We asked Berkeley's students and they told us.

First they gave us the Don'ts. Don't, they said, try to fix things by putting us through three-hour sensitivity sessions designed to raise our consciousness about gender or racial issues or homophobia. Those are too contrived and short-lived to make much of a difference.

And don't force matters by asking different cultures to party together. Black students told us whites are too busy drinking to want to dance up a storm. White students said Chicanos and blacks would rather be raucous than sociable. The perfectly integrated, all-university "We Are The World" dance party is a bad idea, all sides told us, mainly because we don't all like the same music.

What then, did Berkeley's diversity-seekers remember as their most positive experiences when they reflected on their four years here? Again and again, they would describe the time when an instructor had the class break into groups and work on joint projects. Engaged in a collective enterprise, they learned about other students' ways of thinking and problem solving, and sometimes they found friendships forming across the ethnic divide.

A more cooperative approach to learning, then, would breathe some fresh air into the sometimes tense ethnic atmosphere on Berkeley's campus. And a clear explanation and endorsement of the merits of affirmative action by the school administration, something on paper that every student would receive, read, and perhaps debate, would counteract the tension that grows in the present silence. These are two concrete recommendations our report makes.

But Berkeley is not a sealed laboratory, and students don't arrive here as tabulae rasae. They bring their own experiences and expectations; some are angry about injustices they've felt firsthand, while some are blithely unaware of their implications.

What our hundreds of interviews showed is that there is a sharp difference between the ways black and white students feel about racial politics; Asians and Chicanos fall somewhere in between. White students tend to arrive with an almost naive good will, as if they are saying, "I think I'll just go and have some diversity," while music from *Peter and the Wolf* plays in the background. They expect to experience the "other" without conflict, without tension, without anything resembling bitterness or hostility. Meanwhile, many blacks arrive after being told in high school that Berkeley is a tough place, an alien environment, and that in order to survive, they should stick with other black people.

Imagine then what happens in the first few weeks of the first semester. White students looking for diversity run into black students already sure that race is political, so pick your friends carefully. White students seeking easy access to a black group can quickly find their hands slapped. They might say something offensive without knowing it and get called "racist," a word they use to mean prejudging a person because he or she is black. *Why do you call me racist? Hey, I'm willing to talk to you like an ordinary person.*

But when black students use the term, they tend to aim it at a person they see participating in a larger institution that works against black people. *If you're not in favor of affirmative action, that means you're racist.*

The white student retorts: *I'm willing to have dinner with you, talk with you about ideas. I'm not prejudiced.* But the two are talking past each other, the white student describing a style of interaction and friendship, the black student talking about the set of views the white student appears to hold.

It is misunderstandings such as these, arising in an atmosphere of fierce competition, in a setting of remarkable ethnic and racial diversity, that lead some critics to jump gleefully to the conclusion that diversity is not working. But there is another, more hopeful interpretation. Berkeley's students are grappling with one of the most difficult situations in the world: ethnic and racial turf. They are doing this, however modestly, over relatively safe issues such as what kind of music gets played or who sits where in the lunchroom. Perhaps they will learn how to handle conflict, how to divvy up scarce resources, how to adjust, fight, retreat, compromise, and ultimately get along in a future that will no longer be dominated by a single group spouting its own values as the ideal homogenized reality for everyone else. If our students learn even a small bit of this, they will be far better prepared than students tucked safely away in anachronistic single-culture enclaves. And what they learn may make a difference not just for their personal futures, but for a world struggling with issues of nationalism, race and ethnicity.

POSTSCRIPT

Does "Multiculturalism" Debase the Curriculum?

Both sides of the multiculturalism dispute have loose ends in their arguments. One major reason given for why people should study Western civilization is that its themes are transregional: the contention is that these themes touch the central concerns of human beings *anywhere* on earth. Yet advocates often put their case in frankly parochial terms, arguing that it is appropriate for those who live in the Western world to have a thorough grounding in the culture of their region.

D'Souza's argument is developed at greater length and spiced with examples of dubious multicultural experiments in his *Illiberal Education* (Free Press, 1991). Significant segments of the reading public seem receptive to such critiques: D'Souza's book was on the *New York Times* best-seller list for several weeks, as was a book written a few years earlier, Allan Bloom's *The Closing of the American Mind* (Simon & Schuster, 1987), in which Bloom deplored what he saw as politically inspired tampering with the liberal arts curriculum. Other recent books in the same vein include Roger Kimball, *Tenured Radicals* (HarperCollins, 1990), and Charles Sykes, *The Hollow Men* (Regnery Gateway, 1990). For an exchange of different views on multiculturalism, see "The Idea of the University," *Partisan Review* (Special Issue, 1991). Participants include Brigitte Berger, Wilson Moses, Catharine Stimpson, and Jean Elshtain.

For students and educators, politicians and parents, social scientists and policy planners, and the like, the problems associated with defining multiculturalism are more than just a matter of coming up with the right words. It is a question of defining what kind of a society America will be. For a discussion of several points of view on multicultural education, see the Winter 1991 edition of *American Educator,* which contains a special section on various aspects of this debate and what it means in the schools. That edition also contains suggestions for further reading and recommends the following: Arthur Schlesinger, Jr.'s *The Disuniting of America* (W. W. Norton, 1992); "Diversity and Democracy," by Diane Ravitch in the Spring 1990 *American Educator.* For the Afrocentric perspective on this debate, they recommend Molefi Kete Asnate, *The Afrocentric Idea* (Temple University Press, 1988).

ISSUE 2

Are Liberal Values Propagated by the News Media?

YES: William A. Rusher, from *The Coming Battle for the Media* (William Morrow, 1988)

NO: Edward S. Herman and Noam Chomsky, from "Propaganda Mill," *The Progressive* (June 1988)

ISSUE SUMMARY

YES: William A. Rusher, a media analyst and former publisher of the *National Review,* argues that the media are biased against conservatives and that news coverage promotes liberal opinions.
NO: Professors Edward S. Herman and Noam Chomsky critique the mass media from the perspective of the left and find the media to be a "propaganda mill" in the service of the wealthy and powerful.

"A small group of men, numbering perhaps no more than a dozen 'anchormen,' commentators, and executive producers . . . decide what 40 to 50 million Americans will learn of the day's events in the nation and the world." The speaker was Spiro Agnew, vice president of the United States during the Nixon administration. The thesis of Agnew's speech, delivered to an audience of midwestern Republicans in 1969, was that the television news media are controlled by a small group of liberals who foist their liberal opinions on viewers under the guise of "news." The upshot of this control, said Agnew, "is that a narrow and distorted picture of America often emerges from the televised news." Many Americans, even many of those who were later shocked by revelations that Agnew took bribes while serving in public office, agreed with Agnew's critique of the "liberal media."

Politicians' complaints about unfair news coverage go back much further than Spiro Agnew and the Nixon administration. The third president of the United States, Thomas Jefferson, was an eloquent champion of the press, but after six years as president, he could hardly contain his bitterness. "The man who never looks into a newspaper," he wrote, "is better informed than he who reads them, inasmuch as he who knows nothing is nearer to truth than he whose mind is filled with falsehoods and errors."

The press today is much different than it was in Jefferson's day. Newspapers then were pressed in hand-operated frames in many little printing shops around the country; everything was local and decentralized, and each paper averaged only a few hundred subscribers. Today, newspaper chains have taken over most of the once-independent local newspapers. The remaining independents rely heavily on national and international wire services. Almost all major magazines have national circulations; some newspapers, like *USA Today* and the *Wall Street Journal*, do too. Other newspapers, like the *New York Times* and the *Washington Post*, enjoy nation-wide prestige and help set the nation's news agenda. In the case of television, about 70 percent of national news on television comes from three networks whose programming originates in New York City.

A second important difference between the media of the eighteenth century and the media today has to do with the ideal of objectivity. In past eras, newspapers were frankly partisan sheets, full of nasty barbs at the politicians and parties the editors did not like. The ideal of objective journalism is a relatively recent development. It traces back to the early years of the twentieth century. Disgusted with the sensationalist journalism of the time, intellectual leaders urged newspapers to cultivate a core of profes-sionals who would concentrate on accurate reporting and who would leave their opinions to the editorial page. Journalism schools cropped up around the country, helping to promote the ideal of objectivity.

The two historical developments, news centralization and news profes-sionalism, play off against one another in the current debate over news bias. The question of bias was irrelevant when the press was a scatter of little independent newspapers. If you did not like the bias of one paper, you picked another one—or you started your own, which could be done with modest capital outlay. Bias started to become an important question when newspapers became dominated by chains and airwaves by networks, and when a few national press leaders (such as the *New York Times* and the *Washington Post*) began to emerge. When one news anchor can address a nightly audience of 25 million people, the question of bias is no longer irrelevant.

But *is* there bias? If so, *whose* bias? The media constitute a major socializing institution, so these are important questions. Defenders of the press usually concede that journalists, like all human beings, have biases, but they deny that they carry their biases into their writing. Journalists, they say, are professionals, trained to bring us news unembellished by personal opinion. They conclude that bias is in the eye of the beholder: left-wingers think the press is conservative, right-wingers call it liberal; both are unhappy that the press is not biased in *their* direction.

Both the left and the right disagree. The left considers the press conserva-tive because it is tied in with big business, indeed *is* a big business. The right insists that the bias of the press is overwhelmingly liberal because most reporters are liberal. In the following selections, William A. Rusher argues that the media are biased against conservatives, while Edward S. Herman and Noam Chomsky develop a critique of the media from a leftist perspective.

YES
William A. Rusher

THE COMING BATTLE FOR THE MEDIA

It is the conviction of a great many people, not all of them conservative by any means, that news presentation by the media elite is heavily biased in favor of liberal views and attitudes.

It is important, right at the outset, to specify precisely what is being objected to. This is a free country, and journalists are every bit as entitled to their private political opinions as the rest of us. But the average newspaper or television news program, and certainly those we have categorized as the "media elite," purport to be offering us something more than the personal opinions of the reporter, or the chief editor, or even the collective opinions of the journalistic staff. In one way or another, to one extent or another, they all profess to be offering us the "news"—which is to say, an account of as many relevant events and developments, in the period in question, as can be given in the space or time available. Moreover, in offering this account, the media we are discussing implicitly claim to be acting with a reasonable degree of objectivity. Their critics sharply challenge that claim.

But just how much objectivity is it reasonable to expect? The question is more complicated than it may at first appear. There is a school of thought— popular, perhaps naturally, among a certain subcategory of journalists themselves—that a journalist is, or at least ought to be, a sort of vestal virgin: a chalice of total and incorruptible objectivity. But this, of course, is non-sense, and is certainly not expected by any reasonable person.

Journalists too are, after all, sons and daughters of Adam. Their conception was far from immaculate; they share our taint of Original Sin. They were born into our common society, received the same general education we all received, and had roughly the same formative experiences. How likely is it that, simply by choosing to pursue a career in journalism, they underwent some sort of miraculous transformation, to emerge shriven and pure, purged of all bias and dedicated henceforth solely to the pursuit of the unvarnished Truth? . . . Just how does one go about demonstrating that the media elite are, in the matter of their private opinions, overwhelmingly partial to liberal policies and liberal political personalities? A general impression, based on

From William A. Rusher, *The Coming Battle for the Media* (William Morrow, 1988). Copyright © 1988 by William A. Rusher. Reprinted by permission of William Morrow & Company, Inc.

familiarity with their work-product as on display in the *New York Times* or the *Washington Post*, in *Time* or *Newsweek*, or on the evening news programs of one or another of the major networks, is absolutely worthless. You will be told that your perception is distorted by your own partiality to conservative policies and personalities. You will be assured that the liberals complain just as loudly as conservatives about maltreatment by the media (though on inspection it turns out to be the harder left—e.g., Alexander Cockburn—that complains; liberals typically, and understandably, complain very little about distortion by the media elite). You will be referred to news stories in which there was no liberal bias, and to news presentations well and truly balanced—shining exceptions that merely emphasize the rule.

There is, in fact, only one way to ascertain with precision anyone's political leaning, inclination, or prejudice, and that is to interview him or her in depth. Moreover, if the intention is to evaluate the opinions of an entire group, the sample interviewed must be large enough to be dependably representative. Fortunately there have recently been several conscientious surveys of the political views of America's media elite, and the results are thoroughly unambiguous. . . .

[A] remarkable survey, whose results were published in 1981 . . . was conducted in 1979 and 1980 by two professors of political science—S. Robert Lichter of George Washington University and Stanley Rothman of Smith College—as part of a larger inquiry into the attitudes of various elites, under the auspices of the Research Institute on International Change at Columbia University. The survey itself was supervised

by Response Analysis, a survey research organization.

Lichter and Rothman began by defining the following organizations as America's "most influential media outlets": three daily newspapers—the *New York Times*, the *Washington Post*, and the *Wall Street Journal*; three weekly newsmagazines—*Time*, *Newsweek*, and *U.S. News and World Report*; the news departments of four networks—CBS, NBC, ABC, and PBS; and the news departments of certain major independent broadcasting stations.

Within these organizations they then selected at random, from among those responsible for news content, individuals to be approached for interviews. In the print media, these included "reporters, columnists, department heads, bureau chiefs, editors and executives responsible for news content." In the electronic media, those selected included "correspondents, anchormen, producers, film editors and news executives." . . .

It transpires that, of those who voted in these elections at all (and this was 82 percent in 1976, when all but the youngest among those interviewed in 1979–80 would have qualified), *never less than 80 percent of the media elite voted for the Democratic candidate.* . . .

Like many American liberals, the media elite accept the essential free-enterprise basis of the United States economy, but they are devoted to welfarism. Over two thirds (68 percent) believe "the government should substantially reduce the income gap between the rich and the poor," and nearly half (48 percent) think the government should guarantee a job to anyone who wants one.

On sociocultural issues, the media elite's support for liberal positions is overwhelming. Ninety percent believe it is a woman's right to decide whether or not to have an abortion. A solid majority (53 percent) can't even bring itself to affirm that adultery is wrong.

There is far more to the Lichter-Rothman survey than the above brief sample of its findings, but the basic thrust of the study is unmistakable: America's media elite are far to the left of American public opinion in general on the great majority of topics. . . .

THE EFFECT ON THE "NEWS"

Proving statistically that the media's demonstrated liberalism influences their handling of the news is no simple matter. The media clearly aren't going to do us the favor of admitting it, and the formidable human capacity for self-delusion makes it likely that many members of the media don't even realize it, at least not fully. A good many of them undoubtedly think their selection and treatment of stories is governed solely by their acute "news sense," where any objective observer would detect bias. And even when a member of the media knows full well that his handling of news stories is influenced by his biases, he is naturally prone to minimize that influence and make excuses for the residue.

Adding to the difficulty is the fact that evidence of bias, liberal or otherwise, is almost inevitably somewhat subjective. One man's "bias" is another man's "robust journalism," etc. Obvious as the bias may be to many thoughtful people, how can one nail it down?

One of the earliest and still one of the best efforts to do so was made by Edith Efron in her book *The News Twisters* (Nash, 1971). It is said that medieval philosophers had a high old time arguing

over how many teeth a horse has, until some spoilsport ended the game by going out and actually counting them. That was essentially Efron's solution, too. . . .

[Rusher quotes extensively from Efron's discussion of her methodology. She counted the number of words used in prime-time TV news programs that could be classified "for" and "against" the three major candidates for president in 1968: Alabama governor George Wallace (running as an independent), Democrat Hubert Humphrey, and Republican Richard Nixon. —Eds.]

Efron then sets forth, in bar-graph form, the total number of words spoken for and against the three presidential candidates on the three major networks during the period under study. In the case of George Wallace, the result was as follows:

THE EFFECT ON THE "NEWS"

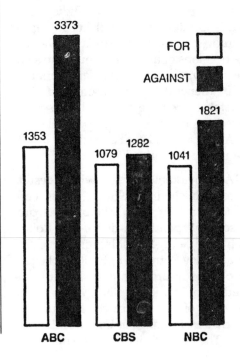

In the case of Hubert Humphrey, the graph looked like this:

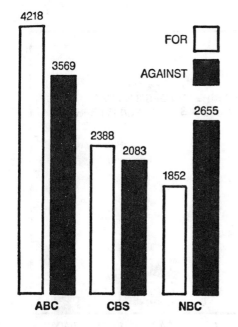

In the case of Richard Nixon, this was the result:

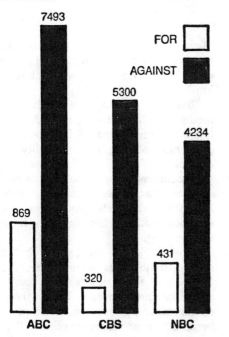

Now, how can the statistics regarding Nixon be interpreted, save as a product of bias? Bear in mind that this was long before Watergate—indeed, that in the next election (1972) Nixon would be re-elected by a landslide. Yet in 1968 the words spoken *against* Nixon on ABC (the network with the smallest imbalance in this respect) outnumbered the words spoken *for* him by nearly nine to one. At NBC the negative proportion was almost ten to one. At CBS it actually exceeded sixteen to one. . . .

Maura Clancey and Michael Robinson conducted another comprehensive study of the media's bias in reporting the "news," in connection with the 1984 presidential election, under the auspices of George Washington University and the American Enterprise Institute. . . .

Clancey and Robinson summed up their findings as follows:

There may be some questions about the validity of our measure, but there can be no question about the lopsidedness of what is uncovered. Assuming that a piece with a positive spin equals "good press," and assuming that negative spin equals "bad press," Ronald Reagan and George Bush proved overwhelmingly to be the "bad press" ticket of 1984. Figure 1 [see next page] contains the number of news seconds we scored as good press or bad press for each of the candidates. Ronald Reagan's bad press total was *ten times greater* than his good press total. (7,230 seconds vs. 730). In other words, his "spin ratio" was ten-to-one negative.

George Bush had a spin ratio that defied computation—1,500 seconds of "bad press" pieces and zero seconds of good press.

Walter Mondale and Geraldine Ferraro, on the other hand, had slightly *positive* spin ratios—1,970 seconds of

Figure 1

News seconds

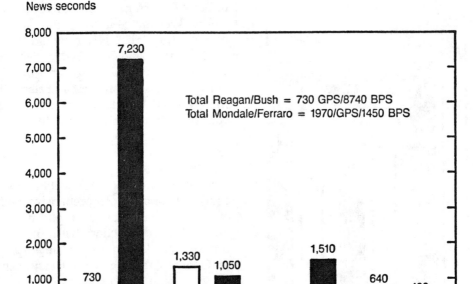

Total Reagan/Bush = 730 GPS/8740 BPS
Total Mondale/Ferraro = 1970/GPS/1450 BPS

	REAGAN		MONDALE		BUSH		FERRARO
GOOD PRESS	BAD PRESS	GOOD PRESS	BAD PRESS	GOOD PRESS	BAD PRESS	GOOD PRESS	BAD PRESS
730	7,230	1,330	1,050	0	1,510	640	400

good press about themselves as people or potential leaders, and 1,450 seconds of bad press. Given what we know about the bad news bias of television, the fact that anyone, let alone any ticket, got more positive spin than negative is news indeed.

But Clancey and Robinson are not even prepared to concede that their own lopsided results in 1984 conclusively demonstrated a liberal bias on the part of the media. On the contrary, they suggest, "liberal bias is not the only explanation, or even the best."

Instead, they posit the existence of what they call "the four I's"—non-ideological reasons for the bad press admittedly accorded Reagan and Bush in 1984. These are:

"Impishness"—a human tendency to want to turn a walkaway into a horse race "to keep one's own work interesting."

"Irritation"—annoyance at what the media perceived as Reagan's glib one-liners and his alleged "Teflon coating" (i.e., his seeming invulnerability to criticism).

"Incumbency"—a sense that the media have "a special mission to warn Americans about the advantages any incumbent has," especially when he is winning big.

"Irrevocability"—the feeling that a double standard is justified because 1984 was the last time Reagan would ever face the electorate. Under those circumstances, giving him a bad press became "a near-messianic mission."

Defenders of the media may well wonder whether pleading them guilty to the above unpleasant set of impulses would actually constitute much of an improvement over admitting that they have a liberal bias. But they can be spared that painful decision, because "the four I's" simply don't survive careful inspection. In pure theory they might explain the media's astonishing bias against Reagan in 1984, but not one of them applies to the equally well-established instance of bias discussed earlier: the media's treatment of Nixon in the 1968 campaign.

That campaign was no "walkaway" for Nixon; it was one of the closest presidential elections in United States history—43.4 percent for Nixon, 42.7 for Humphrey, and 13.5 for Wallace. And Nixon was certainly no Reagan, either in his mastery of glib one-liners or in possessing a "Teflon coating." Moreover, he was not the incumbent, or even the nominee of the incumbent's party. And 1968 was *not* the last time Nixon could or would face the electorate. Yet the media gave him the same biased treatment that Reagan received in 1984. The conclusion is unavoidable that the media's conduct had the same basis in both cases: a liberal bias neatly congruent with the demonstrated liberal preferences of the overwhelming majority of the media elite.

NO

Edward S. Herman and Noam Chomsky

PROPAGANDA MILL

It is a primary function of the mass media in the United States to mobilize public support for the special interests that dominate the Government and the private sector.

This is our conclusion after years of studying the media. Perhaps it is an obvious point—but the common assumption seems to be that the media are independent and committed to discovering and reporting the truth. Leaders of the media claim that their news judgments rest on unbiased, objective criteria. We contend, on the other hand, that the powerful are able to fix the premises of discourse, decide what the general populace will be allowed to see, hear, and think about, and "manage" public opinion by mounting regular propaganda campaigns.

We do not claim this is all the mass media do, but we believe the propaganda function to be a very important aspect of their overall service.

In countries where the levers of power are in the hands of a state bureaucracy, monopolistic control of the media, often supplemented by official censorship, makes it clear that media serve the ends of the dominant elite. It is much more difficult to see a propaganda system at work where the media are private and formal censorship is absent.

This is especially true where the media actively compete, periodically attack and expose corporate and governmental malfeasance, and aggressively portray themselves as spokesmen for free speech and the general community interest. What is not evident (and remains undiscussed in the media) is the severely limited access to the private media system and the effect of money and power on the system's performance.

Critiques of this kind are often dismissed by Establishment commentators as "conspiracy theories," but this is merely an evasion. We don't rely on any kind of conspiracy hypothesis to explain the performance of the media; in fact, our treatment is much closer to a "free-market" analysis.

From Edward S. Herman and Noam Chomsky, "Propaganda Mill," *The Progressive* (June 1988). Adapted from Edward S. Herman and Noam Chomsky, *Manufacturing Consent: The Political Economy of the Mass Media* (Pantheon Books, 1988). Copyright © 1988 by Edward S. Herman and Noam Chomsky. Reprinted by permission of Pantheon Books, a division of Random House, Inc.

Most of the bias in the media arises from the selection of right-thinking people, the internalization of preconceptions until they are taken as self-evident truths, and the practical adaptation of employees to the constraints of ownership, organization, market, and political power.

The censorship practiced within the media is largely self-censorship, by reporters and commentators who adjust to the "realities" as they perceive them. But there are important actors who do take positive initiatives to define and shape the news and to keep the media in line. This kind of guidance is provided by the Government, the leaders of the corporate community, the top media owners and executives, and assorted individuals and groups who are allowed to take the initiative.

The media are not a solid monolith on all issues. Where the powerful are in disagreement, the media will reflect a certain diversity of tactical judgments on how to attain generally shared aims. But views that challenge fundamental premises or suggest that systemic factors govern the exercise of State power will be excluded.

The pattern is pervasive. Consider the coverage from and about Nicaragua. The mass media rarely allow their news columns—or, for that matter, their opinion pages—to present materials suggesting that Nicaragua is more democratic than El Salvador and Guatemala; that its government does not murder ordinary citizens, as the governments of El Salvador and Guatemala do on a routine basis; that it has carried out socioeconomic reforms important to the majority that the other two governments somehow cannot attempt; that Nicaragua poses no military threat to its neighbors but has, in

fact, been subjected to continuous attack by the United States and its clients and surrogates, and that the U.S. fear of the Nicaraguan government is based more on its virtues than on its alleged defects.

The mass media also steer clear of discussing the background and results of the closely analogous attempt of the United States to bring "democracy" to Guatemala in 1954 by means of a CIA-supported invasion, which terminated Guatemalan democracy for an indefinite period. Although the United States supported elite rule and organized terror in Guatemala (among many other countries) for decades, actually subverted or approved the subversion of democracy in Brazil, Chile, and the Philippines (again, among others), is now "constructively engaged" with terror regimes around the world, and had no concern about democracy in Nicaragua so long as the brutal Somoza regime was firmly in power, the media take U.S. Government claims of a concern for "democracy" in Nicaragua at face value.

In contrast, El Salvador and Guatemala, with far worse records, are presented as struggling toward democracy under "moderate" leaders, thus meriting sympathetic approval.

IN CRITICIZING MEDIA BIASES, WE OFTEN draw on the media themselves for at least some of the "facts." That the media provide some information about an issue, however, proves absolutely nothing about the adequacy or accuracy of media coverage. The media do, in fact, suppress a great deal of information, but even more important is the way they present a particular fact—its placement, tone, and frequency of repetition—and the framework of analysis in which it is placed. That a careful reader looking for a fact can sometimes find it, with diligence and a skeptical eye, tells us nothing about whether that fact received the attention and context it deserved, whether it was intelligible to most readers, or whether it was effectively distorted or suppressed.

The standard media pattern of indignant campaigns and suppressions, of shading and emphasis, of carefully selected context, premises, and general agenda, is highly useful to those who wield power. If, for example, they are able to channel public concern and outrage to the abuses of enemy states, they can mobilize the population for an ideological crusade.

Thus, a constant focus on the victims of communism helps persuade the public that the enemy is evil, while setting the stage for intervention, subversion, support for terrorist regimes, an endless arms race, and constant military conflict—all in a noble cause. At the same time, the devotion of our leaders—and our media—to this narrow set of victims raises public patriotism and self-esteem, demonstrating the essential humanity of our nation and our people.

The public does not notice media silence about victims of America's client states, which is as important as the media's concentration on victims of America's enemies. It would have been difficult for the Guatemalan government to murder tens of thousands over the past decade if the U.S. press had provided the kind of coverage it gave to the difficulties of Andrei Sakharov in the Soviet Union or the murder of Jerzy Popieluszko in Poland. It would have been impossible to wage a brutal war against South Vietnam and the rest of Indochina, leaving a legacy of misery and destruction that may never be overcome, if the media had not rallied to the cause,

portraying murderous aggression as a defense of freedom.

Propaganda campaigns may be instituted either by the Government or by one or more of the top media firms. The campaigns to discredit the government of Nicaragua, to support the Salvadoran elections as an exercise in legitimizing democracy, and to use the Soviet shooting down of the Korean airliner KAL 007 as a means of mobilizing support for the arms buildup were instituted and propelled by the Government. The campaigns to publicize the crimes of Pol Pot in Cambodia and the allegations of a KGB plot to assassinate the Pope were initiated by the *Reader's Digest*, with strong follow-up support from NBC television, *The New York Times*, and other major media companies.

Some propaganda campaigns are jointly initiated by the Government and the media; all of them require the media's cooperation.

THE MASS MEDIA ARE DRAWN INTO A SYMbiotic relationship with powerful sources of information by economic necessity and reciprocity of interest. The media need a steady, reliable flow of the raw material of news. They have daily news demands and imperative news schedules. They cannot afford to have reporters and cameras at all places where important stories may break, so they must concentrate their resources where significant news often occurs, where important rumors and leaks abound, and where regular press conferences are held.

The White House, the Pentagon, and the State Department are central nodes of such news activity at the national level. On a local basis, city hall and the police department are regular news beats for reporters. Corporations and trade groups are also regular and credible purveyors of stories deemed newsworthy. These bureaucracies turn out a large volume of material that meets the demands of news organizations for reliable, scheduled flows. They also have the great merit of being recognizable and credible because of their status and prestige.

Another reason for the heavy weight given to official sources is that the mass media claim to be "objective" dispensers of the news. Partly to maintain the image of objectivity, but also to protect themselves from criticism of bias and the threat of libel suits, they need material that can be portrayed as presumptively accurate. This also reduces cost: Taking information from sources that may be presumed credible reduces investigative expense, whereas material from sources that are not *prima facie* credible, or that will draw criticism and threats, requires careful checking and costly research.

The Government and corporate bureaucracies that constitute primary news sources maintain vast public-relations operations that ensure special access to the media. The Pentagon, for example, has a public-information service that involves many thousands of employees, spending hundreds of millions of dollars every year and dwarfing not only the public-information resources of any dissenting individual or group but the aggregate of *all* dissenters.

During a brief interlude of relative openness in 1979 and 1980, the U.S. Air Force revealed that its public-information outreach included 140 newspapers with a weekly total circulation of 690,000; *Airman* magazine with a monthly circulation of 125,000; thirty-four radio and seventeen television stations, primarily overseas; 45,000 headquarters and unit news releases; 615,000 hometown news releases; 6,600 news media interviews; 3,200 news conferences; 500 news media orientation flights; fifty meetings with editorial boards, and 11,000 speeches. Note that this is just the Air Force. In 1982, *Air Force Journal International* indicated that the Pentagon was publishing 1,203 periodicals.

To put this into perspective, consider the scope of public information activities of the American Friends Service Committee and the National Council of the Churches of Christ, two of the largest nonprofit organizations that consistently challenge the views of the Pentagon. The Friends' main office had an information services budget of less than $500,000 and a staff of eleven in 1984–1985. It issued about 200 press releases a year, held thirty press conferences, and produced one film and two or three slide shows. The Council of Churches office of information has an annual budget of about $350,000, issues about 100 news releases, and holds four press conferences a year.

Only the corporate sector has the resources to produce public information and propaganda on the scale of the Pentagon and other Government bodies. These large actors provide the media with facilities and with advance copies of speeches and reports. They schedule news conferences at hours geared to news deadlines. They write press releases in usable language. They carefully organize "photo-opportunity" sessions.

In effect, the large bureaucracies of the powerful subsidize the mass media, and thereby gain special access. They become "routine" news sources, while non-routine sources must struggle for access and may be ignored.

Because of the services they provide, the continuous contact they sustain, and the mutual dependency they foster, the powerful can use personal relationships, threats, and rewards to extend their influence over the news media. The media may feel obligated to carry extremely dubious stories, or to mute criticism, to avoid offending sources and disturbing a close relationship. When one depends on authorities for daily news, it is difficult to call them liars even if they tell whoppers.

Powerful sources may also use their prestige and importance as a lever to deny critics access to the media. The Defense Department, for example, refused to participate in discussions of military issues on National Public Radio if experts from the Center for Defense Information were invited to appear on the same program. Assistant Secretary of State Elliott Abrams would not appear on a Harvard University program dealing with human rights in Central America unless former Ambassador Robert White were excluded. Claire Sterling, a principal propagandist for the "Bulgarian connection" to the plot to assassinate the Pope, refused to take part in television programs on which her critics would appear.

The relation between power and sourcing extends beyond official and corporate provision of news to shaping the supply of "experts." The dominance of official sources is undermined when highly respectable unofficial sources give dissident views. This problem is alleviated by "coopting the experts"—that is, putting them on the payroll as consultants, funding their research, and organizing think tanks that will hire them directly and help disseminate their messages.

The process of creating a body of experts who will confirm and distribute the opinions favored by the Government

and "the market" has been carried out on a deliberate basis and a massive scale. In 1972, Judge Lewis Powell, later elevated to the Supreme Court, wrote a memo to the U.S. Chamber of Commerce in which he urged business "to buy the top academic reputations in the country to add credibility to corporate studies and give business a stronger voice on the campuses."

During the 1970s and early 1980s, new institutions were established and old ones reactivated to help propagandize the corporate viewpoint. Hundreds of intellectuals were brought to these institutions, their work funded, and their output disseminated to the media by a sophisticated propaganda effort.

The media themselves also provide "experts" who regularly echo the official view. John Barron and Claire Sterling are household names as authorities on the KGB and terrorism because the *Reader's Digest* has funded, published, and publicized their work. The Soviet defector Arkady Shevchenko became an expert on Soviet arms and intelligence because *Time*, ABC television, and *The New York Times* chose to feature him despite his badly tarnished credentials. By giving these vehicles of the preferred view much exposure, the media confer status and make them the obvious candidates for opinion and analysis.

Another class of experts whose prominence is largely a function of their serviceability to power consists of former radicals who have "come to see the light." The motives that induce these individuals to switch gods, from Stalin (or Mao) and communism to Reagan and free enterprise, may vary, but so far as the media are concerned, the ex-radicals have simply seen the error of their ways. The former sinners, whose previous work was ignored or ridiculed by the mass media, are suddenly elevated to prominence and anointed as experts.

MEDIA PROPAGANDA CAMPAIGNS HAVE generally been useful to elite interests. The Red Scare of 1919–1920 helped abort the postwar union-organizing drive in steel and other major industries. The Truman-McCarthy Red Scare of the early 1950s helped inaugurate the Cold War and the permanent war economy, and also weakened the progressive coalition that had taken shape during the New Deal years.

The chronic focus on the plight of Soviet dissidents, on enemy killings in Cambodia, and on the Bulgarian Connection helped weaken the Vietnam Syndrome, justify a huge arms buildup and a more aggressive foreign policy, and divert attention from the upward distribution of income that was the heart of the Reagan Administration's domestic economic program. The recent propaganda attacks on Nicaragua have averted eyes from the savageries of the war in El Salvador and helped justify the escalating U.S. investment in counterrevolution in Central America.

Conversely, propaganda campaigns are *not* mobilized where coverage of victimization, though it may be massive, sustained, and dramatic, fails to serve the interests of the elite.

The focus on Cambodia in the Pol Pot era was serviceable, for example, because Cambodia had fallen to the communists and useful lessons could be drawn from the experience of their victims. But the many Cambodian victims of U.S. bombing *before* the communists came to power were scrupulously ignored by the U.S. press. After Pol Pot was ousted by the Vietnamese, the United States quietly shifted its support to this "worse than Hitler" villain, with little or no notice in the press, which once again adjusted to the official political agenda.

Attention to the Indonesian massacres of 1965–1966, or to the victims of the Indonesian invasion of East Timor since 1975, would also be distinctly unhelpful as bases of media campaigns, because Indonesia is a U.S. ally and client that maintains an open door to Western investment. The same is true of the victims of state terror in Chile and Guatemala—U.S. clients whose basic institutional structure, including the state terror system, were put in place by, or with crucial assistance from, the United States.

No propaganda campaigns are mounted in the mass media on behalf of such victims. To publicize their plight would, after all, conflict with the interests of the wealthy and powerful.

POSTSCRIPT

Are Liberal Values Propagated by the News Media?

As the opposing arguments in this section indicate, we can find critics on both the left and the right who agree that the media are biased. What divides such critics is the question of whether the bias is left-wing or right-wing. Defenders of the news media may seize upon this disagreement to bolster their own claim that bias is in the eye of the beholder, meaning that information presented without bias would naturally seem conservative to a liberal and vice versa. But it could also mean that the news media are unfair to both sides. If that were true, however, it would seem to take some of the force out of the argument that the news media have a distinct ideological tilt.

Though published in 1973, Edward Jay Epstein's *News From Nowhere* (Random House, 1973) remains one of the great studies of the factors that influence television news shows. In his book, Epstein uses as an epigraph a statement by Richard Salant, president of CBS News in the 1970s: "Our reporters do not cover stories from *their* point of view. They are presenting them from *nobody's* point of view." Although Salant probably had not intended to be facetious or ironic, the statement so amused Epstein that he parodied it in the title of this book: *News From Nowhere*!

A study by S. Robert Lichter et al., *The Media Elite* (Adler & Adler, 1986), tends to support Rusher's contention that the media slant leftward, while Ben Bagdikian's *The Media Monopoly* (Beacon Press, 1983) lends support to Herman and Chomsky. David Halberstam's *The Powers That Be* (Alfred A. Knopf, 1979), a historical study of CBS, the *Washington Post, Time* magazine, and the *Los Angeles Times,* describes some of the political and ideological struggles that have taken place within major media organizations.

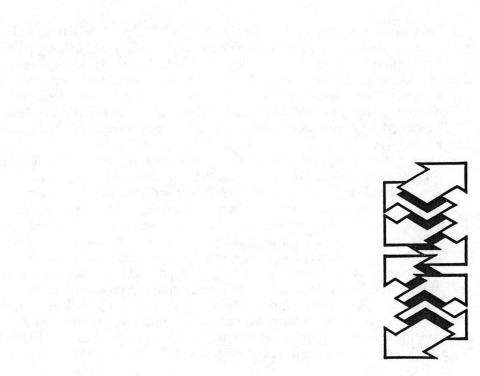

ISSUE 3

Has Individualism Become Excessive?

YES: Robert N. Bellah et al., from *Habits of the Heart: Individualism and Commitment in American Life* (Harper & Row, 1986)

NO: Henry Fairlie, from *The Spoiled Child of the Western World: The Miscarriage of the American Idea in Our Time* (Doubleday, 1975)

ISSUE SUMMARY

YES: Sociologist Robert N. Bellah and his associates argue that the tendency of Americans has been to become absorbed in the self at the expense of transcendent values and the good of the community.

NO: British commentator Henry Fairlie suggests that the critics of "consumerism" fail to appreciate the extraordinary degree of freedom enjoyed by modern "mass man."

Many observers have called attention to the "Lockean" qualities of the American people. The reference is to John Locke, the English philosopher of the seventeenth century, whose writings were much quoted by Americans of the eighteenth century. Parts of America's Declaration of Independence sound like they came almost word for word from Locke. The Declaration reaffirms Locke's belief in "unalienable rights," which are identified as "life, liberty, and the pursuit of happiness" (for Locke there were "life, liberty, and property").

Locke championed individualism. He postulated a "state of nature," in which humans lived before they established governments. In that natural state, human beings were all "free, equal, and independent." Although the raw products of nature (the trees, the fruit, the deer, and so on) belonged to all, the moment a human being "worked on" one of these products—by killing and skinning a deer, by picking a fruit, or otherwise mixing one's labor with the product of nature—the product then became one's own, to do with as one pleased. Not incidentally, the product then became more valuable. The moral: work produces both wealth and private property.

Locke was popular in America because his theory seemed to fit the American experience. Lacking Europe's class distinctions and restrictions on economic activity, America offered unprecedented opportunities to the ambitious and the industrious. Writers like Benjamin Franklin won great renown by showing Americans the "uses of virtue." Franklin demonstrated that thrift, self-denial, temperance, patience, hard work, and other Puritan virtues could bring rewards not only in Heaven but in this world too. The compelling American value became the "pursuit of happiness."

The pursuit was in full swing by the time Alexis de Tocqueville arrived in America in the 1830s. The famous French observer was struck by the driving ambition of Americans. "The passions that stir the Americans most deeply are commercial and not political ones," he noted, adding that "private interest" seems to be the dominant force in the United States. Yet de Tocqueville also noted the tendency of Americans to form associations and work together for common goals. Americans, he said, are farsighted enough to appreciate the individual advantage in common action. "It thus happens that ambition can make a man care for his fellows, and, in a sense, he often finds his self-interest in forgetting about himself."

Perhaps there was a bit of wishful thinking in this analysis. Or, even assuming that de Tocqueville was correct about Americans in the 1830s, is it as obvious today that Americans combine self-seeking and community spirit? If the "pursuit of happiness" is defined as the chase after wealth or whatever else it is that pleases us, won't this individual self-seeking at some point destroy the community? These are not meant to be rhetorical questions. It may well be that individualism and community spirit do fit together, or can be made to fit. But they certainly point different ways. Individualism emphasizes freedom and choice; it prizes incentive, competitiveness, and material reward. Community stresses the need for cooperation, the joy of companionship, and the warmth of familiarity. By the same token, community and individualism both have darker potentialities. Community cooperation can turn into regimentation, and too much familiarity may breed contempt. Yet excessive individualism may lead to the "atomization" of society, in which persons are reduced to faceless and soulless integers. This is the "mass society" that European philosophers have been writing about since the 1930s. Such thinkers as José Ortega y Gasset, Hannah Arendt, and Erich Fromm have warned us that too much individualism lays the groundwork for ugly antidemocratic movements that exploit mass loneliness.

In the following selections, Robert N. Bellah and his colleagues seem to share some of the concerns of the European critics and conclude that individualism has gone too far, causing painful psychic and moral wounds. Henry Fairlie, however, suggests that there is nothing intrinsically wrong, and much that is exciting and liberating, in the way sovereign individuals pursue happiness in America.

YES

Robert N. Bellah et al.

INDIVIDUALISM AND COMMITMENT IN AMERICAN LIFE

How ought we to live? How do we think about how to live? Who are we, as Americans? What is our character? These questions we have asked our fellow citizens in many parts of the country. We engaged them in conversations about their lives and about what matters most to them, talked about their families and communities, their doubts and uncertainties, and their hopes and fears with respect to the larger society. We found them eager to discuss the right way to live, what to teach our children, and what our public and private responsibilities should be, but also a little dismayed by these subjects. These are important matters to those to whom we talked, and yet concern about moral questions is often relegated to the realm of private anxiety, as if it would be awkward or embarrassing to make it public. We hope this book will help transform this inner moral debate, often shared only with intimates, into public discourse. In these pages, Americans speak with us, and indirectly, with one another, about issues that deeply concern us all. As we will see, many doubt that we have enough in common to be able mutually to discuss our central aspirations and fears. it is one of our purposes to persuade them that we do.

The fundamental question we posed, and that was repeatedly posed to us, was how to preserve or create a morally coherent life. But the kind of life we want depends on the kind of people we are—on our character. Our inquiry can thus be located in a longstanding discussion of the relationship between character and society. In the eighth book of the *Republic*, Plato sketched a theory of the relationship between the moral character of a people and the nature of its political community, the way it organizes and governs itself. The founders of the American republic at the time of the Revolution adopted a much later version of the same theory. Since for them, as for Americans with whom we talked, freedom was perhaps the most important value, they were particularly concerned with the qualities of character necessary for the creation of a free republic.

From Robert N. Bellah et al., *Habits of the Heart: Individualism and Commitment in American Life* (University of California Press, 1985). Copyright © 1985 by the Regents of the University of California. Reprinted by permission of the University of California Press.

In the 1830s, the French social philosopher Alexis de Tocqueville offered the most comprehensive and penetrating analysis of the relationship between character and society in America that has ever been written. In his book *Democracy in America,* based on acute observation and wide conversation with Americans, Tocqueville described the mores—which he on occasion called "habits of the heart"—of the American people and showed how they helped to form American character. He singled out family life, our religious traditions, and our participation in local politics as helping to create the kind of person who could sustain a connection to a wide political community and thus ultimately support the maintenance of free institutions. He also warned that some aspects of our character—what he was one of the first to call "individualism"—might eventually isolate Americans one from another and thereby undermine the conditions of freedom.

The central problem of our book concerns the American individualism that Tocqueville described with a mixture of admiration and anxiety. It seems to us that it is individualism, and not equality, as Tocqueville thought, that has marched inexorably through our history. *We are concerned that this individualism may have grown cancerous—that it may be destroying those social integuments that Tocqueville saw as moderating its more destructive potentialities, that it may be threatening the survival of freedom itself.* [emphasis added by editors] We want to know what individualism in America looks and feels like, and how the world appears in its light. . . .

LIVING WELL IS A CHALLENGE. BRIAN PALMER, a successful businessman, lives in a comfortable San Jose suburb and works as a top-level manager in a large corporation. He is justifiably proud of his rapid rise in the corporation, but he is even prouder of the profound change he has made recently in his idea of success. "My value system," he says, "has changed a little bit as the result of a divorce and reexamining life values. Two years ago, confronted with the work load I have right now, I would stay in the office and work until midnight, come home, go to bed, get up at six, and go back in and work until midnight, until such time as it got done. Now I just kind of flip the bird and walk out. My family life is more important to me than that, and the work will wait, I have learned." A new marriage and a houseful of children have become the center of Brian's life. But such new values were won only after painful difficulties.

Now forty-one, his tall, lean body bursting with restless energy, Brian recalls a youth that included a fair amounting of hell-raising, a lot of sex, and a considerable devotion to making money. At twenty-four, he married. Shouldering the adult responsibilities of marriage and children became the guiding purpose of his life for the next few years.

Whether or not Brian felt his life was satisfying, he was deeply committed to succeeding at his career and family responsibilities. He held two full-time jobs to support his family, accepting apparently without complaint the loss of a youth in which, he himself reports, "the vast majority of my time from, say, the age of fifteen to twenty-two or twenty-three was devoted toward giving myself pleasure of one sort or another." Brian describes his reasons for working so hard after he married quite simply. "It seemed like the thing to do at the time," he says. "I couldn't stand not having enough money to get by on, and with my wife unable to contribute to the family income, it seemed like the thing to do. I guess self-reliance is one of the characteristics I have pretty high up in my value system. It was second nature. I didn't even question the thing. I just went out and did it." Brian and his wife came to share very little in their marriage, except, as he thought, good sex, children, and devotion to his career. With his wife's support, he decided to "test" himself "in the Big League," and he made it, although at a great cost to his marriage and family life. "What was my concept of what constituted a reasonable relationship? I guess I felt an obligation to care for materially, provide for, a wife and my children, in a style to which I'd like to see them become accustomed. Providing for my family materially was important. Sharing wasn't important. Sharing of my time wasn't important. I put in extremely long hours, probably averaging sixty to sixty-five hours a week. I'd work almost every Saturday. Always in the office by 7:30. Rarely out of the office before 6:30 at night. Sometimes I'd work until 10:30 or 11. That was numero uno. But I compensated for that by saying, I have this nice car, this nice house, joined the Country Club. Now you have a place you can go, sit on your butt, drink, go into the pool. I'll pay the bills and I'll do my thing at work."

For Brian's wife, the compensations apparently weren't enough. After almost fifteen years of marriage, "One day I came home. In fact, our house was for sale, and we had an offer on the house. My wife said, 'Before you accept this offer, you should probably know that once we sell this house, we will live in different houses.' That was my official notification that she was planning to divorce me."

The divorce, "one of the two or three biggest surprises of my life," led Brian to reassess his life in fundamental ways and to explore the limits of the kind of success he had been pursuing. "I live by establishing plans. I had no plan for being single, and it gave me a lot of opportunity to think, and in the course of thinking, I read for the first time in many, many years. Got back into classical music for the first time since my college years. I went out and bought my first Bach album and a stereo to play it on. Mostly the thinking process of being alone and relating to my children." . . .

The revolution in Brian's thinking came from a reexamination of the true sources of joy and satisfaction in his life. And it is particularly in a marriage to a woman very different from his first wife that Brian has discovered a new sense of himself and a different understanding of what he wants out of life. He has a new sense of what love can be. "To be able to receive affection freely and give affection and to give of myself and know it is a totally reciprocal type of thing. There's just almost a psychological buoyant feeling of being able to be so much more involved and sharing. Sharing experiences of goals, sharing of feelings, working together to solve problems, etc. My viewpoint of a true love, husband-and-wife type of relationship is one that is founded on mutual respect, admiration, affection, the ability to give and receive freely." His new wife, a divorcee his own age, brings four children to their marriage, added to Brian's own three. They have five children still living at home, and a sense of energy, mutual devotion, and commitment sufficient to make their family life a joy.

In many ways, Brian's is an individual success story. He has succeeded materially, and he has also taken hold of the opportunity to reach out beyond material success to a fuller sense of what he wants from life. Yet despite the personal triumph Brian's life represents, despite the fulfillment he seems to experience, there is still something uncertain, something poignantly unresolved about his story.

The difficulty becomes most evident when Brian tries to explain why it is that his current life is, in fact, better than his earlier life built around single-minded devotion to his career. His description of his reasons for changing his life and of his current happiness seems to come down mainly to a shift in his notions of what would make him happy. His new goal—devotion to marriage and children—seems as arbitrary and unexamined as his earlier pursuit of material success. Both are justified as idiosyncratic preference rather than as representing a larger sense of the purpose of life. Brian sees himself as consistently pursuing a utilitarian calculus—devotion to his own self-interest—except that there has been an almost inexplicable change in his personal preferences. In describing the reasons for this change, he begins, "Well, I think I just reestablished my priorities." He sometimes seems to reject his past life as wrong; but at other times, he seems to say he simply got bored with it. "That seems to me not a good way to live. That's not the most important thing to me. I have demonstrated to myself, to my own satisfaction, that I can achieve about what I want to achieve. So the challenge of goal realization does not contain that mystique that it held for me at one time. I just have found that I get a lot of personal reward from being involved in the lives of my children."

American cultural traditions define personality, achievement, and the purpose of human life in ways that leave the individual suspended in glorious, but terrifying, isolation. These are limitations of our culture, of the categories and ways of thinking we have inherited, not limitations of individuals such as Brian who inhabit the culture. People frequently live out a fuller sense of purpose in life than they can justify in rational terms, as we see in Brian's case and many others.

Brian's restless energy, love of challenges, and appreciation of the good life are characteristics of much that is most vital in American culture. They are all qualities particularly well-suited to the hard-driving corporate world in which he works. When Brian describes how he has chosen to live, however, he keeps referring to "values" and "priorities" not justified by any wider framework of purpose or belief. What is good is what one finds rewarding. If one's preferences change, so does the nature of the good. Even the deepest ethical virtues are justified as matters of personal preference. Indeed, *the ultimate ethical rule is simply that individuals should be able to pursue whatever they find rewarding, constrained only by the requirement that they not interfere with the "value systems" of others* [emphasis added by editors]. "I guess I feel like everybody on this planet is entitled to have a little bit of space, and things that detract from other people's space are kind of bad," Brian observes. "One of the things that I use to characterize life in California, one of the things that makes California such a pleasant place to live, is people by and large aren't bothered by other people's value systems as long as they don't infringe upon your own. By and large, the rule of thumb out here is that if you've got the money, honey, you can do your thing as long as your thing doesn't destroy someone else's property, or interrupt their sleep, or bother their privacy, then that's fine. If you want to go in your house and smoke marijuana and shoot dope and get all screwed up, that's your business, but don't bring that out on the street, don't expose my children to it, just do your thing. That works kind of neat." . . .

Each of the individuals that we have described in this chapter is drawn from one of the four research projects on which the book is based.* We are less concerned with whether they are average than with the fact that they represent the ways in which American use private and public life to make sense of their lives. This is the central issue with which our book is concerned. Brian Palmer finds the chief meaning of his life in marriage and family; Margaret Oldham in therapy. Thus both of them are primarily concerned with private life. Joe Gorman gives his life coherence through his active concern for the life of his town; Wayne Bauer finds a similar coherence in his involvement in political activism. Both of them have integrated the public world deeply into their lives. Whether chiefly concerned with private or public life, all four are involved in caring for others. They are responsible and, in many ways, admirable adults. Yet when each of them uses the moral discourse they share, what we call the first language of individualism, they have difficulty articulating the richness of their commitments. In the language they use, their lives sound more isolated and arbitrary than, as we have observed them, they actually are.

*Only Brian Palmer's story is reprinted here. Margaret Oldham, Joe Gorman and Wayne Bauer are the other individuals whose lives are examined in Habits of the Heart.—Eds.

Thus all four of the persons whose voices we have heard assume that there is something arbitrary about the goals of a good life. For Brian Palmer, the goal of a good life is to achieve the priorities you have set for yourself. But how do you know that your present priorities are better than those of your past, or better than those of other people? Because you intuitively appreciate that they are right for you at the present time. For Joe Gorman, the goal of a good life is intimate involvement with the community and family into which he happens to have been born. But how do you know that in this complicated world, the inherited conventions of your community and your family are better and more important, and, therefore, more worthy of your allegiance, than those of other communities and families? In the end, you simply prefer to believe that they are better, at least for you. For Margaret Oldham, the goal of a good life is liberation from precisely the kinds of conventions that Joe Gorman holds dear. But what do you aim for once you have been liberated? Simply what you yourself decide is best for you. For Wayne Bauer, the goal of a good life is participation in the political struggle to create a more just society. But where should political struggle lead us? To a society in which all individuals, not just the wealthy, will have power over their own lives. But what are they going to do with that power? Whatever they individually choose to do, as long as they don't hurt anybody.

The common difficulties these four very different people face in justifying the goals of a morally good life point to a characteristic problem of people in our culture. For most of us, it is easier to think about how to get what we want than to know what exactly we should want. Thus Brian, Joe, Margaret, and Wayne are each in his or her own way confused about how to define for themselves such things as the nature of success, the meaning of freedom, and the requirements of justice. Those difficulties are in an important way created by the limitations in the common tradition of moral discourse they—and we—share. . . .

FREEDOM IS PERHAPS THE MOST RESONANT, deeply held American value. In some ways, it defines the good in both personal and political life. Yet freedom turns out to mean being left alone by others, not having other people's values, ideas, or styles of life forced upon one, being free of arbitrary authority in work, family, and political life. What it is that one might do with that freedom is much more difficult for Americans to define. And if the entire social world is made up of individuals, each endowed with the right to be free of others' demands, it becomes hard to forge bonds of attachment to, or cooperation with, other people, since such bonds would imply obligations that necessarily impinge on one's freedom. . . .

For Margaret, as for others influenced by modern psychological ideals, to be free is not simply to be left alone by others; it is also somehow to be your own person in the sense that you have defined who you are, decided for yourself what you want out of life, free as much as possible from the demands of conformity to family, friends, or community. From this point of view, to be free psychologically is to succeed in separating oneself from the values imposed by one's past or by conformity to one's social milieu, so that one can discover what one really wants. . . .

Joe Gorman and Wayne Bauer both value democratic as well as personal freedom. But even their own political and social definition of freedom—not freedom to be your own person so much as the freedom cherished in a democracy, freedom to speak out, to participate freely in a community, and to have one's rights respected, is highly individualistic. As a traditional American patriot, Joe Gorman deeply cherishes the American ideal of freedom, even though in many ways it is precisely the ideal of freedom that makes his dream of a united Suffolk family impossible to achieve. The success of Suffolk's family spirit depends, as he has discovered, on the willingness of a few people like himself to volunteer freely to sustain community life with their own efforts. Yet he recognizes that very few people in Suffolk are willing to undertake the burdens of shaping community life, and that a man like himself is therefore likely to become exhausted, repeatedly finding himself the only volunteer.

Even more, it is the freedom Joe Gorman values—freedom of each person to live where he wants, do what he wants, believe what he wants, and, certainly, do what he can to improve his material circumstances—that makes community ties so fragile. The freedom of free enterprise makes Suffolk a bedroom community to which the residents are attached mainly by housing prices, while economic opportunities tempt most of its native sons and daughters away. The ideal of freedom Joe Gorman holds most dear makes it difficult even to discuss the question of how a just economy or a good society might best be developed in modern circumstances. For Joe, freedom and community can be reconciled only in the nostalgic dream of an idealized past. . . .

PRIVATE AND PUBLIC

Sometimes Americans make a rather sharp dichotomy between private and public life. Viewing one's primary task as "finding oneself" in autonomous self-reliance, separating oneself not only from one's parents but also from those larger communities and traditions that constitute one's past, leads to the notion that it is in oneself, perhaps in relation to a few intimate others, that fulfillment is to be found. Individualism of this sort often implies a negative view of public life. The impersonal forces of the economic and political worlds are what the individual needs protection against. In this perspective, even occupation, which has been so central to the identity of Americans in the past, becomes instrumental—not a good in itself, but only a means to the attainment of a rich and satisfying private life. But on the basis of what we have seen in our observation of middle-class American life, it would seem that this quest for purely private fulfillment is illusory: it often ends in emptiness instead. On the other hand, we found many people, . . . for whom private fulfillment and public involvement are not antithetical. These people evince an individualism that is not empty but is full of content drawn from an active identification with communities and traditions. Perhaps the notion that private life and public life are at odds is incorrect. Perhaps they are so deeply involved with each other that the impoverishment of one entails the impoverishment of the other. Parker Palmer is probably right when he says that "in a healthy society the private and the public are not mutually exclusive, not in competition with each other. They are, instead, two halves of a whole, two poles of a paradox. They work together dialectically, helping to create and nurture one another." . . .

For all their doubts about the public sphere, Americans are more engaged in voluntary associations and civic organizations than the citizens of most other industrial nations. In spite of all the difficulties, many Americans feel they must "get involved." In public life as in private, we can discern the habits of the heart that sustain individualism and commitment, as well as what makes them problematic. . . .

For several centuries, we have been embarked on a great effort to increase our freedom, wealth, and power. For over a hundred years, a large part of the American people, the middle class, has imagined that the virtual meaning of life lies in the acquisition of ever-increasing status, income, and authority, from which genuine freedom is supposed to come. Our achievements have been enormous. They permit us the aspiration to become a genuinely humane society in a genuinely decent world, and provide many of the means to attain that aspiration. Yet we seem to be hovering on the very brink of disaster, not only from international conflict but from the internal incoherence of our own society. What has gone wrong? How can we reverse the slide toward the abyss?

In thinking about what has gone wrong, we need to see what we can learn from our traditions, as well as from the best currently available knowledge. What has failed at every level—from the society of nations to the national society to the local community to the family—is integration: we have failed to remember "our community as members of the same body," as John Winthrop put it. We have committed what to the republican founders of our nation was the cardinal sin: we have put our own good, as individuals, as groups, as a nation, ahead of the common good. . . .

What we fear above all, and what keeps the new world powerless to be born, is that if we give up our dream of private success for a more genuinely integrated societal community, we will be abandoning our separation and individuation, collapsing into dependence and tyranny. What we find hard to see is that it is the extreme fragmentation of the modern world that really threatens our individuation: that what is best in our separation and individuation, our sense of dignity and autonomy as persons, requires a new integration if it is to be sustained.

The notion of a transition to a new level of social integration, a newly vital social ecology, may also be resisted as absurdly utopian, as a project to create a perfect society. But the transformation of which we speak is both necessary and modest. Without it, indeed, there may be very little future to think about at all. . . .

The question is whether an individualism in which the self has become the main form of reality can really be sustained [emphasis added by editors]. What is at issue is not simply whether self-contained individuals might withdraw from the public sphere to pursue purely private ends, but whether such individuals are capable of sustaining either a public or a private life. If this is the danger, perhaps only the civic and biblical forms of individualism—forms that see the individual in relation to a larger whole, a community and a tradition—are capable of sustaining genuine individuality and nurturing both public and private life.

There are both ideological and sociological reasons for the growing strength of modern individualism at the expense of the civic and biblical traditions. Modern individualism has pursued individual rights and individual autonomy in ever new realms. In so doing, it has come into confrontation with those aspects of biblical and republican thought that accepted, even enshrined, unequal rights and obligations—between husbands and wives, masters and servants, leaders and followers, rich and poor. As the absolute commitment to individual dignity has condemned those inequalities, it has also seemed to invalidate the biblical and republican traditions. And in undermining these traditions, as Tocqueville warned, individualism also weakens the very meanings that give content and substance to the ideal of individual dignity.

We thus face a profound impasse. Modern individualism seems to be producing a way of life that is neither individually nor socially viable, yet a return to traditional forms would be to return to intolerable discrimination and oppression. The question, then, is whether the older civic and biblical traditions have the capacity to reformulate themselves while simultaneously remaining faithful to their own deepest insights. . . .

SIGNS OF THE TIMES

Few of those with whom we talked would have described the problems facing our society in exactly the terms we have just used. But few have found a life devoted to "personal ambition and consumerism" satisfactory, and most are seeking in one way or another to transcend the limitations of a self-centered life. If there are vast numbers of a selfish, narcissistic "me generation" in America, we did not find them, but we certainly did find that the language of individualism, the primary American language of self-understanding, limits the ways in which people think.

Many Americans are devoted to serious, even ascetic, cultivation of the self in the form of a number of disciplines, practices, and "trainings," often of great rigor. There is a question as to whether these practices lead to the self-realization or self-fulfillment at which they aim or only to an obsessive self-manipulation that defeats the proclaimed purpose. But it is not uncommon for those who are attempting to find themselves to find in that very process something that transcends them. For example, a Zen student reported: "I started Zen to get something for myself, to stop suffering, to get enlightened. Whatever it was, I was doing it for myself I had hold of myself and I was reaching for something. Then to do it, I found out I had to give up that hold on myself. Now it has hold of me, whatever 'it' is." What this student found is that the meaning of life is not to be discovered in manipulative control in the service of the self. Rather, through the disciplined practices of a religious way of life, the student found his self more grasped than grasping. It is not surprising that "self-realization" in this case has occurred in the context of a second language, the allusive language of Zen Buddhism, and a community that attempts to put that language into practice.

Many Americans are concerned to find meaning in life not primarily through self-cultivation but through intense relations with others. Romantic love is still idealized in our society. It can, of course, be remarkably self-indulgent, even an excuse to use another for one's own gratification. But it can also be a revelation of the poverty of the self and lead to a genuine humility in the presence of the beloved. . . . As in the case of self-cultivation, there is in the desire for intense relationships with others an attempt to move beyond the isolated self, even though the language of individualism makes that sometimes hard to articulate. . . .

Many of those with whom we talked were locked into a split between a public world of competitive striving and a private world supposed to provide the meaning and love that make competitive striving bearable. Some, however, were engaged in an effort to overcome this split, to make our public and our private worlds mutually coherent. . . . All of these people are drawing on our republican and biblical traditions, trying to make what have become second languages into our first language again. We have spoken of "reappropriating tradition"—that is, finding sustenance in tradition and applying it actively and creatively to our present realities. . . .

On the basis of our interviews, and from what we can observe more generally in our society today, it is not clear that many Americans are prepared to consider a significant change in the way we have been living. The allure of the packaged good life is still strong, though dissatisfaction is widespread. Americans are fairly ingenious in finding temporary ways to counteract the harsher consequences of our damaged social ecology. Livy's words about ancient Rome also apply to us: "We have reached the point where we cannot bear either our vices or their cure." But, as some of the more perceptive of the people to whom we talked believe, the time may be approaching when we will either reform our republic or fall into the hands of despotism, as many republics have done before us.

NO

Henry Fairlie

THE FICTION OF THE MASSES

The masses do not exist. But the idea of "the masses," although it is a fiction, the invention of a few minds, dominates the way in which we both think of our societies and even of ourselves. It helps to nourish both the rebellion of the self and the revolt of the privileged, since everyone would like to distinguish himself from "the masses." None of us believes that he is a mass man, and we do not think of those whom we meet as mass men. We live by anecdote, and anecdotes are about what is particular, an individual or an occasion. We do not say in the evening, "I met a mass man today, called Petermass, and he was exactly like Philipmass, the mass man whom I was telling you about yesterday." If that was all that we had to say, we would have nothing to tell; we would have no anecdote.

We can test this from our own experiences. We all have a story to tell about the conversation of an Italian taxi driver who has just driven us from La Guardia Airport to the centre of Manhattan. No story is ever quite the same; the words of the Italian taxi driver which we report this evening are not the same as the words of the Italian taxi driver who drove us on that evening a week ago. Others interrupt with their own stories of Italian taxi drivers; and, although there is something common to them all, which is a part of their point, they are also all different, which is why we tell them. Again, we notice when one mailman is replaced by another. He performs for us the same service, at about the same time each day, in approximately the same way, as did his predecessor; and we are grateful that he does, it is not eccentricity that we expect of him. But we also notice that there is something different about him, and it is this we mention to our neighbours: "I wish we had the old mailman back, he always had time for a chat." . . . "Thank goodness the old mailman's gone, he always wanted to talk when I was busy."

This is how people talk. They have been touched by individuals during the day, whom they have observed as individuals, and on whose individuality they report in the evening with a story. We call our buses "mass transit"; but we get on a bus in the rush hour, and the driver is either welcoming or he does not have the time of day for us. "He's a sourpuss," we say as we take

From Henry Fairlie, *The Spoiled Child of the Western World: The Miscarriage of the American Idea in Our Time* (Doubleday, 1975). Copyright © 1975, 1976 by Henry Fairlie. Reprinted by permission of Doubleday, a division of Bantam, Doubleday, Dell Publishing Group, Inc. Notes omitted.

our seats, and stick out our tongues behind his back. We do not lament, "Alas and alack! Mass man is driving us today." We know that the next morning the driver may be Irish, with a "top of the morning" for us. In the common situations that we share from day to day, we notice individuals who behave in their own ways, not as a mass.

Unless we are from day to day aware of this—how each retains his individuality, not in the isolation of his-self, but in his dealings with others in our state—we will again be persuaded that as a social being he is inauthentic. We will learn to think of our companions in the estate only as "the masses," and the estate itself only as "mass society." The rebellion of the self will be justified by what we have been taught is the condition of our society. We must be ready to go out each morning and return each evening, and ask ourselves in our ordinary encounters whom we met during the day who was a mass man, who was less of an individual than ourselves; against the ways in which we are taught to imagine our situation, we must bring the evidence of our own senses. . . .

IN DEFENCE OF THE SUPERMARKET

. . . The homogenization of "the masses," as it has been foretold and feared for so long, has not occurred; least of all has it occurred in America, which was described by Ortega as "the paradise of the masses." Instead, there has been the most astonishing individualization of whole classes of people who throughout all previous history have been undifferentiated. Let us consider, for example, "the consumer" in our "consumer societies," which is another of the symbols by which we represent "the masses" in our "mass societies." "The consumer" is commonly taken to be marked by the uniformity of his tastes; but, if we look closely, we will find that his true mark is an increasing individualization of his tastes.

One of the most common symbols of the "consumer society" is, in turn, the replacement of the village (or neighbourhood or corner) shop by the supermarket. One did not know, until one read their writings, that so many of our intellectuals, including some of the most prominent of them, spend so much of their time buying the groceries; or that they suffer such a delicate feeling of estrangement from their fellow men, from society, from nature, from god, or from whatever they feel alienated, when they enter a supermarket. To someone who in fact enjoys trundling his cart round a supermarket. This expression of their feelings is worrying, since it suggests that his own sensibility may be peculiarly dull; and it is even more worrying if he in fact grew up where there were only village (or neighbourhood or corner) shops, and his memory of them, far from being pleasant, is quite the opposite: that they were not pleasant places to go.

Again and again, in the kind of literature we are discussing, we are given a picture of the village woman who used to shop at the village store, where she was served by the village shopkeeper, with whom she discussed the latest gossip, and who is now "at a loss in the metropolitan supermarket where her demands are no longer dictated by her needs, but on the contrary dictated by an abundant supply." At the checkout counter, there is no time for gossip, and she receives only a small slip of paper with the words "Thank you" printed on it, "more for the sake of public than personal relationships. The shopkeeper, focal point in rural face-to-face relationships, has been replaced by machines and anonymous functionaries." The writers seem almost to repeat each other. C. Wright Mills, for example, said that "the small shop serving the neighbourhood is replaced by the anonymity of the national corporation: mass advertisement replaces the personal influence of opinion between merchant and customer."

But the village shop, as one knew it personally, and as one can red about it in fiction, was usually an unattractive place, and frequently a malignant one. The gossip which was exchanged was, as often as not, inaccurate and cruel. Although there were exceptions, one's main memory of the village shopkeeper, man and wife, is of faces which were hard and sharp and mean, leaning forward to whisper into ears that were cocked and turned to hear all that they could of the misfortunes or the disgrace of a neighbour. Whisper! Whisper! Whisper! This has always been the chief commodity of the village shop. And not only whispers, because the village shopkeeper, informed or misinformed, could always apply sanctions against those to whom disgrace or misfortune was imputed.

The anonymity of the supermarket is in fact a gain in privacy, even in the equalization of dignity. Anyone can shop at a supermarket without the whole of his life being known and examined; if he is living in sin, or his daughter is made, or he has dodged the draft, it is of no consequence to the manager or the checkout girl, as long as he can pay the bill.

But let us suppose that the customer is respectable by the standards that prevail: what of the choice, in making a purchase, which is available? There is an impenetrable obscurity in the suggestion that, whereas in the village shop, the customer's demands were dictated by his or her needs, in the supermarket they are dictated by an abundant supply. One really has to do better than that. The demands of most customers at a village shop were dictated, not by their needs, but by their purses; and their purses were very rarely in equation with their needs. The majority of villagers were always poor, and were known to be poor.

It is true that too often at too many supermarkets one may still observe the really poor as they desperately try to balance their purses against their needs, as they rummage for a last penny at the checkout counter. But there is a saving grace in the supermarket even for them. They no longer go into the village shop to be told by the shopkeeper, "Ah! Mrs. Smith, I have saved a few neckbones for you," as if she had no choice, and he was the author of a benefaction. They now enter the supermarket anonymously; no one says to them, "We know what you can afford." They diddle around at the meat counter, as we all do, and even if they in the end have to settle for the neckbones or the chicken feet, they have known, not merely the illusion of choice, as some would say, but something of the experience of choice. The possibility of choice was there, present to them; it was reduced, as they calculated, by the fact of their poverty, but it was not a denial from the beginning, made by others on their behalf, an ordering of the fates, in the person of the village shopkeeper.

What is more, the poor in the supermarket can refuse, with the dignity that anonymity confers, the reduction of their choice. One does not need to imagine, one can remember all too well, Mrs. Smith announcing in a village store that she was tired of cabbage and would try some peas for a change. At once she was reproved by the village shopkeeper—the entertaining fellow—"Ah! Mrs. Smith, you know that the cabbage will go much farther than the peas, with all of those mouths to feed," and before she can remonstrate, the cabbage has been popped into her bag. But in a supermarket one can watch the poor decide for themselves that this week they will waste a little money on a frill, and nobody will challenge or reprove them. . . .

THE RELEASE FROM CUSTOM

But let us leave aside the really poor, and consider the choice that is available at the supermarket to the large majority of Americans, and increasingly to a large number of men and women in comparable societies. Let us watch them also as they shop. Their demands are not dictated by an abundant supply; their demands on the abundant supply are restricted by their purses. The choice of the poor is reduced to the point at which the nature of the choice is changed; the choice of the majority is restricted, but its nature is not affected, it is a limitation only of degree.

Restriction by the purse becomes more serious if the variety of goods that are available is itself restricted. This has always been one of the faults of the village shop. Not only are its goods more expensive than in a supermarket, because its turnover is not so great, but the variety of goods which it carries is limited. This means that the customer is doubly subject to the necessity, week after week, to purchase the same foods, in order to make the same meals. The choice in the supermarket, if the customer wishes to take advantage of it, is much wider. He can determine to spend more on a for-eign cheese—which would probably not be available in the village store in any case—knowing that he can save the extra money that he has spent on the cheese by buying a cheaper vegetable.

These may not seem to be important increases in human freedom, until one considers how astonishingly more varied are the personal tastes of ordinary people than they were even a quarter of a century ago. From this point of view, the recent proliferation of small shops—delicatessens, health-food stores, boutiques—ought to be seen, not as an alternative to the supermarket and the department store, but as an extension of them; they are certainly an extension of the "consumer society," and the true significance of the "consumer society" is this increasing differentiation of tastes. The vegetable counter of almost any supermarket is an invitation to the individual customer to experiment and discriminate with his own taste and, although the significance of this may seem to be slight, it is an expression of individualization, as it is an education in it, far removed from the notion of "the masses."

Not to have to eat the same food that one was brought up to eat, not to have to eat the same food that one ate last week, not to have to eat the same food for all one's life: this is a release from custom, and from its bondage; and there again one can observe how the critics of "the masses" have a point and then misconstrue it. Even in this simple matter of food, the release from custom does indeed mean the destruction of an old culture variety. Germans no longer eat only German food, and German food is no longer eaten only by Germans. When the critics of "mass society" talk of the homogenization of tastes, it is usually to the destruction of this cultural variety that they are referring. But this destruction has been accompanied by an individualization of personal tastes that is elaborately various. German food is not lost to the human memory, the arts of German cooking are not forgotten; they have merely become the property, not of a culture, but of individuals, if that is their taste. What is more, the sharing of individual tastes can then become an opportunity for human companionship and interchange, of associations that are voluntary and not just customary. . . .

"The masses" whom one remembers even from one's own childhood and youth, the working classes and the lower middle classes, ate the same food from day to day, wore the same clothes from year to year, and were uniform in taste and appearance. In contrast, their children or grandchildren are today astonishingly various and colourful in these everyday expressions of their individuality. These gains may seem to be small; but they have their reflections at a more serious level. One does not wish to exaggerate their importance; but it is time that we challenged some of the images in which our society is represented to us, so that we grow to disdain it. The privileged man who was a dandy in the past ought not to be contemptuous or resentful of the construction worker who today is making something of a dandy of himself under his hard hat, which is perched improbably on his mannered tresses, tolerated even by his employer, and now scarcely noticed by passers-by.

THE ROMANTIC IDEALIZATION OF VILLAGE LIFE

If the village shop has been romanticized in contrast to the supermarket, so has the life of the village itself, and the idea of the community which it is supposed to have represented. Villages have usually been, and commonly still are, unattractive and confined, mean in condition and in spirit, unless they are the idealized relics of a rural past which a prosperous and commuting middle class preserves for its quasi-pastoral enjoyments, singing the virtues of a village life that they have urbanized.

Mahmut Makal's bitter description of a village in Anatolia, not in the past but in our own time, can stand for the majority of villages. There is nowhere else to go, even a thought of anywhere else: "the villager has no desire for any other kind of existence; or—more exactly—he believes that 'the best of all days is today.' . . . So the wheel of fate grinds out our lives, turning as it has done for the last thousand years." Custom is never challenged: "In the eyes of the villagers, women are practically of no value whatever. . . . The man can strike her, curse her, beat her, make her weep, cause her pain, and she may not say a word." Religion is only a thrall of suspicion: "Our villagers are born to religion. But they show no interest in that aspect of religion which means unity, friendship, love, and respect for others. . . . A charm for the barren woman, a charm for the child who has broken his leg falling off a roof, a charm to make hair grow on the bald head of a baby, a pinch of salt 'breathed' upon an aching tooth—another charm. Charmers and charms; sorcerers and sorcery; such things are a matter of daily occurrence. So it persists. Frustration, ignorance, destitution; hand in hand, saluting each other, they go straight to hell."

If it is said that this is a picture only of a poor village in a poor region of Anatolia, one must answer that most villages in the past have been like it, that in the world today most villages are still like it, and that even in Europe and America at this moment there are plenty of villages in which, although life has been eased a little, it is still bound to the same wheel. To a greater or lesser degree, the mind and life of the villager are, as Marx said of rural India more than a century ago, "bound in the smallest possible compass," from which there is rarely an escape. . . .

We confront a society, says Robert Nisbet, "composed in ever-increasing numbers of amorphous and incoherent masses, of people who have seen spiritual meanings vanish with the forms of traditional society and who struggle vainly to find re-assimilation." What does he imagine that the spiritual meanings were which the majority of people found in their lives in the past, except fear and incomprehension and an abject submission to what they understood to be their fate? To have released men from fear and imcomprehension and superstition, from submission to gods and kings and popes, is not a loss to them, but the opening of an opportunity, an affirmation such as their ancestors never knew, that they may remake their own lives and their own society.

ONE OF THE DEAD FORMS OF EUROPE

In all these hankerings after the village store and the village, it is the old—and, in particular, the feudal—idea of community that has travelled like a ghost from Europe, in our time, to haunt the new society of America. It is community we have lost, cry the Europeans in their remembrance of times past. It is community we are lacking, echo the Americans

in their uncertainty of times future. European or American, in our ill humour with our own times, we imagine that there were golden ages of community in the past. There was community in Athens—but for whom, in a society "whose division of labour was based on the exploitation of many by man"? There was community in feudalism—but for whom in a society which, in the words of Marc Bloch, the great historian of the Middle Ages, "meant the rigorous economic subjugation of a host of humble folk to a few powerful men . . . whereby men exploited men . . . chiefly to the benefit of an oligarchy of warriors"? . . . The imagination of this European conservatism has never reached beyond the possibility of restoration. In the absence of the old communities of Europe, it has been unable to imagine a society that does not suffer from the atomization of the individual, on the one hand, or the homogenization of "the masses," on the other. It can imagine the individual as self-possessed only in the dead societies of its own past.

THE INDIVIDUAL BECOMES SELF-CONSCIOUS

. . . [I]n the societies of the past that are held up to our admiration, primitive or classical or medieval, the idea of the individual, to say nothing of his sense of his own identity, did not exist. It was not a matter of concern and it was certainly less a matter of concern than it is in our own societies which are supposed to be composed only of the "mass man," anonymous and unidentifiable. . . .

The distinction between the individual and his society, and between his society and the state, has been the work of the modern age, and not only is this double distinction most precious to us, thee is no way in which we can properly understand either ourselves or our societies if we do not strenuously hold to it. When we talk of "the masses" in our "mass societies," we ought to be talking, first, of the individuals who compose them, each equal in his rights and in his claims on his society and, secondly, of the fact that their relations with their society are personal, not mediated by hierarchy or status, by guild or community, by church or even now by family. The relationships of the individual have ceased to be more important than himself. This is the positive gain of the modern age, of which we are the beneficiaries. If we have lost a sense of community, it is because we have gained a sense of the individual. . . .

Only in the American idea has there lain this double affirmation of the individuality of each, and of the equality of each with all: the idea of the I released in the En-Masse. . . .

Amazingly, because it has never before been true in history, the individual who is self-conscious as an individual is the unit round which our societies must organize themselves. He is the man who finds his dignity, as it was put by George Herbert Mead, in the fact that, when he calls upon himself, he finds himself at home. If we are bound to imagine the individual in this manner, we are no less bound to reimagine our societies in such a way that he will be enabled to participate fully as an individual in the common life, so that each may know and feel that he is a citizen. . . .

THE MODEL IN AMERICA

One is not denying that immensity of the challenge—to imagine and then to create a society in which the individual day by day negotiates with it as himself, and it day by day addresses him as an individual—but at least we have a model before us. Whatever its faults, the vast commonalty of the middle class of the United States is a society of individuals, in the sense that we are trying to imagine; it is here that most obviously the I has been released in the En-Masse, with no mediator between the two. The result is not yet rewarding to the individual, or satisfactory to society; but there can be no doubt that here is where the challenge may be met, that it is in "the paradise of the masses" that the I must be established, not only as an individual in his own right, but as fully a citizen.

It ought to be a boast, not a lament, that the example of the En-Masse is being spread by America to the rest of the world, with its power and its commerce. "We do indeed share a common culture," says Edgar Z. Friedenberg of the United States. "And the commonness goes further. American mass gratifications, from soft drinks to comic books and movies, have turned out to be the common coin of the mass culture the world over. This is not conquest, but genuine culture diffusion. All over the world, man in the mass has turned out to be exactly our type of fellow." His point is correct, but the voice is familiar in its disaffection. As always, the emphasis is put only on the material manifestations—and these the grossest—of the culture that is being spread. . . .

The questioning of traditional standards has not proved to be the negation of all standards; the desire to replace has not proved to be an ambition to destroy, the claim of equality has not proved to be a denial of liberty. We have only to look around us in the public estate of America to see that the I released in the En-Masse is neither impatient nor placid, that even in so short a time, year by year, generation after generation, the search is being made for new forms to replace the dead forms of the past. Perhaps it requires an outsider to affirm that the commonalty of the middle class in America is experimental and invigorating and rich in promise, and that it needs only a further exercise of our imaginations to recover for it a sense of direction and a common understanding of its purpose.

POSTSCRIPT

Has Individualism Become Excessive?

Bellah and his associates are critical of Brian Palmer for changing his life-style without being able to justify the change in terms of "a larger sense of the purpose of life." But is that necessary? Do we have to employ widely shared value systems to guide the changes in our lives? Fairlie, on the other hand, cites supermarkets as an example, where people can choose without having to explain their choices. But living our lives is different than picking products from a shelf. "How ought we to live? How do we think about how to live?" Perhaps Bellah and his associates are right to force these questions on us.

America's perennial "Lockeanism" is the theme of Louis Hartz's classic *The Liberal Tradition in America* (Harvest Books, 1955). For the limitations of this approach, see Dorothy Ross, "The Liberal Tradition Revisited and the Republican Tradition Addressed," in John Higham and Paul K. Conking, eds., *New Directions in American Intellectual History* (Johns Hopkins, 1979). Some studies suggest that Americans are quite adept at forming community networks, even in "impersonal" cities. See for example, Claude S. Fischer et al., *Networks and Places* (Free Press, 1977), and Peggy Wireman, *Urban Neighborhoods, Networks, and Families* (Lexington Books, 1984). Others, however, take a more pessimistic view of our capacities for joint action, See, for example, Christopher Lasch, *The Culture of Narcissism* (W. W. Norton, 1979), and Richard Sennett, *The Fall of Public Man* (Alfred A. Knopf, 1976).

The same group that produced *Habits of the Heart* in 1985 produced *The Good Society* in 1991, in which they argue that the "culture of individualism makes the very idea of institutions inaccessible to many of us." Individualistic Americans, therefore, seek to limit the control of institutions over them when they should be shaping institutions to better serve them.

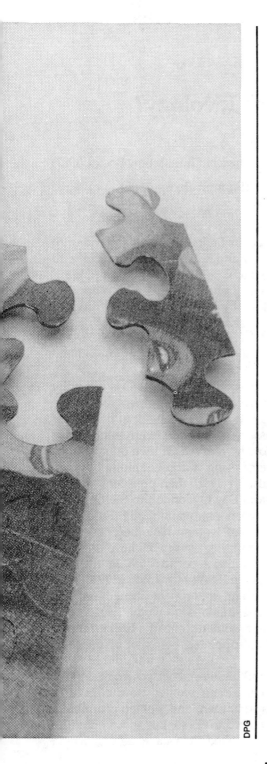

PART 2

Sex Roles and the Family

The modern feminist movement has advanced the cause for the well-being of women to the point where there are now more women in the work force in the United States than ever before. Professions and trades that were traditionally regarded as the province of men have opened up to women, and women have easier access to the education and training necessary to excel in these new areas. But is feminism as a universal philosophy harmful in any way? What are the experiences of women who are balancing careers and families? Do these women need corporate programs to help them maintain that balance? What is happening to sex roles, and what are the effects of changing sex roles? How have related problems such as sexual harassment and the deterioration of the traditional family structure affected these changes? The issues in this part address these sorts of questions.

Is Feminism a Harmful Ideology?
_____

Would a "Mommy Track" Benefit
   Employed Women?
_____

Is Sexual Harassment a Pervasive
   Problem in America?
_____

Should Traditional Families Be
   Preserved?

DPG

ISSUE 4

Is Feminism a Harmful Ideology?

YES: Michael Levin, from *Feminism and Freedom* (Transaction Books, 1987)

NO: Marilyn French, from *Beyond Power* (Summit Books, 1985)

ISSUE SUMMARY

YES: Professor of philosophy Michael Levin faults feminism for trying to impose an inappropriate equality on men and women that conflicts with basic biological differences between the sexes.
NO: Novelist and literary scholar Marilyn French advocates both equality between the sexes and the transformation of existing patriarchal structures to elevate feminine values to the same level as masculine values.

The publication of Betty Friedan's *The Feminine Mystique* in 1963 is generally used to mark the beginning of the modern women's movement, and since that time significant changes have occurred in American society: Occupations and professions, schools, clubs, associations, and governmental positions that were by tradition or law previously reserved for men only are now open to women. Women are found in increasing numbers among lawyers, judges, physicians, and elected officials. In 1981, then-president Ronald Reagan appointed the first woman, Sandra Day O'Connor, to the Supreme Court. In 1983, the first American woman astronaut (Sally Ride) was included in the crew of a space shuttle, and women have been on more recent space shuttle missions as well. The service academies have accepted women since 1976, and women in the military participated in the U.S. invasion of Panama in December 1989 and the Persian Gulf War in 1990–1991. There are ongoing debates in Congress and among the armed services themselves about whether or not to lift restrictions on women serving in combat. Elizabeth Watson became the first woman to head a big city police department when the mayor of Houston appointed her chief of police in January 1990.

These sorts of changes—quantifiable and highly publicized—may signal a change in women's roles, at least to this extent: women now engage in occupations that were previously exclusive to men, and women can pursue the necessary training and education required to do so. But as we enter the decade of the 1990s, to what extent is the United States a society in which females and males have equal standing? Are femininity and femaleness prized or valued the same as maleness or masculinity? What is happening to our concepts of both? Even as changes are occurring in the public world, what is happening on a personal level to the roles of men and women? How do we value the domestic sphere? What is happening to child care? To our concept of the family?

Feminism—an ideology that, in its most basic form, directly opposes sexism by supporting gender equality and portraying women and men as equals—has been a driving force in shaping the modern women's movement. However, because sex differences are at once anatomical and physiological, the significance and implications of these differences are hotly disputed. Among men and women, among feminists and antifeminists, it is hard to arrive at a definition of terms on this issue of sex roles. On the subject of feminism, there is great ambivalence throughout American society. The Equal Rights Amendment to the Constitution (ERA), which would have made gender an irrelevant distinction under the law, and which passed both houses of Congress by overwhelming margins in 1972, failed to win ratification of the required three-fourths of the state legislatures in 1978. Although Congress extended the ratification date to 1982, the amendment—which Betty Friedan had termed "both the symbol and substance of women's rights"—failed to be ratified. That the amendment was not ratified was due in part to the efforts of a coalition of groups, composed overwhelmingly of women, who went to battle against it. In the readings that follow, Michael Levin argues that feminists falsely assume that women are the same as men, so their agenda of eliminating all observable social differences between men and women is doomed to fail, and will inflict more pain than gain in the process. In contrast, Marilyn French argues that the feminist agenda is a sound one and that it needs to be pushed further.

YES

Michael Levin

FEMINISM AND FREEDOM

When the eighty-eight women who took the New York City Fire Department's entrance examination in 1977 failed its physical strength component, they filed a class-action sex discrimination lawsuit in federal court. The court found for the plaintiffs, agreeing in *Berkman v. NYFD* that the strength test was not job-related and therefore in violation of Title VII of the Civil Rights Act. The court thereupon ordered the city to hire forty-five female firefighters and to construct a special, less demanding physical examination for female candidates, with males still to be held to the extant, more difficult—and ostensibly inappropriate—standard. In addition, the court ordered the city to provide special training to the eighty-eight female plaintiffs—but none for the 54 percent of the males who also failed the test—on the grounds that certain "tricks of the trade" available to all male candidates were not available to them.

New York declined to appeal *Berkman* and instructed its regular firemen to maintain public silence. Since *Berkman*, 38 of the original group of 145 women given special training by the NYFD have entered service as firefighters, and almost all personnel actions taken by the NYFD have required the approval of the presiding judge, Charles Sifton. Continuing litigation has resulted in further easing of the physical standards applied to female firefighting applicants.

The use of statistics in *Berkman* is particularly instructive. According to the guidelines of the Equal Employment Opportunity Commission, which are controlling in cases like *Berkman*, a test for a job is presumed to be discriminatory if the passing rate for women is less than 80 percent of that rate for men. The wider the gap, the less defeasible is the presumption. The court accordingly asked how likely it would be, in the absence of discrimination, that none of the eighty-eight women passed while 46 percent of the men did. As the court correctly noted, "the pass rates were separated by

From Michael Levin, *Feminism and Freedom* (Transaction Books, 1987). Copyright © 1987 by Transaction, Inc. Reprinted by permission. Notes omitted.

more than eight standard deviations" (1982 at 205), and the probability that this could happen is so small—less than one in 10 trillion—as to amount to virtual impossibility. The court's conclusion that discrimination must have occurred is entirely cogent, *if strength is assumed to be uncorrelated with sex.* A difference in failure rates on a strength test is consistent with the absence of bias if it is allowed that men are on average stronger than women. The court found an outcome of fewer than thirty-seven passes unacceptably improbable because it adopted the hypothesis that gender and strength are independent variables. Rejecting the hypothesis that gender and strength are in any way connected, the court construed an observed correlation between gender and strength as an artifact to be eliminated by special treatment for one sex. Since women are the same as men, the EEOC and the court reasoned, special steps must be taken to compensate for their manifest differences. . . .

Berkman illustrates as well the extent to which feminism has achieved its effects through the state, particularly unelected officials of the courts and the regulatory agencies, and those elected officials most remote from their constituencies. Gender quotas, limitations on free speech to combat "psychological damage to women" (to cite EEOC guidelines once again), among many other feminist innovations, are all state actions. What is more, the vagueness of such feminist-inspired initiatives as have been passed by elected officials—chiefly civil rights legislation governing gender, and the Equal Rights Amendments of various states—require that they be constantly interpreted, usually by unelected officials.

This, in short, is the thesis of the present book: It is not by accident that femi-nism has had its major impact through the necessarily coercive machinery of the state rather than through the private decisions of individuals. Although feminism speaks the language of liberation, self-fulfillment, options, and the removal of barriers, these phrases invariably mean their opposites and disguise an agenda at variance with the ideals of a free society. Feminism has been presented and widely received as a liberating force, a new view of the relations between the sexes emphasizing openness and freedom from oppressive stereotypes. The burden of the present book is to show in broad theoretical perspective and factual detail that this conventional wisdom is mistaken. Feminism is an antidemocratic, if not totalitarian, ideology.

Feminism is a program for making different beings—men and women—turn out alike, and like that other egalitarian, Procrustes, it must do a good deal of chopping to fit the real world into its ideal. More precisely, feminism is the thesis that males and females are already innately alike, with the current order of things—in which males and females appear to differ and occupy quite different social roles—being a harmful distortion of this fundamental similarity. Recognizing no innate gender differences that might explain observed gender differences and the broad structure of society, feminists are compelled to interpret these manifest differences as artifacts, judged by feminists to benefit men unfairly. Believing that overtly uncoerced behavior is the product of oppression, feminists must devise ever subtler theories about the social pressures "keeping women in their place"—pressures to be detected and cancelled.

The reader may feel an impulse to object that I am talking about radical feminism while ignoring moderate feminism, a more responsible position which concedes innate sex differences and wishes only to correct wrongs undeniably done to women. . . . [But] I believe . . . that complete environmentalism—the denial that innate sex differences have anything to do with the broad structure of society—is central to feminism, and that moderate feminism is a chimera. But even the reader wishing to distinguish moderate from radical feminism must concede that *Berkman* is radical by any standards, and that if radical feminism is sufficiently influential to sway the federal judiciary, its credentials and implications deserve close scrutiny.

The second major contention of this book complements the first. If, as I argue, . . . those broad features of society attributed by feminism to discriminatory socialization are in fact produced by innate gender differences, efforts to eradicate those features must be futile and never-ending. Reforms designed to end when sexism disappears will have to be retained indefinitely, imposing increasingly heavy costs on their nonmalleable subjects. Since innate gender differences express themselves as differences in the typical preferences of men and women, so that people will never freely act in ways which produce a world devoid of sexism, the equalization of the sexes in personal behavior and in the work world demands implacable surveillance and interference. In the end it is impossible to overcome the biological inevitability of sex roles, but it is possible to try—and to violate liberal values in the process. A good summary of my main thesis might run: equality of outcome entails inequality of opportunity. . . .

Despite the propensity of feminists and their commentators to frame issues in terms of the "politics" of women's status, legal reform is of interest to most feminists mainly as an instrument for working wholesale changes on society. Indifference to legal reform is in any case forced on feminists by the absence of anything to reform. Private discrimination against women has been illegal since 1964, and public discrimination at the state and municipal levels has been illegal since 1972. When at the behest of President Ronald Reagan the State of Georgia reviewed its statutes for possible discrimination, it reported that the most serious inequity in the state code was the occurrence of 10,000 "he's" as against 150 "she's." Popular discourse continues to allude to "much outright sex discrimination," but the examples of discrimination cited invariably concern the use of criteria in various activities that men are more likely to meet. Without some showing that these criteria are deployed *for the purpose* of excluding women, or that the discrepant effects of these criteria are *caused by* arbitrary socialization, these effects are not "discriminatory." The actual state of affairs is well illustrated by *Berkman:* extensive institutionalized preference favoring women over men. Feminists who explain their grievance in terms of laws against women driving buses may have a legitimate case, but it is one against Edwardian England, not a society in which female bus drivers are promoted over males with greater seniority.

To be sure, the claim that women do not yet enjoy equal opportunity is most frequently made not in connection with legal barriers but in terms of the tendency of people to think sex-stereotypically and to communicate sex-typed norms to the young. This claim will be considered in due course, but it suffices for now to reflect that, if the formation of stereotypic beliefs is a spontaneous response to perceptions of the world, altering these possibly oppressive beliefs will require manipulation of both the average person's spontaneous tendency to form beliefs and the social environment which prompts them. If the social environment is itself a spontaneous expression of innate sex differences, attempting (and inevitably failing) to alter this environment will require yet further intrusion.

Shifting the locus of unfairness from the realm of law to that of sex role stereotyping involves a shift from what can reasonably be called "political" to the entire range of extra-political institutions and behavior. Most of society's institutions emerge from the myriad uncoordinated decisions of individuals; to call these practices and institutions "political" suggests a disregard for the distinction between public and private and disdain for the private realm itself. It is not surprising that feminists who use the word "political" so expansively also speak as if they believe in an actual worldwide conspiracy against women. Once this usage is adopted, everything from office flirtation to children's horseplay becomes assessable for its tendency to abet the political decision about women's condition. Erstwhile private matters become questions of socially determined rights, and are pulled within the authority of the state.

To deny that women are victims of systematic discrimination is not to assert that contemporary Western civilization is perfect. . . .

The reader may be anxious to inform me of cases known to him of a competent woman being denied a desirable position just because she is a woman. I do not deny that such cases exist, but I ask the reader to remember three points. First, no accumulation of anecdotes can demonstrate an intrinsic societal bias against women. Second, a social arrangement can do no more than treat people better than other possible arrangements; perfect justice is unattainable. Third, the wrongs with which the reader is acquainted must be kept in perspective. Can being denied a merited promotion honestly be compared to being beaten for drinking from a Whites-only fountain, the sort of treatment Blacks experienced two generations ago? . . .

As groundless as the idea that feminism is a movement of liberal reform is the idea that it is passé. The immoderate language of twenty years ago is encountered less frequently today, but no doctrine is more influential in shaping institutional and public life than feminism. Under current federal law, a prospective employer is forbidden to ask a female job applicant if she plans to have children. The Supreme Court has outlawed pension plans that use the greater longevity of women as a factor in computing premiums. . . .

Political leaders of every persuasion reflexively employ gender quotas. The liberal governor of New York State reprimanded a selection committee for not including a female among its candidates for the state's Supreme Court while simultaneously praising all the candidates as "first-rate." A conservative president highly critical of quotas as a private citizen decided that his first Supreme Court appointment had to be a woman. . . . [T]he quota mentality now dominates all phases of employment. . . .

The popular press continues to suggest that wanting to marry and raise children is a curious goal for a woman. It is becoming somewhat more acceptable for a woman to find parenting important, but it is still unacceptable to assert that it is more important for a woman than for a man. . . .

Gender differences will emerge in any human social organization. Since every human activity is either the province of one sex or a joint endeavor of both in which these differences manifest themselves, it is possible to find sexism everywhere. While in that sense feminism conflicts with every human activity, the present book concentrates on the conflict between feminism and those institutions central to a free society. Among the most important are the free market and education. The only way to stifle, or try to stifle, the manifestation of gender differences in people's working lives is through a rigid program of job quotas and pay scales. . . . The only way to stifle, or try to stifle, the manifestation of gender differences in children's perceptions of each other is through a rigid program of exhorting them to disregard their senses. . . .

THE UNIVERSALITY OF MALE DOMINANCE AND SEX-ROLE DIFFERENTIATION

No student of human behavior denies the male advantage in dominance-aggression and its universal correlate, preparedness to use force. After a determinedly skeptical review of the literature, [Eleanor E.] Maccoby and [Carol N.] Jacklin conclude that "the male's greater aggression has a biological component," as evidenced by boys' greater indulgence in mock fighting and "aggressive fantasies," and the greater aggressiveness of male primates. . . .

Every society that has ever existed has associated familial authority with the male and conferred the overwhelming majority of positions of power on males. Efforts to eliminate these features in Israel, Sweden, and the Soviet Union have failed. Male dominance and the sexual division of labor are observed among such reputedly uncorrupted people as the !Kung. !Kung juvenile playgroups are single-sex; boys spend far more time than girls in exploring technology (e.g. digging up termite mounds with arrows) and play rough-and-tumble play. !Kung men hunt and !Kung women gather; although what the women gather accounts for most of the tribe's calories and protein, hunting enjoys greater prestige. Margaret Mead remarked in *Male and Female*: "In every known society, the male's need for achievement can be recognized.". . .

The male advantage in dominance-aggression makes patriarchy inevitable because men will always strive harder than women to reach the top of hierarchies they encounter, and create hierarchies to reach the top of if none exist. Just as the social structure of a gorilla band does not exist apart from the tendencies of individual gorillas to react to each other in various ways, hierarchies exist because of the relational dispositions of individual human beings. That men monopolize leadership positions because they try harder to get them does not mean that men deserve these positions or that men do a better job in them than women would do if they became leaders. The only sense in which male dominance is "right" is that it expresses the free choices of individual men to strive for positions of power and the free choices of individual women to do other things.

. . . [A]ttempts to eliminate patriarchy within a group must sharply limit the freedom of the group's members, and can only be undertaken from without by a stronger group of men. . . .

THE FREE MARKET AND FEMINISM

Judged historically, the free market is the most successful economic arrangement. Permitting people to trade and associate freely for productive purposes has created unparalleled prosperity, along with support for the democratic institutions on which other forms of individual liberty have been found to depend. It is inevitable that feminists reject the free market, however, because they must interpret the expressions of sex differences facilitated by the freedom of the market as products of adverse socialization and discrimination.

Certainly, the observed differences between male and female labor market behavior are not in dispute; men and women do different sorts of work, and women earn lower average wages. It is also widely agreed that the immediate cause of these differences are differences in the motives which lead men and women into the labor market. Most married working women work to supplement their husband's income, which is regarded as the mainstay of the family budget. Working mothers are expected to care for their children as well, or at any rate to supervise the arrangements for their care, an expectation that does not fall nearly so heavily upon fathers. Unmarried women often see work as an interregnum between school and marriage. For these reasons, women gravitate to jobs permitting easy entry, exit and re-entry to and from the workforce. Nor, finally, is it seriously questioned that men tend to seek (although of course not always find) more prestigious jobs and to try to "get ahead" more than women do. In short, men and women invest their human capital differently.

As always, the question is why these things are so. Feminist theory takes them to be consequences of oppression. . . .

This theory is contradicted by the close match between many of the major differences in skills brought by men and women to the workplace and a number of the innate differences discussed [earlier]. Together with the greater innate dominance-aggression of men, which manifests itself economically as greater competitiveness, this match strongly suggests that differences in workplace behavior are not best explained as products of the denial of equal opportunity. . . .

Some innate sex differences correlate closely with aptitude for specific occupations, many of them prestigious, remunerative, and important in industrial society. Spatial ability is requisite for pipe fitting, technical drawing, and wood working, and is the most important component of mechanical ability. Only about 20 percent of girls in the elementary grades reach the average level of male performance on tests of spatial ability, and, according to the U.S. Employment Service, all classes of engineering and drafting as well as a high proportion of scientific and technical occupations require spatial ability in the top 10 percent of the U.S. population. While one should normally be chary of explaining any social phenomenon *directly* in terms of some innate gender dimorphism, male domination of the technical and engineering professions is almost certainly due to the male's innate cognitive advantage rather than to a culturally induced female disadvantage. . . .

However, if one assumes that women would, given the opportunity, be as interested in and as suited for virtually the same work as men, one is compelled to interpret the continuing statistical segregation of the work force as evidencing discrimination. . . .

QUOTAS

Once discrimination is separated from intent, and it is assumed that there should be as many women as men in some position, it becomes natural to seek to replace previously used criteria, including merit (or what employers have regarded as merit) with quotas. . . .

Gender quotas are at this writing the most pervasive influence of feminism on the American economy, although comparable worth has the potential to supersede them. Decisions about employment, union contracts, apprenticeships, admission to professional schools, and the casting and directing of motion pictures are made with an eye toward sex (and skin color). . . .

Quotas deny benefits and impose burdens on individuals not responsible for any wrongs. They cannot be justified as compensation, inspiration, or prevention, and they decrease economic efficiency. . . .

THE FAMILY

The family under patriarchy is a one-sided bargain in which the wife settles for exploitation, brutality, rape, incest, and madness. . . .

The idea that marriage is a spontaneous bond between naturally complementary partners is dismissed out of hand. There is nothing good whatever to be said about male impulses, and the asymmetries of marriage are understood exclusively in terms of the husband's superior physical strength. . . .

Only complete ignorance of male emotions can account for the belief that men invented marriage to force the sexual compliance of women. . . . For most men, sexual arousal vanishes without reciprocation. Even prostitutes find it useful to feign involvement. It would be psychologically impossible for the average man to meet his sexual needs by regularly forcing himself on an unwilling woman. . . .

After increasing for twenty years, the divorce rate has stabilized at the high rate of nearly 5 per 1,000 people in the U.S. One out of two new marriages ends in divorce. This phenomenon has many causes, of which feminism may itself be a further effect, but feminism's ongoing diabolization of marriage is almost certainly a factor. Divorce has been made socially and psychologically more acceptable by the idea that it is a reasonable response to a defective and dying institution. Increased rates of divorce create a feedback loop in which many divorced women embrace a theory which absolves them of blame for an emotional shambles. There are bound to be people for whom the normal frictions of marriage are made unendurable by the message that marriage is oppression. Finally, while I do not see how this could be verified statistically, it seems to me beyond doubt that many households of marriages and affairs vectoring toward marriage have been ruined as couples have tried to conform their sex lives to feminist imperatives. . . .

Feminist ideology encourages a variety of other pressures against marriage. Rates of childlessness, divorce and failure to marry rise steeply for women in careers; to the extent that women are encouraged to pursue careers and defer children, they are being encouraged to be single. There is the related message that women ought to learn to be independent of men. A prominent theme in rationales for nontraditional vocational training for girls is that women will be alone for a good part of their lives, that "millions of women are a divorce away from destitution," and that men are unreliable.

NO
Marilyn French

FEMINISM

Feminism is the only serious, coherent, and universal philosophy that offers an alternative to patriarchal thinking and structures. Feminists believe in a few simple tenets. They believe that women are human beings, that the two sexes are (at least) equal in all significant ways, and that this equality must be publicly recognized. They believe that qualities traditionally associated with women—the feminine principle—are (at least) equal in value to those traditionally associated with men—the masculine principle—and that this equality must be publicly recognized. (I modify these statements with *at least* because some feminists believe in the superiority of women and "feminine" qualities. Indeed, it is difficult not to stress the value of the "feminine" in our culture because it is so pervasively debased and diminished.) Finally, feminists believe the personal is the political—that is, that the value structure of a culture is identical in both public and private areas, that what happens in the bedroom has everything to do with what happens in the boardroom, and vice versa, and that, mythology notwithstanding, at present the same sex is in control in both places.

There are also those who believe they consider women equal to men, but see women as fettered by their traditional socialization and by the expectations of the larger world. These people see women as large children who have talent and energy, but who need training in male modes, male language, and an area of expertise in order to "fit in" in the male world. One philosopher, for example, has commented that women are *not yet ready* for top government posts. This is not just patronizing; it shows a lack of comprehension of feminism. For although feminists do indeed want women to become part of the structure, participants in public institutions; although they want access for women to decision-making posts, and a voice in how society is managed, *they do not want women to assimilate to society as it presently exists but to change it.* Feminism is not yet one more of a series of political movements demanding for their adherents access to existing structures and their rewards. This is how many people see it, however: as a strictly political movement through which women demand entry into the "male" world, a

From Marilyn French, *Beyond Power* (Summit Books, 1985). Copyright © 1985 by Belles-Lettres, Inc. Reprinted by permission of Summit Books, a division of Simon & Schuster, Inc. Notes omitted.

share of male prerogatives, and the chance to be like men. This perception of feminism alienates many nonfeminist women.

Feminism is a political movement demanding access to the rewards and responsibilities of the "male" world, but it is more: it is a revolutionary moral movement, intending to use political power to transform society, to "feminize" it. For such a movement, assimilation is death. The assimilation of women to society as it presently exists would lead simply to the inclusion of certain women (not all, because society as it presently exists is highly stratified) along with certain men in its higher echelons. It would mean continued stratification and continued contempt for "feminine" values. Assimilation would be the cooption of feminism. Yet it must be admitted that the major success of the movement in the past twenty years has been to increase the assimilation of women into the existing structure. This is not to be deplored, but it is only a necessary first step.

There have been many revolutions against various patriarchal forms over the past three or four thousand years, but in each case, what has succeeded an oppressive structure is another oppressive structure. This is inevitable because, regardless of the initial ideas and ideals of rebellious groups, they come to worship power above all: only power, they believe, can overwhelm power; only their greater power can bring them victory over an "enemy" that is the Father. But each victory has increased the power of the *idea* of power, thus each victory has increased human oppression. . . .

If women and men were seen as equal, if male self-definition no longer depended upon an inferior group, other stratifications would also become unnec-

essary. Legitimacy (which has no meaning without the idea of illegitimacy) would no longer be a useful concept, and its disappearance from human minds would lead to the establishment of new structures for social organization. These structures would blur the distinction between public and private spheres, a distinction that was originally created not only to exclude women from a male (public) arena, but to permit discourse which ignored and effectively eliminated from existence the parts of all lives that are bound to nature, that are necessary and nonvolitional. If public and private life were integrated, it would no longer seem incongruous to discuss procreation and weapons systems in the same paragraph. Since pleasure would be the primary value of both personal and public life, harmony (which produces pleasure) would be a universal societal goal, and would no longer have to be manufactured in the ersatz form of coerced uniformity, conformity. Love too would regain its innocence, since it would not be coerced into playing a role within a power structure and thus functioning as an oppression—as it often does in our world.

The foregoing is a sketch of feminist beliefs. It is difficult at present to provide more than a sketch, for to create truly feminist programs we must rid our heads of the power notions that fill them, and that cannot be done in a generation, or even several generations. The sketch may sound utopian: I think it is not. That is, I believe such a world is possible for humans to maintain, to live within, once it is achieved. What may be utopian is the idea that we can achieve it. For to displace power as the highest human value means to supersede patriarchal modes while eschewing traditional power maneuvers as a means. But it is impossible to function in the public world without using power maneuvers; and revolution does imply overthrow of current systems.

Two elements cast a friendly light on feminist goals. One is that the movement is not aimed at overthrow of any particular government or structure, but at the displacement of one way of thinking by another. The other is that feminism offers desirable goals. The first means that the tools of feminism are naturally nonviolent: it moves and will continue to move by influencing people, by offering a vision, by providing an alternative to the cul-de-sacs of patriarchy. The second means that feminism is in a state I call blessed: its ends and its means are identical. Feminism increases the well-being of its adherents, and so can appeal to others on grounds of the possibility of greater felicity. Integration of the self, which means using the full range of one's gifts, increases one's sense of well-being; if integration of one's entire life is not always possible because of the nature of the public world, it is a desirable goal. Patriarchy, which in all its forms requires some kind of self-sacrifice, denial, or repression in the name of some higher good which is rarely (if ever) achieved on earth, stresses nobility, superiority, and victory, the satisfaction of a final triumph. Feminism requires use of the entire self in the name of present well-being, and stresses integrity, community, and the *jouissance* of present experience. . . .

It was probably Betty Friedan's *The Feminine Mystique*, published in 1963, that first galvanized American women into action. Women legislators had seen to it that laws passed to redress wrongs done to blacks were expanded to include women. The Equal Pay Act was passed in 1963; the Civil Rights Act in 1965. Title VII of the latter prohibited discrimination on grounds of sex, race, color, religion, or national origin. The word *sex* was included as a result of maneuvers by Representative Martha Griffiths, Senator Margaret Chase Smith, and a reporter, Mae Craig. In 1965 the Supreme Court held that laws banning contraceptives were unconstitutional, and in 1966 a federal court declared that an Alabama law barring women from juries violated the Fourteenth Amendment (guaranteeing equal protection under the law). In that year too, the National Organization for Woman was founded. . . .

The decade that followed was enormously fertile; the seeds planted then are still bearing fruit. Women scholars began to delve into women's history, to break away from male interpretations and lay the groundwork for an alternative view of anthropology, psychology, sociology, philosophy, and language. Politically oriented groups pressed for legislation granting women equality in education, housing, credit, and promotion and hiring. Other women established feminist magazines, journals, publishing houses, and bookstores. Some strove for political office; some entered the newly open "male" world of business and industry. In the exhilaration of that period, women who had felt crippled found limbs, women who had felt marginal found a center, women who had felt alone found sisters.

It is now less than twenty years since the rising of the "second wave." The difference is astonishing. Women are now working in hundreds of jobs that were closed to them in the past. Women can sign leases, buy cars and houses, obtain credit; they cannot be denied telephone service because they are divorced.

They can be seated in restaurants although they are dining without a man. Although some women's fashions still inhibit mobility, they are no longer *de riguer*. Women are no longer expected to produce elaborate entertainments: life can be easier, more leisurely, for both sexes.

Most important of all, women now possess reproductive freedom. Although men have long had access to condoms, which were and are sold over the counter in every drugstore, women needed doctors' prescriptions to purchase diaphragms and, later, the birth control pill. This is still true, but such prescriptions are widely available now, and women do not have to be married to obtain them. (In France, where men can also obtain condoms easily, women could not purchase contraceptive devices in drugstores until 1967, and such purchases still require the authorization of the minister of social affairs.) Clearly, it is not birth control—or, more accurately, the prevention of conception—per se that is offensive to patriarchal culture, but the placing of that control in the hands of women. Despite continuing attempts to wrest it from them, American women are likely to hold on to this right over their own bodies. But in some Western nations— Ireland, for example—they still do not possess it.

The difference is great for a huge number of women, and because the difference permeates their lives, change may seem complete. But in the scale of things, the change is minimal. Capitalism, under great pressure for almost a hundred and fifty years, has yielded women about what socialism yielded them immediately. But it has managed—as has socialism—to retain its essential character. Capitalism has assimilated women, it

has not broadened itself; it has swallowed women rather than alter itself. And it has done this in accordance with its traditional structures. Thus the women who have benefited most from the changes are well-educated, white, middle-class women, often without children. Thus the divisiveness of racism has pervaded the women's movement itself. Thus women have by and large been kept out of the most sensitive and powerful areas of business and government, so that they have not achieved a voice in the running of our society. And thus women who have not managed to live like men, or with them, have been condemned to the lowest rank in our society: women are the new poor. It is not an exaggeration to say that although feminism in capitalist states has freed many women and improved the lives of others, it has had little effect on the patriarchy, which has simply absorbed a few women who appear acceptable to its purposes, and barred the door for the rest. . . .

. . . [T]he gap between male and female earnings has increased. According to the last census, the mean income of white females was $10,244 (59 cents of a white male dollar), of black females $9,476 (54 cents of a white male dollar), and of Hispanic females $8,466 (49 cents of a white male dollar). Despite differences in the concerns and approaches of women of color and white women, in the realm of economics, women as a caste comprise a lower class.

The poor of America are women: the poor of the world are women. In 1980, in America, the median adjusted income for men was $12,530, for women it was $4,920. In 1980 the poverty level was $8,414 for a nonfarm family of four, and nearly thirty million Americans live beneath it. Seventy percent of these are white, 30 percent black—and we may note that only 12 percent of the population is black—two thirds of them women and children. If we limit these figures to adults, two out of every three poor adults are female. If present trends continue, by the year 2000 the poor of America will be entirely its women.

There are a number of reasons for this. A presidential report published in 1981 claims that women are "systematically underpaid," that "women's work" pays about four thousand dollars a year less than men's work, and that occupational segregation is more pronounced by sex than by race: 70 percent of men and 54 percent of women are concentrated in jobs done only by those of their own sex.

Because women are still held responsible—by themselves and by men—for raising the children, they are forced to take jobs that are close to home, that offer flexible hours (like waitressing), or are part-time; jobs that do not require extended traveling or long hours. They are not able to "compete" in a job market that demands single-minded devotion to work, fast running on a narrow track. For some this is a tolerable situation: some women are not notably ambitious, prefer a balanced life, and have working husbands. But this is not the case for all, or even most, women.

More women than ever in the period covered by American record keeping on this point are living without men: they are single mothers, divorced mothers, and widows, as well as single working women. The reasons for this are complex. Two major reasons, however, are the movement for "sexual liberation" and the feminist movement.

The movement for "sexual liberation" begun in the 1950s was a male campaign, rooted in ideas that seem for the most part honest and beneficial: that sex was good, the body was good; that trading sexual access for financial support degraded sex and the body; that virginity was a questionable good in women and not at all necessary in men; and that the requirement of sexual fidelity in marriage was an oppression. However, the campaign was also extremely self-serving: it was not based on a philosophy that saw a joyous sex life as one element in a life concerned with the pleasure and the good of self and others. It was not a responsible movement: in fact it "masculinized" sex by making it a commodity and by isolating sex from other elements intrinsic to it—affection, connection, and the potential for procreation. To speak lightly, what the sexual revolution accomplished was to change the price of sexual access to a woman from marriage to a dinner.

At the same time, the ties of marriage lost their force—for men. As of 1963, almost all divorces sought in America were initiated (whether openly or not) by men. Divorce—like marriage—is morally neutral. Insofar as it ends a relationship of misery, it is a good; insofar as it ends a long-term intimacy, it is to be lamented. Even when a marriage involves children, it cannot be pre-judged: divorce may be better for the children than the marriage was. It seems reasonable to assume that if one party to a marriage wants a divorce, divorce should occur. But marriage and divorce are both tied to responsibility, and it was this tie that was broken by the "sexual liberation" movement.

If a man—and society in general—requires a woman to set aside ideas of an individual life, and to accept the role of functionary—wife, mother, housekeeper—without payment, then that role must be structured to guarantee that woman a secure life despite her unpaid labor. In cognizance of this contract, traditional divorce laws stipulated alimony. Laws did not, of course, prevent men from abandoning their families completely, or failing in alimony payments. But the new sexual morality was growing in the sixties, a period when feminists were struggling to gain the right to paid employment above the national level, and when many women who had gained such work were initiating divorce themselves. The thinking of legislators and judges underwent an amazing swift change. The new assumption was that women worked, that they earned as much as men, and thus that they did not require alimony—which is rarely granted now, and even more rarely paid. In 1979, only 14 percent of all divorced or separated women were granted alimony or child support, and of those at least 30 percent did not receive what they were awarded.

This situation is unjust to women who have accepted lesser jobs to help their husbands through school, or given up fellowships or promotions to accompany a husband to his new job. It is appallingly unjust to women who have neglected their own potential careers to care for husbands and children. But it becomes outrageous when we consider the statistics (if we need statistics, many women are too well acquainted with the reality behind them) on men's support of their children after divorce.

Although some very rich men use the power of their wealth to take the children away from their mothers after divorce, most men who divorce leave not just a marriage but a family. Men father children; although the degree to which they participate in childraising varies, it seems likely that they have some love and concern for those children. Nevertheless, after divorce they often disappear: they contribute neither emotion, time, nor money to the care of their own children. More than 90 percent of children who live with one parent live with their mothers; in 1978 there were 7.1 million single mothers with custody of their children in the United States. The number of men raising children on their own declined in the decade of the seventies. "The result of divorce, in an overwhelming number of cases, is that men become singles and women become single mothers." Women's incomes decline by 73 percent in the first year after divorce; men's incomes *increase* by 42 percent. The father is better off, the children are often hungry.

In recent years judges have tended not to award child support to mothers with custody; they have denied it to 41 percent of such mothers. Studies of the amounts awarded vary, ranging from as low as an average of $539 per year to an average of $2,110. But over 50 percent of custodial mothers never receive the amounts due them. Lenore Weitzman's research in California shows that only 13 percent of women with custody of pre-school children receive alimony; child support payments (even when they are made) are almost never enough to cover the cost of raising small children. . . .

The women's movement under capitalism has worked almost unbelievably hard and made large gains. Those gains are changes in law and custom, and they affect all women, although they have their greatest effect on middle-class educated women. But feminism has not been able to budge an intransigent establishment bent on destroying the globe; it has not moved us one inch closer to the feminization of society. Indeed, it seems to lose ground with every decade, as the nourishing, procreative, communal, emotional dimensions of experience are increasingly ground into dust, as high technology and more intense pursuit of power are increasingly exalted.

This situation constitutes a quandary for feminists. Only by bringing great numbers of women with feminist values into the institutional structure of the nation can women achieve a voice in the way this country is run. Only by unified political action can women influence the course of the future. But at present, and for the foreseeable future, women are carefully screened, hired in small numbers, and watched for deviance. Women hired by institutions are far more likely to be coopted by institutional policy than to change it; they will assimilate or be fired or quit. Some feminist groups oppose women's efforts to enter the establishment on the ground that women should not contribute to a structure that is sexist, racist, and dedicated to profit and power. On the other hand, to refuse to enter the establishment is to refuse even to try to change it from within and thus to accept the marginal position women have traditionally held. To refuse to enter American institutions may also be to doom oneself to poverty, and poverty is silent and invisible. It has no voice and no face.

For this problem, as for so many others, there is no clear right answer.

POSTSCRIPT

Is Feminism a Harmful Ideology?

"Feminism," says Levin, "is the thesis that males and females are already innately alike." Not so, says French. In her view, feminism insists that the sexes are *not* alike: there are distinctly "feminine values"—nurture, cooperation, nonviolence—that are quite different from the aggressive ways of men, and feminism is an organized effort to force American institutions to give "the feminine principle" the recognition it deserves. But if that is so, how would French stand on the issue of the New York City fire department's entrance exam discussed by Levin? If there are inherent value differences between men and women that should be given institutional recognition, should not our institutions also take cognizance of the inherent *physical* differences between the sexes? This is a problem for feminist theory, though perhaps not an insuperable one, for on some level all sides agree that there are sexual differences; the question really turns upon *which* differences should be considered socially relevant.

French advocates more than just equality. She demands the transformation of society to institutionalize feminine values. Levin, on the other hand, argues that the feminist agenda is "at variance with the ideals of a free society," because it "is a program for making different beings—men and women—turn out alike." As a result it uses the law to force equalizing changes that most women as well as men do not want.

Over the past 30 years, there has been a deluge of books, articles, and periodicals devoted to expounding feminist positions. Among the earliest feminist publications was Betty Friedan's book *The Feminine Mystique* (W. W. Norton, 1963). Friedan later wrote *The Second Stage* (Summit Books, 1981), which was less antagonistic to men and more accepting of motherhood and traditional women's roles. An analytical and historical discussion of women's movements over the past century and a half is provided by Steven M. Buechler in *Women's Movements in the United States: Suffrage, Equal Rights, and Beyond* (Rutgers University Press, 1990). A general work on the position of women in American society is Jessie Bernard, *The Female World* (Free Press, 1981).

Antifeminist works are rarer. Nicholas Davidson charges that it is "extremely difficult to find a publisher for a work critical of feminism"; see Davidson's *The Failure of Feminism* (Prometheus Books, 1988). Still, anyone seeking antifeminist arguments may look to Midge Decter's *The New Chastity and Other Arguments Against Women's Liberation* (Putnam, 1974), which has enjoyed fairly wide circulation, as have George Gilder's *Sexual Suicide* (Times Books, 1973) and Phyllis Schlafly's *The Power of Positive Woman* (Arlington House, 1977).

ISSUE 5

Would a "Mommy Track" Benefit Employed Women?

YES: Felice N. Schwartz, from "Management Women and the New Facts of Life," *Harvard Business Review* (January/February 1989)

NO: Barbara Ehrenreich and Deirdre English, from "Blowing the Whistle on the 'Mommy Track,' " *Ms.* (July/August 1989)

ISSUE SUMMARY

YES: Felice N. Schwartz, president and founder of Catalyst, an organization that advises corporations on the development of women leaders, argues that some women are truly career minded and should be treated just as men are in terms of both demands and opportunities. However, for other women who are not so inclined, corporations should give them a less demanding path with fewer opportunities in order to facilitate their family lives.
NO: Journalists Barbara Ehrenreich and Deirdre English attack Schwartz's suggestion for a less demanding and less rewarding second path as unwarranted not only because Schwartz has no empirical evidence for her premises but also because her suggestion seems to be a justification for not treating women equally.

Should women and men be treated in the same way? Some argue that they should—that identical treatment is indeed warranted. However, others claim that because women are different from men, they should be treated differently in order to be treated fairly. This issue comes to a head in the workplace, especially in management in the corporate world. Two values legitimately converge on this issue: businesses want to utilize personnel wisely so as to make a profit, and women want to have the time and conditions that allow for a rich family life. In addition, four facts in particular affect this issue: (1) women with families generally do most of the housework and childrearing; (2) most mothers have a strong desire to spend time with their children and, as compared to most men, are somewhat less committed to paid work and careers; (3) attractive alternative child-care services are not widely available at reasonable costs; and (4) men have not changed their attitudes toward work as much as women have, nor are most men willing to equally share housework and child-rearing responsibilities. These facts greatly impede women from doing as well in the workplace as men and consequently create stress in women's personal lives. As a result, the women's movement has been trying to change most of these conditioning factors.

Space does not allow a review of the data that establish the four facts just stated, but a few points can help provide a rough outline of where the issue stands and how it is changing. Of particular interest are the results of three surveys of several thousand Americans aged 18 to 65 that were conducted in 1965, 1975, and 1985. In this 20-year period women decreased their housework (excluding childrearing but including the need for more cooking, cleaning, laundry, and so on that comes with having children) from 27 hours in 1965 to 22 in 1975 and 20 in 1985, while men increased their housework from 5 to 7 to 10 hours respectively. Obviously there is a long way to go to parity. Though women do the majority of housework, it should be noted that in the mid-1980s, only 1 in 1,000 young women entering college planned on a career as a housewife, and less than 11 percent of women at that time were traditional housewives, i.e., married with children at home and not in the labor force. Women have moved into the paid labor force in ever-increasing numbers: from 20 percent of women aged 18 and over in 1900, to 31 percent in 1947, to 58 percent in 1986. Attitude changes have accompanied these occupational changes. Only 3 percent of working women regarded their work as a career in 1971, but this percentage increased to 47 percent in 1985, thus closing the gap with men, 57 percent of whom considered their work as a career.

When all these considerations are added up, they provide the following picture: Most women want to work and need to work; in light of the principle of equality, this fact suggests that women should be treated the same as men in the workplace. In other words, they should be given the same opportunities and required to meet the same demands. On the other hand, most women want a rich family life and especially want the time and conditions for mothering young children, women do twice as much housework as men, and acceptable alternative child-care arrangements are in short supply. These facts suggest that less should be demanded of women at the workplace in order to facilitate their family lives. The principle of equality, however, would then require that their rewards and opportunities should be reduced proportionally. The above realities justify two contradictory formulas for the treatment of women in the workplace—two horns of a dilemma.

In the selections that follow, Felice N. Schwartz tries to solve the dilemma by classifying women into two categories—career primary and career and family—and suggests applying the equal treatment formula to the former group and the lenient treatment formula to the latter group. Further, she argues that businesses lose money by treating career-and-family women according to the equal treatment formula. Barbara Ehrenreich and Deirdre English challenge the factual basis of this argument and condemn her proposal as reinforcing rather than solving the problem. The solution, according to Ehrenreich and English, lies in other changes, including getting men to do their fair share of housework and childrearing.

YES

Felice N. Schwartz

MANAGEMENT WOMEN AND THE NEW FACTS OF LIFE

The cost of employing women in management is greater than the cost of employing men. This is a jarring statement, partly because it is true, but mostly because it is something people are reluctant to talk about. A new study by one multinational corporation shows that the rate of turnover in management positions is 2¹/₂ times higher among top-performing women than it is among men. A large producer of consumer goods reports that one half of the women who take maternity leave return to their jobs late or not at all. And we know that women also have a greater tendency to plateau or to interrupt their careers in ways that limit their growth and development. . . .

Career interruptions, plateauing, and turnover are expensive. The money corporations invest in recruitment, training, and development is less likely to produce top executives among women than among men, and the invaluable company experience that developing executives acquire at every level as they move up through management ranks is more often lost. . . .

It is terribly important that employers draw the right conclusions from the studies now being done. The studies will be useless—or worse, harmful—if all they teach us is that women are expensive to employ. What we need to learn is how to reduce that expense, how to stop throwing away the investments we make in talented women, how to become more responsive to the needs of the women that corporations *must* employ if they are to have the best and the brightest of all those now entering the work force. . . .

THE ONE IMMUTABLE, ENDURING DIFFERENCE BETWEEN MEN AND WOMEN IS maternity. Maternity is not simply childbirth but a continuum that begins with an awareness of the ticking of the biological clock, proceeds to the anticipation of motherhood, includes pregnancy, childbirth, physical recuperation, psychological adjustment, and continues on to nursing, bonding, and child rearing. Not all women choose to become mothers, of course, and among those who do, the process varies from case to case depending on the

From Felice N. Schwartz, "Management Women and the New Facts of Life," *Harvard Business Review,* vol. 67, no. 1 (January/February 1989). Copyright © 1988 by the President and Fellows of Harvard College. All rights reserved. Reprinted by permission.

health of the mother and baby, the values of the parents, and the availability, cost, and quality of child care.

In past centuries, the biological fact of maternity shaped the traditional roles of the sexes. Women performed the home-centered functions that related to the bearing and nurturing of children. Men did the work that required great physical strength. Over time, however, family size contracted, the community assumed greater responsibility for the care and education of children, packaged foods and household technology reduced the work load in the home, and technology eliminated much of the need for muscle power at the workplace. Today, in the developed world, the only role still uniquely gender related is childbearing. Yet men and women are still socialized to perform their traditional roles. . . .

In the decades ahead, as the socialization of boys and girls and the experience and expectations of young men and women grow steadily more androgynous, the differences in workplace behavior will continue to fade. At the moment, however, we are still plagued by disparities in perception and behavior that make the integration of men and women in the workplace unnecessarily difficult and expensive.

Let me illustrate with a few broadbrush generalizations. . . .

Men continue to perceive women as the rearers of their children, so they find it understandable, indeed appropriate, that women should renounce their careers to raise families. Edmund Pratt, CEO of Pfizer, once asked me in all sincerity, "Why would any woman choose to be a chief financial officer rather than a full-time mother?" By condoning and taking pleasure in women's traditional behavior, men reinforce it. Not only do they see parenting as fundamentally female, they see a career as fundamentally male—either an unbroken series of promotions and advancements toward CEOdom or stagnation and disappointment. This attitude serves to legitimize a woman's choice to extend maternity leave and even, for those who can afford it, to leave employment altogether for several years. By the same token, men who might want to take a leave after the birth of a child know that management will see such behavior as a lack of career commitment, even when company policy permits parental leave for men.

Women also bring counterproductive expectations and perceptions to the workplace. Ironically, although the feminist movement was an expression of women's quest for freedom from their homebased lives, most women were remarkably free already. They had many responsibilities, but they were autonomous and could be entrepreneurial in how and when they carried them out. And once their children grew up and left home, they were essentially free to do what they wanted with their lives. Women's traditional role also included freedom from responsibility for the financial support of their families. Many of us were socialized from girlhood to expect our husbands to take care of us, while our brothers were socialized from an equally early age to complete their educations, pursue careers, climb the ladder of success, and provide dependable financial support for their families. To the extent that this tradition of freedom lingers subliminally, women tend to bring to their employment a sense that they can choose to change jobs or careers at will, take time off, or reduce their hours.

Finally, women's traditional role encouraged particular attention to the quality and substance of what they did, specifically to the physical, psychological, and intellectual development of their children. This traditional focus may explain women's continuing tendency to search for more than monetary reward—intrinsic significance, social importance, meaning—in what they do. This too makes them more likely than men to leave the corporation in search of other values.

The misleading metaphor of the glass ceiling suggests an invisible barrier constructed by corporate leaders to impede the upward mobility of women beyond the middle levels. A more appropriate metaphor, I believe, is the kind of cross-sectional diagram used in geology. The barriers to women's leadership occur when potentially counterproductive layers of influence on women—maternity, tradition, socialization—meet management strata pervaded by the largely unconscious preconceptions, stereotypes, and expectations of men. Such interfaces do not exist for men and tend to be impermeable for women.

One result of these gender differences has been to convince some executives that women are simply not suited to top management. Other executives feel helpless. If they see even a few of their valued female employees fail to return to work from maternity leave on schedule or see one of their most promising women plateau in her career after the birth of a child, they begin to fear there is nothing they can do to infuse women with new energy and enthusiasm and persuade them to stay. At the same time, they know there is nothing they can do to stem the tide of women into management ranks.

Another result is to place every working woman on a continuum that runs from total dedication to career at one end to a balance between career and family at the other. What women discover is that the male corporate culture sees both extremes as unacceptable. Women who want the flexibility to balance their families and their careers are not adequately committed to the organization. Women who perform as aggressively and competitively as men are abrasive and unfeminine. But the fact is, business needs all the talented women it can get. Moreover, as I will explain, the women I call career-primary and those I call career-and-family each have particular value to the corporation.

WOMEN IN THE CORPORATION ARE ABOUT to move from a buyer's to a seller's market. The sudden, startling recognition that 80% of new entrants in the work force over the next decade will be women, minorities, and immigrants has stimulated a mushrooming incentive to "value diversity."

Women are no longer simply an enticing pool of occasional creative talent, a thorn in the side of the EEO [equal employment opportunity] officer, or a source of frustration to corporate leaders truly puzzled by the slowness of their upward trickle into executive positions. A real demographic change is taking place. The era of sudden population growth of the 1950s and 1960s is over. The birth rate has dropped about 40%, from a high of 25.3 live births per 1,000 population in 1957, at the peak of the baby boom, to a stable low of a little more than 15 per 1,000 over the last 16 years, and there is no indication of a return to a higher rate. The tidal wave of baby boomers that swelled the recruitment pool to overflowing seems to have been a one-time phenomenon. For 20 years, employers had the pick of a very large crop and were able to choose males almost exclusively for the executive track. But if future population remains fairly stable while the economy continues to expand, and if the new information society simultaneously creates a greater need for creative, educated managers, then the gap between supply and demand will grow dramatically and, with it, the competition for managerial talent.

The decrease in numbers has even greater implications if we look at the traditional source of corporate recruitment for leadership positions—white males from the top 10% of the country's best universities. Over the past decade, the increase in the number of women graduating from leading universities has been much greater than the increase in the total number of graduates, and these women are well represented in the top 10% of their classes.

The trend extends into business and professional programs as well. In the old days, virtually all MBAs were male. I remember addressing a meeting at the Harvard Business School as recently as the mid-1970s and looking out at a sea of exclusively male faces. Today, about 25% of that audience would be women. The pool of male MBAs from which corporations have traditionally drawn their leaders has shrunk significantly. . . .

UNDER THESE CIRCUMSTANCES, THERE IS no question that the management ranks of business will include increasing numbers of women. There remains, however, the question of how these women will succeed—how long they will stay, how high they will climb, how completely they will fulfill their promise and poten-

tial, and what kind of return the corporation will realize on its investment in their training and development.

There is ample business reason for finding ways to make sure that as many of these women as possible will succeed. The first step in this process is to recognize that women are not all alike. Like men, they are individuals with differing talents, priorities, and motivations. For the sake of simplicity, let me focus on the two women I referred to earlier, on what I call the career-primary woman and the career-family woman.

Like many men, some women put their careers first. They are ready to make the same trade-offs traditionally made by the men who seek leadership positions. They make a career decision to put in extra hours, to make sacrifices in their personal lives, to make the most of every opportunity for professional development. . . .

The secret to dealing with such women is to recognize them early, accept them, and clear artificial barriers from their path to the top. After all, the best of these women are among the best managerial talent you will ever see. And career-primary women have another important value to the company that men and other women lack. They can act as role models and mentors to younger women who put their careers first. Since upwardly mobile career-primary women still have few role models to motivate and inspire them, a company with women in its top echelon has a significant advantage in the competition for executive talent. . . .

Clearing a path to the top for career-primary women has four requirements:

1. Identify them early.

2. Give them the same opportunity you give to talented men to grow and develop and contribute to company profitability. Give them client and customer

responsibility. Expect them to travel and relocate, to make the same commitment to the company as men aspiring to leadership positions.

3. Accept them as valued members of your management team. Include them in every kind of communication. Listen to them.

4. Recognize that the business environment is more difficult and stressful for them than for their male peers. They are always a minority, often the only woman. The male perception of talented, ambitious women is at best ambivalent, a mixture of admiration, resentment, confusion, competitiveness, attraction, skepticism, anxiety, pride, and animosity. . . .

Stereotypical language and sexist day-to-day behavior do take their toll on women's career development. . . . With notable exceptions, men are still generally more comfortable with other men, and as a result women miss many of the career and business opportunities that arise over lunch, on the golf course, or in the locker room.

THE MAJORITY OF WOMEN, HOWEVER, ARE what I call career-and-family women, women who want to pursue serious careers while participating actively in the rearing of children. These women are a precious resource that has yet to be mined. Many of them are talented and creative. Most of them are willing to trade some career growth and compensation for freedom from the constant pressure to work long hours and weekends.

Most companies today are ambivalent at best about the career-and-family women in their management ranks. They would prefer that all employees were willing to give their all to the company.

They believe it is in their best interests for all managers to compete for the top positions so the company will have the largest possible pool from which to draw its leaders. . . .

These companies lose on two counts. First, they fail to amortize the investment they made in the early training and experience of management women who find themselves committed to family as well as to career. Second, they fail to recognize what these women could do for their middle management.

The ranks of middle managers are filled with people on their way up and people who have stalled. Many of them have simply reached their limits, achieved career growth commensurate with or exceeding their capabilities, and they cause problems because their performance is mediocre but they still want to move ahead. The career-and-family woman is willing to trade off the pressures and demands that go with promotion for the freedom to spend more time with her children. She's very smart, she's talented, she's committed to her career, and she's satisfied to stay at the middle level, at least during the early child-rearing years. . . .

Consider a typical example, a woman who decides in college on a business career and enters management at age 22. For nine years, the company invests in her career as she gains experience and skills and steadily improves her performance. But at 31, just as the investment begins to pay off in earnest, she decides to have a baby. Can the company afford to let her go home, take another job, or go into business for herself? The common perception now is yes, the corporation can afford to lose her unless, after six or eight weeks or even three months of disability and maternity leave, she returns to work on a full-time schedule with the same vigor, commitment, and ambition that she showed before.

But what if she doesn't? What if she wants or needs to go on leave for six months or a year or, heaven forbid, five years? In this worst-case scenario, she works full-time from age 22 to 31 and from 36 to 65—a total of 38 years as opposed to the typical male's 43 years. That's not a huge difference. Moreover, my typical example is willing to work part-time while her children are young, if only her employer will give her the opportunity. There are two rewards for companies responsive to this need: higher retention of their best people and greatly improved performance and satisfaction in their middle management.

The high-performing career-and-family woman can be a major player in your company. She can give you a significant business advantage as the competition for able people escalates. Sometimes, too, if you can hold on to her, she will switch gears in mid-life and re-enter the competition for the top. The price you must pay to retain these women is threefold: you must plan for and manage maternity, you must provide the flexibility that will allow them to be maximally productive, and you must take an active role in helping to make family supports and high-quality, affordable child care available to all women. . . .

For all the women who want to combine career and family—the women who want to participate actively in the rearing of their children and who also want to pursue their careers seriously—the key to retention is to provide the flexibility and family supports they need in order to function effectively.

Time spent in the office increases productivity if it is time well spent, but the fact that most women continue to take the primary responsibility for child care is a cause of distraction, diversion, anxiety, and absenteeism—to say nothing of the persistent guilt experienced by all working mothers. . . .

In its simplest form, flexibility is the freedom to take time off—a couple of hours, a day, a week—or to do some work at home and some at the office, an arrangement that communication technology makes increasingly feasible. At the complex end of the spectrum are alternative work schedules that permit the woman to work less than full-time and her employer to reap the benefits of her experience and, with careful planning, the top level of her abilities.

Part-time employment is the single greatest inducement to getting women back on the job expeditiously and the provision women themselves most desire. A part-time return to work enables them to maintain responsibility for critical aspects of their jobs, keeps them in touch with the changes constantly occurring at the workplace and in the job itself, reduces stress and fatigue, often eliminates the need for paid maternity leave by permitting a return to the office as soon as disability leave is over, and, not least, can greatly enhance company loyalty. The part-time solution works particularly well when a work load can be reduced for one individual in a department or when a full-time job can be broken down by skill levels and apportioned to two individuals at different levels of skill and pay.

I believe, however, that shared employment is the most promising and will be the most widespread form of flexible scheduling in the future. It is feasible at every level of the corporation except at the pinnacle, for both the short and the long term. It involves two people taking responsibility for one job. . . .

Flexibility is costly in numerous ways. It requires more supervisory time to coordinate and manage, more office space, and somewhat greater benefits costs (though these can be contained with flexible benefits plans, prorated benefits, and, in two-paycheck families, elimination of duplicate benefits). But the advantages of reduced turnover and the greater productivity that results from higher energy levels and greater focus can outweigh the costs.

A few hints:

• Provide flexibility selectively. I'm not suggesting private arrangements subject to the suspicion of favoritism but rather a policy that makes flexible work schedules available only to high performers.

• Make it clear that in most instances (but not all) the rates of advancement and pay will be appropriately lower for those who take time off or who work part-time than for those who work full-time. Most career-and-family women are entirely willing to make that trade-off.

• Discuss costs as well as benefits. Be willing to risk accusations of bias. Insist, for example, that half time is half of whatever time it takes to do the job, not merely half of 35 or 40 hours. . . .

FAMILY SUPPORTS—IN ADDITION TO MA-ternity leave and flexibility—include the provision of parental leave for men, support for two-career and single-parent families during relocation, and flexible benefits. But the primary ingredient is child care. The capacity of working mothers to function effectively and without interruption depends on the availability of good, affordable child care. Now that women make up almost half the work force and the growing percent-age of managers, the decision to become involved in the personal lives of employees is no longer a philosophical question but a practical one. To make matters worse, the quality of child care has almost no relation to technology, inventiveness, or profitability but is more or less a pure function of the quality of child care personnel and the ratio of adults to children. These costs are irreducible. Only by joining hands with government and the public sector can corporations hope to create the vast quantity and variety of child care that their employees need. . . .

WE HAVE COME A TREMENDOUS DISTANCE since the days when the prevailing male wisdom saw women as lacking the kind of intelligence that would allow them to succeed in business. For decades, even women themselves have harbored an unspoken belief that they couldn't make it because they couldn't be just like men, and nothing else would do. But now that women have shown themselves the equal of men in every area of organizational activity, now that they have demonstrated they can be stars in every field of endeavor, now we can all venture to examine the fact that women and men are different.

On balance, employing women is more costly than employing men. Women can acknowledge this fact today because they know that their value to employers exceeds the additional cost and because they know that changing attitudes can reduce the additional cost dramatically. Women in management are no longer an idiosyncrasy of the arts and education. They have always matched men in natural ability. Within a very few years, they will equal men in numbers as well in every area of economic activity.

NO

Barbara Ehrenreich and Deirdre English

BLOWING THE WHISTLE ON THE "MOMMY TRACK"

When a feminist has something bad to say about women, the media listen. Three years ago it was Sylvia Hewlett, announcing in her book *A Lesser Life* that feminism had sold women out by neglecting to win child-care and maternity leaves. This year it's Felice Schwartz, the New York–based consultant who argues that women—or at least the mothers among us—have become a corporate liability. They cost too much to employ, she argues, and the solution is to put them on a special lower-paid, low-pressure career track—the now-notorious "mommy track."

The "mommy track" story rated prominent coverage in the New York *Times* and *USA Today,* a cover story in *Business Week,* and airtime on dozens of talk shows. Schwartz, after all, seemed perfectly legitimate. She is the president of Catalyst, an organization that has been advising corporations on women's careers since 1962. She had published her controversial claims in no less a spot than the *Harvard Business Review* ("Management Women and the New Facts of Life," January-February 1989). And her intentions, as she put it in a later op-ed piece, seemed thoroughly benign: "to urge employers to create policies that help mothers balance career and family responsibilities."

Moreover, Schwartz's argument seemed to confirm what everybody already knew. Women haven't been climbing up the corporate ladder as fast as might once have been expected, and women with children are still, on average, groping around the bottom rungs. Only about 40 percent of top female executives have children, compared to 95 percent of their male peers. There have been dozens of articles about female dropouts: women who slink off the fast track, at age 30-something, to bear a strategically timed baby or two. In fact, the "mommy track"—meaning a lower-pressure, flexible, or part-time approach to work—was neither a term Schwartz used nor her invention. It was already, in an anecdotal sort of way, a well-worn issue.

Most of the controversy focused on Schwartz's wildly anachronistic "solution." Corporate employers, she advised, should distinguish between two

From Barbara Ehrenreich and Deirdre English, "Blowing the Whistle on the 'Mommy Track,'" *Ms.,* vol. 18, no. 1 & 2 (July/August 1989). Copyright © 1989 by *Ms.* magazine. Reprinted by permission.

categories of women: "career-primary" women, who won't interrupt their careers for children and hence belong on the fast track with the men, and "career-and-family" women, who should be shunted directly to the mommy track. Schwartz had no answers for the obvious questions: how is the employer supposed to sort the potential "breeders" from the strivers? Would such distinction even be legal? What about *fathers*? But in a sense, the damage had already been done. A respected feminist, writing in a respected journal, had made a case that most women can't pull their weight in the corporate world, and should be paid accordingly.

Few people, though, actually read Schwartz's article. The first surprise is that it contains *no* evidence to support her principal claim, that "the cost of employing women in management is greater than the cost of employing men." Schwartz offers no data, no documentation at all—except for two unpublished studies by two *anonymous* corporations. Do these studies really support her claim? Were they methodologically sound? Do they even exist? There is no way to know.

Few media reports of the "mommy track" article bothered to mention the peculiar nature of Schwartz's "evidence." We, however, were moved to call the *Harvard Business Review* and inquire whether the article was representative of its normal editorial standard. Timothy Blodgett, the executive editor, defended the article as "an expression of opinion and judgment." When we suggested that such potentially damaging "opinions" might need a bit of bolstering, he responded by defending Schwartz: "She speaks with a tone of authority. That comes through."

(The conversation went downhill from there, with Blodgett stating sarcastically,

"I'm sure your article in *Ms.* will be *very* objective." Couldn't fall much lower than the *Harvard Business Review*, we assured him.)

Are managerial women more costly to employ than men? As far as we could determine—with the help of the Business and Professional Women's Foundation and Women's Equity Action League—there is no *published* data on this point. A 1987 government study did show female managerial employees spending less time with each employer than males (5 years compared to 6.8 years), but there is no way of knowing what causes this turnover or what costs it incurs. And despite pregnancy, and despite women's generally greater responsibility for child-raising, they use up on the average only 5.1 sick days per year, compared to 4.9 for men.

The second surprise, given Schwartz's feminist credentials, is that the article is riddled with ancient sexist assumptions—for example, about the possibility of a more androgynous approach to child-raising *and* work. She starts with the unobjectionable statement that "maternity is biological rather than cultural." The same thing, after all, could be said of paternity. But a moment later, we find her defining maternity as " . . . a continuum that begins with an awareness of the ticking of the biological clock, proceeds to the anticipation of motherhood, includes pregnancy, childbirth, physical recuperation, psychological adjustment, and continues on to nursing, bonding, and child-rearing."

Now, pregnancy, childbirth, and nursing do qualify as biological processes. But slipping child-rearing into the list, as if changing diapers and picking up socks were hormonally programmed activities, is an old masculinist trick. Child-raising is a *social* undertaking, which may involve nannies, aunts, grandparents, day-care workers, or, of course, *fathers*.

Equally strange for a "feminist" article is Schwartz's implicit assumption that employment, in the case of married women, is strictly optional, or at least that *mothers* don't need to be top-flight earners. The "career-and-family woman," she tells us, is "willing" and "satisfied" to forgo promotions and "stay at the middle level." What about the single mother, or the wife of a low-paid male? But Schwartz's out-of-date—and class-bound—assumption that every woman is supported by a male breadwinner fits in with her apparent nostalgia for the era of the feminine mystique. "Ironically," she writes, "although the feminist movement was an expression of women's quest for freedom from their home-based lives, *most women were remarkably free already* [emphasis added]."

But perhaps the oddest thing about the "mommy track" article—even as an "expression of opinion and judgment"—is that it is full of what we might charitably call ambivalence or, more bluntly, self-contradictions. Take the matter of the "glass ceiling," which symbolized all the barriers, both subtle and overt, that corporate women keep banging their heads against. At the outset, Schwartz dismisses the glass ceiling as a "misleading metaphor." Sexism, in short, is not the problem.

Nevertheless, within a few pages, she is describing the glass ceiling (not by that phrase, of course) like a veteran. "Male corporate culture," she tells us, sees both the career-primary and the career-and-family woman as "unacceptable." The woman with family responsibilities is likely to be seen as lacking commitment to the organization, while the woman who *is* fully committed to the organiza-tion is likely to be seen as "abrasive and unfeminine." She goes on to cite the corporate male's "confusion, competitive-ness," and his "stereotypical language and sexist . . . behavior," concluding that "with notable exceptions, men are still more comfortable with other men."

And we're supposed to blame *women* for their lack of progress in the corporate world?

Even on her premier point, that women are more costly to employ, Schwartz loops around and rebuts herself. Near the end of her article, she urges corporations to conduct their own studies of the costs of employing women—the two anonymous studies were apparently not definitive after all—and asserts confidently ("of course I believe") that the benefits will end up outweighing the costs. In a more recent New York *Times* article, she puts it even more baldly: "The costs of employ-ing women pale beside the payoffs."

Could it be that Felice Schwartz and the editors of the *Harvard Business Review* are ignorant of that most basic financial management concept, the cost-benefit analysis? If the "payoffs" outweigh the costs of employing women—runny noses and maternity leaves included—then the net cost may indeed be *lower* than the cost of employing men.

In sum, the notorious "mommy track" article is a tortured muddle of feminist perceptions and sexist assumptions, good intentions and dangerous suggestions—unsupported by any acceptable evidence at all. It should never have been taken seriously, not by the media and not by the nation's most prestigious academic business publication. The fact that it was suggests that something serious *is* afoot: a backlash against America's high-status, better paid women, and potentially against all women workers.

We should have seen it coming. For the past 15 years upwardly mobile, managerial women have done everything possible to fit into an often hostile corporate world. They dressed up as non-threatening corporate clones. They put in 70-hour workweeks; and of course, they postponed childbearing. Thanks in part to their commitment to the work world, the birthrate dropped by 16 percent since 1970. But now many of these women are ready to start families. This should hardly be surprising; after all, 90 percent of American women do become mothers.

But while corporate women were busily making adjustments and concessions, the larger corporate world was not. The "fast track," with its macho camaraderie and toxic work load, remains the only track to success. As a result, success is indeed usually incompatible with motherhood—as well as with any engaged and active form of fatherhood. The corporate culture strongly discourages *men* from taking parental leave even if offered. And how many families can afford to have both earners on the mommy track?

Today there's an additional factor on the scene—the corporate women who *have* made it. Many of them are reliable advocates for the supports that working parents need. But you don't have to hang out with the skirted-suit crowd for long to discover that others of them are impatient with, and sometimes even actively resentful of, younger women who are trying to combine career and family. Recall that 60 percent of top female executives are themselves childless. Others are of the "if I did it, so can you" school of thought. Felice Schwartz may herself belong in this unsisterly category. In a telling anecdote in her original article, she describes her own problems with an executive employee seeking maternity leave, and the "somewhat awkward conversations" that ensued.

SOONER OR LATER, CORPORATIONS WILL have to yield to the pressure for paid parental leave, flextime, and child care, if only because they've become dependent on female talent. The danger is that employers—no doubt quoting Felice Schwartz for legitimization—will insist that the price for such options be reduced pay and withheld promotions, i.e., consignment to the mommy track. Such a policy would place a penalty on parenthood, and the ultimate victims—especially if the policy trickles down to the already low-paid female majority—will of course be children.

Bumping women—or just fertile women, or married women, or whomever—off the fast track may sound smart to cost-conscious CEOs, but eventually it is the corporate culture itself that needs to slow down to a human pace. No one, male or female, works at peak productivity for 70 hours a week, year after year, without sabbaticals or leaves. Think of it this way. If the price of success were exposure to a toxic chemical, would we argue that only women should be protected? Work loads that are incompatible with family life are themselves a kind of toxin—to men as well as women, and ultimately to businesses as well as families.

POSTSCRIPT

Would a "Mommy Track" Benefit Employed Women?

Schwartz mentions a study by one corporation that shows a 2.5 times higher turnover rate among high-level women than among men. Ehrenreich and English point out that this one study by an anonymous corporation is flimsy evidence for the conclusion that high-level women have high turnover rates relative to men and are therefore less profitable to corporations than men. Other studies, however, do show that more women than men drop out of management positions and become self-employed (often part-time) or drop out of the work force altogether. Alex Taylor III reviews a number of relevant studies in "Why Women Managers Are Bailing Out," *Fortune* (August 18, 1986). Schwartz's critics ask, "What about *fathers?*" Her solution assigns the responsibility of child care to women. If there is to be a mommy track for the noble reasons that Schwartz suggests, then should there also be a daddy track? Why should corporate policies reinforce traditional gender ideals when many women are trying to change them? Furthermore, her solution condemns women to second-class status in accepting the conflict between work and family as a women's problem.

The focus of this debate is on the adjustment of the corporate world to the tension between work and family today. Part of the problem, however, is political in that the United States has not passed legislation that provides social support for working families that comes close to European programs. This failure is analyzed by Sylvia Ann Hewlett in *A Lesser Life: The Myth of Women's Liberation in America* (William Morrow, 1986). For information on other countries, see Joan Aldos and Wilfried Dumon, eds., *The Politics and Programs of Family Policy* (University of Notre Dame Press, 1980), and Joni Seager and Ann Olson, *Women in the World: An International Atlas* (Simon & Schuster, 1986). Valerie Polakow Suransky discusses the pros and cons of day-care centers based on her observational study of five centers in *The Erosion of Childhood* (University of Chicago Press, 1982).

The major work discussing the conflict of men and women over housework is Arlie Hochschild, *The Second Shift: Working Parents and the Revolution at Home* (Viking, 1989). A rare book on house husbands is William R. Beer, *House Husbands: Men and Housework in American Families* (Praeger, 1983). An excellent work on the choices for women is Kathleen Gerson, *Hard Choices: How Women Decide About Work, Career, and Motherhood* (University of California Press, 1985).

ISSUE 6

Is Sexual Harassment a Pervasive Problem in America?

YES: Catharine R. Stimpson, from "Over-Reaching: Sexual Harassment and Education," *Initiatives* (vol. 52, no. 3)

NO: Gretchen Morgenson, from "May I Have the Pleasure," *National Review* (November 18, 1991)

ISSUE SUMMARY

YES: Catharine R. Stimpson, graduate dean at Rutgers University, argues that sexual harassment is a form of male domination in America and that the real problem is not wrongful accusations of harassment but the refusal of the wronged to file complaints.

NO: Gretchen Morgenson, senior editor of *Forbes* magazine, argues that the notion of pervasive sexual harassment in the workplace is largely the product of hype by an "anti-harassment industry" and its supporters.

Relations between the sexes and society's expectations concerning men's and women's roles have changed considerably over the past 30 years. Indeed, some sociologists argue that this area has witnessed some of the most significant social changes in our time. For women, one aspect of their changing roles has been increased participation in the paid labor force and the increased likelihood that they view their work experience as a career. It is within this work context that we look at the issue of sexual harassment—a relatively new term that came into popular, current usage in the period 1975 to 1980.

Rape and sexual assault have always been outlawed in the United States, but these offenses involve physical acts. Sexual harassment need not; it can consist of words, gestures, even facial expressions. Sexual harassment occupied the headlines in the fall of 1991: During Senate confirmation hearings on Supreme Court justice nominee Judge Clarence Thomas, law professor Anita Hill charged that she had been sexually harassed by Thomas when she worked for him. Thomas had served for a time as head of the Equal Employment Opportunity Commission (EEOC), which over a decade ago was the federal agency responsible for developing workplace guidelines on sexual harassment. In 1980 the EEOC defined sexual harassment as any "unwelcome sexual conduct that is a term or condition of employment," and the EEOC ruled that it constituted a form of sexual discrimination outlawed by Title VII of the Civil Rights Act of 1964. This raises a tricky question: what is "unwelcome"? It seems to vary with time, place, and social circles. Certain kinds of male behavior that were not uncommon in the 1950s—whistling, winking, commenting on a woman's figure, or calling her a "girl" or a "chick"—are taboo in enlightened circles today, though perhaps not everywhere in America.

In defining *sexual harassment*, the EEOC delineated two basic types. The first type is the quid pro quo (something for something) variety, in which an employer or some other empowered individual in the workplace suggests to an employee that sexual favors will be rewarded while withholding sexual favors will be punished. The second general category of sexual harassment defined by the EEOC is the so-called hostile environment: The boss or co-workers engage in sexually oriented behavior that unreasonably interferes with an employee's job performance. Such behavior might include sexual ridicule, sexual pranks, and the use of sexually charged words or gestures that threaten or demean. The importance of this second form of sexual harassment was underscored by the U.S. Supreme Court in a 1986 decision, *Meritor Savings Bank v. Vinson*. The Court said that to win a sexual harassment suit against a company, an employee does not have to prove quid pro quo; it is enough if she can prove that she was subjected to a hostile working environment. "Title VII," the Court said, "affords employees the right to work in an atmosphere free from discrimination, intimidation, ridicule, and insult."

The Court's conclusion caused little debate, yet even some of those whose business it is to guard against sexual harassment admit that there is danger of pushing its application too far. In its 1980 guidelines the EEOC warned against confusing sexual harassment with ordinary workplace flirtations: "Only unwelcome sexual conduct that is a term or condition of employment constitutes a violation." The EEOC added, "Because sexual attraction may often play a role in the day-to-day social exchange between employees," the distinction between sexual conduct that is uninvited but not necessarily unwelcome and clearly unwelcome sexual conduct is sometimes difficult to discern, "but this distinction is essential because sexual conduct becomes unlawful only when it is unwelcome." The distinction is useful, but it raises questions of its own. *How* unwelcome must conduct be to constitute a violation? And since "unwelcomeness" is a subjective feeling, in what ways is that feeling to be expressed in order to register an objective public meaning? If certain types of behavior are tolerated by the victims, does that mean that we can assume it to be welcome—or at least not too "unwelcome"—by EEOC standards?

In the following selections, Catharine R. Stimpson contends that much more still needs to be done to combat sexual harassment, while Gretchen Morgenson worries that the limits of the tolerable are being overly constricted by an "anti-harassment industry" and its supporters.

YES

Catharine R. Stimpson

OVER-REACHING: SEXUAL HARASSMENT AND EDUCATION

Sexual harassment is an ancient shame that has become a modern embarrassment. Largely because of the pressure of feminism and feminists, such a shift in status took place during the 1970s. Today, the psychological and social pollution that harassment spews out is like air pollution. No one defends either of them. We have classified them as malaises that damage people and their environments. For this reason, both forms of pollution are largely illegal. In 1986, in *Meritor Savings Bank v. Vinson*, the Supreme Court held an employer liable for acts of sexual harassment that its supervisory personnel might commit.

Yet, like air pollution, the psychological and social pollution of sexual harassment persists. In the stratosphere, chlorofluorocarbons from aerosol sprays and other products break apart and help to destroy the ozone layer. Well below the stratosphere, in classrooms and laboratories sexual louts refuse to disappear, imposing themselves on a significant proportion of our students.[1] As the graduate dean at a big public university, I experience, in my everyday life, the contradiction between disapproval of sexual harassment and the raw reality of its existence. I work, with men and women of good will, to end harassment. We must work, however, because the harassers are among us.

Inevitably, then, we must ask why sexual harassment persists, why we have been unable to extirpate this careless and cruel habit of the heartless. As we know, but must continue to repeat, a major reason is the historical strength of the connections among sexuality, gender, and power. But one demonstration of the force of these connections, sexual harassment, floats at the mid-point of an ugly, long-lasting continuum. At the most glamorous end of the continuum is a particular vision of romance, love, and erotic desire. Here men pursue women for their mutual pleasure. That promise of pleasure masks the inequities of power. "Had we but world enough, and time," a poet [Andrew Marvell] sings, "This coyness, Lady, were no crime." But for the poet, there is not enough world, not enough time. The lady, then, must

From Catharine R. Stimpson, "Over-Reaching: Sexual Harassment and Education," *Initiatives*, vol. 52, no. 3, pp. 1-5. Copyright by *Initiatives*. Reprinted by permission.

submit to him before " . . . Worms shall try/That long preserv'd Virginity." At the other end of the continuum is men's coercion of women's bodies, the brutalities of incest and of rape, in which any pleasure is perverse.

In the mid-nineteenth century, Robert Browning wrote a famous dramatic monologue, "Andrea Del Sarto." In the poem, a painter is using his wife as a model. As he paints, he speaks, muses, and broods. He is worried about his marriage, for his model/wife is apparently faithless, a less than model wife. He is worried about his art, for his talents may be inadequate. He is, finally, worried about his reputation, for other painters may be gaining on and surpassing him. In the midst of expressing his fears, he declares, "Ah, but a man's reach should exceed his grasp/Or what's a heaven for. . . ." Traditional interpretations of his poem have praised Browning for praising the necessity of man's ambitions, of man's reaching out for grandeur. Indeed, Del Sarto, in an act of minor blasphemy, casts heaven not as God's space but as man's reminder that he has not yet achieved his personal best. Unhappily, these interpretations go on, women can hurt men in their noble quests. Fickle, feckless, the feminine often embarks on her own quest, a search-and-destroy mission against male grandeur.

A revisionary interpretation of "Andrea Del Sarto," however, can find the poem a different kind of parable about sexuality, gender, and power. In this reading, a man has at least two capacities. First, he can reach out and move about in public space and historical time. Del Sarto goes after both canvas and fame. Next, he can define a woman's identity, here through talking about her and painting her portrait. Del Sarto literally shapes the image of his wife. Iron-

ically, he wants to believe that he is a victim. He exercises his powers in order to demonstrate that he is powerless. A man, he projects himself as a poor baby who cannot shape up his mate.

A sexual harasser in higher education reveals similar, but more sinister, capacities. The hierarchical structure of institutions sends him a supportive message: the arduous climb up the ladder is worth it. The higher a man goes, the more he deserves and ought to enjoy the sweetness and freedoms of his place.[2] First, a man reaches out for what he wants. He makes sexual "advances." His offensive weapons can be linguistic (a joke, for example) or physical (a touch). He warns the powerless that he has the ability to reach out in order to grasp and get what he wants. He also demonstrates to himself that he is able to dominate a situation. As the psychoanalyst Ethel Spector Person has pointed out, for many men, sexuality and domination are inseparable. To be sexual is to dominate and to be reassured of the possession of the power to dominate (Person, 1980).[3]

Usually, women compose the powerless group, but it may contain younger men as well, the disadvantages of age erasing the advantages of gender. One example: a 1986 survey at the University of Illinois/Champaign-Urbana found that 19 percent of the female graduate students, 10 percent of the undergraduates, and 8 percent of the professional school students had experienced harassment. So, too, had 5 percent of the male respondents. In all but one incident, the harasser was another man (Allen & Okawa, 1987).

Second, the harasser assumes the right to define the identity of the person whom he assaults. To him, she is not mind, but body; not student, not professional, but sexual being. She is who and what the harasser says she is. Ironically, like Andrea Del Sarto, many academics project their own power onto a woman and then assert that she, not he, has power.[4] He, not she, is powerless. Her sexuality seduces and betrays him. This psychological maneuver must help to explain one fear that people express about sexual harassment policies—that such policies will permit, even encourage, false complaints against blameless faculty and staff. A recent study found 78 percent of respondents worried about loss of due process and about the fate of innocent people who might be accused of misconduct. Yet, the study concluded, less than 1 percent of all sexual harassment complaints each year *are* false. The deep problem is not wrongful accusations against the innocent, but the refusal of the wronged to file any complaint at all. In part, they believe they should handle sexual matters themselves. In part, they hope the problem will go away if they ignore it. In part, they fear retaliation, punishment for stepping out of line (Robertson, Dyer, & Campbell, 1988).

The unreasonable fear about false complaints is also a symptom of the blindness of the powerful to the realities of their own situation. They enjoy its benefits but are unable to see its nature and costs to other people. They are like a driver of an inherited sports car who loves to drive but refuses to learn where gas and oil come from, who services the car when it is in the garage, or why pedestrians might shout when he speeds through a red light. In a probing cssay, Molly Hite (1988) tells a story about a harasser on a United States campus, a powerful professor who abused his authority over female graduate students. He damaged several women, psychologically and professionally. Yet even after that damage became public knowledge, he survived, reputation intact, although he did discreetly move to another campus. Hite inventories the responses of her colleagues to this event. Men, no matter what their academic rank, tended to underplay the seriousness of his behavior. They thought that he had acted "normally," if sometimes insensitively, that the women had acted abnormally and weakly. Women, no matter what their academic rank, tended to sympathize with the female victims. They could identify with powerlessness. Hite writes, "The more the victim is someone who could be you, the easier it is to be scared. By the same reasoning, it's possible to be cosmically un-scared, even to find the whole situation trivial to the point of absurdity, if you can't imagine ever being the victim" (p. 9).

So far, higher education has participated in building at least four related modes of resistance to sexual harassment. First, we have named the problem *as a problem*. We have pushed it into public consciousness as an issue. The Equal Employment Opportunity Commission guidelines, in particular, have provided a citable, national language with which to describe harassment, a justifiable entry in the dictionary of our concerns. Next, we have learned how much administrative leadership has mattered in urging an institution to address this concern. Not surprisingly, faculties have not moved to reform themselves. Next, workshops that educate people about the nature of harassment do seem to reduce its virulence. Finally, we have created grievance procedures with which we can hear complaints, investigate them, and punish harassers.[5] The most carefully designed in themselves help to empower women. The process does not itself perpetuate her sense of self as victim (Hoffman, 1986).

These modes of resistance, good in themselves, have also done good. They have shown an institution's commitment to a fair, non-polluting social environment. They have warned potential harassers to stop. They have offered some redress to the harassed. Resistance will, however, be of only limited good unless a rewriting of the historical connections among sexuality, gender, and power accompanies it. Similarly, putting up traffic lights on crowded streets is a good. Lights are, however, of only limited good unless drivers believe in the rights of other drivers, in safety, and in the limits of their machines.

In such a rewriting, an act of "overreaching" will be interpreted not as aspiration and desire, but as an invasion of another person's body, dignity, and livelihood. No one will feel the approaching grasp of the harasser as a welcome clasp. Over-reaching will be a sign not of grace but of disgrace, not of strength but of callousness and, possibly, anxiety, not of virility but of moral and psychological weakness. It will not be a warm joke between erotic equals, but a smutty titter from an erotic jerk. The rhetoric of neither romance nor comedy will be able to paint over the grammar of exploitation.[6]

One consequence of this rewriting will be to expand our modes of resistance to include a general education curriculum, not simply about harassment as a phenomenon, but about power itself, which harassment symptomizes. This will mean teaching many men to cut the ties among selfhood, masculinity, and domination. It will mean teaching many women to cut the ties among self, femininity, and intimacy at any price, including the price of submission. Occasionally, reading a sexual harassment complaint from a young woman, I have asked myself, in some rue

and pain, why she has acted *like a woman*. By that, I have meant that her training for womanhood has taught her to value closeness, feeling, relationships. Fine and dandy, but too often, she takes this lesson to heart above all others.

The first part of the curriculum, for women, will remind them of their capacity for resistance, for saying no. Telling a harasser to stop can be effective.[7] Speaking out, acting verbally, can also empower an individual woman. Less fortunately, these speech acts reconstitute the traditional sexual roles of man as hunter, woman as prey. Unlike a rabbit or doe, she is responsible for setting the limits of the hunt, for fencing in the game park. If the hunter violates these limits, it is because she did not uphold them firmly enough. Moreover, saying no to the aggressor also occurs in private space. Because of this location, both harasser and harassed can forget that these apparently private actions embody, in little, grosser structures of authority.

The second part of the curriculum will be for men and women. Fortunately, women's studies programs are now developed enough to serve as a resource for an entire institution that chooses to offer lessons about gender and power. These lessons will do more than anatomize abuses. They will also present an ethical perspective, which the practices of colleges and universities might well represent. This ethic will cherish a divorce between sexuality and the control of another person, an unbridgeable distance between a lover's pleasure and a bully's threat. This ethic will also ask us to cherish our capacities to care for each other, to attend to each other's needs without manipulating them.[8] We will reach out to each other without grasping, hauling, pushing, mauling.

The struggle against sexual harassment, then, is part of a larger struggle to replant the moral grounds of education. Our visionary hope is that we will, in clear air, harvest new gestures, laws, customs, and practices. We will still take poets as our prophets. When we do so, however, we might replace the dramatic monologue of a fraught, Renaissance painter with that of a strong-willed, late twentieth-century feminist. In 1977, in "Natural Resources," Adrienne Rich spoke for those who stubbornly continue to believe in visionary hope:

"My heart is moved by all I cannot save:
so much has been destroyed.
I have to cast my lot with those
who age after age, perversely,
with no extraordinary power,
reconstitute the world."

NOTES

1. The authors of a survey of 311 institutions of higher education, conducted in 1984, estimate that one woman out of four experiences some form of harassment as a student (Robertson et al., 1988). A survey of a single institution, a large public research university, found that 31 percent of the more than 700 respondents had been subjected to "sex-stereotyped jokes, remarks, references, or examples" ("Survey documents," 1988, pp. 41–42).

2. As Robertson et al. comment, "individuals in positions of authority . . . (are) used to viewing professional status as expanding privilege rather than increasing responsibility and obligation" (p. 808). An anecdote illustrates this generalization. Recently, I was chairing a meeting of the graduate faculty of my university. Our agenda item was a proposal to conduct a periodic review of faculty members, program by program, to help insure they were still qualified to be graduate teachers. A professor, well-known for his decency, stood up in opposition. He said, "When I got tenure, I became a member of a club, and no one is going to tell me what to do. If I don't want to publish, that's my business."

3. Not coincidentally, most of the sexual harassers whom I have had to investigate as graduate dean have had streaks of arrogance, flare-ups

of vanity. In contrast, the men who have been most sympathetic to the necessity of my investigations have had a certain ethical poise, a balance of standards and stability.

4. An obvious parallel is a traditional response to rape, in which women are held culpable for being raped. Moreover, like versions of Jezebel, they are thought only too likely to cry rape in order to cover up their own sins.

5. I am grateful to Robertson et al. (1988) for their description of various modes of resistance to harassment. Their study also explores the reasons why public institutions have been more sensitive than private institutions. More specifically, Beauvais (1986) describes workshops that deal with harassment for residence hall staff at the University of Michigan.

6. Disguising the language of harassment as humor has several advantages. First, it draws on our old, shrewd assessment of much sexual behavior as funny and comic. Next, it simultaneously inflates the harasser to the status of good fellow, able to tell a joke, and deflates the harassed to the status of prude, unable to take one.

7. Allen and Okawa (1987) say that this worked for two-thirds of the respondents in their study of harassment at the University of Illinois.

8. Tronto (1987) suggestively outlines a theory of care that educational institutions might adopt.

REFERENCES

Allen, D., & Okawa, J. B. (1987). A counseling center looks at sexual harassment. *Journal of the National Association for Women Deans, Administrators, and Counselors,* 51(1), 9–16.

Beauvais, K. (1986). Workshops to combat sexual harassment: A case study of changing attitudes. *Signs,* 12(1), 130–145.

Hite, M. (1988). Sexual harassment and the university community. Unpublished manuscript.

Hoffman, F. L. (1986). Sexual harassment in academia. *Harvard Educational Review,* 56(2), 105–121.

Person, E. (1980). Sexuality as the mainstay of identity. In C. R. Stimpson & E. S. Person (eds.), *Women: Sex and sexuality.* Chicago: University of Chicago Press.

Robertson, C., Dyer, C. C., & Campbell, D'A. (1988). Campus harassment: Sexual harassment policies and procedures at institutions of higher learning. *Signs,* 13(4), 792–812.

Survey documents sexual harassment at U Mass. (1988). *Liberal Education,* 74(2), 41–2.

Tronto, J. C. (1987). Beyond gender differences to a theory of care. *Signs,* 12(4), 644–663.

NO

Gretchen Morgenson

MAY I HAVE THE PLEASURE

On October 11, in the middle of the Anita Hill/Clarence Thomas contretemps, the *New York Times* somberly reported that sexual harassment pervades the American workplace. The source for this page-one story was a *Times*/CBS poll conducted two days earlier in which a handful (294) of women were interviewed by telephone. Thirty-eight per cent of respondents confirmed that they had been at one time or another "the object of sexual advances, propositions, or unwanted sexual discussions from men who supervise you or can affect your position at work." How many reported the incident at the time it happened? Four per cent.

Did the *Times* offer any explanation for why so few actually reported the incident? Could it be that these women did not report their "harassment" because they themselves did not regard a sexual advance as harassment? Some intelligent speculation on this matter might shed light on a key point: the vague definitions of harassment that make it easy to allege, hard to identify, and almost impossible to prosecute. Alas, the *Times* was in no mood to enlighten its readers.

It has been more than ten years since the Equal Employment Opportunity Commission (EEOC) wrote its guidelines defining sexual harassment as a form of sexual discrimination and, therefore, illegal under Title VII of the Civil Rights Act of 1964. According to the EEOC there are two different types of harassment: so-called *quid pro quo* harassment, in which career or job advancement is guaranteed in return for sexual favors, and environmental harassment, in which unwelcome sexual conduct "unreasonably interferes" with an individual's working environment or creates an "intimidating, hostile, or offensive working environment."

Following the EEOC's lead, an estimated three out of four companies nationwide have instituted strict policies against harassment; millions of dollars are spent each year educating employees in the subtleties of Title VII etiquette. Men are warned to watch their behavior, to jettison the patronizing pat and excise the sexist comment from their vocabularies.

Yet, if you believe what you read in the newspapers, we are in the Stone Age where the sexes are concerned. A theme common to the media,

From Gretchen Morgenson, "May I Have the Pleasure . . . ," *National Review* (November 18, 1991). Copyright © 1991 by National Review, Inc., 150 East 35th Street, New York, NY 10016. Reprinted by permission.

plaintiff's lawyers, and employee-relations consultants is that male harassment of women is costing corporations millions each year in lost productivity and low employee morale. "Sexual harassment costs a typical Fortune 500 Service or Manufacturing company $6.7 million a year" says a sexual-harassment survey conducted late in 1988 for *Working Woman* by Klein Associates. This Boston consulting firm is part of a veritable growth industry which has sprung up to dispense sexual-harassment advice to worried companies in the form of seminars, videos, and encounter groups.

But is sexual harassment such a huge problem in business? Or is it largely a product of hype and hysteria? The statistics show that sexual harassment is less prevalent today than it was five years ago. According to the EEOC, federal cases alleging harassment on the job totaled 5,694 in 1990, compared to 6,342 in 1984. Yet today there are 17 per cent more women working than there were then.

At that, the EEOC's figures are almost certainly too high. In a good many of those complaints, sexual harassment may be tangential to the case; the complaint may primarily involve another form of discrimination in Title VII territory: race, national origin, or religious discrimination, for example. The EEOC doesn't separate cases involving sexual harassment alone; any case where sexual harassment is mentioned, even in passing, gets lumped into its figures.

Many of the stories depicting sexual harassment as a severe problem spring from "consultants" whose livelihoods depend upon exaggerating its extent. In one year, DuPont spent $450,000 on sexual-harassment training programs and materials. Susan Webb, president of Pacific Resources Development Group, a Seattle consultant, says she spends 95 per cent of her time advising on sexual harassment. Like most consultants, Miss Webb acts as an expert witness in harassment cases, conducts investigations for companies and municipalities, and teaches seminars. She charges clients $1,500 for her 35-minute sexual-harassment video program and handbooks.

UNFELT NEEDS

Corporations began to express concern on the issue back in the early Eighties, just after the EEOC published its first guidelines. But it was *Meritor Savings Bank v. Vinson*, a harassment case that made it to the Supreme Court in 1985, that really acted as an employment act for sex-harassment consultants. In *Vinson*, the Court stated that employers could limit their liability to harassment claims by implementing anti-harassment policies and procedures in the workplace. And so, the anti-harassment industry was born.

Naturally, the consultants believe they are filling a need, not creating one. "Harassment is still as big a problem as it has been because the workplace is not integrated," says Susan Webb. Ergo, dwindling numbers of cases filed with the EEOC are simply not indicative of a diminution in the problem.

Then what do the figures indicate? Two things, according to the harassment industry. First, that more plaintiffs are bringing private lawsuits against their employers than are suing through the EEOC or state civil-rights commissions. Second, that the number of cases filed is a drop in the bucket compared to the number of actual, everyday harassment incidents.

It certainly stands to reason that a plaintiff in a sexual-harassment case would prefer bringing a private action against her employer to filing an EEOC claim. EEOC and state civil-rights cases allow plaintiffs only compensatory damages, such as back pay or legal fees. In order to collect big money—punitive damages—from an employer, a plaintiff must file a private action.

Yet there's simply no proof that huge or increasing numbers of private actions are being filed today. No data are collected on numbers of private harassment suits filed, largely because they're brought as tort actions—assault and battery, emotional distress, or breach of contract. During the second half of the Eighties, the San Francisco law firm of Orrick, Herrington, and Sutcliffe monitored private sexual-harassment cases filed in California. Its findings: From 1984 to 1989, the number of sexual-harassment cases in California that were litigated through a verdict totaled a whopping 15. That's in a state with almost six million working women.

Of course, cases are often settled prior to a verdict. But how many? Orrick, Herrington partner Ralph H. Baxter Jr., management co-chairman of the American Bar Association's Labor Law Committee on Employee Rights and Responsibilities, believes the number of private sexual-harassment cases launched today is greatly overstated. "Litigation is not as big a problem as it's made out to be; you're not going to see case after case," says Mr. Baxter. "A high percentage of matters go to the EEOC and a substantial number of cases get resolved."

Those sexual-harassment actions that do get to a jury are the ones that really grab headlines. A couple of massive awards have been granted in recent years—five plaintiffs were awarded $3.8 million by a North Carolina jury—but most mammoth awards are reduced on appeal. In fact, million-dollar sexual-harassment verdicts are still exceedingly rare. In California, land of the happy litigator, the median jury verdict for all sexual-harassment cases litigated between 1984 and 1989 was $183,000. The top verdict in the sate was just under $500,000, the lowest was $45,000. And California, known for its sympathetic jurors, probably produces higher awards than most states.

Now to argument number two: that the number of litigated harassment cases is tiny compared to the number of actual incidents that occur. Bringing a sexual-harassment case is similar to filing a rape case, consultants and lawyers say; both are nasty proceedings which involve defamation, possible job loss, and threats to both parties' family harmony.

It may well be that cases of perceived harassment go unfiled, but is it reasonable to assume that the numbers of these unfiled cases run into the millions? Consider the numbers of cases filed that are dismissed for "no probable cause." According to the New York State human-rights commission, almost two-thirds of the complaints filed in the past five years were dismissed for lack of probable cause. Of the two hundred sexual-harassment cases the commission receives a year, 38 per cent bring benefits to the complainant.

What about private actions? No one keeps figures on the percentage of cases nationwide won by the plaintiff versus the percentage that are dismissed. However, the outcomes of private sexual-harassment suits brought in California from 1984 to 1989 mirror the public figures from New York. According to Orrick, Herrington, of the 15 cases litigated to a verdict in California from 1984 to 1989, slightly less than half were dismissed and slightly more than half (53 per cent) were won by the plaintiff.

Are California and New York anomalies? Stephen Perlman, a partner in labor law at the Boston firm of Ropes & Gray, who has 15 years' experience litigating sexual-harassment cases, thinks not: "I don't suppose I've had as many as a dozen cases go to litigation. Most of the cases I've seen—the vast majority—get dismissed. They don't even have probable cause to warrant further processing."

WHAT IS HARASSMENT?

A major problem is the vague definition of harassment. If "environmental harassment" were clearly defined and specifiable, lawyers would undoubtedly see more winnable cases walk through their doors. Asking a subordinate to perform sexual favors in exchange for a raise is clearly illegal. But a dirty joke? A pin-up? A request for a date?

In fact, behavior which one woman may consider harassment could be seen by another as a non-threatening joke. The closest thing to harassment that I have experienced during my 15-year career occurred in the early Eighties when I was a stockbroker-in-training at Dean Witter Reynolds in New York City. I had brought in the largest personal account within Dean Witter's entire retail brokerage system, an account which held roughly $20 million in blue-chip stocks. Having this account under my management meant I had a larger capital responsibility than any of my colleagues, yet I was relatively new to the business. My fellow brokers were curious, but only one was brutish enough to walk right up to me and pop the question: "How did you get that account? Did you sleep with the guy?"

Instead of running away in tears, I dealt with him as I would any rude person. "Yeah," I answered. "Eat your heart out." He turned on his heel and never bothered me again. Was my colleague a harasser, or just practicing Wall Street's aggressive humor, which is dished out to men in other ways? Apparently, I am in the minority in thinking the latter. But the question remains. Whose standards should be used to define harassment?

Under tort law, the behavior which has resulted in a case—such as an assault or the intent to cause emotional distress—must be considered objectionable by a "reasonable person." The EEOC follows this lead and in its guidelines defines environmental harassment as that which "unreasonably interferes with an individual's job performance."

Yet, sexual-harassment consultants argue that any such behavior—even that which is perceived as harassment only by the most hypersensitive employee—ought to be considered illegal and stamped out. In fact, they say, the subtler hostile-environment cases are the most common and cause the most anguish. Says Frieda Klein, the Boston consultant: "My goal is to create a corporate climate where every employee feels free to object to behavior, where people are clear about their boundaries and can ask that objectionable behavior stop."

Sounds great. But rudeness and annoying behavior cannot be legislated out of existence; nor should corporations be forced to live under the tyranny of a hypersensitive employee. No woman should have to run a daily gauntlet of sexual innuendo, but neither is it reasonable for women to expect a pristine work environment free of coarse behavior.

Susan Hartzoge Gray, a labor lawyer at Haworth, Riggs, Kuhn, and Haworth in Raleigh, North Carolina, believes that hostile-environment harassment shouldn't be actionable under Title VII. "How can the law say one person's lewd and another's nice?" she asks. "There are so many different taste levels. . . . We condone sexual jokes and innuendos in the media—a movie might get a PG rating— yet an employer can be called on the carpet because the same thing bothers someone in an office."

But changing demographics may do more to eliminate genuine sexual harassment than all the apparatus of law and consultancy. As women reach a critical mass in the workforce, the problem of sexual harassment tends to go away. Frieda Klein says the problem practically vanishes once 30 per cent of the workers in a department, an assembly line, or a company are women.

Reaching that critical mass won't take long. According to the Bureau of Labor Statistics, there will be 66 million women to 73 million men in the workplace by 2000. They won't all be running departments or heading companies, of course, but many will.

So sexual harassment will probably become even less of a problem in the years ahead than it is today. But you are not likely to read that story in a major newspaper anytime soon. Indeed, sexual harassment has all the earmarks of an issue Democrats will use to try to steal voters, particularly women, from the GOP. Such tactics are more likely to worsen the Democrats' already woeful standing with male voters, who went 58 per cent Republican in the last presidential election. The likelihood of losing more than they stand to gain from highlighting sexual harassment probably won't stop the Democrats—unless George Bush has saved them by endorsing the feminist agenda of punitive damages for vaguely defined sex-harassment charges in his new litigation-boosting civil-rights bill.

POSTSCRIPT

Is Sexual Harassment a Pervasive Problem in America?

"The harassers are among us," says Stimpson. "Sexual louts refuse to disappear." Morgenson suggests that such alarms are "largely a product of hype and hysteria." Both writers cite statistics, provide examples, and give advice on how to repel unwelcome advances. Yet they come to very different conclusions about the pervasiveness of the problem. Perhaps the differences between the two of them result from causes deeper than the immediate issue of sexual harassment. Stimpson seems to have in mind a larger agenda, or as she says, "a larger struggle to replant the moral grounds of education." It is probably safe to say that Morgenson would be very wary of this replanting project—and might even enlist herself on the opposite side of the struggle.

Michele A. Paludi, director of the women's studies program at Hunter College of the City University of New York, is the author of *Academic and Workplace Sexual Harassment: A Resource Manual* (State University of New York Press, 1991) and the editor of *Ivory Power: Sexual Harassment on Campus* (State University of New York Press, 1991). Catharine A. MacKinnon's *Sexual Harassment of Working Women: A Case of Sex Discrimination* (Yale University Press, 1979) was an early and highly influential argument for placing sexual harassment under the legal category of sexual discrimination. Like MacKinnon, Susan Faludi, in *Backlash: The Undeclared War Against American Women* (Random House, 1991), argues that sexual harassment is virtually pandemic in our society. The argument is disputed and defended by various writers in the May/June 1991 issue of *Society*, which features the topic of sexual harassment.

There may be some signs of a backlash against charges of sexual harassment. Some men have already brought defamation suits, charging that their reputations have been seriously harmed. More than a dozen major corporations, including General Motors, AT&T, and DuPont, have been sued by male employees who were dismissed on grounds of sexual harassment. Few of the suits have been successful so far, perhaps in part because firms have pulled out all the stops in fighting them.

ISSUE 7

Should Traditional Families Be Preserved?

YES: David Popenoe, from "Breakup of the Family: Can We Reverse the Trend?" *USA Today Magazine,* a publication of the Society for the Advancement of Education (May 1991)

NO: Judith Stacey, from *Brave New Families: Stories of Domestic Upheaval in Late Twentieth Century America* (Basic Books, 1990)

ISSUE SUMMARY

YES: Sociologist David Popenoe decries the demise of the traditional nuclear family, explains its causes, and recommends corrective actions.
NO: Sociologist Judith Stacey argues that the falsely labeled traditional family with the wife confined to the home is not an option for many women and is not the preferred family practice for a majority of women.

The crisis of the American family deeply concerns many Americans. About 50 percent of marriages end in divorce, and only 27 percent of children born in 1990 are expected to be living with both parents when they reach age 17. Most Americans, therefore, are affected personally or are close to people who are affected by structural changes in the family. Family problems in the form of violence and celebrity divorces are standard fare for news programs. Magazine articles decrying the breakdown of the family appear frequently. Most politicians try to address the problems of the family. Academics affirm that the family crisis has numerous significant negative effects on children, spouses, and the larger society.

Sociologists pay attention to the role that the family plays in the functioning of society. Procreation and socialization are two vital roles that families traditionally have performed. For a society to survive, its population must reproduce (or take in many immigrants), and its young must be trained to perform adult roles and to have the values and attitudes that will motivate them to contribute to society. Families are the units that performed both these tasks. In addition, the family provides economic and emotional support for its members, and this support is vital to their effective functioning in society.

Today the performance of the family is disappointing in all these areas. Procreation outside of marriage has become rather common, often leading to less than ideal conditions for raising children. The scorecard on American family socialization is hard to assess, but complaints are common about such issues as parents' declining time with and influence on their children and the large population of latchkey children. The prevalence of poverty among single-parent families and the potential for financial difficulties within families that have only one income earner indicate that the modern family is failing economically unless both spouses work. The high divorce rate and the frequency of child and spouse abuse indicate that the modern family fails to provide adequate social and emotional support.

Although most experts agree that the American family is in crisis, there is little agreement about what, if anything, should be done about it. After all, most of these problems result from the choices that people make to increase their happiness. People end unhappy marriages. Married women work for fulfillment or money that is perceived as needed. Unwed mothers decide to keep their children. The number of couples who choose to remain childless is growing rapidly. More people are choosing to have sex before marriage, which further redefines the role of marriage in a way that pleases individuals but weakens the institutions of marriage and family. The widespread practice of abortion has similar effects.

Individual choices are not the only factors that have contributed to the weakening of the family (economic and legal changes have also played an important role), but this trend cannot be changed unless people start choosing differently. There is no sign, however, that people are going to choose differently. Does this mean that the weakening of the family is desirable? Few would advocate such an idea, but it is a reasonable position if free choice is a leading value. However, sociologists recognize that the free choices of individuals do not always produce good results at the aggregate or societal level. For example, people smoke, drink, and take drugs by choice for their pleasure, but the costs in lost production, medical services, and socially harmful behaviors are immense. Is the family crisis this type of problem?

In the readings that follow, David Popenoe argues that the weakening of the traditional family is a trend that *must* be reversed. Judith Stacey argues that the traditional family needed to be changed. She does not applaud all the changes that have taken place, but she supports many of the choices (and the right to make those choices) that have resulted in the variety of family structures that exist in the United States today.

YES

David Popenoe

BREAKUP OF THE FAMILY: CAN WE REVERSE THE TREND?

As a social institution, the family has been "in decline" since the beginning of world history. It gradually has been becoming weaker through losing social functions and power to other institutions such as church, government, and school. Yet, during the past 25 years, family decline in the U.S., as in other industrialized societies, has been both steeper and more alarming than during any other quarter-century in our history. Although they may not use the term decline, most scholars now agree—though for many this represents a recent change of viewpoint—that the family has undergone a social transformation during this period. Some see "dramatic and unparalleled changes," while others call it "a veritable revolution."

I believe, in short, that we are witnessing the end of an epoch. Today's societal trends are bringing to a close the cultural dominance of the traditional nuclear family—one situated apart from both the larger kin group and the workplace, and focused on procreation. It consists of a legal, lifelong, sexually exclusive, heterosexual, monogamous marriage, based on affection and companionship, in which there is a sharp division of labor (separate spheres), with the female as full-time housewife and the male as primary provider and ultimate authority. Lasting for only a little more than a century, this family form emphasized the male as "good provider," the female as "good wife and mother," and the paramount importance of the family for childbearing. (Of course, not all families were able to live up to these cultural ideals.) During its heyday, the terms family, home, and mother ranked extraordinarily high in the hierarchy of cultural values.

In certain respects, this family form reached its apogee in the middle of the 20th century. By the 1950's—fueled in part by falling maternal and child mortality rates, greater longevity, and a high marriage rate—a larger percentage of children than ever before were growing up in stable, two-parent families. Similarly, this period witnessed the highest-ever proportion of women who married, bore children, and lived jointly with their husbands until at least age 50.

From David Popenoe, "Breakup of the Family: Can We Reverse the Trend?" *USA Today Magazine* (May 1991). Copyright © 1991 by the Society for the Advancement of Education. Reprinted by permission.

In the 1960's, however, four major social trends emerged to signal a widespread "flight" from both the ideal and the reality of the traditional nuclear family: rapid fertility decline, the sexual revolution, the movement of mothers into the labor force, and the upsurge in divorce. None of these changes was new to the 1960's; each represents a tendency that already was in evidence in earlier years. What happened in the 1960's was a striking acceleration of the trends, made more dramatic by the fact that, during the 1950's, they had leveled off and, in some cases, even reversed direction.

First, fertility declined in the U.S. by almost 50% between 1960 and 1989, from an average of 3.7 children per woman to only 1.9. Although births have been diminishing gradually for several centuries (the main exception being the two decades following World War II), the level of fertility during the past decade was the lowest in U.S. history and below that necessary for the replacement of the population.

A growing dissatisfaction with parenthood is now evident among adults in our culture, along with a dramatic decrease in the stigma associated with childlessness. Some demographers predict that 20–25% of today's young women will remain completely childless, and nearly 50% will be either childless or have only one offspring.

Second, the sexual revolution has shattered the association of sex and reproduction. The erotic has become a necessary ingredient of personal well-being and fulfillment, both in and outside of marriage, as well as a highly marketable commodity. The greatest change has been in the area of premarital sex. From 1971 to 1982 alone, the proportion of unmarried females in the U.S. aged 15–19 who engaged in premarital sexual intercourse jumped up from 28 to 44%. This behavior reflects a widespread change in values; in 1967, 85% of Americans condemned premarital sex as morally wrong, compared to 37% in 1979.

The sexual revolution has been a major contributor to the striking increase in unwed parenthood. Nonmarital births jumped from five percent of all births in 1960 (22% of black births) to 22% in 1985 (60% of black births). This is the highest rate of nonmarital births ever recorded in the U.S.

Third, although unmarried women long have been in the labor force, the past quarter-century has witnessed a striking movement into the paid work world of married women with children. In 1960, only 19% of married women with children under the age of six were in the labor force (39% with children between six and 17); by 1986, this figure had climbed to 54% (68% of those with older children).

Fourth, the divorce rate in the U.S. over the past 25 years (as measured by the number of divorced persons per 1,000 married persons) has practically quadrupled, going from 35 to 130. This has led many to refer to a divorce revolution. The probability that a marriage contracted today will end in divorce ranges from 44 to 66%, depending upon the method of calculation.

These trends signal a widespread retreat from the traditional nuclear family in its dimensions of a lifelong, sexually exclusive unit, focused on children, with a division of labor between husband and wife. Unlike most previous change, which reduced family functions and diminished the importance of the kin group, that of the past 25 years has tended to break up the nucleus of the family unit—the bond between husband and wife. Nuclear units, therefore, are losing ground to single-parent households, serial and step-families, and unmarried and homosexual couples.

The number of single-parent families, for example, has grown sharply—the result not only of marital breakup, but also of marriage decline (fewer persons who bear children are getting married) and widespread male abandonment. In 1960, only nine percent of U.S. children under 18 were living with a lone parent; by 1986, this figure had climbed to nearly one-quarter of all children. (The comparable figures for blacks are 22 and 53%.) Of children born during 1950–54, only 19% of whites (48% of blacks) had lived in a single-parent household by the time they reached age 17. For children born in 1990, however, the figure is projected to be 70% (94% for blacks).

The psychological character of the marital relationship also has changed substantially over the years. Traditionally, marriage has been understood as a social obligation—an institution designed mainly for economic security and procreation. Today, marriage is understood mainly as a path toward self-fulfillment. One's self-development is seen to require a significant other, and marital partners are picked primarily to be personal companions. Put another way, marriage is becoming deinstitutionalized. No longer comprising a set of norms and social obligations that are enforced widely, marriage today is a voluntary relationship that individuals can make and break at will. As one indicator of this shift, laws regulating marriage and divorce have become increasingly more lax.

As psychological expectations for marriage grow ever higher, dashed expectations for personal fulfillment fuel our society's high divorce rate. Divorce also feeds upon itself. With more divorce, the more "normal" it becomes, with fewer negative sanctions to oppose it and more potential partners available. In general, psychological need, in and of itself, has proved to be a weak basis for stable marriage.

Trends such as these dramatically have reshaped people's lifetime connectedness to the institution of the family. Broadly speaking, the institution of the family has weakened substantially over the past quarter-century in a number of respects. Individual members have become more autonomous and less bound by the group, and the latter has become less cohesive. Fewer of its traditional social functions are now carried out by the family; these have shifted to other institutions. The family has grown smaller in size, less stable, and with a shorter life span; people are, therefore, family members for a smaller percentage of their lives. The proportion of an average person's adulthood spent with spouse and children was 62% in 1960, the highest in our history. Today, it has dropped to a low of 43%.

The outcome of these trends is that people have become less willing to invest time, money, and energy in family life. It is the individual, not the family unit, in whom the main investments increasingly are made.

These trends are all evident, in varying degrees, in every industrialized Western society. This suggests that their source lies not in particular political or economic systems, but in a broad cultural shift that has accompanied industrialization and urbanization. In these societies, there clearly has emerged an ethos of radical individualism in which personal autonomy, individual rights, and social equality have gained in supremacy as cultural ideals. In keeping with these ideals, the main goals of personal behavior have shifted from commitment to social units of all kinds (families, communities, religions, nations) to personal choices, lifestyle options, self-fulfillment, and personal pleasure.

SOCIAL CONSEQUENCES

How are we to evaluate the social consequences of recent family decline? Certainly, one should not jump immediately to the conclusion that it is necessarily bad for our society. A great many positive aspects to the recent changes stand out as noteworthy. During this same quarter-century women and many minorities clearly have improved their status and probably the overall quality of their lives. Much of women's status gain has come through their release from family duties and increased participation in the labor force. In addition, given the great emphasis on psychological criteria for choosing and keeping marriage partners, it can be argued persuasively that those marriages today which do endure are more likely than ever before to be true companionships that are emotionally rewarding.

This period also has seen improved health care and longevity, as well as widespread economic affluence that has produced, for most people, a material standard of living that is historically unprecedented. Some of this improvement is due to the fact that people no longer are dependent on their families for health care and economic support or imprisoned by social class and family obligation. When in need, they now can rely more on public care and support, as well as self-initiative and self-development.

Despite these positive aspects, the negative consequences of family decline are real and profound. The greatest negative effect of recent trends, in the opinion of nearly everyone, is on children. Because they represent the future of a society, any negative consequences for them are especially significant. There is substantial, if not conclusive, evidence that, partly due to family changes, the quality of life for children in the past 25 years has worsened. Much of the problem is of a psychological nature, and thus difficult to measure quantitatively.

Perhaps the most serious problem is a weakening of the fundamental assumption that children are to be loved and valued at the highest level of priority. The general disinvestment in family life that has occurred has commonly meant a disinvestment in children's welfare. Some refer to this as a national "parent deficit." Yet, the deficit goes well beyond parents to encompass an increasingly less child-friendly society.

The parent deficit is blamed all too easily on newly working women. Yet, it is men who have left the parenting scene in large numbers. More than ever before, fathers are denying paternity, avoiding their parental obligations, and absent from home. (At the same time, there has been a slow, but not offsetting, growth of the "house-father" role.)

The breakup of the nuclear unit has been the focus of much concern. Virtually every child desires two biological parents for life, and substantial evidence exists that childrearing is most successful when it involves two parents, both of whom are strongly motivated to the task. This is not to say that other family forms can not be successful, only that, as a group, they are not as likely to be so. This also is not to claim that the two strongly motivated parents must be organized in the patriarchal and separate-sphere terms of the traditional nuclear family.

Regardless of family form, there has been a significant change over the past quarter-century in what can be called the social ecology of childhood. Advanced societies are moving ever further from what many hold to be a highly desirable childrearing environment, one consisting of a relatively large family that does a lot of things together, has many routines and traditions, and provides a great deal of quality contact time between adults and children; regular contact with relatives, active neighboring in a supportive neighborhood, and contact with the adult world of work; little concern on the part of children that their parents will break up; and the coming together of all these ingredients in the development of a rich family subculture that has lasting meaning and strongly promulgates such values as cooperation and sharing.

AGENDAS FOR CHANGE

What should be done to counteract or remedy the negative effects of family decline? This is the most controversial question of all, and the most difficult to answer. Among the agendas for change that have been put forth, two extremes stand out as particularly prominent in the national debate. The first is a return to the structure of the traditional nuclear family characteristic of the 1950's; the second is the development of extensive governmental policies.

Aside from the fact that it probably is impossible to return to a situation of an earlier time, the first alternative has major drawbacks. It would require many women to leave the workforce and, to some extent, become "de-liberated," an unlikely occurrence indeed. Economic conditions necessitate that even more women take jobs, and cultural conditions stress ever greater equality between the sexes.

In addition to such considerations, the traditional nuclear family form, in today's world, may be fundamentally flawed. As an indication of this, one should realize that the young people who led the transformation of the family during the 1960's and 1970's were brought up in 1950's households. If the 1950's families were so wonderful, why didn't their children seek to emulate them? In hindsight, the 1950's seem to have been beset with problems that went well beyond patriarchy and separate spheres. For many families, the mother-child unit had become increasingly isolated from the kin group, the neighborhood and community, and even from the father, who worked a long distance away. This was especially true for women who were fully educated and eager to take their place in work and public life. Maternal childrearing under these historically unprecedented circumstances became highly problematic.

Despite such difficulties, the traditional nuclear family is still the one of choice for millions of Americans. They are comfortable with it, and for them it seems to work. It is reasonable, therefore, at least not to place roadblocks in the way of couples with children who wish to conduct their lives according to the traditional family's dictates. Women who freely desire to spend much of their lives as mothers and housewives, outside of the labor force, should not be penalized economically by public policy for making that choice. Nor should they be denigrated by our culture as second-class citizens.

The second major proposal for change that has been stressed in national debate is the development of extensive governmental programs offering monetary support and social services for families, especially the new "non-nuclear" ones. In some cases, these programs assist with functions these families are unable to perform adequately; in others, the functions are taken over, transforming them from family to public responsibilities.

This is the path followed by the European welfare states, but it has been less accepted by the U.S. than by any other industrialized nation. The European welfare states have been far more successful than the U.S. in minimizing the negative economic impact of family decline, especially children. In addition, many European nations have established policies making it much easier for women (and increasingly men) to combine work with childrearing. With these successes in mind, it seems inevitable that the U.S. will (and I believe should) move gradually in the European direction with respect to family policies, just as we are now moving gradually in that direction with respect to medical care.

There are clear drawbacks, however, in moving too far down this road. If children are to be served best, we should seek to make the family stronger, not to replace it. At the same time that welfare states are minimizing some of the consequences of decline, they also may be causing further breakup of the family unit. This phenomenon can be witnessed today in Sweden, where the institution of the family probably has grown weaker than anywhere else in the world. On a lesser scale it has been seen in the U.S. in connection with our welfare programs. Fundamental to successful welfare state programs, therefore, is keeping uppermost in mind that the ultimate goal is to strengthen families.

While each of the above alternatives has some merit, I suggest a third one. It is premised on the fact that we can not return to the 1950's family, nor can we depend on the welfare state for a solution. Instead, we should strike at the heart of the cultural shift that has occurred, point up its negative aspects, and seek to reinvigorate the cultural ideals of family, parents, and children within the changed circumstances of our time. We should stress that the individualistic ethos has gone too far, that children are getting woefully shortchanged, and that, over the long run, strong families represent the best path toward self-fulfillment and personal happiness. We should bring again to the cultural forefront the old ideal of parents living together and sharing responsibility for their children and for each other.

What is needed is a new social movement whose purpose is the promotion of families and their values within the new constraints of modern life. It should point out the supreme importance to society of strong families, while at the same time suggesting ways they can adapt better to the modern conditions of individualism, equality, and the labor force participation of both women and men. Such a movement could build on the fact that the overwhelming majority of young people today still put forth as their major life goal a lasting, monogamous, heterosexual relationship which includes the procreation of children. It is reasonable to suppose that this goal is so pervasive because it is based on a deep-seated human need.

The time seems ripe to reassert that strong families concerned with the needs of children are not only possible, but necessary.

NO

Judith Stacey

THE POSTMODERN FAMILY,
FOR BETTER AND WORSE

BACKWARD TOWARD THE POSTMODERN FAMILY

Two centuries ago leading white, middle-class families in the newly united American states spearheaded a family revolution that replaced the pre-modern gender order with a modern family system. But "modern family" was an oxymoronic label for the peculiar institution, which dispensed modernity to white, middle-class men only by withholding it from women. The former could enter the public sphere as breadwinners and citizens, because their wives were confined to the newly privatized family realm. Ruled by an increasingly absent patriarchal landlord, the modern, middle-class family, a woman's domain, soon was sentimentalized as "traditional."

It took most of the subsequent two centuries for substantial numbers of white working-class men to achieve the rudimentary economic passbook to "modern" family life—a male family wage. By the time they had done so, however, a second family revolution was well underway. Once again middle-class, white families appeared to be in the vanguard. This time women were claiming the benefits and burdens of modernity, a status we could achieve only at the expense of the "modern" family itself. Reviving a long-dormant feminist movement, frustrated middle-class homemakers and their more militant daughters subjected modern domesticity to a sustained critique. At times this critique displayed scant sensitivity to the effects our antimodern family ideology might have on women for whom full-time domesticity had rarely been feasible. Thus, feminist family reform came to be regarded widely as a white, middle-class agenda, and white, working-class families its most resistant adversaries.

I shared these presumptions before my fieldwork among Silicon Valley families radically altered my understanding of the class basis of the post-modern family revolution. White, middle-class families, I have come to believe, are less the innovators than the propagandists and principal bene-

From Judith Stacey, *Brave New Families: Stories of Domestic Upheaval in Late Twentieth Century America* (Basic Books, 1990). Copyright © 1990 by Basic Books, Inc. Reprinted by permission of Basic Books, a division of HarperCollins Publishers. Notes omitted.

ficiaries of contemporary family change. African-American women and white, working-class women have been the genuine postmodern family pioneers, even though they also suffer most from its most negative effects. Long denied the mixed benefits that the modern family order offered middle-class women, less privileged women quietly forged alternative models of femininity to that of full-time domesticity and mother-intensive child rearing. Struggling creatively, often heroically, to sustain oppressed families and to escape the most oppressive ones, they drew on "traditional" premodern kinship resources and crafted untraditional ones, lurching backward and forward into the postmodern family.

Rising divorce and cohabitation rates, working mothers, two-earner households, single and unwed parenthood, and matrilineal, extended, and fictive kin support networks appeared earlier and more extensively among poor and working-class people. Economic pressures more than political principles governed these departures from domesticity, but working women . . . soon found additional reasons to appreciate paid employment. Eventually white, middle-class women, sated and even sickened by our modern family privileges, began to emulate, elaborate, and celebrate many of these alternative family practices. . . .

FAMILY QUARRELS

Recent books with such titles as *Falling from Grace* and *Fear of Falling* convey widespread suffering and anxiety among once-settled, middle-class Americans. And Americans, as historian Linda Gordon noted, recurrently frame social anxieties in familial terms. Sociologists may attempt to reassure an anxious populace that family life is "here to stay," but, as political analyst Andrew Hacker once observed, "it is hardly news that families are not what they used to be." The modern family system has lost the cultural and statistical dominance it long enjoyed, and no new family order has arisen to supplant it. The postmodern family is a site of disorder instead, a contested domain.

The passionate public response to the [Daniel Patrick] Moynihan report [on minority families] of the 1960s signaled a prolonged era of national conflict and confusion over which gender and kinship relationships are to count as "families" in postindustrial America. And in this family quarrel, gender and sexual politics occupy pride of place. Which relationships between and among women and men will receive legal recognition, social legitimacy, institutional and cultural support? In the postmodern period, a truly democratic gender and kinship order, one that does not favor male authority, heterosexuality, a particular division of labor, or a singular household or parenting arrangement became thinkable for the first time in history. And during the past several decades, family visionaries and reformers have been organizing struggles to bring it to fruition. They have met, however, with fierce resistance, and, as feminists have learned with great pain, it is not men alone who resist.

Why do many people of both genders recoil from the prospect of a fully democratic family regime? While there are multiple motives, including theological ones, this [selection] suggests compelling sociological sources of popular ambivalence about family reform. Not only would a democratic kinship system threaten vested gender and class interests, but even under the most benevolent of social orders, it promises also to bring its own kind of costs. A fully voluntary marriage system, as this century's experience with divorce rates indicates, . . . institutionalizes conjugal and thus parental instability. A normless gender order, one in which parenting arrangements, sexuality, and the distribution of work, responsibility, and resources all are negotiable and constantly renegotiable, can also invite considerable conflict and insecurity. These inescapable "burdens of freedom" have been magnified monstrously, however, under the far-from-benevolent social conditions of this turbulent, conservative period.

Many men, African-American men most of all, have suffered from postindustrialization and the eroding modern family order, while, thanks to feminism, numerous women, particularly white, middle-class ones, have achieved substantial gains. The resilient gender inequality of the transitional period, however, places the vast majority of women at disproportionate risk. In exchange for subordination and domestic service, the modern family promised women a number of customary protections and privileges, principal among these, lifelong support from a male breadwinner. Scarcely had working-class women . . . achieved access to this "patriarchal bargain," however, before it collapsed in a postindustrial deluge. With few social protections provided to replace the precarious "private" ones that the modern family once offered, many women have found good cause to mistrust the terms postmodern conditions appear to offer in its place. Women have been adding the burdens and benefits of paid labor to their historic domestic responsibilities, but men seem less eager to share the responsibilities and rewards of child rearing and house-

work. Moreover, as feminists have demonstrated in depressing detail, women have suffered numerous unexpected, and disturbing, consequences of egalitarian family reforms, such as no-fault divorce, joint custody provisions, shared parenting, and sexual liberation. Consequently, as Deirdre English, former editor of *Mother Jones* once observed, many women have come to "fear that feminism will free men first."

The insecure and undemocratic character of postmodern family life fuels nostalgia for the fading modern family, now recast as the "traditional" family. Capitalizing on this nostalgia, a vigorous, antifeminist "profamily" movement was able to score impressive political victories in the 1980s. It successfully, if incorrectly, identified feminism as the primary cause of the demise of the modern family, rather than the mopping-up operation for postindustrial transformations that were long underway. Defining the ERA [Equal Rights Amendment] and abortion rights as threats to the family, it placed feminists in the same defensive posture that housewives had come to assume. And partly because the profamily movement could draw on the volunteer labors of the disproportionate numbers of housewives it attracted to its political ranks, the backlash movement was able to achieve political visibility and victories far in excess of its numerical strength. Former President Reagan assured this movement a profound and lasting political legacy by rewarding its contribution to his "revolution" with antifeminist appointments to the Supreme Court and the federal judiciary who promise to inhibit the progress of democratic family reform well into the twenty-first century.

Many feminists, like myself, were caught off guard by the retreat from feminist activism and the resurgence of profamilialism that characterized the 1980s. During the 1970s family instability seemed to swell the ranks of the women's liberation movement. Feminist ideology, disseminated not only by the media but in flourishing grass-roots community activities and women's reentry programs, served [many] women . . . well to ease the exit from, or the reform of, unhappy modern marriages. Even older women in successful long-term marriages . . . employed feminist principles to improve their relationships. Second-wave feminism also supported women's efforts to develop independent work lives and career goals. With high divorce rates and women's paid work continuing throughout the eighties, feminist activism and family reforms might have been expected to progress apace.

Yet optimistic projections like these did not reckon with the ravages of postindustrialism. Neither feminism nor other progressive family reform movements have been as useful in addressing the structural inequalities of postindustrial occupational structure or the individualist, fast-track culture that makes all too difficult the formation of stable intimate relations on a democratic, or any other basis. . . .

WHOSE FAMILY CRISIS?

Ironically, while women are becoming the new proletariat and some men are increasing their participation in housework and childwork, the postmodern family, even more than the modern family it is replacing, is proving to be a woman-tended domain. There is some empirical basis for the enlightened father imagery celebrated by films like "Kramer versus Kramer." Indeed my fieldwork corroborates evidence that the determined efforts by many working women and feminists to reintegrate men into family life have had some success. There are data, for example, indicating that increasing numbers of men would sacrifice occupational gains in order to have more time with their families, just as there are data documenting actual increases in male involvement in child care. The excessive media attention which the faintest signs of new paternity enjoy, however, may be symptomatic of a deeper, far less comforting reality it so effectively obscures. We are experiencing, as demographer Andrew Cherlin aptly puts it, "the feminization of kinship." Demographers report a drastic decline in the average numbers of years that men live in households with young children. Few of the women who assume responsibility for their children in 90 percent of divorce cases in the United States today had to wage a custody battle for this privilege. We hear few proposals for a "daddy track." And few of the adults providing care to sick and elderly relatives are male. Yet ironically, most of the alarmist, nostalgic literature about contemporary family decline impugns women's abandonment of domesticity, the flipside of our tardy entry into modernity. Rarely do the anxious outcries over the destructive effects on families of working mothers, high divorce rates, institutionalized child care, or sexual liberalization scrutinize the family behaviors of men. Anguished voices, emanating from all bands on the political spectrum, lament state and market interventions that are weakening "the family." But whose family bonds are fraying? Women have amply demonstrated our continuing commitment to sustaining kin ties. If there is a family crisis, it is a male family crisis.

The crisis cannot be resolved by reviving the modern family system. While nostalgia for an idealized world of *Ozzie and Harriet* and *Archie Bunker* families abounds, little evidence suggests that most Americans genuinely wish to return to the gender order these symbolize. On the contrary, the vast majority . . . are actively remaking family life. Indeed a 1989 survey conducted by *The New York Times* found more than two-thirds of women, including a substantial majority of even those living in "traditional"—that is to say, "modern"—households, as well as a majority of men agreeing that "the United States continues to need a strong women's movement to push for changes that benefit women." Yet many seem reluctant to own their family preferences. . . . [T]hey cling to images of themselves as "back from the old days," while venturing ambivalently but courageously into the new.

Responding to new economic and social insecurities as well as to feminism, higher percentages of families in almost all income groups have adopted a multiple-earner strategy. Thus, the household form that has come closer than any other to replacing the modern family with a new cultural and statistical norm consists of a two-earner, heterosexual married couple with children. It is not likely, however, that any single household type will soon achieve the measure of normalcy that the modern family long enjoyed. Indeed, the postmodern success of the voluntary principle of the modern family system precludes this. The routinization of divorce and remarriage generates a diversity of family patterns even greater than was characteristic of the premodern period when death prevented family stability or household homogeneity. Even cautious demographers judge the new family diversity to be "an intrinsic feature . . . rather than a temporary aberration" of contemporary family life.

"The family" is *not* "here to stay." Nor should we wish it were. On the contrary, I believe that all democratic people, whatever their kinship preferences, should work to hasten its demise. An ideological concept that imposes mythical homogeneity on the diverse means by which people organize their intimate relationships, "the family" distorts and devalues this rich variety of kinship stories. And, along with the class, racial, and heterosexual prejudices it promulgates, this sentimental fictional plot authorizes gender hierarchy. Because the postmodern family crisis ruptures this seamless modern family script, it provides a democratic opportunity. Efforts to expand and redefine the definition of family by feminists and gay liberation activists and by many minority rights organizations are responses to this opportunity, seeking to extend social legitimacy and institutional support to the diverse patterns of intimacy that Americans have already forged.

If feminist identity threatens many and seems out of fashion, struggles to reconstitute gender and kinship on a just and democratic basis are more popular than ever. If only a minority of citizens are willing to grant family legitimacy to gay domestic partners, an overwhelming majority subscribe to the postmodern definition of a family by which the New York Supreme Court validated a gay man's right to retain his deceased lover's apartment. "By a ratio of 3-to-1" people surveyed in a Yale University study defined the family as "a group of people who love and care for each other." And while a majority of those surveyed gave negative ratings to the quality of American family life in general, 71 percent declared themselves "at least very satisfied" with their own family lives.

There is bad faith in the popular lament over family decline. Family nostalgia deflects social criticism from the social sources of most "personal troubles." Supply-side economics, governmental deregulation, and the right-wing assault on social welfare programs have intensified the destabilizing effects of recent occupational upheavals on flagging modern families and emergent postmodern ones alike. This [selection] is not the first to expose the bitter irony of right-wing politicians manipulating nostalgia for eroding working-class families while instituting policies that deepened their distress. Indeed, the ability to provide financial security was the chief family concern of most surveyed in the Yale study. If the postmodern family crisis represents a democratic opportunity, contemporary economic and political conditions enable only a minority to realize its tantalizing potential.

The bad faith revealed in the discrepant data reported in the Yale study indicates how reluctant most Americans are to fully own the genuine ambivalence we feel about family and social change. Yet ambivalence, as sociologist Alan Wolfe suggests, is an underappreciated but responsible moral stance, and one well suited for democratic citizenship: "Given the paradoxes of modernity, there is little wrong, and perhaps a great deal right, with being ambivalent—especially when there is so much to be ambivalent about."

Certainly . . . there are good grounds for ambivalence about postmodern family conditions. Even were a feminist family revolution to succeed, it could never eliminate all family distress. At best, it would foster a social order that could invert Tolstoy's aphorism by granting happy families the freedom to differ, and even to suffer. Truly postfeminist families, however, would suffer only the "common unhappiness" endemic to intimate human relationships; they would be liberated from the "hysterical misery" generated by social injustice. No nostalgic movement to restore the modern family can offer as much. For better and/or worse, the postmodern family revolution is here to stay.

POSTSCRIPT

Should Traditional Families Be Preserved?

Popenoe admits that there are many positive aspects to the recent changes that have affected families, but he sees the negative consequences, especially for children, as necessitating actions to counter them. He recognizes that it is impossible to return to the 1950s family pattern and that a government welfare approach would weaken family values further, as has been found where it has been tried. Instead he recommends a propaganda campaign to sell family values and preach against the individualistic ethos. He hopes for a family-oriented social movement. Is this a pie-in-the-sky solution? Remember that social movements arise spontaneously. Governments can encourage them, but they cannot manufacture them. It should also be remembered that social movements (the women's movement and the sexual revolution) created the crisis of the family in the first place, and many agree with Stacey in applauding these changes. Finally, one cannot be encouraged by a theory that maintains that the only acceptable solution requires a change of heart of the American people, because such a widespread and thoroughgoing change is generally unlikely.

Both authors agree that great changes have taken place in the American family, but this observation has not gone uncontested. Theodore Caplow and others replicated a study first conducted in the 1920s in Muncie, Indiana, and found many continuities and relatively few changes in family patterns. See *Middletown Families: Fifty Years of Change and Continuity* (University of Minnesota Press, 1983). They find little evidence of the disintegration of the family as an institution, a theme also developed by Mary Jo Bane in *Here to Stay: American Families in the Twentieth Century* (Basic Books, 1976). Continuity is also the theme in the collection of essays on women's familial roles, *Women and the Family: Two Decades of Change*, edited by Beth B. Hess and Marvin B. Sussman (Haworth Press, 1984), while change is emphasized in Andrew Cherlin's two books *Marriage, Divorce, Remarriage* (Harvard University Press, 1981) and *The Changing American Family and Public Policy* (Urban Institute Press, 1988). For a major statistical analysis of changing family patterns, see James A. Sweet and Larry L. Bumpass, *American Families and Households* (Russell Sage Foundation, 1987). For a long-term view of changes in the American family, see Steven Mintz and Susan Kellogg, *Domestic Revolutions: A Social History of American Family Life* (Free Press, 1989).

Most of the literature on the family tends to be alarmist. For example, in 1970 David Cooper wrote *The Death of the Family* (Vintage). Maxine L. Margolis relates changes in the American economy to transformations in the way the lives of women (especially their familial roles) are viewed in *Mothers and Such: Views of American Women and Why They Have Changed* (University of California Press, 1984). Barbara Ehrenreich argues a radical view that the male revolt against his traditional role of family breadwinner has spawned the women's movement for greater independence in *The Hearts of Men: American Dreams and the Flight from Commitment* (Anchor, 1983). Finally, David Popenoe documents the many negative consequences of family decline in *Disturbing the Nest: Sweden and the Decline of Families in Modern Society* (Aldine de Gruyter, 1988).

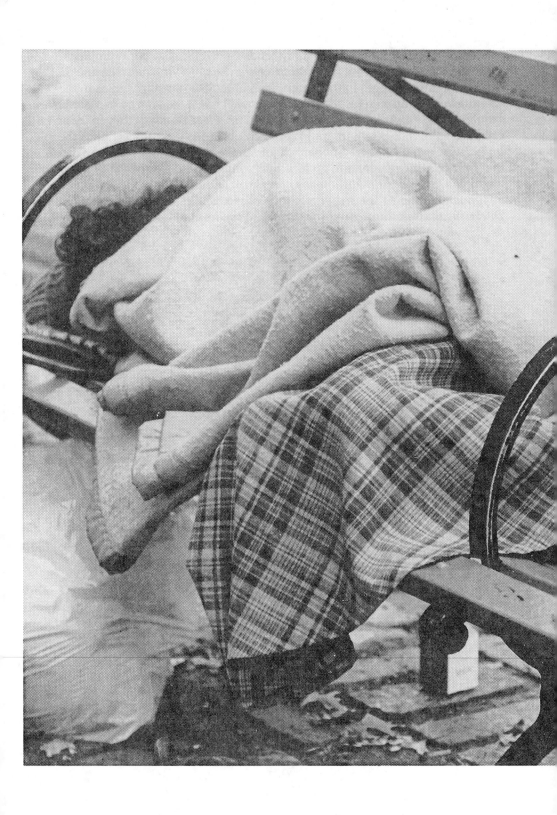

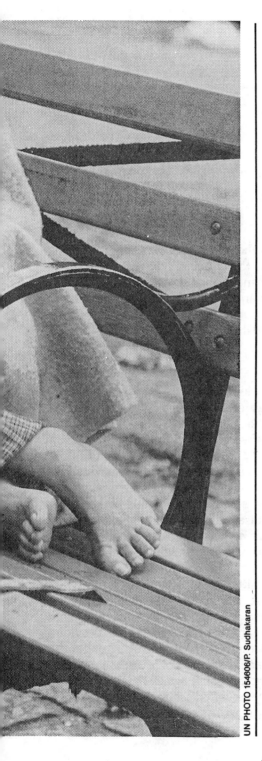

UN PHOTO 154606/P. Sudhakaran

PART 3

Stratification and Inequality

Although the ideal of equal opportunity for all is strong in the United States, many charge that inequities in the U.S. political and economic system do exist. Various affirmative action programs have been implemented to remedy inequalities, but some argue that this is discrimination in reverse. Others argue that minorities should depend on themselves, not the government, to overcome differences in equality. Does poverty continue to exist in the United States despite public assistance programs because it has become a deeply ingrained way of life? Or is poverty as well as homelessness a result of the failure of policymakers to live up to U.S. egalitarian principles? Social scientists debate these questions in this part.

Is Economic Inequality Beneficial to Society?

Does "Lower-Class" Culture Perpetuate Poverty?

Is Black Self-Help the Solution to Racial Inequality?

Is Affirmative Action Reverse Discrimination?

Helping the Homeless: Do We Need More Government Regulation?

ISSUE 8

Is Economic Inequality Beneficial to Society?

YES: George Gilder, from *Wealth and Poverty* (Basic Books, 1981)

NO: William Ryan, from *Equality* (Pantheon Books, 1981)

ISSUE SUMMARY

YES: Social critic George Gilder praises the American political economy that provides so many incentives for people to get ahead and make money. He maintains that the economy is dynamic and that all classes of people benefit.
NO: Professor of psychology William Ryan contends that income inequalities in America are excessive and immoral because they vastly exceed differences of merit and result in tremendous hardships for the poor.

Few people think that the president of the United States should be paid the same salary as a professor of sociology or a teaching assistant. Everyone benefits when the financial rewards for being president are large enough to motivate the most capable members of society to compete for the job. A society is better off with income inequality than with income equality as long as everyone has an equal opportunity to compete for the high-paying jobs. Pay differentials are needed to get the best possible fit between people and jobs. But how much income inequality is desirable? On this issue, people strongly disagree, and they carry their disagreement into the political arena.

Income inequality, however, should be viewed as only one type of inequality. Four other essential dimensions of equality/inequality are the degree of equality of opportunity, legal rights, political power, and social status. The American creed is fully committed to equality of opportunity and equality of legal and political rights. We believe everyone should have an equal opportunity to compete for jobs and awards. Laws that forbid discrimination and free public school education are two major means for providing equal opportunities to U.S. citizens. Whether society should also compensate for handicaps such as disadvantaged family backgrounds or the ravages of past discrimination, however, is a knotty issue, which has divided the country. Policies such as Head Start, income-based scholarships, quotas, and affirmative action are hotly debated. Equality of legal rights has been promoted by the civil rights and women's movements. A major debate in this area, of course, is the Equal Rights Amendment (ERA). However, the disagreement is not over the principle of equality but over whether ERA is good or bad for women. America's commitment to political equality is strong in principle, though less strong in practice. Everyone over eighteen gets one vote, and all votes are counted equally, but the political system tilts in the direction of special interest groups; those who belong to no such groups are seldom heard. Furthermore, money plays an increasingly important role in political campaigns. Clearly, there is room for improvement here. The final dimension of equality/inequality is status. Inequality of status involves differences in prestige, and it is arguable as to whether or not it can or should be eliminated. Ideally, the people who contribute the most to society are the most highly esteemed. The reader can judge the extent to which this principle holds true in the United States.

The Declaration of Independence proclaims that "all men are created equal," and the Founding Fathers who wrote the Declaration of Independence went on to base the laws of the land on the principle of equality. The equality they were referring to was equality of opportunity and legal and political rights for white, property-owning males. They did not mean equality of income or status, though they recognized that too much inequality of income would jeopardize democratic institutions. In the two centuries following the signing of the Declaration, nonwhites and women struggled for and won considerable equality of opportunity and rights. Meanwhile, income gaps in the United States have been widening (except from 1929 to 1945 when the stock market crash harmed the wealthy and wartime full employment favored the poor).

Should America now move toward greater income equality? Must this dimension of inequality be rectified in order for society to be just? George Gilder strongly believes that people must try hard, work hard, innovate, compete, aspire, accept risks, and be rewarded for their efforts. He maintains that welfare, public enterprise, highly progressive taxes, and many other egalitarian measures are sapping American initiative, crippling American enterprise, slowing the American economy, and perpetuating the poverty of the poor. According to Gilder, the free enterprise system, with all of its inequalities, stimulates individual effort and enterprise, and this is what makes America great and prosperous. On the other hand, William Ryan makes the case that the existing income inequalities are obscene and offensive to moral sensibilities. He believes some reduction of inequalities is essential to social justice. Ryan contends that the rich and their propagandists justify existing inequalities by claiming that the system is fair and the inequalities result largely from differential effort, skill, and achievement. He argues that this justification is weak.

YES
George Gilder

THE DIRGE OF TRIUMPH

The most important event in the recent history of ideas is the demise of the socialist dream. Dreams always die when they come true, and fifty years of socialist reality, in every partial and plenary form, leave little room for idealistic reverie. In the United States socialism chiefly rules in auditoria and parish parlors, among encounter groups of leftist intellectuals retreating from the real world outside, where socialist ideals have withered in the shadows of Stalin and Mao, Sweden and Tanzania, gulag and bureaucracy.

The second most important event of the recent era is the failure of capitalism to win a corresponding triumph. For within the colleges and councils, governments and churches where issue the nebulous but nonetheless identifiable airs and movements of new opinion, the manifest achievements of free enterprise still seem less comely than the promise of socialism betrayed. . . .

A prominent source of trouble is the profession of economics. Smith entitled Book One of *The Wealth of Nations*, "Of the Causes of Improvement in the productive Powers of Labour and the Order according to which its Produce is naturally distributed among the different Ranks of the people." He himself stressed the productive powers, but his followers, beginning with David Ricardo, quickly became bogged down in a static and mechanical concern with distribution. They all were forever counting the ranks of rich and poor and assaying the defects of capitalism that keep the poor always with us in such great numbers. The focus on distribution continues in economics today, as economists pore balefully over the perennial inequalities and speculate on brisk "redistributions" to rectify them.

This mode of thinking, prominent in foundation-funded reports, best-selling economics texts, newspaper columns, and political platforms, is harmless enough on the surface. But its deeper effect is to challenge the golden rule of capitalism, to pervert the relation between rich and poor, and to depict the system as "a zero-sum game" in which every gain for someone implies a loss for someone else, and wealth is seen once again to create poverty. As Kristol has said, a free society in which the distributions are

From George Gilder, *Wealth and Poverty* (Basic Books, 1981). Copyright © 1981 by George Gilder. Reprinted by permission of Basic Books, Inc., Publishers, New York.

widely seen as unfair cannot long survive. The distributionist mentality thus strikes at the living heart of democratic capitalism.

Whether of wealth, income, property, or government benefits, distributions always, unfortunately, turn out bad: highly skewed, hugely unequal, presumptively unfair, and changing little, or getting worse. Typical conclusions are that "the top 2 percent of all families own 44 percent of all family wealth, and the bottom 25 percent own none at all"; or that "the top 5 percent get 15.3 percent of the pretax income and the bottom 20 percent get 5.4 percent." . . .

Statistical distributions, though, can misrepresent the economy in serious ways. They are implicitly static, like a picture of a corporate headquarters, towering high above a city, that leaves out all the staircases, escalators, and elevators, and the Librium® on the executive's desk as he contemplates the annual report. The distribution appears permanent, and indeed, like the building, it will remain much the same year after year. But new companies will move in and out, executives will come and go, people at the bottom will move up, and some at the top will leave their Librium® and jump. For example, the share of the tobacco industry commanded by the leading four firms has held steady for nearly thirty years, but the leader of the 1950s is now nearly bankrupt. The static distributions also miss the simple matter of age; many of the people at the bottom of the charts are either old, and thus beyond their major earning years, or young, and yet to enter them. Although the young and the old will always be with us, their low earnings signify little about the pattern of opportunity in a capitalist system.

Because blacks have been at the bottom for centuries now, economists often miss the dynamism within the American system. The Japanese, for example, were interned in concentration camps during World War II, but thirty years later they had higher per capita earnings than any other ethnic group in America except the Jews. Three and one-half million Jewish immigrants arrived on our shores around the turn of the century with an average of nine dollars per person in their pockets, less than almost any other immigrant group. Six decades later the mean family income of Jews was almost double the national average. Meanwhile the once supreme British Protestants (WASPs) were passed in per capita earnings after World War II not only by Jews and Orientals but also by Irish, Italians, Germans, and Poles (which must have been the final Polish joke), and the latest generation of black West Indians.

It is a real miracle that learned social scientists can live in the midst of these continuing eruptions and convulsions, these cascades and cataracts of change, and declare in a tone of grim indignation that "Over the last fifty years there has been no shift in the distribution of wealth and income in this country." . . .

The income distribution tables also propagate a statistical illusion with regard to the American rich. While the patterns of annual income changed rather little in the 1970s, there was a radical shift in the distribution of wealth. In order to understand this development, it is crucial to have a clear-eyed view of the facts and effects of inflation, free of the pieties of the Left and the Right: the familiar rhetoric of the "cruelest tax," in which all the victims seem to be widows and orphans. In fact, widows and orphans—at least the ones who qualified for full social security and welfare benefits—did rather well under inflation. Between 1972 and 1977, for example, the median household income of the elderly rose from 80 to 85 percent of the entire population's. As Christopher Jencks of Harvard University and Joseph Minarek of the Brookings Institution, both men of the Left, discovered in the late 1970s, inflation hit hardest at savers and investors, largely the rich. . . .

Wealth consists of assets that promise a future stream of income. The flows of oil money do not become an enduring asset of the nation until they can be converted into a stock of remunerative capital—industries, ports, roads, schools, and working skills—that offer a future flow of support when the oil runs out. Four hundred years ago, Spain was rich like Saudi Arabia, swamped by a similar flood of money in the form of silver from the mines of Potosi in its Latin American colonies. But Spain failed to achieve wealth and soon fell back into its previous doldrums, while industry triumphed in apparently poorer parts of Europe.

A wealthy country must be able to save as well as to consume. Saving is often defined as deferred consumption. But it depends on investment: the ability to produce consumable goods at that future date to which consumption has been deferred. Saving depends on having something to buy when the deposit is withdrawn. For an individual it sounds easy; there must always be *something* to buy after all. But for a nation, with many savers, real wealth is hard work, requiring prolonged and profitable production of goods. . . .

Work, indeed, is the root of wealth, even of the genius that mostly resides in sweat. But without a conception of goals and purposes, well-paid workers consume or waste all that they earn. Pop singers rocking and rolling in money, rich basketball stars who symbolize wealth to millions, often end up deep in debt with nothing solid to show for their efforts, while the poorest families can often succeed in saving enough to launch profitable businesses. The old adages on the importance of thrift are true not only because they signify a quantitative rise in investible funds, but because they betoken imagination and purpose, which make wealth. Few businesses begin with bank loans, and small businesses almost never do. Instead they capitalize labor.

For example, ten years ago a Lebanese family arrived in Lee, Massachusetts, with a few dollars and fewer words of English. The family invested the dollars in buying a woebegone and abandoned shop beside the road at the edge of town, and they started marketing vegetables. The man rose at five every morning to drive slowly a ramshackle truck a hundred miles to farms in the Connecticut Valley, where he purchased the best goods he could find as cheaply as possible to sell that morning in Lee. It was a classic entrepreneurial performance, arbitrage, identifying price differentials in different markets, and exploiting them by labor. But because both the labor and the insight was little compensated, it was in a sense invisibly saved and invested in the store. All six children were sources of accumulating capital as they busily bustled about the place. The store remained open long hours, cashed checks of locals, and began to build a clientele. A few years later one had to fight through the crowds around it in summer, when the choice asparagus or new potted plants went on sale. Through the year it sold flowers and Christmas trees, gas and dry goods, maple syrup and blackberry jam, cider and candies, and wines and liquors, in the teeth of several supermarkets, innumerable gas stations, and other shops of every description, all better situated, all struggling in an overtaxed and declining Massachusetts economy.

The secret was partly in the six children (who placed the family deep in the statistics of per capita poverty for long after its arrival) and in the entrepreneurial vision of the owner, which eluded all the charts. Mr. Michael Zabian is the man's name, and he recently bought the biggest office building in the town, a three-story structure made of the same Lee marble as the national capitol building. He owns a large men's clothing store at street level and what amounts to a small shopping center at his original site; and he preens in three-piece suits in the publicity photos at the Chamber of Commerce.

As extraordinary as may seem his decade of achievement, though, two other Lebanese have performed similar marvels in the Berkshires and have opened competing shops in the area. Other immigrants in every American city—Cubans in Miami, Portuguese in Providence and Newark, Filipinos in Seattle, Koreans in Washington, D.C., and New York, Vietnamese in Los Angeles, to mention the more recent crop—have performed comparable feats of commerce, with little help from banks or government or the profession of economics.

Small firms, begun by enterprising men, can rise quickly to play important roles in the national economy. Berkshire Paper Company, for example, was started by Whitmore (Nick) Kelley of Glendale, Massachusetts, as a maker of scratch pads in the rural town of Great Barrington. One of the array of paper manufacturers along the Housatonic River, the firm endured repeated setbacks, which turned into benefits, and, by 1980, it was providing important capital and consumer goods to some of the nation's largest and fastest growing corporations, though Kelley himself had no inherited wealth or outside support.

From the onset, the company's capital consisted mostly of refuse. Like the copper and steel companies thriving on the contents of slag heaps, Berkshire Paper Company employed paper, machinery, and factory space rejected as useless by other companies. Berkshire Paper, in fact, was launched and grew with almost no recourse to resources or capital that was accorded by any value at all in any national economic accounts. Yet the company has now entered the semiconductor industry and holds virtual monopolies in three sophisticated products. The story of its rise from scratch pads to semiconductor products shows the irrelevance of nearly all the indices of economic value and national wealth employed by the statisticians of our economy.

As a sophomore in college, Nick Kelley used to visit his stepfather at Clark-Aiken, a manufacturer of papermaking machine tools in Lee, Massachusetts. Within and around the factory, he noticed random piles of paper and asked his stepfather what was done with them. He was told they were leftovers from machinery tests and would be loaded into a truck and taken to the Lee dump. Kelley asked whether he could have them instead.

He took a handful of paper to an office-supply store, Gowdy's in Pittsfield, and asked the proprietor what such paper was good for. Scratch pads, he was told. After long trial and error, and several visits to a scratch pad factory in the guise of a student, he figured out how to make the pads. With the help of his stepfather he purchased and repaired a broken paper-cutting machine, and he even found a new method of applying glue, replacing the usual paintbrush with a paint roller. He then scoured much of the Northeast for markets and created a thriving scratch pad business that, again with his stepfather's help, even survived Kelley's stint in Southeast Asia during the Vietnam War.

In every case, setbacks led to innovation and renewed achievement. Deprived of paper from Clark-Aiken, he learned how to purchase it from jobbers in New York. Discovering that it cost two cents a pound more in sheets than in rolls (nine cents rather than seven cents), he computed that the two pennies represented a nearly 30 percent hike in cost and determined to contrive a sheeter out of old equipment. Finally, his worst setback drove him out of the scratch pad business altogether and allowed him to greatly expand his company.

Attempting to extend his marketing effort to Boston, Kelley approached the buyer for a large office-supply firm. The buyer said he doubted that Kelley could meet the competition. Kelley demanded to know how anyone could sell them for less, when the raw materials alone cost some fourteen cents a pound, and he sold the pads for eighteen cents. He went off to investigate his rival, a family firm run by Italians in Somerville. Kelley found a factory in an old warehouse, also filled with old equipment, but organized even more ingeniously than Kelley's own. He had to acknowledge that the owner was "the best." "He had me beat." Kelley said, "I decided then and there to go out of scratch pad manufacturing." Instead he resolved to buy pads from the Somerville factory and use his

own marketing skills to sell them. He also purchased printing equipment and began adding value to the pads by printing specified lines and emblems on them.

This effort led to a request from Schweitzer, a large paper firm in the Berkshires, that Kelley print up legal pads, and then later, in a major breakthrough, that he cut up some tea bag paper that the Schweitzer machines could not handle. Although Kelley had only the most crude cutting machinery, he said sure, he could process tea bags. He took a pile of thin paper and spent several days and nights at work on it, destroying a fourth of the sheets before his machine completely jammed and pressed several of the layers together so tightly that he found he could easily cut them. This accident gave Kelley a reputation as a worker of small miracles with difficult and specialized papermaking tasks, and the large companies in the area began channeling their most difficult production problems to him.

These new assignments eventually led to three significant monopolies for the small Berkshire firm. One was in making women's fingernail mending tissue (paper with long fibers that adhere to the nail when it is polished) for cosmetic firms from Avon to Revlon. Another was in manufacturing facial blotting tissue (paper that cleans up dirt and makeup without rubbing) for such companies as Mary Kaye and Bonne Belle. His third and perhaps most important project, though—a task that impelled Kelley to pore endlessly through the literature of semiconductor electronics, trafficking in such concepts as microns (one-thousandth of a centimeter) and angstroms (one thousandth of a micron)—was production of papers for use in the manufacture of microprocessors and other semiconductor devices. This required not only the creation of papers sufficiently lint free to wrap a silicon wafer in (without dislodging an electron), but also a research effort to define for the companies precisely what impurities and "glitches" might remain. Kelley now provides this paper, along with the needed information, to all leading semiconductor companies, from National Semiconductor to Intel and Motorola, and he continues research to perfect his product.

Throughout his career, Kelley had demonstrated that faith and imagination are the most important capital goods in the American economy, that wealth is a product less of money than of mind.

The official measures miss all such sources of wealth. When Heilbroner and Thurow claim that 25 percent of American households owned zero net wealth in 1969, they are speaking of families that held above 5 billion dollars' worth of automobiles, 16 billion dollars of other consumer durables, such as washers and television sets, 11 billion dollars' worth of housing (about one-third had cars and 90 percent TVs), as well as rights in Medicaid, social security, housing, education, and other governmental benefits. They commanded many billions of dollars' worth of human capital, some of it rather depreciated by age and some by youthful irresponsibilities (most of these poor households consisted either of single people or abandoned mothers and their offspring). Their net worth was zero, because their debts exceeded their calculable worth. Yet some 80 percent of these people who were poor in 1969 escaped poverty within two years, only to be replaced in the distributions by others too young, too old, too improvident, or too beset with children to manage a positive balance in their asset accounts.

Now it may be appropriate to exclude from the accounting such items as rights in government welfare and transfer programs, which often destroy as much human worth as they create. But the distribution tables also miss the assets of the greatest ultimate value. For example, they treated as an increment of poverty, bereft of net worth, the explosive infusion of human capital that arrived on our shores from Lebanon in the guise of an unlettered family.

Families of zero wealth built America. Many of the unincorporated businesses that have gained some 500 billion dollars in net value since World War II (six times more than all the biggest corporations combined) were started in households of zero assets according to the usual accounts. The conception of a huge and unnegotiable gap between poverty and wealth is a myth. In the Berkshires, Zabian moving up passed many scions of wealth on their way down. . . .

In the second tier of wealth-holders, in which each member would average nearly 2 million dollars net worth in 1970 dollars, 71 percent reported no inherited assets at all, and only 14 percent reported substantial inheritance. Even in the top group of multimillionaires, 31 percent received no inherited assets, and 9 percent only small legacies. Other studies indicate that among the far larger and collectively more important group of wealth-holders of more than $60,000 in 1969, 85 percent of the families had emerged since 1953. With a few notable exceptions, which are always in the news, fast movement up or down in two generations has been the fate of the American rich. . . .

In attacking the rich, tax authorities make great use of the concept of "unearned income," which means the returns from money earned earlier, heavily taxed, then saved or invested. Inheritances receive special attention, since they represent undemocratic transfers and concentrations of power. But they also extend the time horizons of the economy (that is, business), and retard the destruction of capital. That inheritance taxes are too high is obvious from the low level of revenue they collect and the huge industry of tax avoidance they sustain. But politically these levies have long been regarded as too attractive to forgo at a time of hostility toward the rich.

Nonetheless, some of the most catalytic wealth in America is "unearned." A few years before Michael Zabian arrived on our shores, Peter Sprague, now his Berkshire neighbor, inherited 400,000 dollars, largely from the sale of Sprague Electric Company stock. Many heirs of similar legacies have managed to lose most of it in a decade or so. But Sprague set out on a course that could lose it much faster. He decided on a career in venture capital. To raise the odds against him still further, he eventually chose to specialize in companies that faced bankruptcy and lacked other sources of funds.

His first venture was a chicken hatchery in Iran, which taught him the key principles of entrepreneurship—chiefly that nothing happens as one envisions it in theory. The project had been based on the use of advanced Ralston-Purina technology, widely tested in Latin America, to tap the rapidly growing poultry markets of the Middle East. The first unexpected discovery was two or three feet of snow; no one had told him that it *snowed* in Iran. Snow ruined most of the Ralston-Purina equipment. A second surprise was chicanery (and sand) in the chicken feed business. "You end up buying two hundred pounds of stone for every hundred pounds of grain." But after some seven years of similar setbacks, and a growing capital of knowledge, Sprague began to make money in Iran; growing a million trees fertilized with chicken manure, cultivating mushrooms in abandoned ice houses, and winding up with the largest cold storage facilities in the country. The company has made a profit through most of the seventies.

In 1964, three years after starting his Iranian operations, Sprague moved in on a failing electronics company called National Semiconductor. Sprague considered the situation for a week, bought a substantial stake, and became its chairman. The firm is now in the vanguard of the world-wide revolution in semiconductor technology and has been one of America's fastest growing firms, rising from 300 employees when Sprague joined it to 34,000 in 1980.

Also in the mid-sixties Sprague bought several other companies, including the now fashionable Energy Resources, and rescued Design Research from near bankruptcy (the firm finally folded in 1976). In 1969, he helped found Auton Computing Company, a firm still thriving in the business of detecting and analyzing stress in piping systems in nuclear and other power plants, and in 1970 he conducted a memorably resourceful and inventive but finally unsuccessful Republican campaign for the New York City congressional seat then held by Edward Koch. . . .

He then entered the latest phase of his career rescuing collapsing companies. A sports car buff, he indicated to some friends an interest in reviving Aston-Martin, which had gone out of business six months earlier, in mid-1974. Arriving in England early in 1975 with a tentative plan to investigate the possibilities, he was besieged by reporters and TV cameras. Headlines blared: MYSTERY YANK FINANCIER TO SAVE ASTON MARTIN. Eventually he did, and the company is now securely profitable. . . .

A government counterpart of Sprague's investment activity was Wedgewood Benn's National Enterprise Board in England, which spent some 8 billion dollars attempting to save various British companies by drowning them in money. Before Sprague arrived in England Benn had adamantly refused to invest in Aston-Martin—dismissing the venerable firm as a hopeless case—and instead subsidized a large number of other companies, most of which, unlike Aston, still lose money, and some of which ended up bankrupt. The British, however, did find 104 million dollars—fifty times more than Sprague had to invest in Aston-Martin—to use in luring John DeLorean's American luxury car project to Northern Ireland and poured 47.8 million dollars into the effort to create Ininos, a British nationalized semiconductor firm that has yet to earn any money and technologically remains well in the wake of Sprague's concern. With 400,000 dollars inheritance and his charismatic skills, Sprague has revived many times more companies than Wedgewood Benn with the British Treasury. One entrepreneur with energy, resolution, and charisma could turn 400,000 dollars into a small fortune for himself and a bonanza for the economy, accomplishing more than any number of committee-bound foundations, while a government agency usually requires at least 400,000 dollars to so much as open an office.

Nonetheless, considering the sometimes unedifying spectacle of the humpty-dumpty heirs of wealth—and often focusing on the most flamboyant and newsworthy consumers of cocaine and spouses—it is all too easy to forget that the crucial role of the rich in a capitalist economy is not to entertain and titillate the classes below, but to invest: to provide unencumbered and unbureaucratized cash. The broad class of rich does, in fact, perform this role. Only a small portion of their money is consumed. Most of it goes to productive facilities that employ labor and supply goods to consumers. The rich remain the chief source of discretionary capital in the economy.

These are the funds available for investment outside the largely sterile channels of institutional spending. This is the money that escapes the Keynesian trap of compounded risk, created by the fact that a bank, like an entrepreneur, may lose most of its investment if an enterprise fails, but only the entrepreneur can win the large possible payoff that renders the risk worthwhile. Individuals with cash comprise the wild card—the mutagenic germ—in capitalism, and it is relatively risky investments that ultimately both reseed the economy and unseat the rich. . . .

The risk-bearing role of the rich cannot be performed so well by anyone else. The benefits of capitalism still depend on capitalists. The other groups on the pyramid of wealth should occasionally turn from the spectacles of consumption long enough to see the adventure on the frontiers of the economy above them—an adventure not without its note of nobility, since its protagonist families will almost all eventually fail and fall in the redeeming struggle of the free economy.

In America the rich should not be compared to the Saudi Arabians or be seen in the image of Midas in his barred cage of gold. . . . Under capitalism, when it is working, the rich have the anti-Midas touch, transforming timorous liquidity and unused savings into factories and office towers, farms and laboratories, orchestras and museums—turning gold into goods and jobs and art. That is the function of the rich: fostering opportunities for the classes below them in the continuing drama of the creation of wealth and progress. . . .

THE NATURE OF POVERTY

To get a grip in the problems of poverty, one should also forget the idea of overcoming inequality by redistribution. Inequality may even grow at first as poverty declines. To lift the incomes of the poor, it will be necessary to increase the rates of investment, which in turn will tend to enlarge the wealth, if not the consumption, of the rich. The poor, as they move into the work force and acquire promotions, will raise their incomes by a greater percentage than the rich; but the upper classes will gain by greater absolute amounts, and the gap between the rich and the poor may grow. All such analyses are deceptive in the long run, however, because they imply a static economy in which the *numbers* of the rich and the middle class are not growing.

In addition, inequality may be favored by the structure of a modern economy as it interacts with demographic changes. When the division of labor becomes more complex and refined, jobs grow more specialized; and the increasingly specialized workers may win greater rents for their rare expertise, causing their incomes to rise relative to common labor. This tendency could be heightened by a decline in new educated entrants to the work force, predictable through the 1990s, and by an enlarged flow of immigration, legal and illegal. Whatever the outcome of these developments, an effort to take

income from the rich, thus diminishing their investment, and to give it to the poor, thus reducing their work incentives, is sure to cut American productivity, limit job opportunities, and perpetuate poverty.

Among the beneficiaries of inequality will be the formerly poor. Most students of the problems of poverty consider the statistics of success of previous immigrant groups and see a steady incremental rise over the years, accompanied by the progressive acquisition of educational credentials and skills. Therefore, programs are proposed that foster a similar slow and incremental ascent by the currently poor. But the incremental vision of the escape from poverty is mostly false, based on a simple illusion of statistical aggregates that conceals everything important about upward mobility. Previous immigrants earned money first by working hard; their children got the education.

The rising average incomes of previous groups signify not the smooth progress of hundreds of thousands of civil-service or bureaucratic careers, but the rapid business and professional successes of a relative few, who brought their families along and inspired others to follow. Poor people tend to rise up rapidly and will be damaged by a policy of redistribution that will always hit new and unsheltered income and wealth much harder than the elaborately concealed and fortified winnings of the established rich. The poor benefit from a dynamic economy full of unpredictable capital gains (they have few capital losses!) more than from a stratified system governed by educational and other credentials that the rich can buy.

The only dependable route from poverty is always work, family, and faith. The first principle is that in order to move up, the poor must not only work, they must work harder than the classes above them. Every previous generation of the lower class has made such efforts. But the current poor, white even more than black, are refusing to work hard. Irwin Garfinkel and Robert Haveman, authors of an ingenious and sophisticated study of what they call *Earning Capacity Utilization Rates*, have calculated the degree to which various income groups use their opportunities—how hard they work outside the home. This study shows that, for several understandable reasons, the current poor work substantially less, for fewer hours and weeks a year, and earn less in proportion to their age, education, and other credentials (even *after* correcting the figures for unemployment, disability, and presumed discrimination) than either their predecessors in American cities or those now above them on the income scale (the study was made at the federally funded Institute for Research on Poverty at the University of Wisconsin and used data from the census and the Michigan longitudinal survey). The findings lend important confirmation to the growing body of evidence that work effort is the crucial unmeasured variable in American productivity and income distribution, and that current welfare and other subsidy programs substantially reduce work. The poor choose leisure not because of moral weakness, but because they are paid to do so.

A program to lift by transfers and preferences the incomes of less diligent groups is politically divisive—and very unlikely—because it incurs the bitter resistance of the real working class. In addition, such an effort breaks the psychological link between effort and reward, which is crucial to long-run upward mo-

bility. Because effective work consists not in merely fulfilling the requirements of labor contracts but "in putting out" with alertness and emotional commitment, workers have to understand and feel deeply that what they are given depends on what they give—that they must supply work in order to demand goods. Parents and schools must inculcate this idea in their children both by instruction and example. Nothing is more deadly to achievement than the belief that effort will not be rewarded, that the world is a bleak and discriminatory place in which only the predatory and the specially preferred can get ahead. Such a view in the home discourages the work effort in school that shapes earnings capacity afterward. As with so many aspects of human performance, work effort begins in family experiences, and its sources can be best explored through an examination of family structure.

Indeed, after work the second principle of upward mobility is the maintenance of monogamous marriage and family. Adjusting for discrimination against women and for child-care responsibilities, the Wisconsin study indicates that married men work between two and one-third and four times harder than married women, and more than twice as hard as female family heads. The work effort of married men increases with their age, credentials, education, job experience, and birth of children, while the work effort of married women steadily declines. Most important in judging the impact of marriage, husbands work 50 percent harder than bachelors of comparable age, education, and skills.

The effect of marriage, thus, is to increase the work effort of men by about half. Since men have higher earnings capacity to begin with, and since the female capacity-utilization figures would be even lower without an adjustment for discrimination, it is manifest that the maintenance of families is the key factor in reducing poverty.

Once a family is headed by a woman, it is almost impossible for it to greatly raise its income even if the woman is highly educated and trained and she hires day-care or domestic help. Her family responsibilities and distractions tend to prevent her from the kind of all-out commitment that is necessary for the full use of earning power. Fewer women with children make earning money the top priority in their lives.

A married man, on the other hand, is spurred by the claims of family to channel his otherwise disruptive male aggressions into his performance as a provider for a wife and children. These sexual differences alone, which manifest themselves in all societies known to anthropology, dictate that the first priority of any serious program against poverty is to strengthen the male role in poor families.

These narrow measures of work effort touch on just part of the manifold interplay between family and poverty. Edward Banfield's *The Unheavenly City* defines the lower class largely by its lack of an orientation to the future. Living from day to day and from hand to mouth, lower class individuals are unable to plan or save or keep a job. Banfield gives the impression that short-time horizons are a deep-seated psychological defect afflicting hundreds of thousands of the poor.

There is no question that Banfield puts his finger on a crucial problem of the poor and that he develops and documents his theme in an unrivaled classic of disciplined social science. But he fails to show how millions of men, equally present oriented, equally buffeted by impulse and blind to

the future, have managed to become far-seeing members of the middle classes. He also fails to explain how millions of apparently future-oriented men can become dissolute followers of the sensuous moment, neglecting their jobs, dissipating their income and wealth, pursuing a horizon no longer than the most time-bound of the poor.

What Banfield is in fact describing in his lower-class category is largely the temperament of single, divorced, and separated men. The key to lower-class life in contemporary America is that unrelated individuals, as the census calls them, are so numerous and conspicuous that they set the tone for the entire community. Their congregation in ghettos, moreover, magnifies greatly their impact on the black poor, male and female (though, as Banfield rightly observes, this style of instant gratification is chiefly a male trait).

The short-sighted outlook of poverty stems largely from the breakdown of family responsibilities among fathers. The lives of the poor, all too often, are governed by the rhythms of tension and release that characterize the sexual experience of young single men. Because female sexuality, as it evolved over the millennia, is psychologically rooted in the bearing and nurturing of children, women have long horizons within their very bodies, glimpses of eternity within their wombs. Civilized society is dependent upon the submission of the short-term sexuality of young men to the extended maternal horizons of women. This is what happens in monogamous marriage; the man disciplines his sexuality and extends it into the future through the womb of a woman. The woman gives him access to his children, otherwise forever denied him; and he gives her the product of his labor, otherwise dissipated on temporary pleasures. The woman gives him a unique link to the future and a vision of it; he gives her faithfulness and a commitment to a lifetime of hard work. If work effort is the first principle of overcoming poverty, marriage is the prime source of upwardly mobile work.

It is love that changes the short horizons of youth and poverty into the long horizons of marriage and career. When marriages fail, the man often returns to the more primitive rhythms of singleness. On the average, his income drops by one-third and he shows a far higher propensity for drink, drugs, and crime. But when marriages in general hold firm and men in general love and support their children, Banfield's lower-class style changes into middle-class futurity. . . .

Adolph A. Berle, contemplating the contrast between prosperous and dominantly Mormon Utah and indigent, chiefly secular Nevada next door, concluded his study of the American economy with the rather uneconomic notion of a "transcendental margin," possibly kin to Leibenstein's less glamorous X-efficiency and Christopher Jencks's timid "luck." Lionel Tiger identifies this source of unexplained motion as "evolutionary optimism—the biology of hope," and finds it in the human genes. Ivan Light, in his fascinating exploration of the sources of difference between entrepreneurial Orientals and less venturesome blacks, resolved on "the spirit of moral community." Irving Kristol, ruminating on the problems of capitalism, sees the need for a "transcendental justification." They are all addressing, in one way or another, the third principle of upward mobility, and that is faith.

Faith in man, faith in the future, faith in the rising returns of giving, faith in the mutual benefits of trade, faith in the providence of God are all essential to successful capitalism. All are necessary to sustain the spirit of work and enterprise against the setbacks and frustrations it inevitably meets in a fallen world; to inspire trust and cooperation in an economy where they will often be betrayed; to encourage the forgoing of present pleasures in the name of a future that may well go up in smoke; to promote risk and initiative in a world where the rewards all vanish unless others join the game. In order to give without the assurance of return, in order to save without the certainty of future value, in order to work beyond the requirements of the job, one has to have confidence in a higher morality: a law of compensations beyond the immediate and distracting struggles of existence.

NO   William Ryan

EQUALITY

It should not surprise us . . . that the clause "all men are created equal" can be interpreted in quite different ways. Today, I would like to suggest, there are two major lines of interpretation: one, which I will call the "Fair Play" perspective, stresses the individual's right to pursue happiness and obtain resources; the other, which I will call the "Fair Shares" viewpoint, emphasizes the right of access to resources as a necessary condition for equal rights to life, liberty and happiness.

Almost from the beginning, and most apparently during the past century or so, the Fair Play viewpoint has been dominant in America. This way of looking at the problem of equality stresses that each person should be equally free from all but the most minimal necessary interferences with his right to "pursue happiness." . . . Given significant differences of interest, of talents, and of personalities, it is assumed that individuals will be variably successful in their pursuits and that society will consequently propel to its surface what Jefferson called a "natural aristocracy of talent," men who because of their skills, intellect, judgment, character, will assume the leading positions in society that had formerly been occupied by the hereditary aristocracy—that is, by men who had simply been born into positions of wealth and power. In contemporary discussions, the emphasis on the individual's unencumbered pursuit of his own goals is summed up in the phrase "equality of opportunity." Given at least an approximation of this particular version of equality, Jefferson's principle of a natural aristocracy—spoken of most commonly today as the idea of "meritocracy"—will insure that the ablest, most meritorious, ambitious, hardworking, and talented individuals will acquire the most, achieve the most, and become the leaders of society. The relative inequality that this implies is seen not only as tolerable, but as fair and just. Any effort to achieve what proponents of Fair Play refer to as "equality of results" is seen as unjust, artificial, and incompatible with the more basic principle of equal opportunity.

The Fair Shares perspective, as compared with the Fair Play idea, concerns itself much more with equality of rights and of access, particularly the

From William Ryan, *Equality* (Pantheon Books, 1981), pp. 8-20, 26-32. Copyright © 1981 by William Ryan. Reprinted by permission of Pantheon Books, a division of Random House, Inc.

implicit rights to a reasonable share of society's resources, sufficient to sustain life at a decent standard of humanity and to preserve liberty and freedom from compulsion. Rather than focusing on the individual's pursuit of his own happiness, the advocate of Fair Shares is more committed to the principle that all members of the society obtain a reasonable portion of the goods that society produces. From his vantage point, the over-zealous pursuits of private goals on the part of some individuals might even have to be bridled. From this it follows, too, that the proponent of Fair Shares has a different view of what constitutes fairness and justice, namely, an appropriate distribution throughout society of sufficient means for sustaining life and preserving liberty.

So the equality dilemma is built into everyday life and thought in America; it comes with the territory. Rights, equality of rights—or at least interpretations of them—clash. The conflict between Fair Play and Fair Shares is real, deep, and serious, and it cannot be easily resolved. Some calculus of priorities must be established. Rules must be agreed upon. It is possible to imagine an almost endless number of such rules:

• Fair Shares until everyone has enough; Fair Play for the surplus

• Fair Play until the end of a specified "round," then "divvy up" Fair Shares, and start Fair Play all over again (like a series of Monopoly games)

• Fair Play all the way, except that no one may actually be allowed to starve to death.

The last rule is, I would argue, a perhaps bitter parody of the prevailing one in the United States. Equality of opportunity and the principle of meritocracy are the clearly dominant interpretation of

"all men are created equal," mitigated by the principle (usually defined as charity rather than equality) that the weak, the helpless, the deficient will be more or less guaranteed a sufficient share to meet their minimal requirements for sustaining life.

FAIR PLAY AND UNEQUAL SHARES

The Fair Play concept is dominant in America partly because it puts forth two most compelling ideas: the time-honored principle of distributive justice and the cherished image of America as the land of opportunity. At least since Aristotle, the principle that rewards should accrue to each person in proportion of his worth or merit has seemed to many persons one that warrants intuitive acceptance. The more meritorious person—merit being some combination of ability and constructive effort—*deserves* a greater reward. From this perspective it is perfectly consistent to suppose that *unequal* shares could well be *fair* shares; moreover, within such a framework, it is very unlikely indeed that equal shares could be fair shares, since individuals are not equally meritorious.

The picture of America as the land of opportunity is also very appealing. The idea of a completely open society, where each person is entirely free to advance in his or her particular fashion, to become whatever he or she is inherently capable of becoming, with the sky the limit, is a universally inspiring one. This is a picture that makes most Americans proud.

But is it an accurate picture? Are these two connected ideas—unlimited opportunity and differential rewards fairly distributed according to differences in individual merit—congruent with the facts of life? The answer, of course, is yes and no. Yes, we see some vague congruence here and there—some evidence of upward mobility, some kinds of inequalities that can appear to be justifiable. But looking at the larger picture, we must answer with an unequivocal "No!" The fairness of unequal shares and the reality of equal opportunity are wishes and dreams, resting on a mushy, floating, purely imaginary foundation. Let us look first at the question of unequal shares.

Fair Players and Fair Sharers disagree about the meaning, but not about the fact, of unequal shares and of the significant degree of inequality of wealth and income and of everything that goes along with wealth and income—general life conditions, health, education, power, access to services and to cultural and recreational amenities, and so forth. Fair Sharers say that this fact is the very *essence* of inequality, while Fair Players define the inequalities of condition that Fair Sharers decry as obvious and necessary *consequences* of equality of opportunity. Fair Players argue, furthermore, that such inequalities are for the most part roughly proportional to inequalities of merit. . . .

There [are] some patterns of ownership that are reasonably consistent with the Fair Play paradigm. In the distribution of such items as automobiles, televisions, appliances, even homes, there are significant inequalities, but they are not extreme. And if the Fair Player is willing to concede that many inequities remain to be rectified—and most Fair Players are quite willing, even eager, to do so—these inequalities can, perhaps, be swallowed.

It is only when we begin to look at larger aspects of wealth and income—aspects that lie beyond our personal vision—that the extreme and, I believe, gross inequalities of condition that pre-vail in America become evident. Let us begin with income. How do we divide up the shares of what we produce annually? In 1977 about one American family in ten had an income of less than $5,000 and about one in ten had an income of $35,000 a year and up ("up" going all the way to some unknown number of millions). It is difficult to see how anyone could view such a dramatic disparity as fair and justified. One struggles to imagine any measure of merit, any sign of membership in a "natural aristocracy," that would manifest itself in nature in such a way that one sizable group of persons would "have" eight or ten or twenty times more of it—whatever "it" might be—than another sizeable group has.

Income in the United States is concentrated in the hands of a few: one-fifth of the population gets close to half of all the income, and the top 5 percent of this segment get almost one-fifth of it. The bottom three-fifths of the population—that is, the majority of us—receive not much more than one-third of all income. . . .

As we move [to] the reality of living standards, the pertinent questions are: How much do people spend and on what? How do the groups at the different tables, that is, different income groups in America, live? Each year the Bureau of Labor Statistics [BLS] publishes detailed information on the costs of maintaining three different living standards, which it labels "lower," "intermediate," and "higher"; in less discreet days it used to call the budgets "minimum," "adequate," and "comfortable." The adequate, intermediate budget is generally considered to be an index of a reasonably decent standard of living. It is on this budget, for example, that newspapers focus when they write their annual stories on the BLS budgets.

To give some sense of what is considered an "intermediate" standard of living, let me provide some details about this budget as it is calculated for a family of four—mother, father, eight-year-old boy, and thirteen-year-old girl. As of the autumn of 1978, for such a family the budget allows $335 a month for housing, which includes rent or mortgage, heat and utilities, household furnishings, and all household operations. It allows $79 a week for groceries, which extends to cleaning supplies, toothpaste, and the like. It allows $123 a month for transportation, including car payments. It allows $130 a month for clothing, clothing care or cleaning, and all personal-care items.

In his book *The Working Class Majority*, Andrew Levinson cites further details about this budget from a study made by the UAW:

A United Auto Workers study shows just how "modest" that budget is: The budget assumes, for example, that a family will own a toaster that will last for thirty-three years, a refrigerator and a range that will each last for seventeen years, a vacuum cleaner that will last for fourteen years, and a television set that will last for ten years. The budget assumes that a family will buy a two-year-old car and keep it for four years, and will pay for a tune-up once a year, a brake realignment every three years, and front-end alignment every four years. . . . The budget assumes that the husband will buy one year-round suit every four years . . . and one topcoat every eight and a half years. . . . It assumes that the husband will take his wife to the movies once every three months and that one of them will go to the movies alone once a year. The average family's two children are each al-lowed one movie every four weeks. A total of two dollars and fifty-four cents per person per year is allowed for admission to all other events, from football and baseball games to plays or concerts. . . . The budget allows nothing whatever for savings.

This budget, whether labeled intermediate, modest, or adequate, is perhaps more accurately described by those who call it "shabby but respectable." . . .

In 1978 the income needs by an urban family of four in order to meet even this modest standard of living was $18,622. This is a national average; for some cities the figure was much higher: in Boston, it was $22,117, in metropolitan New York, $21,587, in San Francisco, $19,427. More than *half* of all Americans lived *below* this standard. As for the "minimum" budget (which, by contrast with the "intermediate" budget, allows only $62 rather than $79 for groceries, $174 rather than $335 for housing, $67 rather than $123 for transportation, and $93 rather than $130 for clothing and personal care), the national average cost for an urban family in 1978 was $11,546. Three families out of ten could not afford even *that* standard, and one family in ten had an income below $5,000 which is *less than half enough* to meet minimum standards.

These dramatically *unequal* shares are —it seems to me—clearly *unfair* shares. Twenty million people are desperately poor, an additional forty million don't get enough income to meet the minimal requirements for a decent life, the great majority are just scraping by, a small minority are at least temporarily comfortable, and a tiny handful of persons live at levels of affluence and luxury that most persons cannot even imagine.

The myth that America's income is symmetrically distributed—an outstanding few at the top getting a lot, an inadequate few at the bottom living in poverty, and the rest clustered around the middle—could hardly be more false. The grotesquely lopsided distribution of our yearly production of goods and services is well illustrated by Paul Samuelson's famous image:

> A glance at the income distribution in the United States shows how pointed is the income pyramid and how broad its base. "There's always room at the top" is certainly true; this is so because it is hard to get there, not easy. If we make an income pyramid out of a child's blocks, with each layer portraying $1000 of income, the peak would be far higher than the Eiffel Tower, but almost all of us would be within a yard of the ground.

When we move from income to wealth—from what you *get* to what you *own*—the *degree* of concentration makes the income distribution look almost fair by comparison. About one out of every four Americans owns *nothing*. Nothing! In fact, many of them *owe* more than they have. Their "wealth" is actually negative. The persons in the next quarter own about 5 percent of all personal assets. In other words, half of us own 5 percent, the other half own 95 percent. But it gets worse as you go up the scale. Those in the top 6 percent own half of all the wealth. Those in the top 1 percent own one-fourth of all the wealth. Those in the top 1/2 percent own one-fifth of all the wealth. That's one-half of 1 percent—about one million persons, or roughly 300,000 families.

And even this fantastic picture doesn't tell the whole story, because "assets" include homes, cars, savings accounts, cash value of life insurance policies—the kinds of assets that the very rich don't bother with very much. The very rich put their wealth into the ownership of things that produce more wealth—corporate stocks and bonds, mortgages, notes, and the like. Two-thirds of their wealth is in this form and the top 1 percent owns 60 percent of all that valuable paper. The rest of it is owned by only an additional 10 percent, which means that nine people out of ten own none of it—and, if they're like me, they probably have never seen a real stock certificate in their lives.

America, we are sometimes told, is a nation of capitalists, and it is true that an appreciable minority of its citizens have a bank account here, a piece of land there, along with a few shares of stock. But quantitative differences become indisputably qualitative as one moves from the ownership of ten shares of General Motors to the ownership of ten thousand. There are capitalists, and then there are capitalists. . . .

Another way of grasping the extreme concentration of wealth in our society is to try to imagine what the ordinary person would have if that wealth were evenly distributed rather than clumped and clotted together in huge piles. Assuming that all the personal wealth was divided equally among all the people in the nation, we would find that every one of us, man, woman, and child, would *own* free and clear almost $22,000 worth of goods: $7,500 worth of real estate, $3,500 in cash, and about $5,000 worth of stocks and bonds. For a family of four that would add up to almost $90,000 in assets, including $30,000 equity in a house, about $14,000 in the bank, and about $20,000 worth of stocks and bonds. That much wealth would also bring in an extra $3,000 or $4,000 a year in income.

If you have any doubts about the reality of grossly unequal shares, compare the utopian situation of that imaginary "average" family with your own actual situation. For most of us, the former goes beyond our most optimistic fantasies of competing and achieving and getting ahead. Actually only about ten million persons in the country own as much as that, and, as I suggested before, the majority of us have an *average* of less than $5,000 per family including whatever equity we have in a home, our car and other tangible assets, and perhaps $500 in the bank.

Still another way of thinking about this is to remark that the fortunate few at the top, and their children, are more or less guaranteed an opulent standard of living because of what they own, while the majority of American families are no more than four months' pay away from complete destitution.

All of this, of course, takes place in the wealthiest society the world has ever known. If we extended our horizons further and began to compare the handful of developed, industrial nations with the scores of underdeveloped, not to say "over-exploited," nations, we would find inequalities that are even more glaring and appalling. . . .

THE VULNERABLE MAJORITY

Stripped down to its essentials, the rule of equal opportunity and Fair Play requires only that the best man win. It doesn't necessarily specify the margin of victory, merely the absence of unfair barriers. The practical test of equal opportunity is *social mobility*—do talented and hardworking persons, whatever their backgrounds, actually succeed in rising to higher social and economic positions?

The answer to that of course, is that they do. Remaining barriers of discrimination notwithstanding, it is plain that many persons climb up the social and economic ladder and reach much higher rungs than those their parents attained and than those from which they started. Fair Players prize these fortunate levitations as the ultimate justification of their own perspective and as phenomena that must be protected against any erosion caused by excessive emphasis upon Fair Shares.

It is necessary, then, to look seriously at the question of mobility. Among the questions to be asked are the following:

• How much mobility can we observe? No matter how rigidly hierarchical it might be, every society permits some mobility. How much movement up and down the scale is there in ours?

• How far do the mobile persons move?

• Is mobility evident across the whole social and economic range? Do the very poor stay poor, or do they, too, have an equal chance to rise? Are the very rich likely to slide *down* the ladder very often?

Given our great trove of rags-to-riches mythology, our creed that any child (well, any man-child) can grow up to be president—if not of General Motors, at least of the United States—we clearly assume that our society is an extraordinarily open one. And everyone knows, or has a friend who knows, a millionaire or someone on the way to that envied position: the patient, plodding peddler who transformed his enterprise into a great department store; the eccentric tinkerer in his garage whose sudden insight produced the great invention that everyone had been saving his pennies to buy.

At lesser levels of grandeur, we all know about the son of the illiterate cobbler who is now a wealthy neurosurgeon, the daughter of impoverished immigrants who sits in a professional chair at Vassar or Smith—or even Princeton. In America social mobility is an unquestioned fact.

But how many sons of illiterate cobblers become physicians, on the other hand, and how many become, at best, literate cobblers? And how many settle for a job on the assembly line or in the sanitation department? And all of those daughters of impoverished immigrants—how many went on to get Ph.D.'s and become professors? Very few. A somewhat larger number may have gone to college and gotten a job teaching sixth grade. But many just finished high school and went to work for an insurance company for a while, until they married the sons of other impoverished immigrants, most of them also tugging at their bootstraps without much result.

About all of these facts there can be little dispute. For most people, there is essentially no social mobility—for them, life consists of rags to rags and riches to riches. Moreover, for the relatively small minority who do rise significantly in the social hierarchy, the *distance* of ascent is relatively short. Such a person may start life operating a drill press and eventually become a foreman or even move into the white-collar world by becoming a payroll clerk or perhaps an accountant. Or he may learn from his father to be a cobbler, save his money, and open a little cobbler shop of his own. He hardly ever starts up a shoe factory. It is the son of the owner of the shoe factory who gets to do that. So there is mobility—it is rather common, but also rather modest, with only an occasional dramatic rise from rags to riches.

To provide some specific numbers, it has been calculated that for a young man

born into a family in which the father does unskilled, low-wage manual work, the odds against his rising merely to the point of his becoming a nonmanual white-collar worker are at least three or four to one; the odds against his rising to the highest level and joining the wealthy upper class are almost incalculable. For the son of a middle-level white-collar worker, the odds against his rising to a higher-level professional or managerial occupation are two or three to one. On the other hand, the odds are better than fifty to one that the son of a father with such a high-level occupation will not descend the ladder to a position as an unskilled or semiskilled manual worker. Upward mobility is very limited and usually involves moving only one or two levels up the hierachy. . . .

Finally, we have to look carefully to see that, for all our social mobility, the very rich almost all stay at the top and welcome only a select handful to their ranks. The rich of one generation are almost all children of the rich of the previous generation, partly because more than half of significant wealth is inherited, partly because all the other prerogatives of the wealthy are sufficient to assure a comfortable future for Rockefeller and Du Pont toddlers. It may well take more energy, ingenuity, persistence, and single-mindedness for a rich youngster to achieve poverty than for a poor one to gain wealth.

The dark side of the social-mobility machine is that it is, so to speak, a reciprocating engine—when some parts go up, others must come *down*. Downward mobility is an experience set aside almost exclusively for the nonrich, and it is grossly destructive of the quality of life. The majority of American families are constantly vulnerable to economic disaster—to downward mobility to the point where they lack sufficient income to meet their most basic needs—food, shelter, clothing, heat, and medical care. Included in this vulnerable majority, who have at least an even chance of spending some portion of their lives in economic distress, are perhaps three out of four Americans.

This does not accord with the common view of poverty. We have been given to understand that "the poor" form a fairly permanent group in our society and that those who are above the poverty line are safe and perhaps even on their way up. This thought is comforting but false. A number of small studies have raised serious questions about this static picture; recently we have received massive evidence from one of the most comprehensive social and economic investigations ever mounted. This study, under the direction of James Morgan, has traced the life trajectories of five thousand American families over a period, to date, of eight years, concentrating on the nature of and possible explanations for economic progress or the lack of it.

Five Thousand American Families indicates that over a period of eight years, although only one in ten families is poor during *every one* of the eight years, over one-third of American families are poor for *at least one* of those eight years.

From the Michigan study, the census data, and other sources, we can readily estimate that a few are permanently protected against poverty because they *own things*—property, stocks, bonds—that provide them with income sufficient to meet their needs whether or not they work or have any other source of income. Another small minority of Americans own only *rights*—virtual job tenure, a guaranteed pension—but these rights also give

effective protection against poverty. At the bottom of the pyramid, there are a few who might be called permanently poor. Between these extremes come persons whose income is primarily or wholly dependent on salaries or wages. This is the core of the vulnerable majority—not poor now, but in jeopardy. In any given year one family out of six in that vulnerable majority will suffer income deficit, will go through a year of poverty. Over a five-year period nearly half of them will be poor for at least one year. If we project this over ten or fifteen years, we find that well over half will be poor for at least one year. On adding this group to the permanently poor, we arrive at the startling fact that a *substantial majority* of American families will experience poverty at some point during a relatively short span of time.

Several elements in our socioeconomic structure help account for income deficiency. Let us consider, for example, those who are more or less permanently poor. Why do they stay mired in poverty? The answer in most cases is simple: they remain poor because it has been deliberately *decided* that they should remain poor. They are, for the most part, dependent on what we impersonally call transfer payments—mostly Social Security, some private pensions, some welfare. To put it as simply as possible, these transfer payments are not enough to live on, not enough to meet basic needs. Countrywide, public assistance payments provide income that is only 75 percent of what is required to pay for sufficient food, adequate shelter, clothing, and fuel; the percentage decreases as the size of the family increases. For very large families, welfare provides only half of what is needed to live on. The poverty of the permanently poor is thus easily explained by the fact that the income assistance that we provide them is simply too small.

For the vulnerables, however, economic hills and valleys are created by the job situation. Economic status, progress, and deficit are determined by what social scientists call "family composition and participation in the labor force." In plain English that means they depend on the number of mouths to be fed and on the number of people working—that is, on how many children there are, on whether both wife and husband are working, and so forth. But this, of course, is only synonymous with the natural ebb and flow in the life of almost any family. It should not be an economic catastrophe, after all, when people get married and have children. . . . So, children are born and they grow up, sometimes work awhile, and then leave home. One parent, usually the mother, is tied to the home during some periods, free to work during others. A family member finds a job, loses a job, gets sick or injured, sometimes dies tragically young. All of these events are the landmarks in the life of a family, most of them are common enough, and some are inevitable sources of joy or sorrow. Yet these ordinary occurrences have a drastic impact on families, because they lead to greater changes in one or both sides of the ratio of income and needs. In most cases they are direct causes of most of the economic progress or distress that a family experiences. . . .

WHY NOT FAIR SHARES?

I have been trying to show, in a preliminary way, that the beliefs and assumptions associated with the Fair Play rendering of equality are quite inconsistent with the facts of life as we know them, although its principles are paraded as a version—in fact, the correct version—of equality and are widely accepted as quite plausible, indeed obvious. To the extent that there is any competition between Fair Players and Fair Sharers for the mind of the public, the former usually win hands down. Yet, as we have seen, the Fair Play idea appears to condone and often to endorse conditions of inequality that are blatant and, I would say, quite indefensible. Such equal opportunities for advancing in life as do exist are darkly overshadowed by the many head starts and advantages provided to the families of wealth and privilege. As for the workings out of the solemnly revered principles of meritocracy, they are—like many objects of reverence—invisible to most persons and rarely discernible in the lives of the vulnerable majority of us. Barely two centuries after its most persuasive formulation, the Fair Play concept of equality has shriveled to little more than the assertion that a few thousand individuals are fully licensed to gather and retain wealth at the cost of the wasteful, shameful, and fraudulent impoverishment of many millions. . . .

A Fair Shares egalitarian would hold that all persons have a *right* to a reasonable share of material necessities, a right to do constructive work, and a right of unhindered access to education, to gratifying social memberships, to participation in the life and decisions of the community, and to all the major amenities of society. This principle doesn't lend itself to the calculation of "equal results," and it certainly doesn't imply a demand for uniformity of resources. No one in his right mind would entertain some cockeyed scheme in which everyone went to school for precisely thirteen years; consumed each year 19,800 grams of protein and 820,000 calories; read four works of fiction and six of non-fiction; attended two concerts, one opera, and four basketball games, and voted in 54 percent of the elections. . . . Unfortunately, many persons who are upset about the present state of inequality tend to talk vaguely about the need "to redistribute income" or even "to redistribute wealth." When such ideas are tossed out without consideration of the fact that they will then be discussed within the framework of Fair Play, we have a surefire prescription for disaster. From that viewpoint, which is, after all, the dominant one in America, such ideas appear both extremely inpracticable and not particularly desirable. For example, are we to take redistribution of income to mean that every individual will somehow receive the same compensation, no matter what work he or she does or whether he works at all? And would we try to redistribute wealth by giving every person, say, a share of stock in GM, Exxon, IBM, and the local paperbag factory? Hardly. Fair Players can make mincemeat of such silly ideas, and they love to pretend that that's what Fair Share egalitarians are proposing. I don't think many of us have strong objections to inequality of monetary income as such. A modest range, even as much as three or four to one, could, I suspect, be tolerable to almost everybody. (And one would suppose that, given some time for adjustment and perhaps some counseling and training in homemaking and budgeting skills, those who now get a lot more could learn to scrape by on something like eight or nine hundred dollars a week.) The current range in annual incomes—from perhaps $3,000 to some unknown number of *millions*—is, however, excessive and intolerable, impossible to justify rationally, and plain inhuman.

The problem of wealth is more fundamental. Most of the evils of inequality derive from the reality that a few thousand families control almost all the necessities and amenities of life, indeed the very conditions of life. The rest of us, some 200 million, have to pay tribute to them if we want even a slight illusion of life, liberty, and the pursuit of happiness. But the solution to this problem is certainly not simply the fragmentation of ownership into tiny units of individual property. This naive solution has been well criticized by serious proponents of equality, perhaps most gracefully by R. H. Tawney:

> It is not the division of the nation's income into eleven million fragments, to be distributed, without further ado, like cake as a school treat, among its eleven million families. It is, on the contrary, the pooling of its surplus resources by means of taxation, and use of the funds thus obtained to make accessible to all, irrespective of their income, occupation, or social position, the conditions of civilization which, in the absence of such measures, can only be enjoyed by the rich. . . .
>
> It can generalize, by collective action, advantages associated in the past with ownership of property. . . . It can secure that, in addition to the payments made to them for their labour, its citizens enjoy a social income, which is provided from the surplus remaining after the necessary cost of production and expansion have been met, and is available on equal terms for all its members. . . .

The central problem of inequality in America—the concentration of wealth and power in the hands of a tiny minority—cannot, then, be solved, as Tawney makes clear, by any schemes that rest on the process of long division. We need, rather, to accustom ourselves to a different method of holding resources, namely, holding them in common, to be *shared* amongst us all—not divided up and parceled out, but shared. That is the basic principle of Fair Shares, and it is not at all foreign to our daily experience. To cite a banal example, we share the air we breathe, although some breathe in penthouses or sparsely settled suburbs and others in crowded slums. In a similar fashion, we share such resources as public parks and beaches, although, again, we cannot overlook the gross contrast between the size of vast private waterfront holdings and the tiny outlets to the oceans that are available to the public. No one in command of his senses would go to a public beach, count the number of people there, and suggest subdividing the beach into thirty-two-by-twenty-six-foot lots, one for each person. Such division would not only be unnecessary, it would ruin our enjoyment. If I were assigned to Lot No. 123, instead of enjoying the sun and going for a swim, I might sit and watch that sneaky little kid with the tin shovel to make sure he did not extend the sand castle onto my beach. We own it in common; it's *public;* and we just plain *share* it.

We use this mode of owning and sharing all the time and never give it a second thought. We share public schools, streets, libraries, sewers, and other public property and services, and we even think of them as being "free" (many libraries even have the word in their names). Nor do we need the "There's no such thing as a free lunch" folks reminding us that they're not really free; everyone is quite aware that taxes support them. We don't feel any need to divide up all the books in the library among all the citizens. And there's no sensible way of looking at the use of libraries in terms of "equal opportunity" as opposed to "equal results." Looking at the public library as a tiny example of what Fair Shares equality is all about, we note that it satisfies the principle of equal access if no one is *excluded* from the library on the irrelevant grounds of not owning enough or of having spent twelve years in school learning how not to read. And "equal results" is clearly quite meaningless. Some will withdraw many books; some, only a few; some will be so unwise as to never even use the facility.

The *idea* of sharing, then, which is the basic idea of equality, and the *practice* of sharing, which is the basic methodology of Fair Shares equality, are obviously quite familiar and acceptable to the American people in many areas of life. There are many institutions, activities, and services that the great majority believe should be located in the public sector, collectively owned and paid for, and equally accessible to everyone. We run into trouble when we start proposing the same system of ownership for the resources that the wealthy have corralled for themselves. . . .

Most of the good things of life have either been provided free by God (nature, if you prefer) or have been produced by the combined efforts of many persons, sometimes many generations. As all share in the making, so all should share in the use and the enjoyment. This may help convey a bit of what the Fair Shares idea of equality is all about.

POSTSCRIPT

Is Economic Inequality Beneficial to Society?

The spirit of personal initiative seems to be alive in the hearts of Michael Zabian, the vegetable stand owner, Nick Kelley, the scratch paper dealer, and Peter Sprague, the venture capitalist, whose success stories are related by Gilder. But how typical are their experiences? What about the government's bail-outs of Lockheed and Chrysler and the trials of U.S. Steel, General Motors, and many other corporations? What about the limitation of individual initiative in countless corporations guided by decisions made by committees and teams of experts? And what about the issues of fairness raised by Ryan? Perhaps the basic question is: "Can the system be made more just, fair and humane without squelching enterprise and drive?"

Stratification and social mobility are two of the central concerns of sociology, and much literature has been produced discussing these issues. Two major publications of research on census statistics are Peter M. Blau and Otis Dudley Duncan's *The American Occupational Structure* (John Wiley & Sons, 1967) and Robert M. Hauser and David L. Featherman's *The Process of Social Stratification* (Academic Press, 1972). For general works, see Gerhard Lenski's *Power and Privilege* (McGraw-Hill, 1966) and Leonard Beeghley's *Social Stratification in the United States* (Goodyear, 1978). Many have written about the rich and their power, including Ferdinand Lundberg in *The Rich and the Super Rich* (Lyle Stuart, 1968); E. Digby Baltzell, *The Protestant Establishment* (Random House, 1964); G. William Dornhoff in *Who Rules America?* (Prentice Hall, 1967) and *The Higher Circles* (Random House, 1970); and Michael Patrick Allen, *The Founding Fortunes: A New Anatomy of the Super-Rich Families in America* (E. P. Dutton, 1987). A number of important works look at the poor and their disadvantages, including Joe Feagin's *Subordinating the Poor* (Prentice Hall, 1975); Richard Sennett and Jonathan Cobbs, *The Hidden Injuries of Class* (Alfred A. Knopf, 1973); Michael Harrington's *The Other America* (Macmillan, 1962) and *The New American Poverty* (Holt, Rinehart and Winston, 1984); William Wilson's *The Truly Disadvantaged* (University of Chicago Press, 1987); and Elliot Liebow's *Tally's Corner* (Little, Brown, 1967).

Some studies of the social origins of elites include Suzanne Keller's *Beyond the Ruling Class* (Random House, 1963) and Floyd Warner and James Abegglen's *Big Business Leaders in America* (Harper, 1955). An interesting study of how the rich view themselves and the poor and income inequalities is *Equality in America: The View from the Top*, by Sidney Verber and Gary Orren (Harvard University Press, 1985). Two valuable resources on stratification are *Research in Social Stratification and Mobility: A Research Annual* and *Research in Inequality and Social Conflict: A Research Annual*.

ISSUE 9

Does "Lower-Class" Culture Perpetuate Poverty?

YES: Edward Banfield, from *The Unheavenly City* (Little, Brown, 1970)

NO: William Ryan, from *Blaming the Victim* (Pantheon Books, 1971)

ISSUE SUMMARY

YES: Sociologist Edward Banfield suggests that it is the cultural outlook of the poor that tends to keep them in poverty.
NO: Professor of psychology William Ryan responds that attacking the culture of the poor is a form of "blaming the victims" for the conditions that surround them.

The Declaration of Independence proclaims the right of every human being to "life, liberty, and the pursuit of happiness." It never defines happiness, but Americans have put their own gloss on the term. Whatever else happiness means, Americans tend to agree that it includes doing well, getting ahead in life, and maintaining a comfortable standard of living.

The fact, of course, is that millions of Americans do not do well and do not get ahead. They are mired in poverty and seem unable to get out of it. On the face of it, this fact poses no contradiction to America's commitment to the pursuit of happiness. To pursue is not necessarily to catch; it certainly does not mean that everyone should feel entitled to a life of material prosperity. "Equality of opportunity," the prototypical American slogan, is vastly different from the socialist dream of "equality of condition," which perhaps is one reason socialism has so few adherents in America.

The real difficulty in reconciling the American ideal with American reality is not the problem of income differentials but of the *persistence* of poverty from generation to generation. Often, parent, child, and grandchild seem to be locked into a hopeless cycle of destitution and dependence. One explanation is that a large segment of the poor do not really try to get out of poverty. In its more vicious form this view portrays these people as lazy, stupid, or base. Their poverty is not to be blamed on defects of American society but on their own defects. After all, many successful Americans have worked their way up from humble beginnings, and many immigrant groups have made progress in one generation. Therefore, the United States provides opportunities for all who will work hard and make something of themselves. Another explanation, however, could be that the poor have few opportunities and many obstacles to overcome to climb out of poverty. If so, then America is not the land of opportunity for the poor and the American dream is reserved for the more fortunate.

The first explanation for the persistence of poverty holds that among some groups there is a *culture* that breeds poverty because it is antithetical to the self-discipline and hard work that enable others to climb out of their poverty. In other words, the poor have a culture all their own that is at variance with middle-class culture and hinders their success. While it may keep people locked into what seems to be an intolerable life, this culture nevertheless has its own compensations and pleasures: It is full of "action" and it does not demand that people postpone pleasure, save money, or work hard. It is, for the most part, tolerable to those who live in it. Furthermore, according to this argument, not all poor people embrace the culture of poverty, and those who embrace middle-class values should be given every workable form of encouragement—material and spiritual—for escaping poverty. But for those poor who embrace lower-class culture, very little can be done. These poor will always be with us.

According to the second explanation of poverty, most of the poor will become self-supporting if they are given a decent chance. Their most important need is for decent jobs that can go somewhere. But often they cannot find jobs, and when they do, the jobs are dead-end or degrading. Some need job training or counseling to give them more self-confidence before navigating the job market. Others need temporary help through programs such as rent supplements, inexpensive housing, income supplements, protection from crime, medical services, or better education to help them help themselves.

The culture of poverty thesis shields the economic system from blame for poverty and honors Americans who are better off. But most of the poor are as committed to taking care of themselves and their families through hard work as is the middle class, and a sense of dignity is common to all classes. Critics judge the culture of poverty thesis to be a smug, self-righteous justification by spokesmen for the middle and upper classes for the economic system that rewards them so handsomely while subjecting the poor to an intolerable existence. The culture of the poor is similar to the culture of the middle class. Where they do differ, however, the difference is because the culture of the poor is materially different. Change their material conditions and their culture will change rather quickly.

Proponents of the culture of poverty thesis maintain that it is not the material that controls the culture but the other way around; only the abandonment of lower-class culture will get the poor out of poverty. This is Edward Banfield's argument. On the other side is William Ryan, who says that the Banfield approach is a typical case of "blaming the victim."

YES
Edward Banfield

THE FUTURE OF THE LOWER CLASS

So long as the city contains a sizable lower class, nothing basic can be done about its most serious problems. Good jobs may be offered to all, but some will remain chronically unemployed. Slums may be demolished, but if the housing that replaces them is occupied by the lower class it will shortly be turned into new slums. Welfare payments may be doubled or tripled and a negative income tax instituted, but some persons will continue to live in squalor and misery. New schools may be built, new curricula devised, and the teacher-pupil ratio cut in half, but if the children who attend these schools come from lower-class homes, they will be turned into blackboard jungles, and those who graduate or drop out from them will, in most cases, be functionally illiterate. The streets may be filled with armies of policemen, but violent crime and civil disorder will decrease very little. If, however, the lower class were to disappear—if, say, its members were overnight to acquire the attitudes, motivations, and habits of the working class—the most serious and intractable problems of the city would all disappear with it.

[The] serious problems of the city all exist in two forms—a normal-class and a lower-class form—which are fundamentally different from each other. In its normal-class form, the employment problem, for example, consists mainly of young people who are just entering the labor market and who must make a certain number of trials and errors before finding suitable jobs; in its lower-class form, it consists of people who prefer the "action" of the street to any steady job. The poverty problem in its normal-class form consists of people (especially the aged, the physically handicapped, and mothers with dependent children) whose only need in order to live decently is money; in its lower-class form it consists of people who live in squalor and misery even if their incomes were doubled or tripled. The same is true with the other problems—slum housing, schools, crime, rioting; each is really two quite different problems.

The lower-class forms of all problems are at bottom a single problem: the existence of an outlook and style of life which is radically present-oriented and which therefore attaches no value to work, sacrifice, self-improvement, or service to family, friends, or community. Social workers, teachers, and law-

From Edward Banfield, *The Unheavenly City* (Little, Brown, 1970). Copyright © 1968, 1970 by Edward C. Banfield. Reprinted by permission of Waveland Press, Inc.

enforcement officials—all those whom Gans calls "caretakers"—cannot achieve their goals because they can neither change nor circumvent this cultural obstacle. . . .

Robert Hunter described it in 1904:

They lived in God only knows what misery. They ate when there were things to eat; they starved when there was lack of food. But, on the whole, although they swore and beat each other and got drunk, they were more contented than any other class I have happened to know. It took a long time to understand them. Our Committees were busy from morning until night in giving them opportunities to take up the fight again, and to become independent of relief. They always took what we gave them; they always promised to try; but as soon as we expected them to fulfill any promises, they gave up in despair, and either wept or looked ashamed, and took to misery and drink again,—almost, so it seemed to me at times, with a sense of relief.

In Hunter's day these were the "undeserving," "unworthy," "depraved," "debased," or "disreputable" poor; today, they are the "troubled," "culturally deprived," "hard to reach," or "multiproblem." In the opinion of anthropologist Oscar Lewis, their kind of poverty "is a way of life, remarkably stable and persistent, passed down from generation to generation among family lines." This "culture of poverty," as he calls it, exists in city slums in many parts of the world, and is, he says, an adaptation made by the poor in order to defend themselves against the harsh realities of slum life.

The view that is to be taken here [is that] there is indeed such a culture, but that poverty is its effect rather than its cause. (There are societies even poorer than the ones Lewis has described— primitive ones, for example—in which nothing remotely resembling the pattern of behavior here under discussion exists.) Extreme present-orientedness, not lack of income or wealth, is the principal cause of poverty in the sense of "the culture of poverty." Most of those caught up in this culture are unable or unwilling to plan for the future, to sacrifice immediate gratifications in favor of future ones, or to accept the disciplines that are required in order to get and to spend. Their inabilities are probably culturally given in most cases—"multi-problem" families being normal representatives of a class culture that is itself abnormal. No doubt there are also people whose present-orientedness is rationally adaptive rather than cultural, but these probably comprise only a small part of the "hard core" poor.

Outside the lower class, poverty (in the sense of hardship, want, or destitution) is today almost always the result of external circumstances—involuntary unemployment, prolonged illness, the death of a breadwinner, or some other misfortune. Even when severe, such poverty is not squalid or degrading. Moreover, it ends quickly once the (external) cause of it no longer exists. Public or private assistance can sometimes remove or alleviate the cause—for example, by job retraining or remedial surgery. Even when the cause cannot be removed, simply providing the nonlower-class poor with sufficient income is enough to enable them to live "decently."

Lower-class poverty, by contrast, is "inwardly" caused (by psychological inability to provide for the future, and all that this inability implies). Improvements in external circumstances can affect this poverty only superficially: One problem of a "multiproblem" family is no sooner solved than another arises. In principle, it is possible to eliminate the poverty (material lack) of such a family, but only at great expense, since the capacity of the radically improvident to waste money is almost unlimited. Raising such a family's income would not necessarily improve its way of life, moreover, and could conceivably even make things worse. Consider, for example, the H. family:

> Mrs. H. seemed overwhelmed with the simple mechanics of dressing her six children and washing their clothes. The younger ones were running around in their underwear; the older ones were unaccounted for, but presumably were around the neighborhood. Mrs. H. had not been out of the house for several months; evidently her husband did the shopping. The apartment was filthy and it smelled. Mrs. H. was dressed in a bathrobe, although it was mid-afternoon. She seemed to have no plan or expectations with regard to her children; she did not know the names of their teachers and she did not seem to worry about their school work, although one child had been retained one year and another two years. Mrs. H. did seem to be somewhat concerned about her husband's lack of activity over the weekend—his continuous drinking and watching baseball on television. Apparently he and she never went out socially together nor did the family ever go anywhere as a unit.

If this family had a very high income—say, $50,000 a year—it would not be considered a "culture of poverty" case. Mrs. H. would hire maids to look after the small children, send the others to boarding schools, and spend her time at fashion shows while her husband drank and watched TV at his club. But with an income of only moderate size—say 100 percent above the poverty line—they would probably be about as badly off as they are now. They might be even worse off, for Mrs. H. would be able to go to the dog races, leaving the children alone, and Mr. H. could devote more time to his bottle and TV set. . . .

Welfare agencies, recognizing the difference between "internally" and "externally" caused poverty, have long been trying first by one means and then another to improve the characters or, as it is now put, to "bring about personal adjustment" of the poor. In the nineteenth century, the view was widely held that what the lower class individual needed was to be brought into a right relation with God or (the secular version of the same thing) with the respectable (that is, middle- and upper-class) elements of the community. The missionary who distributed tracts door to door in the slums was the first caseworker; his—more often, her—task was to minister to what today would be called "feelings of alienation."

> The stranger, coming on a stranger's errand, becomes a friend, discharging the offices and exerting the influence of a friend. . . .

Secularized, this approach became the "friendly visitor" system under which "certain persons, under the direction of a central board, pledge themselves to take one or more families who need counsel, if not material help, on their visiting list, and maintain personal friendly relations with them." The system did not work; middle- and upper-class people might be "friendly," but they could not sympathize, let alone communicate, with the lower class. By the beginning of the twentieth century the friendly visitor had been replaced by the "expert." The idea now was that the authority of "the facts" would bring about desired changes of attitude, motive, and habit. As it happened, however, the lower class did not recognize the authority of the facts. The expert then became a supervisor, using his (or her) power to confer or withhold material benefits in order to force the poor to do the things that were supposed to lead to "rehabilitation" (that is, to a middle-class style of life). This method did not work either; the lower class could always find ways to defeat and exploit the system. They seldom changed their ways very much and they never changed them for long. Besides, there was really no body of expertise to tell caseworkers how to produce the changes desired. As one caseworker remarked recently in a book addressed to fellow social service professionals:

> Despite years of experience in providing public aid to poor families precious little is yet known about how to help truly inadequate parents make long term improvements in child care, personal maturity, social relations, or work stability.

Some people understood that if the individual's style of life was to be changed at all, it would be necessary to change that of the group that produced, motivated, and constrained him. Thus, the settlement house. As Robert A. Woods explained:

> The settlements are able to take neighborhoods in cities, and by patience bring back to them much of the healthy village life, so that the people shall again know and care for one another. . . .

When it became clear that settlement houses would not change the culture of slum neighborhoods, the group approach was broadened into what is called "community action." In one type of community action ("community development"), a community organizer tries to persuade a neighborhood's informal leaders to support measures (for instance, measures for delinquency control) that he advances. In another form of it ("community organization"), the organizer tries to promote self-confidence, self-respect, and attachment to the group (and, hopefully, to normal society) among lower-class people. He attempts to do this by encouraging them in efforts at joint action, or by showing them how to conduct meetings, carry on discussions, pass resolutions, present requests to politicians, and the like. In still another form ("community mobilization"), the organizer endeavors to arouse the anger of lower-class persons against the local "power structure," to teach them the techniques of mass action—strikes, sit-ins, picketing, and so on—and to show them how they may capture power. The theory of community organization attributes the malaise of the poor to their lack of self-confidence (which is held to derive largely from their "inexperience"); community mobilization theory, by contrast, attributes it to their feelings of "powerlessness." According to this doctrine, the best cure for poverty is to give the poor power. But since power is not "given," it must be seized.

The success of the group approach has been no greater than that of the caseworker approach. Reviewing five years of effort on the part of various community action programs, Marris and Rein conclude:

> . . . the reforms had not evolved any reliable solutions to the intractable problems with which they struggled. They had not discovered how in general to override the intransigent autonomy of public and private agencies, at

any level of government; nor how to use the social sciences practically to formulate and evaluate policy; nor how, under the sponsorship of government, to raise the power of the poor. Given the talent and money they had brought to bear, they had not even reopened very many opportunities.

If the war on poverty is judged by its ability "to generate major, meaningful and lasting social and economic reforms in conformity with the expressed wishes of poor people," writes Thomas Gladwin, " . . . it is extremely difficult to find even scattered evidence of success." . . .

Although city agencies have sent community organizers by the score into slum neighborhoods, the lower-class poor cannot be organized. In East Harlem in 1948, five social workers were assigned to organize a five-block area and to initiate a program of social action based on housing, recreation, and other neighborhood needs. After three years of effort, the organizers had failed to attract a significant number of participants, and those they did attract were upwardly mobile persons who were unrepresentative of the neighborhood. In Boston a "total community" delinquency control project was found to have had "negligible impact," an outcome strikingly like that of the Cambridge-Somerville experiment— a "total caseworker" project—a decade earlier. Even community mobilization, despite the advantages of a rhetoric of hate and an emphasis on "action," failed to involve lower-class persons to a significant extent. Gangsters and leaders of youth gangs were co-opted on occasion, but they did not suffer from feelings of powerlessness and were not representative of the class for which mobilization was to provide therapy. No matter how hard they have tried to appeal to people

at the very bottom of the scale, community organizers have rarely succeeded. Where they have appeared to succeed, as, for example, in the National Welfare Rights Organization, it has been by recruiting people who had some of the *outward* attributes of the lower class— poverty, for example—but whose outlook and values were not lower class; the lower-class person (as defined here) is incapable of being organized. Although it tried strenuously to avoid it, what the Mobilization for Youth described as the general experience proved to be its own experience as well:

> Most efforts to organize lower-class people attract individuals on their way up the social-class ladder. Persons who are relatively responsible about participation, articulate and successful at managing organizational "forms" are identified as lower-class leaders, rather than individuals who actually reflect the values of the lower-class groups. Ordinarily the slum's network of informal group associations is not reached.

NO

William Ryan

BLAMING THE VICTIM

Twenty years ago, Zero Mostel used to do a sketch in which he impersonated a Dixiecrat Senator conducting an investigation of the origins of World War II. At the climax of the sketch, the Senator boomed out, in an excruciating mixture of triumph and suspicion, "What was Pearl Harbor *doing* in the Pacific?" This is an extreme example of Blaming the Victim.

Twenty years ago, we could laugh at Zero Mostel's caricature. In recent years, however, the same process has been going on every day in the arena of social problems, public health, anti-poverty programs, and social welfare. A philosopher might analyze this process and prove that, technically, it is comic. But it is hardly ever funny.

Consider some victims. One is the miseducated child in the slum school. He is blamed for his own miseducation. He is said to contain within himself the causes of his inability to read and write well. The shorthand phrase is "cultural deprivation," which, to those in the know, conveys what they allege to be inside information: that the poor child carries a scanty pack of cultural baggage as he enters school. He doesn't know about books and magazines and newspapers, they say. (No books in the home: the mother fails to subscribe to *Reader's Digest.*) They say that if he talks at all—an unlikely event since slum parents don't talk to their children—he certainly doesn't talk correctly. Lower-class dialect spoken here, or even—God forbid!—Southern Negro. (*Ici on parle nigra.*) If you can manage to get him to sit in a chair, they say, he squirms and looks out the window. (Impulse-ridden, these kids, motoric rather than verbal.) In a word he is "disadvantaged" and "socially deprived," they say, and this, of course, accounts for his failure (*his* failure, they say) to learn much in school.

Note the similarity to the logic of Zero Mostel's Dixiecrat Senator. What is the culturally deprived child *doing* in the school? What is wrong with the victim? In pursuing this logic, no one remembers to ask questions about the collapsing buildings and torn textbooks, the frightened, insensitive teachers, the six additional desks in the room, the blustering, frightened principals, the relentless segregation, the callous administrator, the irrelevant curriculum, the bigoted or cowardly members of the school board, the insulting

From William Ryan, *Blaming the Victim* (Pantheon Books, 1971), pp. 3-9, 121-125, 236-237. Copyright © 1971 by William Ryan. Reprinted by permission of Pantheon Books, a division of Random House, Inc.

history book, the stingy taxpayers, the fairy-tale readers, or the self-serving faculty of the local teachers' college. We are encouraged to confine our attention to the child and to dwell on all his alleged defects. Cultural deprivation becomes an omnibus explanation for the educational disaster area known as the inner-city school. This is Blaming the Victim.

Pointing to the supposedly deviant Negro family as the "fundamental weakness of the Negro community" is another way to blame the victim. Like "cultural deprivation," "Negro family" has become a shorthand phrase with stereotyped connotations of matriarchy, fatherlessness, and pervasive illegitimacy. Growing up in the "crumbling" Negro family is supposed to account for most of the racial evils in America. Insiders have the word, of course, and know that this phrase is supposed to evoke images of growing up with a long-absent or never-present father (replaced from time to time perhaps by a series of transient lovers) and with bossy women ruling the roost, so that the children are irreparably damaged. This refers particularly to the poor, bewildered male children, whose psyches are fatally wounded and who are never, alas, to learn the trick of becoming upright, downright, forthright all-American boys. Is it any wonder the Negroes cannot achieve equality? From such families! And, again, by focusing our attention on the Negro family as the apparent *cause* of racial inequality, our eye is diverted. Racism, discrimination, segregation, and the powerlessness of the ghetto are subtly, but thoroughly, downgraded in importance.

The generic process of Blaming the Victim is applied to almost every American problem. The miserable health care of the poor is explained away on the grounds that the victim has poor motivation and lacks health information. The problems of slum housing are traced to the characteristics of tenants who are labeled as "Southern rural migrants" not yet "acculturated" to life in the big city. The "multiproblem" poor, it is claimed, suffer the psychological effects of impoverishment, the "culture of poverty," and the deviant value system of the lower classes; consequently, though unwittingly, they cause their own troubles. From such a viewpoint, the obvious fact that poverty is primarily an absence of money is easily overlooked or set aside.

The growing number of families receiving welfare are fallaciously linked together with the increased number of illegitimate children as twin results of promiscuity and sexual abandon among members of the lower orders. Every important social problem—crime, mental illness, civil disorder, unemployment—has been analyzed within the framework of the victim-blaming ideology. In the following pages, I shall present in detail nine examples that relate to social problems and human services in urban areas.

It would be possible for me to venture into other areas—one finds a perfect example in literature about the underdeveloped countries of the Third World, in which the lack of prosperity and technological progress is attributed to some aspect of the national character of the people, such as lack of "achievement motivation"—but I plan to stay within the confines of my own personal and professional experience, which is, generally, with racial injustice, social welfare, and human services in the city.

I have been listening to the victim-blamers and pondering their thought processes for a number of years. That process is often very subtle. Victim-blaming is cloaked in kindness and concern, and bears all the trappings and statistical furbelows of scientism; it is obscured by a perfumed haze of humanitarianism. In observing the process of Blaming the Victim, one tends to be confused and disoriented because those who practice this art display a deep concern for the victims that is quite genuine. In this way, the new ideology is very different from the open prejudice and reactionary tactics of the old days. Its adherents include sympathetic social scientists with social consciences in good working order, and liberal politicians with a genuine commitment to reform. They are very careful to dissociate themselves from vulgar Calvinism or crude racism; they indignantly condemn any notions of innate wickedness or genetic defect. "The Negro is *not born* inferior," they shout apoplectically. "Force of circumstance," they explain in reasonable tones, "has *made* him inferior." And they dismiss with self-righteous contempt any claims that the poor man in America is plainly unworthy or shiftless or enamored of idleness. No, they say, he is "caught in the cycle of poverty." He is trained to be poor by his culture and his family life, endowed by his environment (perhaps by his ignorant mother's outdated style of toilet training) with those unfortunately unpleasant characteristics that make him ineligible for a passport into the affluent society.

Blaming the Victim is, of course, quite different from old-fashioned conservative ideologies. The latter simply dismissed victims as inferior, genetically defective, or morally unfit; the emphasis is on the intrinsic, even hereditary, defect. The former shifts its emphasis to the environmental causation. The old-fashioned conservative could hold firmly to the belief that the oppressed and the victimized were born that way—that way being defective or inadequate in character or ability. The new ideology attributes defect and inadequacy to the malignant nature of poverty, injustice, slum life, and racial difficulties. The stigma that marks the victim and accounts for his victimization is an acquired stigma, a stigma of social, rather than genetic, origin. But the stigma, the defect, the fatal difference—though derived in the past from environmental forces—is still located *within* the victim, inside his skin. With such an elegant formulation, the humanitarian can have it both ways. He can, all at the same time, concentrate his charitable interest on the defects of the victim, condemn the vague social and environmental stresses that produced the defect (some time ago), and ignore the continuing effect of victimizing social forces (right now). It is a brilliant ideology for justifying a perverse form of social action designed to change, not society, as one might expect, but rather society's victim.

As a result, there is a terrifying sameness in the programs that arise from this kind of analysis. In education, we have programs of "compensatory education" to build up the skills and attitudes of the ghetto child, rather than structural changes in the schools. In race relations, we have social engineers who think up ways of "strengthening" the Negro family, rather than methods of eradicating racism. In health care, we develop new programs to provide health information (to correct the supposed ignorance of the poor) and to reach out and discover cases of untreated illness and disability (to compensate for their supposed unwillingness to seek treatment). Meanwhile, the gross inequities of our medical care delivery systems are left completely unchanged. As we might expect, the logical outcome of analyzing social problems in terms of the deficiencies of the victim is the development of programs aimed at correcting those deficiencies. The formula for action becomes extraordinarily simple: change the victim.

All of this happens so smoothly that it seems downright rational. First, identify a social problem. Second, study those affected by the problem and discover in what ways they are different from the rest of us as a consequence of deprivation and injustice. Third, define the differences as the cause of the social problem itself. Finally, of course, assign a government bureaucrat to invent a humanitarian action program to correct the differences.

Now no one in his right mind would quarrel with the assertion that social problems are present in abundance and are readily identifiable. God knows it is true that when hundreds of thousands of poor children drop out of school—or even graduate from school—they are barely literate. After spending some ten thousand hours in the company of professional educators, these children appear to have learned very little. The fact of failure in their education is undisputed. And the racial situation in America is usually acknowledged to be a number one item on the nation's agenda. Despite years of marches, commissions, judicial decisions, and endless legislative remedies, we are confronted with unchanging or even widening racial differences in achievement. In addition, despite our assertions that Americans get the best health care in the world, the poor stubbornly remain unhealthy. They lose more work because of illness, have more carious teeth, lose more babies as a result of both miscarriage and infant death, and die considerably younger than the well-to-do.

The problems are there, and there in great quantities. They make us uneasy. Added together, these disturbing signs reflect inequality and a puzzlingly high level of unalleviated distress in America totally inconsistent with our proclaimed ideals and our enormous wealth. This thread—this rope—of inconsistency stands out so visibly in the fabric of American life, that it is jarring to the eye. And this must be explained, to the satisfaction of our conscience as well as our patriotism. Blaming the Victim is an ideal, almost painless, evasion.

The second step in applying this explanation is to look sympathetically at those who "have" the problem in question, to separate them out and define them in some way as a special group, a group that is *different* from the population in general. This is a crucial and essential step in the process, for that difference is in itself hampering and maladaptive. The Different Ones are seen as less competent, less skilled, less knowing—in short, less human. . . .

The ultimate effect is always to distract attention from the basic causes and to leave the primary social injustice untouched. And, most telling, the proposed remedy for the problem is, of course, to work on the victim himself. Prescriptions for cure, [are] invariably conceived to revamp and revise the victim, never to change the surrounding circumstances. They want to change his attitudes, alter his values, fill up his cultural deficits, energize his apathetic soul, cure his character defects, train him and polish him and woo him from his savage ways.

. . . The old, reactionary exceptionalistic formulations are replaced by new progressive, humanitarian exceptionalistic formulations. In education, the outmoded and unacceptable concept of racial or class differences in basic inherited intellectual ability simply gives way to the new notion of cultural deprivation: there is very little functional difference between these two ideas. In taking a look at the phenomenon of poverty, the old concept of unfitness or idleness or laziness is replaced by the newfangled theory of the culture of poverty. In race relations, plain Negro inferiority—which was good enough for old-fashioned conservatives—is pushed aside by fancy conceits about the crumbling Negro family. With regard to illegitimacy, we are not so crass as to concern ourselves with immorality and vice, as in the old days; we settle benignly on the explanation of the "lower-class pattern of sexual behavior," which no one condemns as evil, but which is, in fact, simply a variation of the old explanatory idea. Mental illness is no longer defined as the result of hereditary taint or congenital character flaw; now we have new causal hypotheses regarding the ego-damaging emotional experiences that are supposed to be the inevitable consequence of the deplorable child-rearing practices of the poor.

In each case, of course, we are persuaded to ignore the obvious: the continued blatant discrimination against the Negro, the gross deprivation of contraceptive and adoption services to the poor, the heavy stresses endemic in the life of the poor. And almost all our make-believe liberal programs aimed at correcting our urban problems are off target; they are designed either to change the poor man or to cool him out. . . .

But, in any case, are the poor really all that different from the middle class? Take a common type of study, showing that ninety-one percent of the upper class, compared to only sixty-eight percent of the poor, prefer college education for their children. What does that tell us about the difference in values between classes?

First, if almost seventy percent of the poor want their children to go to college, it doesn't make much sense to say that the poor, as a group, do not value education. Only a minority of them—somewhat less than one-third—fail to express a *wish* that their children attend college. A smaller minority—one in ten—of the middle class give similar responses. One might well wonder why this small group of the better-off citizens of our achieving society reject higher education. They have the money; many of them have the direct experience of education; and most of them are aware of the monetary value of a college degree. I would suggest that the thirty percent of the poor who are unwilling to express a wish that their children go to college are easier to understand. They know the barriers—financial, social, and for black parents, racial—that make it very difficult for the children of the poor to get a college education. That seven out of ten of them nevertheless persist in a desire to see their children in a cap and gown is, in a very real sense, remarkable. Most important, if we are concerned with cultural or subcultural differences, it seems highly illogical to emphasize the values of a small minority of one group and then to attribute these values to the whole group. I simply cannot accept the evidence. If seventy percent of a group values education, then it is completely illogical to say that the group as a whole does *not* value education.

A useful formulation is to be found in Hyman Rodman's conception of the "lower class value stretch" which, to give a highly oversimplified version, proposes that members of the lower class *share* the dominant value system but *stretch* it to include as much as possible of the variations that circumstances force upon them. Rodman says:

> Lower class persons in close interaction with each other and faced with similar problems do not long remain in a state of mutual ignorance. They do not maintain a strong commitment to middle class values that they cannot attain, and they do not continue to respond to others in a rewarding or punishing way simply on the basis of whether these others are living up to the middle class values. A change takes place. They come to tolerate and eventually to evaluate favorably certain deviations from the middle class values. In this way they need not be continually frustrated by their failure to live up to unattainable values. The resultant is a stretched value system with a low degree of commitment to all the values within the range, including the dominant, middle class values.

In Rodman's terms, then, differences in range of values and commitments to specific elements within that range occur primarily as an *adaptive* rather than as a *cultural* response. . . .

The most recent, and in many ways the best information on [the related issue of child rearing] comes to us from the Hylan Lewis child-rearing studies, which I have mentioned before. Lewis has demonstrated (finally, one hopes) that there really *is* no "lower class child-rearing pattern." There are a number of such patterns—ranging from strict and over-controlled parenting, to permissiveness, to down-right neglect—just as in Lewis' sample there are a variety of different kinds of families—ranging from those

with rigid, old-fashioned standards of hard work, thrift, morality and obsessive cleanliness, to the disorganized and disturbed families that he calls the "clinical poor." Lewis says:

> . . . it appears as a broad spectrum of pragmatic adjustments to external and internal stresses and deprivation. . . . Many low income families appear here as, in fact, the frustrated victims of what are thought of as middle class values, behavior and aspirations.

We return, finally, to where we began: the concept of Deferred Need Gratification. The simple idea that lower class folk have, as a character trait, a built-in deficiency in ability to delay need gratification has been explored, analyzed and more or less blown apart by Miller, Riessman, and Seagull. They point out that the supposed commitment of the middle classes to the virtues of thrift and hard work, to the practices of planning and saving for every painfully-chosen expenditure is, at this point in time, at best a surviving myth reflecting past conditions of dubious prevalence. The middle classes of today are clearly consumption-minded and debt-addicted. So the comparison group against which the poor are judged exists largely as a theoretical category with a theoretical behavior pattern. They go on to raise critical questions, similar to those I have raised earlier in this chapter. For example, on the question of what one would do with a two thousand dollar windfall, there was a difference between class groups of only five percent—about seventy percent of the middle class said they would save most of it, compared with about sixty-five percent of the lower class. On the basis of this small difference (which was statistically, but not practically, significant), the researchers, you will remember, had concluded that working-class people had less ability to defer need gratification. This conclusion may reflect elegant research methodology, but it fails the test of common sense. . . .

As for the idea that the poor share a culture in the sense that they subscribe to and follow a particular, deviant prescription for living—a poor man's blueprint for choosing and decision-making which accounts for the way he lives—this does not deserve much comment. Every study—with the exception of the egregious productions of Walter Miller—shows that, at the very least, overwhelming numbers of the poor give allegiance to the values and principles of the dominant American culture.

A related point—often the most overlooked point in any discussion of the culture of poverty—is that there is not, to my knowledge, *any evidence whatever* that the poor perceive their way of life as good and preferable to that of other ways of life. To make such an assertion is to talk pure nonsense. . . .

Perhaps the most fundamental question to ask of those who are enamored of the idea that the poor have one culture and the rich another is to ask, simply, "So what?" Suppose the mythical oil millionaire behaves in an unrefined "lower class" manner, for example. What difference does that make as long as he owns the oil wells? Is the power of the Chairman of the Ways and Means Committee in the state legislature diminished or enhanced in any way by his taste in clothing or music? And suppose every single poor family in America set as its long-range goal that its sons and daughters would get a Ph.D.—who would pay the tuition?

The effect of tastes, child-rearing practices, speech patterns, reading habits, and other cultural factors is relatively small in comparison to the effect of wealth and influence. What I am trying to suggest is that the inclusion in the analytic process of the elements of social stratification that are usually omitted—particularly economic class and power—would produce more significant insights into the circumstances of the poor and the pressures and deprivations with which they live. The simplest—and at the same time, the most significant—proposition in understanding poverty is that it is caused by lack of money. The overwhelming majority of the poor are poor because they have, first: insufficient income; and second: no access to methods of increasing that income—that is, no power. They are too young, too old, too sick; they are bound to the task of caring for small children, or they are simply discriminated against. The facts are clear, and the solution seems rather obvious—raise their income and let their "culture," whatever it might be, take care of itself.

The need to avoid facing this obvious solution—which is very uncomfortable since it requires some substantial changes and redistribution of income—provides the motivation for developing the stabilizing ideology of the culture of poverty which acts to sustain the *status quo* and delay change. The function of the ideology of lower class culture, then, is plainly to maintain inequality in American life.

The millionaire, freshly risen from the lower class, whose crude tongue and appalling table manners betray the newness of his affluence, is a staple of American literature and folklore. He comes on stage over and over, and we have been taught exactly what to expect with each entrance. He will walk into the parlor in his undershirt, gulp tea from a saucer, spit into the Limoges flower pot, and, when finally invited to the society garden party, disgrace his wife by saying "bullshit" to the president of the bank. When I was growing up, we had daily lessons in this legend from Jiggs and Maggie in the comic strip.

This discrepancy between *class* and *status*, between possession of economic resources and life style, has been a source of ready humour and guaranteed fascination for generations. The centrality of this mythical strain in American thought is reflected again in the strange and perverse ideas emerging from the mouths of many professional Pauper Watchers and Victim Blamers.

In real life, of course, Jiggs' character and behavior would never remain so constant and unchanging over the decades. The strain between wealth and style is one that usually tends to be quickly resolved. Within a fairly short time, Jiggs would be coming into the parlor first with a shirt, then with a tie on, and, finally, in one of his many custom-made suits. He would soon be drinking tea from a Limoges cup, and for a time he would spit in an antique cuspidor, until he learned not to spit at all. At the garden party, he would confine his mention of animal feces to a discussion of the best fertilizer for the rhododendron. In real life, style tends to follow close on money, and money tends to be magnetized and attracted to power. Those who try to persuade us that the process can be reversed, that a change in style of life can lead backward to increased wealth and greater power, are preaching nonsense. To promise that improved table manners can produce a salary increase; that more elegant taste in clothes will lead to the acquisition of stock in IBM; that an expanded vocabulary will automatically generate an enlargement of community influence—these are pernicious as well as foolish. There is no record in history of any *group* having accomplished this wondrous task. (There may be a few clever individuals who have followed such artful routes to money and power, but they are relatively rare.) The whole idea is an illusion of fatuous social scientists and welfare bureaucrats blinded by the ideology I have painstakingly tried to dissect in the previous chapters.

POSTSCRIPT

Does "Lower-Class" Culture Perpetuate Poverty?

The debate over the culture of poverty thesis is as strong today as it was over 20 years ago when Banfield and Ryan were debating. In 1981 George Gilder incorporated the culture of poverty thesis in his book *Wealth and Poverty* (Basic Books) and argued that hard work is the tried and true path from poverty to wealth. He also agrees that many welfare programs perpetuate poverty by breeding dependence and supporting the culture of poverty. This criticism of welfare has been forcefully argued with ample statistics by Charles Murray in *Losing Ground* (Basic Books, 1984). Both Gilder and Murray view the welfare system as an important contributor to the culture of poverty, whereas Banfield sees the culture of poverty as virulent long before welfare became a major factor in the lives of poor people.

There are countless works that describe the crushing and numbing conditions of the poor. The nineteenth-century English novelist Charles Dickens was a crusader for the poor, and many of his novels, still in print and certainly considered classics, graphically depict the wretchedness of poverty. Michael Harrington (1929–1989), a prominent political theorist and socialist, is one example of a more contemporary writer whose works call attention to the poor in our society. He described poverty in America in his influential nonfiction book *The Other America* (Macmillan, 1963) at a time when most of the country was increasingly affluent. He helped launch the War on Poverty of the Kennedy-Johnson administrations. Thomas Gladwin, in *Poverty USA* (Little, Brown, 1967), and Nick Katz, in *Let Them Eat Promises* (Prentice Hall, 1969), sought to maintain national concern about poverty in the late 1960s by documenting its prevalence even though the poverty rate dropped from 30 percent in 1950 to 13 percent in 1970. In 1968, however, the administration changed and the crusade against poverty died down. Nevertheless, public welfare expenditures rose mainly because Social Security, Medicare, and Medicaid kept expanding.

The antipoverty crusaders have new concerns with more recent developments, such as the increase in the number of female-headed single-parent families living below the poverty line and the increase throughout the 1980s in the number of homeless. Michael Harrington chronicled these changes in the condition of the poor in *The New American Poverty* (Holt, Rinehart and Winston, 1984). More recently, William Julius Wilson has written about the macroeconomic forces at work on the poor in *The Truly Disadvantaged* (University of Chicago Press, 1987).

ISSUE 10

Is Black Self-Help the Solution to Racial Inequality?

YES: Glenn C. Loury, from "A Prescription for Black Progress," *The Christian Century* (April 30, 1986)

NO: John E. Jacob, from "The Future of Black America," *Vital Speeches of the Day* (August 1, 1988)

ISSUE SUMMARY

YES: Professor of political economy Glenn C. Loury contends that government programs aimed at relieving black poverty often become job programs for middle-class professionals and argues that, historically, self-help has been the key to black progress.
NO: National Urban League president John E. Jacob argues that the notion of blacks pulling themselves out of poverty by their own bootstraps is a myth without basis in fact or in history.

In 1968, following four years of urban riots by blacks in several major U.S. cities, a presidential commission headed by Illinois governor Otto Kerner tried to determine the causes of the disorders. In its report the Kerner Commission offered this conclusion: "Our nation is moving toward two societies, one black, one white—separate and unequal." Ironically, this gloomy diagnosis came near the close of one of the most progressive periods in American race relations, for within the four previous years, between 1964 and 1968, Congress passed three major civil rights bills and added a new civil rights amendment to the Constitution. These new laws banned racial discrimination in employment, public accommodations, and housing, and removed the remaining obstacles to black voting rights. Federal judges began to vigorously enforce laws against racial discrimination, in some cases ordering busing and other actions to remedy the long-term effects of discrimination. Yet this great rights revolution, launched with vigor and high hopes, was culminating in violence, arson, and looting. Why?

The Kerner Commission attributed it to a combination of white racism and black frustration. Racism, the Commission said, produced the ghettos where crime, drug addiction, and welfare dependency flourished; it also lay behind the white suburban exodus that sapped the cities of funds and services needed by blacks. White racism produced the "frustrated hopes" and "the frustrations of powerlessness," which in turn produced the black riots. To cure what it saw as the underlying malaise, the Kerner Commission urged a massive new program of state and federal involvement in the black community: job creation, education, training, urban aid, welfare, housing, and new studies.

The Kerner Commission report was startling at the time, but today most major civil rights organizations have incorporated its conclusions into their platforms. Like the Kerner Commission, they say that civil rights must go much further than the attainment of legal equality. They focus upon the persistence of social inequality between the races, as measured in the statistics on everything from joblessness to maternal and child health. They conclude, as did the Kerner Commission, that white racism created these problems and only a massive commitment by government can solve them.

There exists, however, another perspective. It was also foreshadowed by a report written in the 1960s, although this report began with a different set of premises and pointed toward a different conclusion than that of the Kerner Commission. In 1965, Assistant Secretary of Labor Daniel Patrick Moynihan, now a U.S. senator from New York, wrote a report entitled "The Negro Family: The Case for National Action," in which he suggested that one reason for the persistence of social inequality between the races was the breakdown of the black family. Early pregnancies, illegitimacies, and the absence of a father were factors that he claimed contribute to a culture of poverty and dependency among urban blacks. Moynihan emphasized that these pathologies were ultimately rooted in a history of high unemployment and racial discrimination, but he suggested that they had taken on a life of their own. Although, as the subtitle of his report makes clear, Moynihan urged that the government play a role in helping the black family, the Moynihan report has been widely interpreted as suggesting the need for black self-help.

At the time, the Moynihan report provoked angry denunciation—critics saw it as a classic case of "blaming the victim"—but in recent years the theme of black self-help has won support from some black writers and activists. Robert L. Woodson, head of the national Center for Neighborhood Enterprise, and Roy Innis, director of the Congress of Racial Equality (CORE), are outspoken self-help activists. Even some black liberals, such as law professor Eleanor Holmes Norton, have endorsed the Moynihan report (Norton notes that the deterioration of the black family has become much worse since the report was written) and have urged a rediscovery of what Norton calls the "enduring values" of black America: hard work, education, and respect for family. Many civil rights spokespersons, however, worry that simplistic theories of "self-help" may be used as excuses for abandoning social programs that help poor blacks.

In the selections that follow, Glenn C. Loury makes the case for self-help, while John E. Jacob insists on the need for a major government role in narrowing the social differences between the races in the United States.

YES

Glenn C. Loury

A PRESCRIPTION FOR BLACK PROGRESS

Black Americans confront a great challenge, and an enormous opportunity. The black struggle for equality, born in the dark days of slavery and nurtured with the courage and sacrifices of generations who would not silently accept second-class citizenship, now threatens to falter and come to a stop—short of its historic goal. Throughout America, in the rural counties of the Black Belt, in the slums of Harlem, in North Philadelphia, on the west side of Chicago, on the east side of Detroit, in south-central Los Angeles, in East St. Louis, Illinois, in the ghettos of Houston, Oakland, Newark and scores of smaller cities and towns, literally millions of blacks live in poverty and, all too often, despair.

Of course, it is not only blacks who experience poverty or who deserve our concern. I focus on this group for two reasons. First, the problems associated with civic exclusion are especially severe for blacks and originate from a unique history of central importance to our nation. Second, I am convinced that group cohesion, identity and mutual concern are key assets in the struggle for equality. So I address the situation of this particular group—my group. Undoubtedly much of what I say can be applied to other groups as well.

The great challenge facing black America today is the task of taking control of its own future by exerting the necessary leadership, making the required sacrifices, and building the needed institutions so that black social and economic development becomes a reality. No matter how windy the debate becomes among white liberals and conservatives as to what should be done, meeting this self-creating challenge ultimately depends on black action.

It is unwise (and dangerous) to suppose that any state or federal government would, over the long haul, remain sufficiently committed to such a program of black revitalization. It is to make a mockery of the ideal of freedom to hold that, as free men and women, blacks must sit back and wait for white Americans, of whatever political persuasion, to come to the rescue. A people who languish in dependency, while the means through which they might work for their advancement exist, have surrendered their claim to

From Glenn C. Loury, "A Prescription for Black Progress," *The Christian Century* (April 30, 1986). Copyright © 1986 by the Christian Century Foundation. Reprinted by permission.

dignity. A genuinely free people must accept responsibility for their fate. Black America's political leaders have too often failed to face up to this fact.

One way of framing the choice now confronting blacks is to ask, "What does it mean today to be an advocate for the poor?" I propose a different answer to this question than one could infer from the historic practices of those now most widely recognized as "black leaders." My central theme is that poor black people have the wherewithal to begin to make fundamental improvements in their lives, given the opportunity. An advocate for the poor, from this perspective, is one who provides the means for poor people to help themselves develop to their full potential. An advocate for the poor is not someone who perpetuates the dependency of poor people, teaching them by example that their only option is to hold out their hands to accept gifts from others.

In order for the black self-help movement to flourish and prosper, several forces which work to impede or distract this effort must be recognized. As a case in point, some elected officials at the state and federal level are unwilling to consider efforts that would spur self-help activities because of their attachment to past, misguided programs. These legislators retard progress when, for example, they oppose even trying urban enterprise zones in areas of high urban unemployment, but instead urge a return to massive Great Society schemes which have no chance of passage in this era of $200 billion deficits.

Another impediment and distraction is the array of groups who graft their interests on to those of the economically disenfranchised. A poor people's march is seldom held without the participation of radical feminists, gay rights activists, environmentalists and communist apologists, who have twisted the misfortune of the inner-city poor to their own ends.

Yet another major obstacle to the goal of black empowerment is the quality of leadership supplied by many black elected officials. In local, state and federal elections around the country, the black masses are constantly told that sending a black elected official to the mayor's office, the state capital or Congress will lead to the solution of their plight, simply because the candidate is black. Yet, in many cities around the country where blacks are in positions of power, the same lack of economic development can be observed in the black ghettos (which constitute the politicians' key political base) that can be seen in white-controlled cities. It is not suggested that all black politicians are unworthy of their people's support; but there should be mechanisms to evaluate and discipline indifferent political leaders so that they would be forced to adopt positions and pursue programs that contribute to the economic and social advancement of their constituents. The sad fact is that these disciplining forces are few in number.

Unfortunately, poor blacks seldom seem willing to exercise this kind of critical judgment of the performance of their leaders. Black elected officials who have done little, other than parrot the lines of white liberals, seem to be re-elected regularly. Because of the long history of racism, many blacks mistakenly place group solidarity and considerations of loyalty above a common-sense evaluation of a politician's on-the-job performance. Many black incumbents seem immune to challenge by another black, since it is easy to cast the challenger as somehow being "a white man's nigger."

Some of these rascal incumbents should be voted out of office. But even before that, poor blacks should structure an ongoing system of monitoring a politician's day-to-day performance. Regularly scheduled public political forums and community-based newsletters are but two examples of how to match deed with need.

JOHN L. McKNIGHT, ASSOCIATE DIRECTOR of the Center for Urban Affairs and Policy Research at Northwestern University, has made an accurate assessment of how our society views its poor: "What we have done for many poor people is to say to them you are sentenced to be a consumer and a client, you are denied the privileges to create, to solve problems, and to produce; you have the most degraded status our society will provide."

McKnight, recounting an experience he had in a low-income community during the 1960s, tells of "poverty experts" who came into a town of 20,000 residents to conduct "needs surveys." All too predictably, they discovered there were severe problems in the areas of housing, education, jobs, crime and health.

In his role as a community organizer, McKnight took note of the "public-policy experts" from both the public and private sectors who were sent in to "solve" the community's problems. They included public housing officials, land clearance experts, housing development counselors, daily-living skills advisers, rodent removal experts, weatherization counselors, teacher's aides, audiovisual specialists, urban curriculum developers, teacher trainers, school security advisers, civil rights consultants, job developers, job counselors, job classifiers, job location specialists, relocation program specialists, job trainees, small business advisers, police aides, correctional system designers, rehabilitation specialists, a juvenile counselor, diversion specialists, social workers, psychologists, psychiatrists, health outreach workers, health educators, sex educators, environmental reform workers, caseworkers, home-budget management trainers, lead inspectors, skills trainers, and administrators and managers to coordinate all of these activities. In short, overkill. McKnight termed this situation an example of an economic development plan for people who *don't* live in the neighborhood.

McKnight concluded his observation by remarking with bull's-eye accuracy:

> I know from years in the neighborhoods that we can rely on community creativity. You have heard about it today over and over again. It is the most exciting thing that's happening in America. America is being reinvented little by little in the little places, but there is much more wealth that could be freed up, made available, if we understood that we have a big investment in the poor but their income is radically misdirected into the hands of service professionals [*Revitalizing Our Cities: New Approaches to Solving Urban Problems*, ed. Marc Lipsitz (Fund for American Renaissance and the National Center for Neighborhood Enterprise, 1986) pp. 101–102].

McKnight's example is all too familiar to those who are aware of the profusion of misdirected and misinformed approaches to "solving" the problems of the country's low-income citizens. This miscalculation of black capabilities is not by any means restricted to white America.

Some of the most eminent black thinkers, with close links to the civil rights establishment, no longer voice the same confidence they once did regarding the capabilities of black people. A great turning point was reached in the history of black Americans when, in 1934, the brilliant black thinker W. E. B. DuBois was dismissed from the editorship of *Crisis*, the journal of the National Association for the Advancement of Colored People, because of his view that the drive for integration at all costs undermined black people's confidence in their own institutions and capacities. Fearing that the fight against segregation (which he often led) had become a crusade to mix with whites for its own sake, DuBois wrote: "Never in the world should our fight be against association with ourselves because by that very token we give up the whole argument that we are worth association with."

Just 20 years after these words were written, however, black psychologist Kenneth Clark managed to convince the justices of the Supreme Court that segregation was inherently damaging to the personalities of black children. Unless whites were willing to mix with blacks, Clark seemed to argue, the result would inevitably be that black children would suffer self-image problems. The belief that development and self-respect for blacks is inherently impossible without "integration" might itself be considered damaging to the personalities of black children. As famed civil rights leader Floyd McKissick noted sarcastically, it seems to mean "if you put Negro with Negro you get stupidity." Such apparent expressions of black insecurity and inferiority bore out DuBois's fears. When the civil rights struggle moved from ending de facto segregation to forcing racial mixing, blacks often seemed to be rejecting the very possibility of beneficial association with themselves.

THIS LACK OF CONFIDENCE VOICED BY THE black intelligentsia about their own people extended to the capacity of black institutions to confront successfully the development problems that black people face. Many examples of this could be given, but one in the area of education should make the point. Recent experience in Chicago, Philadelphia and Washington, D.C., confirms the potential of developing independent black schools in the inner cities. These schools show that the education of poor black children can be improved with very limited resources, when there are parents and teachers willing to make the children's education an urgent priority. Yet so deeply entrenched is the civil rights mentality that in some communities black children are permitted to languish with limited skills while their "advocates" seek ever more farfetched versions of "integration," tacitly rejecting the option of positively promoting the education of their children themselves.

In 1977, black parents in Ann Arbor, Michigan, faced a difficult educational problem. Their children in the early grades were not learning how to read, though white students were. A group of civil rights lawyers and educators convinced these parents to sue the public schools, alleging discrimination, because white teachers in Ann Arbor failed to take due account of the fact that the black children spoke a distinct dialect of the English language called "black English." Two years later, a federal judge ordered the Ann Arbor schools to provide reading teachers with sensitivity training in "black English" so as to better teach reading to the black students. Now, seven years after the court order, it appears that young blacks in Ann Arbor continue to lag far behind their white counterparts in reading ability—but they have won their discrimination lawsuit, and are duly instructed by teachers "sensitized" to their "foreign" dialect.

All of this would be amusing if it weren't so tragically sad. Civil rights advocates won themselves a symbolic victory, but what did they do for those children? While years of legal wrangling went on, the opportunity of the Ann Arbor community to address directly the needs of the poor black students went unexploited. Apparently, it never occurred to those parents or their "advocates" that, rather than cast their problem as one of discrimination, their children might benefit more from a straightforward effort to tutor them in reading. With 35,000 students at the University of Michigan's Ann Arbor campus, a sizable number of whom are black, one imagines that sufficient volunteers for such a tutoring effort could have been found. That such an effort was rejected in favor of the far-fetched "black English" argument suggests the kind of intellectual malaise of which DuBois warned a half-century ago.

Blacks must examine their past objectively, taking what is valuable from it and rejecting those notions that have proven unworkable. Over many decades and under much more adverse circumstances than exist today, blacks have made impressive progress—without the benefit of the civil rights laws and welfare transfers that now exist. I do not suggest repeal of those laws. I merely urge that we not permit ourselves to become wholly dependent on them.

There are many examples of the impressive accomplishments which our ancestors managed under difficult conditions. The literacy rate among blacks rose steadily after emancipation, though free public schools were virtually unknown in the South. Independent black businesses and entire black towns flourished in the late 19th century. Modern research has shown that despite the terrible economic and social oppression to which the slaves were subjected, they created a vibrant familial, religious and cultural tradition which continues to enrich black America.

Among the black migrant communities in the North in the early years of this century, the kind of social dislocation and family instability that plagues today's black ghettos was virtually unknown. In 1925 in Harlem, 85 per cent of black families were intact, and single, teenage mothers were virtually unknown. In Buffalo, New York, in 1910, blacks exhibited similarly strong family structures, despite the virulent racism which they faced at that time. The point is that without liberal apologists to tell them what little they could do for themselves or how inevitable their misery, poor black folk in years past were able to maintain their communities and establish a firm foundation for their children's progress.

This heritage is the underpinning of a collective black strength waiting to be tapped today. To revive a value system that nurtured and enriched the lives of yesterday's black America, a dynamic and continuing process of economic, political and social development must be initiated to furnish the soil in which the seeds of black pride and accomplishment can take root and sprout. Some activists, like Robert Woodson of the National Center for Neighborhood Enterprise in Washington, D.C., have begun to explore the components of an economic rejuvenation process that could launch such a large-scale self-help movement. To be successful, however, these suggested programs must be built upon, expanded, revised and adapted to the varying conditions of local communities. We must, in the words of Chairman Mao, "let a hundred flowers bloom!" The time is now ripe for blacks to spearhead such an effort. With everything to gain and little to lose, a spirit of black adventurism could lift the community beyond dependency to self-sufficiency.

It is important to understand that I am *not* arguing here against the ancient and still valid notion that there is a public responsibility in a decent society to contribute to the alleviation of poverty, black or otherwise. In the areas of education, employment training, and provision of minimal subsistence to the impoverished, the government must be involved. Some of the most innovative and useful private efforts are sustained by public funds. There are publicly supported programs—preschool education, for one—which are expensive, but which research has shown pay an even greater dividend. It is a tragic error that those of us who make the self-help argument in dialogue concerning alternative development strategies for blacks are often construed by the political right as making a case for "benign neglect."

Black America cannot lift itself by its bootstraps into great wealth overnight. But there is a great unexploited potential for change at the level of the black individual and the local black community. In the current environment it is evident that blacks must exploit this dormant opportunity. The self-help approach—more a philosophy of life than a list of specific projects—must be initiated as a matter of necessity, not ideology.

Religious leadership at the grass-roots level, through committed ministries and active church congregations, can play a useful role in the process of collective uplift that I envision. It is the natural province of the religious institutions within a community to provide moral leadership, to set and enforce standards of behavior. In *Where Do We Go from Here: Chaos or Community?* (Beacon, 1968) Martin Luther King, Jr., recognized the crucial role that the then-emerging black middle class, through its churches, would have to play in the process of improving conditions for the group as a whole. He wrote:

> It is time for the Negro haves to join hands with the Negro have-nots and, with compassion, journey into that other country of hurt and denial. It is time for the Negro middle class to rise up from its stool of indifference, to retreat from its flight into unreality and to bring its full resources—its heart, its mind and its checkbook—to the aid of the less fortunate brother [p. 132].

Concerning moral leadership King added:

> It is not a sign of weakness, but a sign of high maturity, to rise to the level of self-criticism. Through group unity we must convey to one another that our women must be respected, and that life is too precious to be destroyed in a Saturday night brawl, or a gang execution. Through community agencies and religious institutions we must develop a positive program through which Negro youth can become adjusted to urban living and improve their general level of behavior [p. 125].

I believe that, were King at the helm of the civil rights movement today, it is in this direction that he would be taking us.

The task of narrowing class schisms within the black community should have priority. Blacks must not be afraid to make judgments about faults and failings in their community. Blacks must abandon the pernicious and self-destructive tendency arbitrarily to empower the "man" with ultimate control over their destiny. This is an almost criminal abdication of responsibility. Precisely because racism is a fact of life not likely to disappear soon, *all* blacks are "in the same lifeboat." This being the case, it is in the individual black's interest to contribute time and resources to the advancement of those least well off in the community. It is politically and morally irresponsible to sit back in disgust, as so many veterans of past struggles are fond of doing, constantly decrying the problems, doing little or nothing to solve them, shouting epithets and threats at whites who grow weary of being "generous and understanding," while the black poor sink deeper and deeper into despair.

It is crucial that blacks not become so caught up in seeking welfare state handouts that we lose our own souls. The very important, but essentially private, matter of the indignities our ancestors suffered due to their race must not be allowed to become a vehicle for cheap brokering with the welfare state. The generations of blacks who suffered under Jim Crow deserve something more than simply having their travails used as an excuse for current failures. Our work today is not to change the *minds* of white people, but to involve ourselves in the *lives* of black people. Past black sufferings should not be hauled out to gain guilt money. Such a posture is pitiful and unbecoming of black America's proud heritage. Dependency, even when one is dependent on sympathetic and generous souls, is destructive of dignity—and dignity is a necessary precondition of genuine freedom and equality.

NO

John E. Jacob

THE FUTURE OF BLACK AMERICA

I'm honored to be here and I look forward to this opportunity to present my views on the future prospects for black Americans and to engage in some dialogue with you.

Today I want to begin by briefly sketching what the Urban League is, and going on from there to discuss the plight of black citizens. Along the way, I'd like to look back at some of the things America has done to deal with its racial problems. And I'd like to look ahead as well, to suggest some of the things we can do to secure the future for black people and for all Americans.

Most of you are familiar with the work of the National Urban League. We have affiliates in 112 cities—and that means most of your districts and states include at least one Urban League.

We're based on three principles—and we've held fast to them since our founding 78 years ago.

One is advocacy on behalf of black citizens and all poor people. We are a repository of research, ideas, and experiences that the nation needs in framing policies that affect the third of our population that is black or poor.

Second, we are a community-based service delivery organization. Urban League job and skills training programs, education and health and housing programs, and a host of others, serve one-and-a-half million people who come to Urban League offices each year.

Currently, we are concentrating on mobilizing black and minority communities around a national Education Initiative designed to radically improve black students' academic achievement. We are also concentrating resources on the plight of female-headed households, teenage pregnancy, crime, and citizenship education.

Third, the National Urban League is a bridge-builder between the races. We are believers in an open, integrated, pluralistic society, and our activities support that goal. Our staffs and boards are integrated, and we work very hard at improving race relations in America.

I am clearly here today in our advocacy role, and I have to tell you that the state of black Americans is very bad. In fact, our future is at risk.

From John E. Jacob, "The Future of Black America," *Vital Speeches of the Day* (August 1, 1988). Copyright © 1988 by *Vital Speeches of the Day*. Reprinted by permission.

In January [1988], the National Urban League published its annual State of Black America report. It documents continuing black disadvantage.

Let me share with you some of the facts about black life in America. I know that this knowledgeable audience is familiar with them—but I also know that they cannot be repeated often enough.

- Half of all black children grow up in poverty.
- Over a third of all blacks are poor—two million more blacks became poor in the past dozen years.
- Almost two million black workers are jobless—over twelve percent of the black work force, and a rate two-and-a-half times that for whites.
- Black family income is only 58 percent that of whites; the typical black family earns less than the government itself says is needed for a decent but modest living standard.
- Black households have less than one-tenth the wealth of white households.

In this high-tech, information age, black dropout rates in some cities are higher than black graduation rates, and there has been an alarming decline in the numbers of blacks entering college.

In virtually all of those areas, black disadvantage is worse than it has been at any time since the mid-1970s.

At the same time, I should acknowledge the fact that some blacks have made extraordinary progress.

Today, black judges preside over court rooms where civil rights demonstrators were once sentenced in the 1950s. Black executives now help shape policies of corporations that once wouldn't hire blacks. Black professionals live in formerly all-white suburbs and earn middle class incomes.

But they share with their poorer brothers and sisters the bond of blackness—the fact that whether affluent or disadvantaged, all blacks suffer from racism.

Racism need not be violent, like the murder of a black truck driver in Texas by police officers, or the actions of a mob in Howard Beach.

It can take subtler forms that affect all blacks—from the teenage kid denied a job in a downtown store because of racial stereotypes to the son of the black doctor who's stopped by police because he's driving his Dad's Mercedes and they just assume a young black behind the wheel of that kind of car stole it.

Recently, we've seen surveys that document the harassment of black managers in corporate America, and their perceptions of a racial ceiling that limits their potential.

So despite the often-proclaimed statements that we are finally a color-blind society, I have to tell you that we are very far . . . very far . . . from achieving that goal.

And let me take this opportunity to say that Congress' action last week in overriding the veto of the Civil Rights Restoration Act helps move us just that little bit closer to our goal.

Your vote to override is important for the future of black people and the entire nation. It endorsed the proposition that federal money should not subsidize discrimination in any of its forms.

And it sends a bi-partisan message that when it comes to civil rights, America will allow no loopholes.

To the extent that black people have made progress, we have to credit the civil rights revolution of the 1960s and the effects of the Great Society programs that are now out of fashion.

The laws, executive orders and judicial decisions of the 1960s empowered black people and removed many of the barriers in their way. Social welfare programs assisted many black people to get the incomes, health and nutrition care, and education they needed to enter the mainstream.

Some of those programs may not have worked as well as they should. Too often, programs were not targeted sharply enough and resources intended by Congress for the poorest of the poor found their way into middle-class neighborhoods instead.

The Urban League carefully monitored training programs and urban aid programs, and we found a consistent pattern of diverting funds away from community-based programs that could have helped those most in need.

Part of the problem has been the lack of patience with those programs—the drive for instant results. So we had a lot of skimming—helping people who would be likely to succeed anyway so the numbers look better, rather than attempting to work with the most impacted of the poor.

Other programs worked well by any standard. The Job Corps, Head Start, Chapter One remedial education, nutrition programs, and others.

Where those programs did not work as well as they should, it was most often due to underfunding and restrictive eligibility procedures that prevented them from reaching all in need. It is notorious that such proven programs as Medicaid, food stamps and others reached only about half of the poor. Head Start enrolls only about a fifth of eligible children—and similar figures apply to nutrition and training and health programs.

In the 1980s, there was an extraordinary increase in poverty, in homelessness, and in other indexes of disadvantaged among blacks and other minorities.

This was due to two factors.

One was the deep cuts in government social programs. The Center on Budget and Policy Priorities studied funding for low-income programs other than entitlements and found that spending was cut by 54 percent after inflation since 1981. Subsidized housing was cut by 81 percent and training and employment services by 68 percent.

A second factor is the economic shift in our society.

The elimination of a substantial part of America's manufacturing base has hit black workers hardest. Studies show they are concentrated in the most vulnerable industries and are more likely to be laid off and less likely to find comparable jobs.

And there has been an extraordinary shrinkage in lower level jobs available to people without high educational credentials. That is the single most important factor in the troubles of the black family.

Twenty-five years ago, three out of four black men in America were working and three out of four black families were intact. Today, just a little over half of all black men are working and just over half of all black families are intact.

Anyone concerned about the rise of single-parent families in the black community doesn't have to look further for the reason. Unemployment and underemployment is tearing black families apart. And it is responsible for the inability of many young people to begin families.

Last year [1987], the Children's Defense Fund released a study that further confirms this thesis. In the early 1970s about 60 percent of all young men earned enough to lift a family of three above the poverty line. By the mid-1980s, only about 40 percent earned that much. Between the mid-1970s and the mid-1980s, the marriage rate for young men was cut by one-half.

And those are overall, national figures for all races. For blacks, and especially for young black men who do not finish school, the figures are far worse. Only one out of nine black dropouts, for example, earns enough to support a family of three above the poverty line.

So there have been worsening economic prospects for a majority of young blacks at the same time that the props of federal education, training and social supports have been cut or removed.

We've found that black people with skills, education and strong family backgrounds are able to enter the mainstream today. But the other half—blacks without skills and suffering from educational deficiencies and social deficits, are increasingly locked out.

There is a powerful myth today that the answer to such problems is self-help—that it is the sole responsibility of the black community to eradicate dysfunctional behavior and to pull itself into the mainstream.

That's just a myth—without basis in fact or in history. I have little patience with the people who tell us to look at other groups that are making it. Black people did not come here voluntarily. No other group came in chains. Today's successful immigrant groups came to these shores with education, with a belief in the American Dream, and with substantial internal community financial resources.

Black people have made it in America despite overwhelming odds—the rise of the new black middle class is proof of that. But far too many of us are trapped in the hopelessness and despair of urban ghettos with little hope to escape. Too many of our kids are seduced by the underground economy and sucked into crack and crime.

While many ask why they don't stop such behavior, I have to ask what kind of society creates an environment of hopelessness and despair that drives young children into self-destructive behavior.

The Urban League knows all about self-help and pulling yourself up by your bootstraps. That's what we've been about for 78 years. But we also know that conditions have changed in many of our communities—changed to the point where our efforts cannot possibly succeed without government intervention.

It's all right to talk about pulling yourself by your bootstraps but not when you're talking to people who don't have boots. The conditions that allowed previous generations of black people to pull themselves up have changed. Today's young generation is too concerned with simple survival to think about long-term career choices.

In Chicago's Cabrini public housing project, the big question for kids is: have the gangs stopped shooting so I can go out of the house. We're talking about kids whose parents keep them away from the windows so they won't be hit by stray bullets. We're talking about kids whose classmates tote automatic weapons.

It's a new ball game out there, and those people in positions of power who won't do anything about it and who preach self-help are adding to the problem, not solving it.

The black community today is mobilizing to deal with those issues. Last week I attended a meeting of community leaders drawn from across the nation to find ways to save young black men—America's most endangered group.

The Urban League and other community-based agencies and groups are working very hard to turn things around—but we're just whistling in the dark unless government is on our side.

The problem is simply not amenable to solution through self-help alone. Let me give you two examples drawn from the *New York Times* of March 16th.

Page One headline: "Reliance on Temporary Jobs Hints at Economic Fragility." The story went on to talk about the shift to part-time and temporary jobs that are likely to disappear at the first hint of recession. The dark side of the well-publicized job boom is that many of those jobs are low-paying, and are temporary.

Black people who used to get steady work at low-skill jobs are now either unemployed or working part-time and unable to support their families or to serve as role models for their kids.

Another page one headline the same day: "Carnegie Report Urges Crusade for Bypassed Urban Schools."

That story reported that the school reforms of the past five years have bypassed ghetto schools, which are still sunk in a morass of failure. It reports about students there—our black kids—quote: "No one notices if they drop out because no one noticed when they dropped in."

Twenty years after the Kerner Commission [which, under the chairmanship of Illinois governor Otto Kerner, was established in 1967 to study the increasing number of civil disorders in America; the resulting report indicated that the nation was moving toward "two societies, separate and unequal"], we're finding not only that we're moving to two separate societies—one black, one white—but also two societies within the black community—one middle class and

aspiring, the other desperately poor and increasingly without hope.

That is not simply a problem for black people—this is a national problem that will affect the future of our economy.

In the past, America could write off young black people . . . relegate them to the margins . . . deny them training and opportunities.

In the future, doing that will amount to committing economic suicide.

The Labor Department's Workforce 2000 study says that there will be 25 percent fewer young adults entering the workforce than there were in the 1980s. The least-skilled jobs will disappear and the most highly skilled jobs will grow rapidly.

And up to a third of new workers will be minority—in other words, the core of our future workforce will come from groups that are most at-risk today.

We face a surplus of people without the skills to be productive in a post-industrial, information-based economy. And we face a shortage of people to fill the growing number of jobs required to remain competitive in a global marketplace.

David Kearns is chairman and CEO of the Xerox Corporation and a former chairman of the National Urban League. David is concerned about the huge training costs imposed on industry just to bring people up to the point where they can hold entry-level jobs.

And he's asking the question: "Who is going to do the work that needs to be done to keep this economy running?"

The demographics are putting America at a competitive disadvantage in this global economy. Unless we take the problems of minority youth seriously—unless we assure that each and every young black and brown person has the education and skills our economy needs— we're going to wind up colonized by foreign competitors.

At this point, I suppose I'm expected to present a shopping list of solutions—a want list that you as Congresspeople would be asked to legislate and fund.

The only problem with that is that the Reagan Revolution has created such awesome deficits and such a huge national debt that any proposals for new funding initiatives are unlikely.

But I'd like to suggest that ducking the problems we face by pointing to the deficits is irresponsible. Inaction won't save endangered black youth . . . won't make us more competitive in the future . . . won't prevent the inequalities in our society from growing to the point where they endanger our democracy.

Who among us can expect the homeless to remain silent forever . . . the unemployed to accept their lot quietly forever . . . the despairing to contain their anger forever?

We're sitting on a social and economic powderkeg, and future generations will be harsh on those who did nothing, when they had the power and the responsibility to act constructively.

Frankly, I see those huge deficits as an *excuse* to do nothing, not as a reason.

I find it incredible to hear that a trillion dollar budget can't accommodate investments that cut poverty and create opportunities. I find it incredible that a five trillion dollar economy can't support programs that cut inequality and invest in the human resources that represent our best hope for the future.

Politics and governing are based on reasoned choices among alternatives. One choice we have is to redirect spending away from areas that are marginal to areas that are crucial.

We found it within our capabilities, for example, to spend some two trillion dollars on the Pentagon over the past eight years. As one expert has written: "We manufacture weapons that are not needed, that cost too much, and that don't work, while we fail to meet other, more basic defense needs."

We need to tailor military spending to a realistic defense posture in a multipolar world. That would most likely result in savings that could be diverted to domestic investment in human capital.

Those people programs are cheap by comparison. The B-1B bomber cost $28 billion for a fleet of 100 planes that don't do what they were supposed to do. That's more than enough to assure training every disadvantaged young person in marketable skills.

A nation with the lowest rates in the industrial world can increase taxes to levels commensurate with its needs. A modest tax on oil would not only keep the OPEC cartel at bay—it would finance Head Start and Chapter One remedial education programs for every disadvantaged child, and enough would be left over to beef up child health programs.

With a 28 percent top tax rate, can anyone really argue that a surtax or a third bracket at 35 percent is unreasonable at a time of huge national needs?

Any prudent person invests in the future and any responsible government does the same. There's a strange notion around that when government builds a bridge it is making a capital investment in the future, but when it invests in a job training program, it is current spending. It's not—it is a long-term investment in human capital.

By not making those investments today, we're increasing tomorrow's deficits. Between 700,000 and 900,000 kids drop out of school every year, and the ultimate cost to society in lost earnings and lost tax revenues comes to $240 billion over their lifetimes! And that doesn't even include the bill for crime, social welfare programs, and other costs.

I find it hard to explain why so many businessmen understand that while others do not. The Committee for Economic Development includes some of the top corporate leaders, and they've urged heavy investments in child development programs and in education.

They point out that one dollar spent in child health programs—the same programs the Administration wants to cut—saves almost $5 in expenditures down the road.

When hard-nosed businessmen start talking about the need for nutrition, health, and education programs, you know the message is beginning to get across that government action is necessary. Only government can train and educate our young people, keep them healthy, and give them access to the social services they've got to have if they're to make decent lives for themselves.

That should also be clear to people in government and to the public. In fact, we're seeing a shift in the public's mood today—toward greater compassion and more realism about enabling all Americans to be more productive and more competitive.

We're really confronted with two scenarios today. One is based on the continuation of present policies. That will inevitably lead to greater inequality and the formation of a permanent underclass that threatens America's social stability and economic foundations.

A second scenario would be an activist government role in equipping disadvantaged people to make it in our society.

That scenario would shrink the poverty population, and increase the numbers of young blacks entering college and moving into the middle class. The result would be a stronger black community and an America that retains its world primacy.

That second scenario could be implemented by a number of steps:

One, a national effort to create jobs or training opportunities for every disadvantaged person.

Two, a national education program that fully funds early childhood education for the disadvantaged, and provides incentives to local school districts to provide whatever assistance is necessary to bring quality education to disadvantaged students.

Three, transformation of the welfare system to provide decent living standards for the poor and incentives to work and to get the education and training necessary to be productive.

There are further unmet needs in housing, health and other areas that must also be addressed.

This is hardly the time or the place to go into detailed specifics of such programs. The National Urban League has a Washington Operations Office headed by our Vice President, Doug Glasgow, and we'd be very happy to work with you and with your staffs to help you address the specifics of such issues. We have already worked with some of you on key legislation in the past and hope to continue and expand that relationship.

But today, I do want to suggest that such investments in the nation's future make sense . . . are do-able . . . and should cross party and ideological lines.

Winston Churchill is the model of a conservative statesman, and he once said: "There is no finer investment for any community than putting milk into babies."

And George Will, the conservative columnist, wrote: "It is cheaper to feed the child than jail the man. Persons who do not understand this are not conservatives, just dim."

So I don't want to see the fate of black Americans embroiled in false liberal versus conservative ideological disputes. I would hope that all of us have the sense to understand that government has the responsibility and the ability to solve the social problems that endanger our economy and our society.

And I would hope that all of us have the compassion and the human concern to want to do something about children who face bleak futures and adults who have no jobs, no homes, no hope.

Social and economic policy has been in a state of paralysis over the past decade.

We now find ourselves having to make up for lost time and lost resources. A generation of young black people was lost in the 1980s—doomed to failure and to marginality because they didn't have access to the opportunities they needed to become functioning members of our changing society.

We can't let that wastage of human resources continue. We can't let our society continue to drift apart, separated by unbridgeable gaps in education, income, skills, class and race.

We are at a period in time when the currents of the past and future converge . . . when we are positioned to make decisions and implement policies that determine whether future generations of poor and black people are consigned to the outer borders of society or are drawn into the mainstream.

As Congressmen, as leaders, and as citizens, you have the power to make the right choices and the right decisions.

I have faith that you will.

POSTSCRIPT

Is Black Self-Help the Solution to Racial Inequality?

Both Loury and Jacob seem to agree that government transfer payments are not the solution in the long term to the problem of social inequality. Both also agree that, in Loury's words, "there is a public responsibility in a decent society to contribute to the alleviation of poverty." It is clear that both favor government investment in education and training for the poor, especially for young people. (Both praise Operation Head Start, a program for pre-schoolers.) But Loury insists that private volunteer work is the real key to helping the black poor, while Jacob insists that government involvement is essential. It seems beyond dispute that both approaches are needed; the question is where to place the emphasis.

Loury quotes with approval some of the advice given by Martin Luther King, Jr., and W. E. B. Du Bois, but one black leader from the early years of the twentieth century whose views (or at least some of them) he might have quoted was Booker T. Washington. Much praised during his lifetime, scorned later as an "Uncle Tom," Washington has made something of a comeback in recent years because of his philosophy—and personal example—of black self-help. His autobiographical *Up From Slavery* (1900), available in a number of editions, is still inspirational. Du Bois was an early critic of Washington. See his *The Souls of Black Folk* (1903, Reprint, New American Library, 1969). One of the best anthologies of different views on such questions is that of Herbert Storing, ed., *What Country Have I?* (St. Martin's Press, 1970). Two seminal historical studies may lend support to the conclusion that black family breakdown is a relatively new phenomenon not caused by slavery or segregation. *Roll, Jordan, Roll*, by Eugene Genovese (Random House, 1976), is a record of the resilience and cohesion of black families during the darkest days of slavery. (Somewhat surprisingly for a Marxist historian, Genovese attributes much of their strength to their religion.) Herbert G. Gutman's *The Black Family in Slavery and Freedom* (Random House, 1977) also shows how strong the black family remained during the nineteenth and early twentieth centuries. Still another perspective, not necessarily contradictory, is provided by J. Owens Smith in *The Politics of Racial Inequality* (Greenwood Press, 1987), which stresses the importance of a legal framework guaranteeing civil rights. Reynolds Farley and Walter Allen, *The Color Line and the Quality of Life in America* (Russell Sage, 1987), use census data to demonstrate the progress of blacks and the remaining gap between the races.

ISSUE 11

Is Affirmative Action Reverse Discrimination?

YES: Shelby Steele, from *The Content of Our Character* (St. Martin's Press, 1990)

NO: Herman Schwartz, from "In Defense of Affirmative Action," *Dissent* (Fall 1984)

ISSUE SUMMARY

YES: Associate professor of English Shelby Steele contends that instead of solving racial inequality problems, affirmative action mandates have generated racial discrimination in reverse.
NO: Professor of law Herman Schwartz argues that we must somehow undo the cruel consequences of racism that still plague our society and its victims.

In America, equality is a political principle as basic as liberty. "All men are created equal" is the most famous phrase in the Declaration of Independence. More than half a century later, Alexis de Tocqueville examined democracy in America and concluded that its most essential ingredient was the equality of condition. Today we know that the "equality of condition" that de Tocqueville perceived did not exist for women, blacks, Native Americans, and other racial minorities, nor for other disadvantaged social classes. Nevertheless, the ideal persisted. When slavery was abolished after the Civil War, the Constitution's newly ratified Fourteenth Amendment proclaimed: "No State shall . . . deny to any person within its jurisdiction the equal protection of the laws."

Equality has been a long time coming. For nearly a century after the abolition of slavery, American blacks were denied equal protection by law in some states and by social practice nearly everywhere. One-third of the states either permitted or forced schools to become racially segregated, and segregation was achieved elsewhere through housing policy and social behavior. In 1954 the Supreme Court reversed a 58-year-old standard that had found "separate but equal" schools compatible with equal protection of the law. A unanimous decision in *Brown v. Board of Education* held that separate is *not* equal for the members of the discriminated-against group when the segregation "generates a feeling of inferiority as to their status in the community that may affect their hearts and minds in a way unlikely ever to be undone." The 1954 ruling on public elementary education has been extended to other areas of both governmental and private conduct, including housing and employment.

Even if judicial decisions and congressional statutes could end all segregation and racial discrimination, would this achieve equality—or simply perpetuate the status quo? The unemployment rate for blacks today is more than twice that of whites. Disproportionately higher numbers of blacks experience poverty, brutality, broken homes, physical and mental illness, and early deaths, while disproportionately lower numbers of them have reached positions of affluence and prestige. It seems likely that much of this inequality results from 300 years of slavery and segregation. Is termination of this ill treatment enough to end the injustices? No, say the proponents of "affirmative action."

Affirmative action has had an uneven history in U.S. federal courts. In *Regents of the University of California v. Bakke* (1978), which marked the first time the Supreme Court directly dealt with the merits of affirmative action, a 5-4 majority ruled that a white applicant to a medical school had been wrongly excluded in favor of a less qualified black applicant due to the school's affirmative action policy; yet the majority also agreed that "race-conscious" policies may be used in admitting candidates—as long as they do not amount to fixed quotas. The ambivalence of *Bakke* has run through the Court's treatment of the issue since 1978. Decisions have gone one way or the other depending on the precise circumstances of the case (such as whether it was a federal or state policy, whether or not it was mandated by a congressional statute, and whether quotas were required or simply permitted). Recent decisions suggest that the Court is beginning to take a dim view of affirmative action. In 1989, for example, the Court ruled that a city council could *not* set aside a fixed percentage of public construction projects to minority contractors.

In the following selections, Shelby Steele and Herman Schwartz debate the merits of affirmative action. In Steele's view, affirmative action represents a distortion of the original aims of the civil rights revolution, while Schwartz considers it an essential means of undoing the effects of white racism.

YES

Shelby Steele

AFFIRMATIVE ACTION: THE PRICE OF PREFERENCE

In a few short years, when my two children will be applying to college, the affirmative action policies by which most universities offer black students some form of preferential treatment will present me with a dilemma. I am a middle-class black, a college professor, far from wealthy, but also well-removed from the kind of deprivation that would qualify my children for the label "disadvantaged." Both of them have endured racial insensitivity from whites. They have been called names, have suffered slights, and have experienced firsthand the peculiar malevolence that racism brings out in people. Yet, they have never experienced racial discrimination, have never been stopped by their race on any path they have chosen to follow. Still, their society now tells them that if they will only designate themselves as black on their college applications, they will likely do better in the college lottery than if they conceal this fact. I think there is something of a Faustian bargain [sacrificing values for material gain] in this.

Of course, many blacks and a considerable number of whites would say that I was sanctimoniously making affirmative action into a test of character. They would say that this small preference is the meagerest recompense for centuries of unrelieved oppression. And to these arguments other very obvious facts must be added. In America, many marginally competent or flatly incompetent whites are hired everyday—some because their white skin suits the conscious or unconscious racial preference of their employer. The white children of alumni are often grandfathered into elite universities in what can only be seen as a residual benefit of historic white privilege. Worse, white incompetence is always an individual matter, while for blacks it is often confirmation of ugly stereotypes. The Peter Principle [which states that in a hierarchy, every employee tends to rise to the level of his or her incompetence] was not conceived with only blacks in mind. Given that unfairness cuts both ways, doesn't it only balance the scales of history that my children now receive a slight preference over whites? Doesn't this repay,

From Shelby Steele, *The Content of Our Character* (St. Martin's Press, 1990). Copyright © 1990 by Shelby Steele. Reprinted by permission of St. Martin's Press, Inc., New York, NY.

in a small way, the systematic denial under which their grandfather lived out his days?

So, in theory, affirmative action certainly has all the moral symmetry that fairness requires—the injustice of historical and even contemporary white advantage is offset with black advantage; preference replaces prejudice, inclusion answers exclusion. It is reformist and corrective, even repentent and redemptive. And I would never sneer at these good intentions. Born in the late forties in Chicago, I started my education (a charitable term in this case) in a segregated school and suffered all the indignities that come to blacks in a segregated society. My father, born in the South, only made it to the third grade before the white man's fields took permanent priority over his formal education. And though he educated himself into an advanced reader with an almost professorial authority, he could only drive a truck for a living and never earned more than ninety dollars a week in his entire life. So yes, it is crucial to my sense of citizenship, to my ability to identify with the spirit and the interests of America, to know that this country, however imperfectly, recognizes its past sins and wishes to correct them.

Yet good intentions, because of the opportunity for innocence they offer us, are very seductive and can blind us to the effects they generate when implemented. In our society, affirmative action is, among other things, a testament to white goodwill and to black power, and in the midst of these heavy investments, its effects can be hard to see. But after twenty years of implementation, I think affirmative action has shown itself to be more bad than good and that blacks— whom I will focus on in this essay—now stand to lose more from it than they gain.

In talking with affirmative action administrators and with blacks and whites in general, it is clear that supporters of affirmative action focus on its good intentions while detractors emphasize its negative effects. Proponents talk about "diversity" and "pluralism"; opponents speak of "reverse discrimination," the unfairness of quotas and set-asides. It was virtually impossible to find people outside either camp. The closest I came was a white male manager at a large computer company who said, "I think it amounts to reverse discrimination, but I'll put up with a little of that for a little more diversity." I'll live with a little of the effect to gain a little of the intention, he seemed to be saying. But this only makes him a halfhearted supporter of affirmative action. I think many people who don't really like affirmative action support it to one degree or another anyway.

I believe they do this because of what happened to white and black Americans in the crucible of the sixties when whites were confronted with their racial guilt and blacks tasted their first real power. In this stormy time white absolution and black power coalesced into virtual mandates for society. Affirmative action became a meeting ground for these mandates in the law, and in the late sixties and early seventies it underwent a remarkable escalation of its mission from simple anti-discrimination enforcement to social engineering by means of quotas, goals, timetables, set-asides and other forms of preferential treatment.

Legally, this was achieved through a series of executive orders and EEOC [Equal Employment Opportunity Commission] guidelines that allowed racial imbalances in the workplace to stand as proof of racial discrimination. Once it could be assumed that discrimination explained racial imbalances, it became easy to justify group remedies to presumed discrimination, rather than the normal case-by-case redress for proven discrimination. Preferential treatment through quotas, goals, and so on is designed to correct imbalances based on the assumption that they always indicate discrimination. This expansion of what constitutes discrimination allowed affirmative action to escalate into the business of social engineering in the name of anti-discrimination, to push society toward statistically proportionate racial representation, without any obligation of proving actual discrimination.

What accounted for this shift, I believe, was the white mandate to achieve a new racial innocence and the black mandate to gain power. Even though blacks had made great advances during the sixties without quotas, these mandates, which came to a head in the very late sixties, could no longer be satisfied by anything less than racial preferences. I don't think these mandates in themselves were wrong, since whites clearly needed to do better by blacks and blacks needed more real power in society. But, as they came together in affirmative action, their effect was to distort our understanding of racial discrimination in a way that allowed us to offer the remediation of preference on the basis of mere color rather than actual injury. By making black the color of preference, these mandates have reburdened society with the very marriage of color and preference (in reverse) that we set out to eradicate. The old sin is reaffirmed in a new guise.

But the essential problem with this form of affirmative action is the way it leaps over the hard business of developing a formerly oppressed people to the point where they can achieve proportionate representation on their own (given

equal opportunity) and goes straight for the proportionate representation. This may satisfy some whites of their innocence and some blacks of their power, but it does very little to truly uplift blacks.

A white female affirmative action officer at an Ivy League university told me what many supporters of affirmative action now say: "We're after diversity. We ideally want a student body where racial and ethnic groups are represented according to their proportion in society." When affirmative action escalated into social engineering, diversity became a golden word. It grants whites an egalitarian fairness (innocence) and blacks an entitlement to proportionate representation (power). *Diversity* is a term that applies democratic principles to races and cultures rather than to citizens, despite the fact that there is nothing to indicate that real diversity is the same thing as proportionate representation. Too often the result of this on campuses (for example) has been a democracy of colors rather than of people, an artificial diversity that gives the appearance of an educational parity between black and white students that has not yet been achieved in reality. Here again, racial preferences allow society to leapfrog over the difficult problem of developing blacks to parity with whites and into a cosmetic diversity that covers the blemish of disparity—a full six years after admission, only about 26 percent of black students graduate from college.

Racial representation is not the same thing as racial development, yet affirmative action fosters a confusion of these very different needs. Representation can be manufactured; development is always hard-earned. However, it is the music of innocence and power that we hear in affirmative action that causes us to cling to it and to its distracting emphasis on representation. The fact is that after twenty years of racial preferences, the gap between white and black median income is greater than it was in the seventies. None of this is to say that blacks don't need policies that ensure our right to equal opportunity, but what we need more is the development that will let us take advantage of society's efforts to include us.

I think that one of the most troubling effects of racial preferences for blacks is a kind of demoralization, or put another way, an enlargement of self-doubt. Under affirmative action the quality that earns us preferential treatment is an implied inferiority. However this inferiority is explained—and it is easily enough explained by the myriad deprivations that grew out of our oppression—it is still inferiority. There are explanations, and then there is the fact. And the fact must be borne by the individual as a condition apart from the explanation, apart even from the fact that others like himself also bear this condition. In integrated situations where blacks must compete with whites who may be better prepared, these explanations may quickly wear thin and expose the individual to racial as well as personal self-doubt.

All of this is compounded by the cultural myth of black inferiority that blacks have always lived with. What this means in practical terms is that when blacks deliver themselves into integrated situations, they encounter a nasty little reflex in whites, a mindless, atavistic reflex that responds to the color black with alarm. Attributions may follow this alarm if the white cares to indulge them, and if they do, they will most likely be negative—one such attribution is intellectual ineptness. I think this reflex and the attributions that may follow it embarrass most

whites today, therefore, it is usually quickly repressed. Nevertheless, on an equally atavistic level, the black will be aware of the reflex his color triggers and will feel a stab of horror at seeing himself reflected in this way. He, too, will do a quick repression, but a lifetime of such stabbings is what constitutes his inner realm of racial doubt.

The effects of this may be a subject for another essay. The point here is that the implication of inferiority that racial preferences engender in both the white and black mind expands rather than contracts this doubt. Even when the black sees no implication of inferiority in racial preferences, he knows that whites do, so that—consciously or unconsciously—the result is virtually the same. The effect of preferential treatment—the lowering of normal standards to increase black representation—puts blacks at war with an expanded realm of debilitating doubt, so that the doubt itself becomes an unrecognized preoccupation that undermines their ability to perform, especially in integrated situations. On largely white campuses, blacks are five times more likely to drop out than whites. Preferential treatment, no matter how it is justified in the light of day, subjects blacks to a midnight of self-doubt, and so often transforms their advantage into a revolving door.

Another liability of affirmative action comes from the fact that it indirectly encourages blacks to exploit their own past victimization as a source of power and privilege. Victimization, like implied inferiority, is what justifies preference, so that to receive the benefits of preferential treatment one must, to some extent, become invested in the view of one's self as a victim. In this way, affirmative action nurtures a victim-focused identity in blacks. The obvious irony here is that we become inadvertently invested in the very condition we are trying to overcome. Racial preferences send us the message that there is more power in our past suffering than our present achievements—none of which could bring us a *preference* over others.

When power itself grows out of suffering, then blacks are encouraged to expand the boundaries of what qualifies as racial oppression, a situation that can lead us to paint our victimization in vivid colors, even as we receive the benefits of preference. The same corporations and institutions that give us preference are also seen as our oppressors. At Stanford University minority students—some of whom enjoy as much as $15,000 a year in financial aid—recently took over the president's office demanding, among other things, more financial aid. The power to be found in victimization, like any power, is intoxicating and can lend itself to the creation of a new class of super-victims who can feel the pea of victimization under twenty mattresses. Preferential treatment rewards us for being underdogs rather than for moving beyond that status—a misplacement of incentives that, along with its deepening of our doubt, is more a yoke than a spur.

But, I think, one of the worst prices that blacks pay for preference has to do with an illusion. I saw this illusion at work recently in the mother of a middle-class black student who was going off to his first semester of college. "They owe us this, so don't think for a minute that you don't belong there." This is the logic by which many blacks, and some whites, justify affirmative action—it is something "owed," a form of reparation. But this logic overlooks a much harder and less digestible reality, that it is impossible to repay blacks living today for the historic suffering of the race. If all blacks were given a million dollars tomorrow morning it would not amount to a dime on the dollar of three centuries of oppression, nor would it obviate the residues of that oppression that we still carry today. The concept of historic reparation grows out of man's need to impose a degree of justice on the world that simply does not exist. Suffering can be endured and overcome, it cannot be repaid. Blacks cannot be repaid for the injustice done to the race, but we can be corrupted by society's guilty gestures of repayment.

Affirmative action is such a gesture. It tells us that racial preferences can do for us what we cannot do for ourselves. The corruption here is in the hidden incentive *not* to do what we believe preferences will do. This is an incentive to be reliant on others just as we are struggling for self-reliance. And it keeps alive the illusion that we can find some deliverance in repayment. The hardest thing for any sufferer to accept is that his suffering excuses him from very little and never has enough currency to restore him. To think otherwise is to prolong the suffering. . . .

The mandates of black power and white absolution out of which preferences emerged were not wrong in themselves. What was wrong was that both races focused more on the goals of these mandates than on the means of the goals. Blacks can have no real power without taking responsibility for their own educational and economic development. Whites can have no racial innocence without earning it by eradicating discrimination and helping the disadvantaged to develop. Because we ignored the means, the goals have not been reached, and the real work remains to be done.

NO

Herman Schwartz

IN DEFENSE OF AFFIRMATIVE ACTION

The Reagan administration's assault on the rights of minorities and women has focused on the existing policy of affirmative action. This strategy may be shrewd politics but it is mean-spirited morally and insupportable legally. . . .

Affirmative action has been defined as "a public or private program designed to equalize hiring and admission opportunities for historically disadvantaged groups by taking into consideration those very characteristics which have been used to deny them equal treatment." The controversy swirls primarily around the use of numerical goals and timetables for hiring or promotion, for university admissions, and for other benefits. It is fueled by the powerful strain of individualism that runs through American history and belief.

It is a hard issue, about which reasonable people can differ. Insofar as affirmative action is designed to compensate the disadvantaged for past racism, sexism, and other discrimination, many understandably believe that today's society should not have to pay for their ancestors' sins. But somehow we must undo the cruel consequences of the racism and sexism that still plague us, both for the sake of the victims and to end the enormous human waste that costs society so much. Civil Rights Commission Chairman Pendleton has conceded that discrimination is not only still with us but is, as he put it, "rampant." As recently as January 1984, the dean of faculty at Amherst College wrote in the *New York Times:*

> In my contacts with a considerable range of academic institutions, I have become aware of pervasive residues of racism and sexism, even among those whose intentions and conscious beliefs are entirely nondiscriminatory. Indeed, I believe most of us are afflicted with such residues. Beyond the wrongs of the past are the wrongs of the present. Most discriminatory habits in academia are nonactionable; affirmative action goals are our only instrument for focusing sustained attention.

The plight of black America not only remains grave, but in many respects, it is getting worse. The black unemployment rate—21 percent in early 1983— is double that for whites and the gap continues to increase. For black

From Herman Schwartz, "In Defense of Affirmative Action," *Dissent* (Fall 1984). Adapted from Herman Schwartz, "In Defense of Affirmative Action," in Leslie Dunbar, ed., *Minority Report* (Pantheon Books, 1984). Copyright © 1984 by Herman Schwartz. Reprinted by permission of Pantheon Books, a division of Random House, Inc.

20- to 24-year-old males, the rate—an awful 30 percent—is almost triple that for whites; for black teenagers the rate approaches 50 percent. More than half of all black children under three years of age live in homes below the poverty line. The gap between white and black family income, which prior to the '70s had narrowed a bit, has steadily edged wider, so that black-family income is now only 55 percent of that of whites. Only 3 percent of the nation's lawyers and doctors are black and only 4 percent of its managers, but over 50 percent of its maids and garbage collectors. Black life expectancy is about six years less than that of whites; the black infant mortality rate is nearly double.

Although the situation for women, of all races, is not as bad, the average earnings of women still, at most, are only two-thirds of those of their male counterparts. And the economic condition of black women, who now head 41 percent of the 6.4 million black families, is particularly bad; a recent Wellesley study found that black women are not only suffering in the labor market, but they receive substantially less public assistance and child support than white women. The economic condition of female household heads of any race is just as deplorable: 90 percent of the 4 million single-parent homes are headed by women, and more than half are below the poverty line. Bureau of Labor Statistics data reveal that in 1983 women actually earned *less* than two-thirds of their male counterparts' salaries, and black women earned only 84 percent of the white female incomes. In his 1984 State of the Union address, President Reagan claimed dramatic gains for women during the 1983 recovery. A *Washington Post* analysis the next day charitably described his claims as "overstated," noting that the Bureau of Labor Statistics reports (on which the president relied) showed that "there was no breakthrough. The new jobs which the president cited included many in sales and office work, where women have always found work" and are paid little.

We must close these gaps so that we do not remain two nations, divided by race and gender. Although no one strategy can overcome the results of centuries of inequity, the use of goals and timetables in hiring and other benefit distribution programs has helped to make modest improvements. Studies in 1983 show, for example, that from 1974 to 1980 minority employment with employers subject to federal affirmative action requirements rose 20 percent, almost twice the increase elsewhere. Employment of women by covered contractors rose 15 percent, but only 2 percent among others. The number of black police officers nationwide rose from 24,000 in 1970 to 43,500 in 1980; that kind of increase in Detroit produced a sharp decline in citizen hostility toward the police and a concomitant increase in police efficiency. There were also large jumps in minority and female employment among firefighters, and sheet metal and electrical workers.

Few other remedies work as well or as quickly. As the New York City Corporation Counsel told the Supreme Court in the *Fullilove* case about the construction industry (before Mayor Edward Koch decided that affirmative action was an "abomination"), "less drastic means of attempting to eradicate and remedy discrimination have been attempted repeatedly and continuously over the past decade and a half. They have all failed."

What, then, is the basis for the assault on affirmative action?

Apart from the obvious political expediency and ideological reflex of this administration's unvarying conclusion that the "haves" deserve government help and the "have-nots" don't, President Reagan and his allies present two related arguments: (1) hiring and other distributional decisions should be made solely on the basis of individual merit; (2) racial preferences are always evil and will take us back to *Plessy vs. Ferguson* and worse.

Quoting Dr. Martin Luther King Jr., Thurgood Marshall, and Roy Wilkins to support the claim that anything other than total race neutrality is "discriminatory," Assistant Attorney General Reynolds warns that race consciousness will "creat[e] . . . a racial spoils system in America," "stifle the creative spirit," erect artificial barriers, and divide the society. It is, he says, unconstitutional, unlawful, and immoral.

Midge Decter, writing in the *Wall Street Journal* a few years ago, sympathized with black and female beneficiaries of affirmative action programs for the "self-doubts" and loss of "self-regard" that she is sure they suffer, "spiritually speaking," for their "unearned special privileges."

Whenever we take race into account to hand out benefits, declares Linda Chavez, the new executive director of the Reagan Civil Rights Commission, we "discriminate," "destroy[ing] the sense of self."

The legal position was stated by Morris Abram, in explaining why the reshaped Commission hastened to do Reagan's bidding at its very first meeting by withdrawing prior Commission approval of goals and timetables:

I do not need any further study of a principle that comes from the basic bedrock of the Constitution, in which the words say that every person in the land shall be entitled to the equal protection of the law. Equal means equal. Equal does not mean you have separate lists of blacks and whites for promotion, any more than you have separate accommodations for blacks and whites for eating. Nothing will ultimately divide a society more than this kind of preference and this kind of reverse discrimination.

In short, any form of race preference is equivalent to racism.

All of this represents a nadir of "Newspeak," all too appropriate for this administration in Orwell's year. For it has not only persistently fought to curtail minority and women's rights in many contexts, but it has used "separate lists" based on color, sex, and ethnic origin whenever politically or otherwise useful.

For example, does anyone believe that blacks like Civil Rights Commission Chairman Clarence Pendleton or Equal Employment Opportunities Commission Chairman Clarence Thomas were picked because of the color of their eyes? Or that Linda Chavez Gersten was made the new executive director for reasons having nothing to do with the fact that her maiden and professional surname is Chavez?

Perhaps the most prominent recent example of affirmative action is President Reagan's selection of Sandra Day O'Connor for the Supreme Court. Obviously, she was on a "separate list," because on any unitary list this obscure lower-court state judge, with no federal experience and no national reputation, would never have come to mind as a plausible choice for the highest court. (Incidentally, despite Ms. Decter's, Mr. Reynolds's, and Ms. Chavez's concern about the loss of "self-regard" suffered by beneficiaries of such preferences, "spiritually speaking" Justice O'Connor seems to be bearing her loss and spiritual pain quite easily.) And, like so many other beneficiaries of affirmative action given an opportunity that would otherwise be unavailable, she may perform well.

This is not to say that Reagan should not have chosen a woman. The appointment ended decades of shameful discrimination against women lawyers, discrimination still practiced by Reagan where the lower courts are concerned, since he has appointed very few female federal judges apart from Justice O'Connor—of 123 judgeships, Reagan has appointed no women to the courts of appeals and only 10 to the district benches. Of these judgeships, 86 percent went to white males. But the choice of Sandra O'Connor can be explained and justified only by the use of affirmative action and a separate list, not by some notion of neutral "individual merit" on a single list.

But is affirmative action constitutional and legal? Is its legal status, as Mr. Abram claims, so clear by virtue of principles drawn from the "basic bedrock of the Constitution" that no "further study" is necessary?

Yes, but not in the direction that he and this administration want to go. Affirmative action is indisputably constitutional. Not once but many times the Supreme Court has upheld the legality of considering race to remedy the wrongs of prejudice and discrimination. In 1977, for example, in *United Jewish Organizations vs. Carey*, the Supreme Court upheld a New York statute that "deliberately increased the nonwhite majorities in certain districts in order to enhance the opportunity for election of nonwhite representatives from those districts," even if it disadvan-taged certain white Jewish communities. Three members of the Court including Justice Rehnquist explained that "no racial slur or stigma with respect to whites or any other race" was involved. In the *Bakke* case, five members of the Court upheld the constitutionality of a state's favorable consideration of race as a factor in university admissions, four members would have sustained a fixed 16 percent quota. In *United Steelworkers of America vs. Weber*, a 5:2 majority held that private employers could set up a quota system with separate lists for selecting trainees for a newly created craft program. In *Fullilove vs. Klutznick*, six members of the Court led by Chief Justice Burger unequivocally upheld a congressional set-aside of 10 percent for minority contractors on federal public works programs.

All members of the present Court except for Justice O'Connor have passed on affirmative action in one or more of these four cases, and each has upheld it at one time or another. Although the decisions have been based on varying grounds, with many differing opinions, the legal consequence is clear: affirmative action is lawful under both the Constitution and the statutes. To nail the point home, the Court in January 1984 not once but *twice* rejected the Justice Department's effort to get it to reconsider the issue where affirmative action hiring plans are adopted by governmental bodies (the Detroit Police Department and the New York State Corrections system), an issue left open in *Weber*, which had involved a private employer.

The same result obtains on the lower-court levels. Despite the persistent efforts of Reagan's Justice Department, all the courts of appeals have unanimously and repeatedly continued to sustain hiring quotas.

Nor is this anything new. Mr. Reynolds told an audience of prelaw students in January 1984 that the Fourteenth Amendment was intended to bar taking race into account for any purpose at all, and to ensure race neutrality. "That was why we fought the Civil War," he once told the *New York Times*. If so, he knows something that the members of the 1865–66 Congress, who adopted that amendment and fought the war, did not.

Less than a month after Congress approved the Fourteenth Amendment in 1866 the very same Congress enacted eight laws exclusively for the freedman, granting preferential benefits regarding land, education, banking facilities, hospitals, and more. No comparable programs existed or were established for whites. And that Congress knew what it was doing. The racial preferences involved in those programs were vigorously debated with a vocal minority led by President Andrew Johnson, who argued that the preferences wrongly discriminated against whites.

All these governmental actions reflect the obvious point that, as Justice Harry Blackmun has said, "in order to get beyond racism, we must first take account of race. There is no other way." Warren Burger, our very conservative chief justice, had made the point even clearer in the prophetic commentary on this administration's efforts to get the courts to ignore race when trying to remedy the ravages of past discrimination. Striking down in 1971 a North Carolina statute that barred considerations of race in school assignments, the chief justice said:

> The statute exploits an apparently neutral form to control school assignments' plans by directing that they be "color blind"; *that requirement, against the back-*

ground of segregation, would render illusory the promise of Brown. Just as the race of students must be considered in determining whether a constitutional violation has occurred so also must race be considered in formulating a remedy . . . [color blindness] would deprive school authorities of the one tool [race consideration] absolutely essential to fulfillment of their constitutional obligation to eliminate existing dual school systems. . . . [Emphasis added.]

But what of the morality of affirmative action? Does it amount to discrimination? Is it true, as Brian Weber's lawyer argued before the Supreme Court, that "you can't avoid discrimination by discriminating"? Will racially influenced hiring take us back to *Plessy vs. Ferguson*, as Pendleton and Reynolds assert? Were Martin Luther King, Jr., Thurgood Marshall, Roy Wilkins, and other black leaders against it?

Hardly. Indeed, it is hard to contain one's outrage at this perversion of what Dr. King, Justice Marshall, and others have said, at this manipulation of their often sorrow-laden eloquence, in order to deny a handful of jobs, school admissions, and other necessities for a decent life to a few disadvantaged blacks out of the many who still suffer from discrimination and would have few opportunities otherwise.

No one can honestly equate a remedial preference for a disadvantaged (and qualified) minority member with the brutality inflicted on blacks and other minorities by Jim Crow laws and practices. The preference may take away some benefits from some white men, but none of them is being beaten, lynched, denied the right to use a bathroom, a place to sleep or eat, being forced to take the dirtiest jobs or denied any work at all, forced to attend dilapidated and mind-killing schools, subjected to brutally unequal justice, or stigmatized as an inferior being.

Setting aside, after proof of discrimination, a few places a year for qualified minorities out of hundreds and perhaps thousands of employees, as in the Kaiser plant in the *Weber* case, or 16 medical-school places out of 100 as in *Bakke*, or 10 percent of federal public work contracts as in *Fullilove*, or even 50 percent of new hires for a few years as in some employment cases—this has nothing in common with the racism that was inflicted on helpless minorities, and it is a shameful insult to the memory of the tragic victims to lump together the two.

This administration claims that it does favor "affirmative action" of a kind: "employers should seek out and train minorities," Linda Chavez told a *Washington Post* interviewer. Apart from the preference involved in setting aside money for "seeking out" and "training" minorities (would this include preference in training programs like the *Weber* plan, whose legality Mr. Reynolds said was "wrongly decided"?), the proposed remedy is ineffectual—it just doesn't work. As the "old" Civil Rights Commission had reported, "By the end of the 1960s, enforcement officials realized that discernible indicators of progress were needed." Consequently, "goals and timetables" came into use. . . .

There are indeed problems with affirmative action, but not of the kind or magnitude that Messrs. Reynolds and Abram claim: problems about whether these programs work, whether they impose heavy burdens, how these burdens can be lightened, and the like. They are not the basis for charges that affirmative action is equivalent to racism and for perverting the words of Dr. King and others.

"Equal is equal" proclaims Morris Abram, and that's certainly true. But it is just as true that equal treatment of unequals perpetuates and aggravates inequality. And gross inequality is what we still have today. As William Coleman, secretary of transportation in the Ford administration, put it,

> For black Americans, racial equality is a tradition without a past. Perhaps, one day America will be color-blind. It takes an extraordinary ignorance of actual life in America today to believe that day has come. . . . [For blacks], there is another American "tradition"—one of slavery, segregation, bigotry, and injustice.

POSTSCRIPT

Is Affirmative Action Reverse Discrimination?

Much of the argument between Steele and Schwartz turns on the question of color blindness. To what extent should U.S. laws be color-blind? During the 1950s and early 1960s, civil rights leaders were virtually unanimous on this point. "I have a dream," said Martin Luther King, "[that white and black people] will not be judged by the color of their skin but on the content of their character." This was the consensus view in 1963, but today Schwartz seems to be suggesting that the statement needs to be qualified. In order to *bring about* color blindness, it may be necessary to become temporarily color conscious. But for how long? And is there a danger that this temporary color consciousness may become a permanent policy?

Robert M. O'Neil, in *Discriminating Against Discrimination* (Indiana, 1975), studies preferential admission to universities and supports preferential treatment without racial quotas. Steven L. Carter's *Reflections of an Affirmative Action Baby* (Basic Books, 1991) is based on the author's own experiences under affirmative action. Frederick R. Lynch's *Invisible Victims: White Males and the Crisis of Affirmative Action* (Greenwood Press, 1989) traces some of the effects of affirmative action on society and other groups within it. Lee Sigelman and Susan Welch, *Black Americans' Views of Racial Inequality: The Dream Deferred* (Cambridge University Press, 1991), argue that blacks and whites have basically different perspectives of the racial situation, though they also note that there is little agreement in the black community about how government should address the problem of inequality. The focus of Allan P. Sindler's *Bakke, DeFunis, and Minority Admissions* (Longman, 1978) is on affirmative action in higher education.

Whatever the Supreme Court says today or in the future, it will not be easy to lay to rest the issue of affirmative action. There are few issues on which opposing sides are more intransigent. It appears as if there is no easily found compromise that can satisfy the passionately held convictions of both sides.

ISSUE 12

Helping the Homeless: Do We Need More Government Regulation?

YES: Peter Dreier and Richard Appelbaum, from "American Nightmare: Homelessness," *Challenge* (March/April 1991)

NO: William Tucker, from "How Housing Regulations Cause Homelessness," *The Public Interest* (Winter 1991)

ISSUE SUMMARY

YES: Peter Dreier, a housing authority administrator, and sociologist Richard Appelbaum explain homelessness as largely due to skyrocketing housing prices and federal housing cuts. The solution to the housing crisis lies not in freeing up the market but in implementing government programs, including subsidies.
NO: *Forbes* magazine staff writer William Tucker blames the housing crisis and homelessness in large part on government policies, particularly rent control.

Sleeping in cars or alleyways, begging in the streets, inhabiting bus and train stations, America's homeless have become a national scandal. Nobody knows for sure how many there are. The estimates range from a low of about a quarter of a million cited by the Department of Housing and Urban Development in a 1984 study to a high of 2 or 3 million, cited by homeless advocacy groups. Nobody is even certain of what causes homelessness, although there are plenty of hypotheses. These tend to vary according to ideology. Leftists attribute homelessness to structural failures of American capitalism, which, they claim, make the rich richer and the poor poorer. Liberals blame it on penny-pinching Republican economics, which led to cutbacks in government housing programs. Social conservatives say it comes from the breakdown of families and from the "deinstitutionalization" of the sixties and early seventies, which emptied the inmates of mental institutions into city streets. Economic conservatives blame rent control and other well-intended government interventions in the market economy. All of these explanations probably contain at least grains of truth, and some of them a good deal more. The U.S. economy has not been able to suppress its cyclical ups and downs, and during recession periods the homelessness problem gets worse. Even during good times, policymakers have not been able to find a satisfactory answer to the problem of the "underclass," the chronically unemployed and dependent. Even for those who do work there is a shortage of affordable housing in some major American cities. But homelessness has other roots as well. The mentally ill have been deinstitutionalized in large numbers since the 1960s. The major purpose of this policy was to improve the quality of life of the patients, but for many of these former inmates the results turned out to be disastrous. Assumptions about the kind of care that they could receive in the community proved false, or the released patients failed to avail themselves of the services provided. Drug addicts also swelled the population of the homeless (some estimates put them at a third of New York City's homeless population), adding to the sense that homelessness is a kind of social disease and increasing much of the public's desire to solve the problem by "sweeping the streets" of the homeless.

Clearly, then, the tragedy of homelessness is multifaceted. One part of the solution is to increase the housing supply. During the Reagan administration, Congress, at the urging of the president, diminished the money allocated to build low-income housing, but Reagan increased the funds available for rent vouchers. Vouchers or low-income housing could be made part of a new housing agenda. If low-income housing is tried, some means must be found to prevent it from deteriorating into crime-ridden "projects." Affordable housing is also constricted at the local level by tangles of bureaucratic regulations, often enforced by incompetent and corrupt officials. Local laws may also have the unintended effect of causing the deterioration, abandonment, and destruction of buildings. Lawmakers may need to reexamine existing political structures, laws, and financial commitments in order to make housing available to those who live in it and take care of it. But a significant percentage of the homeless need more than that. They need to be taken in from the streets and cared for in proper institutions. Aside from the staggering costs involved, which the public seems increasingly reluctant to assume, it has become almost impossible to legally confine people against their will unless it can be proven that they pose *immediate* danger to themselves or others.

A comprehensive approach to homelessness, then, may require sacrifices from many different quarters. Civil libertarians may have to modify their opposition to enforced confinement of the mentally ill and screening policies for admission to low-income housing; taxpayers may have to dig deeper into their pockets in order to expand housing, institutionalization, and drug treatment programs; and residents may have to tolerate different classes of people moving into their neighborhoods. In the meantime, there is much to be learned about the nature and the causes of homelessness—to which both of the readings presented here make significant contributions. Peter Dreier and Richard Appelbaum point to the inevitable bad effects of an unfettered housing and land speculation market and call for government regulations and programs. William Tucker, arguing that government regulations and programs have created the housing crisis in the first place, concludes that deregulation and vouchers provide the best means of reducing the problem.

YES

Peter Dreier and
Richard Appelbaum

AMERICAN NIGHTMARE: HOMELESSNESS

In the worst housing crisis since the Depression, many families face the spectre of homelessness. Restoring the homeownership dream means shifting national spending priorities and taking housing out of the speculative market.

During the 1980s, a new ingredient was added to the landscape of America's cities—millions of people sleeping in alleyways and subways, in cars and on park benches.

The spectacle of homeless Americans living literally in the shadow of luxury condos and yuppie boutiques symbolized the paradox of the decade: It was a period of both outrageous greed and outrageous suffering. The media gave us "lifestyles of the rich and famous," but they also offered cover stories about homeless families. And while the 1980s were often characterized as the "me decade"—an orgy of selfishness and self-interest—more Americans were involved in social issues, as volunteers and activists, than at any time in recent memory.

These contrasts are even more striking in light of the billions of dollars invested in speculative commercial real estate during the 1980s, which has led, according to a recent Salomon Brothers report, to an unprecedented high office vacancy rate. Rampant real estate speculation also contributed to the savings-and-loan debacle. The S&L bailout, perhaps the biggest rip-off in American history, may cost taxpayers over $500 billion, a regressive burden that will divert funds from much-needed economic and social recovery programs. Meanwhile, housing starts—particularly construction of low-rent apartments—have reached a postwar low while, according to a new U.S. Conference of Mayors survey, demand for emergency shelter continues to grow.

What will the 1990s bring?

Everyone from President Bush to the late advocate for the homeless Mitch Snyder has agreed that homelessness is a national tragedy and an embarrassment to America in the court of world opinion. Most Americans acknowl-

Excerpted from Peter Dreier and Richard Appelbaum, "American Nightmare: Homelessness," *Challenge*, vol. 34, no. 2 (March/April 1991). Copyright © 1991 by M. E. Sharpe, Inc., Armonk, NY 10504. Reprinted by permission.

edge that something must be done, that no great and affluent nation should tolerate such fundamental misery. And public opinion polls show that a vast majority of Americans now put solving the problem of the homeless near the top of the national agenda. According to these polls, Americans are even willing to pay higher taxes, if the funds go to assist the homeless.

It is clear to most Americans that "a thousand points of light" cannot stem the rising tide of homelessness. Public policy was responsible for creating this epidemic, and changes in public policy will be required to resolve this mounting problem. But as long as politicians, housing activists, and academic experts disagree on how many people are homeless, who they are, and why America suddenly found itself with so many people living on the streets, it will be difficult to forge a consensus on what to do. In this article, we seek to answer these questions.

MIDDLE CLASS CRISIS

No other major industrial nation has such widespread homelessness. Even Canada, a country quite similar to ours in most political and economic features, has neither the slums to match the physical and social deterioration of our inner cities, nor the level of homeless people sleeping in shelters, streets, and subways. This suggests that there is something unique about the way the United States deals with its most needy citizens; but it also suggests that a solution is within reach. Indeed, there is no reason why the United States cannot solve its homeless problem by the end of the twentieth century, if we can mobilize the political will to do so.

The growing epidemic of homelessness is only the tip of the iceberg. The United States faces its worst housing crisis since the Great Depression. The underlying problem is a widening gap between what Americans can afford to pay and what it costs to build and maintain housing. This has always been a problem for the poor; now it is a growing problem for the middle class.

The "American Dream" of homeownership is fading fast for a large segment of the middle class. Thanks to postwar federal housing programs, the rate of homeownership rose steadily for three decades, from 43.4 percent in the late 1940s to 65.6 percent in 1980. Since then, however, it has steadily declined, reaching 64.0 percent in 1989. The problem is particularly troubling for young families. For example, among twenty-five to thirty-four-year-olds, the homeownership rate dropped from 52.3 percent in 1980 to 45.2 percent in 1989. The median price of a new single-family home climbed from $69,300 in 1982 to about $120,000 today. While in 1973 it took roughly one-quarter of the median income of a young family with children to carry a new mortgage on average-priced housing, today it takes over half of a young family's income. In some regions of the country, housing prices have started to drop, but because of wage and employment trends as well as interest rates, this has not made a significant dent in overall housing affordability.

High rents make it impossible for most young families to save money for a downpayment. As a result, about the only people who can afford to purchase a home are those who already own one. Even among those who manage to buy a home, a growing number are in danger of losing their homes to foreclosure by banks.

Rents have reached a two-decade peak, according to a recent Harvard University study. This is especially a problem for the poor, who are now competing with the middle class for scarce apartments. Some 85 percent of low-income renters (5.8 million households) are paying at least 30 percent of their income for housing. Two-thirds of the poor are paying at least half of their income just for housing. The typical young single mother pays over 70 percent of her meager income just to keep a roof over her children's heads.

Perhaps the most important statistic is this: Only one-quarter of poor households receive any kind of housing subsidy—the lowest level of any industrial nation in the world. The swelling waiting lists for even the most deteriorated subsidized housing projects are telling evidence of the desperation of the poor in the private housing market.

Is it any wonder that the ranks of the homeless are growing?

FUNDAMENTAL ECONOMIC SHIFTS

The initial stereotype of the homeless person was an alcoholic or mentally ill middle-aged man or "bag lady"—many of them victims of deinstitutionalization resulting from the Community Mental Health Act of 1963. But when more low-rent housing was available, including many rooming houses that have since been lost to gentrification, even people on the margins of society could afford a roof over their heads.

The homelessness crisis is not, as some suggest, primarily a problem of personal pathology. It is, rather, a symptom of some fundamental shifts in the nation's economy.

The most important involves the deindustrialization and gentrification of our urban areas. The past fifteen years have been characterized by a tremendous flight of previously high-wage industries to low-wage countries. Since the early 1970s, the electronics revolution has hastened the development of a global economy. Footloose firms have moved their manufacturing operations to more favorable locations—with low wages, lax environmental laws, tax breaks, and other subsidies—whether these be in suburbs, rural areas, or Third World countries.

As a result of this geographic realignment, it is unlikely that American industry will soon again enjoy the once-privileged postwar position that enabled our standard of living to rise steadily for almost three decades. Many American cities have still not recovered from the loss of blue-collar industry and jobs. As factories closed down, tax bases declined, waterfronts were left vacant, and downtown department stores went out of business, some cities began to resemble ghost towns.

During the past decade, many observers have hailed the "services revolution" as the savior of cities. It is true that many cities have now shifted from what University of North Carolina sociologist John Kasarda calls "centers of production and distribution of goods to centers of administration, finance and information exchange." Cities sought to revitalize their downtown areas with new office buildings, medical and educational complexes, hotels, urban shopping malls, convention centers, and even sports complexes. But such efforts, even when successful, do not stem the growing tide of poverty only blocks away from the glittering glass and steel. In the shadow of its downtown skyscrapers, Los Angeles resembles a Third World city, its streets teeming with economically precarious low-wage workers and homeless men, women, and children.

Why? Because the services economy is predominantly a low-wage economy, and most of its jobs offer no career ladder or upward mobility. According to Bennett Harrison and Barry Bluestone, in the *The Great U-Turn*, the majority of jobs created since the 1970s have offered poverty-level wages. Working full-time is no longer a guarantee of escaping poverty. Even relatively low levels of unemployment in some cities mask the deepening poverty and desperation.

As Robert Reich has noted, the American economy has two escalators—a small one moving upward and a much larger one moving downward. More than 33 million Americans—one out of seven—now live below the poverty line. The figure for children is even more alarming: one of every four (and one-half of all black children) live in poverty. Today's poor people are poorer and likely to remain poor for longer periods of time. During the 1980s, both the minimum wage and Aid For Dependent Children (AFDC) benefit levels fell far behind the rate of inflation.

Not surprisingly, more and more of America's homeless are families with children and people with jobs. A survey released in December 1990 by the U.S. Conference of Mayors found that almost one-quarter of the homeless work, but have wages too low to afford permanent housing. Apart from those who live on the streets or in shelters, there are millions more who live doubled-up or tripled-up in overcrowded apartments, and millions of others who pay more than they can reasonably afford for substandard housing. As a result of this situation, millions of low-income Americans are only one rent increase, one hospital stay, one layoff away from becoming homeless.

Things are getting worse for the middle class as well. In recent years, the average middle class American has seen family income stagnate. In 1960, the typical thirty-year-old head of household could expect family income to increase by 50 percent during the next decade. Today, he or she can expect family income (real buying power) to decline. According to a recent Children's Defense Fund report, young families (headed by someone under thirty) have seen their incomes erode by one-quarter over the past fifteen years; among Hispanics, the decline has been one-third; among Blacks, one-half.

For a small, but very visible, segment of the population, however, these new economic forces have led to the up-escalator. The services economy has created a stratum of highly-educated, well-paid management and professional workers. They, along with top-level executives and owners of wealth, did well during the decade of corporate takeovers and leveraged buyouts. The share of national income now going to the wealthiest 20 percent is the highest since World War II. Meanwhile, the share going to the poorest 40 percent is the lowest in that period. By dramatically lowering tax rates of the affluent and big business, the Reagan Administration exacerbated these trends and redistributed income from the working class to the wealthy. President Bush's proposal to cut capital gains taxes would continue this trend.

All this pertains directly to housing. While America was witnessing a growing disparity of incomes, the affluent began viewing a house less as a home than as an investment, as valuable for its tax benefits as for its Victorian details. Young baby boom generation professionals moved into urban neighborhoods, especially those close to the downtown core, where they found work in the growing service sector. Housing that had been abandoned or devalued decades earlier became more attractive to so-called "yuppies." As the affluent and the poor began to compete for scarce inner-city housing, prices skyrocketed. Low-rent apartments were converted to high-priced condominiums. Rooming houses, the last refuge of the poor, were torn down or turned into upscale apartments. Businesses catering to the poor and working class families were replaced by high-priced shops and restaurants.

The housing market failed to expand significantly the overall number of apartments, because it simply isn't profitable to build housing for the poor. The situation was made worse when the Reagan Administration removed the two props that once served to entice some private investors into providing low-rent housing—subsidies which bring housing costs and poor peoples' incomes into line, and tax shelters which indirectly produce the same result.

THE ROLE OF GOVERNMENT

The dramatic escalation of housing prices during the 1980s—and the ongoing affordability gap—stems from three basic factors. First, nearly everyone involved in housing is trying to maximize profits—including land development, materials manufacture, construction, rentals, and capital gains. For example, the average price of a residential lot has increased 813 percent in the past twenty years, from $5,200 in 1969 to $42,300 in 1989; more than half of that increase occurred in the last five years alone. Second, the cost of credit (the money borrowed to build and buy housing) adds a large and permanent cost to every housing unit. For homeowners, roughly two out of every three housing dollars goes to pay off the mortgage. For renters (who pay these costs indirectly), the proportion is often higher. Third, because housing is viewed as an investment by developers, landlords, and most homeowners, home prices and rents are often much higher than what it actually costs to build and operate housing. Both homeowners and landlords expect to sell their buildings for much more than they paid for them— a psychological and economic factor known as speculation. Government policies can exacerbate or curb these market-driven forces.

One way for the federal government to help close the gap between incomes and housing expenses is through a variety of consumer and developer subsidies. The magnitude of federal housing resources was never adequate, but the Reagan Administration made the situation worse. Housing shouldered the largest burden of the Reagan budget axe. Since 1981, federal housing assistance has been slashed from about $33 billion to less than $8 billion a year. The number of new federally subsidized apartments built each year dwindled from over 200,000 in the 1970s to less than 15,000 last year. To put this in perspective, in 1981 the federal government was spending seven dollars for defense for every one dollar it spent on housing. By 1989, it spent over forty dollars on defense for every housing dollar.

The increase in homelessness parallels these federal housing cuts. And although President Bush and Housing and Urban

Development (HUD) Secretary Jack Kemp have promised to deal with the nation's homelessness scandal, the Bush Administration actually proposed further housing cutbacks in its 1991 budget proposal, but was rebuffed by Congress. Bush's 1992 budget proposed further housing cuts.

The single housing subsidy that did *not* fall to the Reagan (and now Bush) budget axe is the one that goes to the very rich. The federal tax code allows homeowners to deduct all property tax and mortgage interest from their income taxes. This cost the federal government $34 billion in 1990 alone—more than four times the HUD budget for low-income housing. Over three-quarters of the foregone tax revenue goes to the 15.1 percent of taxpayers who earn over $50,000 annually; one-third of this subsidy goes to the 3.1 percent of taxpayers with incomes over $100,000. Over half of all homeowners do not claim deductions at all. Tenants, of course, don't even qualify. In other words, our nation's housing subsidies disproportionately benefit homeowners with high incomes, often with two homes. The *Washington Post* recently revealed, for example, that Sen. John D. (Jay) Rockefeller of West Virginia receives a tax subsidy worth about $223,000 a year just on his $1.5-million Washington mansion.

Another housing role for federal and state governments is to regulate lenders in order to guarantee a supply of credit for builders and homeowners. The government can control interest rates, require banks to meet community credit needs, and protect savings-and-loans to guarantee credit for the average homeowner. The Reagan Administration, however, dismantled most of the federal policies designed to regulate lenders. Reagan's policies resulted in a frenzy of speculative lending, mismanagement, and corruption by the nation's savings-and-loan industry during the past decade. President Bush has proposed a bailout of failing savings-and-loans which will fall primarily on low- and middle-income taxpayers, and which now looks as if it will swell to over $500 billion. And Bush's new plan to restructure the nation's banks does nothing to promote lending for homeownership or to encourage community development.

Finally, state and local governments can regulate land use, through zoning laws, to promote affordable housing development. Instead, most localities, particularly suburbs, use these regulations ("snob zoning") to keep out the poor. They can establish codes regulating the safety and health of new and existing buildings, but few state or local governments allocate adequate resources to enforce these laws, particularly in poor neighborhoods. They can also protect consumers by regulating rents, evictions, and condominium conversions. However, only a few local politicians are willing to buck the powerful real estate industry.

THE POLITICS OF HOUSING

In the past, the major political force for housing programs was the real estate industry—developers, mortgage bankers, landlords, and brokers. They, of course, wanted Congress to enact policies to help build more housing for the middle class or to provide subsidies to make it lucrative to house the poor. Developers, realtors, and mortgage bankers have been the most generous contributors to congressional and presidential candidates, and their national associations have strong political action committees, deep pockets, and effective local networks. In turn, many members of Congress have ties to developers and have lobbied HUD or bank regulators on their behalf.

But even the housing industry's clout couldn't offset the Reagan Administration's determination to slash federal housing funds, which suffered the biggest cuts of any domestic program. Recently, some conservative politicians and editorial writers have cynically used the corruption scandal at HUD as an excuse to dismantle federal housing programs even further. House Minority Whip Newt Gingrich (R-Ga.), *The Wall Street Journal*, and *The New Republic* have called for folding up HUD's tent and replacing it with a voucher program, an approach long-advocated by HUD Secretary Jack Kemp. But rent vouchers, on their own, won't solve the problem. About one million low-income households already receive such vouchers, which are intended to help them pay rent for apartments in the private market. But in cities with low rental vacancy rates, handing out vouchers is like providing food stamps when the grocery shelves are empty. About half the low-income tenants who now receive vouchers return them unused because apartments are so scarce. Clearly, we must increase the overall *supply* of low-income housing.

The Bush Administration has never acknowledged that more affordable housing is the only workable solution to homelessness. His proposed budget significantly *reduced* funding for new housing, while providing only minimal increases for emergency shelters and vouchers. In October, Congress enacted legislation that called for a slight increase in new housing funds. In January, however, Bush unveiled a 1992 budget proposal that called for *reduced* funding for new housing,

while providing only minimal increases for emergency shelters and vouchers.

Ironically, one hopeful sign is that Jack Kemp's political ambitions have made him the most vocal and visible HUD Secretary in memory. In sharp contrast to his predecessor, Samuel Pierce, Kemp has been a high-profile Cabinet member, although his clout within the Bush Administration does not appear to parallel his public visibility. He visits shelters, meets with advocates and builders, and testifies before Congress. Although his approach to urban housing problems (vouchers, selling off public housing, creating "enterprise zones" in inner cities) and his budget proposals are woefully inadequate, his enthusiasm and visibility have helped keep the housing issue in the media. History suggests that social movements and social reform are best sown in the soil of "rising expectations." Kemp's rhetoric is clearly setting the stage for a revolt against broken promises. . . .

THE PROGRESSIVE HOUSING AGENDA

In light of the HUD scandal, the public is correctly skeptical of programs that offer big profits to politically connected developers and consultants in the name of housing the poor. However, the solution is not to scrap federal housing programs, but to build on the cost-effective successes that have recently emerged in communities across the country.

The key to a successful housing policy is to increasingly remove housing from the speculative market and transform it into limited equity, resident-controlled housing, funded through direct capital grants rather than long-term debt. That is how a significant segment of the housing industry in Canada, Sweden, and other social democratic countries is organized. In the United States, the non-profit (or "social") sector is relatively small, but it has grown significantly during the past decade.

Congressman Ron Dellums of California already has sponsored legislation tailored to this goal. The National Comprehensive Housing Act, drafted by an Institute for Policy Studies task force, calls for an annual expenditure of $50 billion. The federal government would make direct capital grants to non-profit groups to build and rehabilitate affordable housing, as well as to purchase existing, privately owned housing for transfer to non-profit organizations. These homes would remain in the "social" sector, never again to be burdened with debt. Occupants would pay only the operating costs, which would dramatically lower what poor and working class families are currently paying for housing. The Dellums bill is clearly a visionary program—a standard for judging progress on long-term housing goals—but not yet a winnable bill in the current political climate.

In fact, the major housing bill passed in Congress in October and signed by President Bush in November, if fully funded, is a mix of good and bad news. After a decade of housing cutbacks, Congress would finally increase the federal commitment to housing. After months of political wrangling, the House and Senate agreed on legislation to add only $3 billion to the current housing budget. The bill, a compromise of versions sponsored by Senator Alan Cranston (D-Cal.) and Rep. Henry Gonzalez (D-Tex.), would provide some funding to assist first-time homebuyers, to preserve the existing inventory of public and subsidized housing, to expand housing vouchers for the poor, and to expand the capacity of non-profit builders. But it would not even restore the commitment of federal government to the pre-Reagan level of housing assistance, much less move us forward. The bill incorporates a progressive initiative, the Community Housing Partnership Act, sponsored by Rep. Joseph Kennedy (D-Mass.) at the urging of Boston Mayor Ray Flynn. It targets federal funds specifically to the non-profit "social" housing sector.

This year, housing advocates hope to make the Mickey Leland Housing Assistance Act the centerpiece of their efforts. Named after the late Texas Congressman, the bill would add $125 billion in new housing funds over a five-year period.

In broad terms, there are five key areas in national housing policy that need attention:

• Expanding the supply of low- and moderate-income housing, particularly through the vehicle of non-profit housing builders. We need to build at least five million new units (500,000 a year) this decade.

• Preserving the existing inventory of public housing (1.3 million units) and subsidized private housing (two million units), which are at risk because of expiring subsidies and long-term neglect—and giving residents a greater role in management.

• Providing adequate income subsidies to the seven-to-eight million low-income families who currently receive no housing assistance and cannot afford market rents.

• Providing working class and lower-middle class young families opportunities for homeownership, in part by putting a cap on the homeownership tax subsidy for the affluent while expanding it for the rest.

• Strengthening the government's regulation of banks and other financial institutions, particularly in terms of allocating credit for homebuyers, eliminating discrimination in lending, making the wealthy pay for the S&L bail-out and putting consumer representatives on the Federal Reserve Bank.

In light of the war in the Persian Gulf, there is no guarantee that we will see a "peace dividend" to invest in housing, child care, health care, education, rebuilding the infrastructure, and other much-needed domestic programs. Without it, however, the nation cannot address its other gulf crises—the widening gulf between the wealthy and the rest of America, as well as the growing gulf in competitiveness between the United States and the rest of the world. There is no question that we must shift national spending priorities to solve our formidable domestic crises, including the lack of adequate housing for our population. This is the most urgent political issue we face today. And whether the nation's leaders seize this historic moment to act effectively in our best domestic national interests, is a question of political will, not resources.

NO

William Tucker

HOW HOUSING REGULATIONS CAUSE HOMELESSNESS

The problem of homelessness in the 1980s has puzzled liberals and conservatives alike. Both have tended to fit the problem into their preconceived views, without looking at what is new and different about the phenomenon.

For liberals, the issue has been fairly straightforward. Homelessness, they say, stems from a lack of government effort and compassion. Reacting almost reflexively, liberals have blamed homelessness on federal spending cuts and the heartlessness of the Reagan administration. The most commonly cited figure is that budget authorizations for the Department of Housing and Urban Development (HUD) were cut 75 percent in the Reagan years, from $32 billion in 1981 to $8 billion in 1988. Everything else is presumably self-explanatory. This compelling logic has even been repeated in the *Wall Street Journal*.

Conservatives, on the other hand, have taken two approaches. Either they deny the problem's existence or they assert that homelessness is almost always the result of personal pathologies. On the first count, it has often been argued (as in Martin Morse Wooster's June 1987 *Reason* article, "The Homeless: An Adman's Dream") that homelessness is really no worse than it ever was, but that the problem has been exaggerated to justify increases in government spending. On the other, conservatives have also argued that most of the homeless are insane, alcoholics, or drug addicts, and that their personal failings make it impossible for them to find housing, even when it is available.

UNPERSUASIVE EXPLANATIONS

But these arguments, whether liberal or conservative, do not really hold up under close scrutiny.

The most obviously flawed explanation lies in the figures that seem to indicate a massive federal cutback in housing assistance. There has been no such cutback. Federal low-income housing assistance actually *increased* from $5.7 billion in 1980 to $13.8 billion in 1988. The number of households

From William Tucker, "How Housing Regulations Cause Homelessness," *The Public Interest*, no. 102 (Winter 1991), pp. 78–88. Copyright © 1991 by National Affairs, Inc. Reprinted by permission of *The Public Interest* and the author.

receiving low-income housing assistance also rose, going from 3.1 million to 4.2 million during the same period.

The commonly cited "cutback" from $32 billion to $8 billion is the figure for HUD's future authorizations. This figure has nothing to do with actual housing assistance, however, since it only indicates the amount of money that Congress authorized HUD to spend in the future. These authorizations often run forty years in advance—and much of the money is never spent anyway.

The reason for this cutback has been the changeover from a program centered around public-housing construction to one centered around housing vouchers. When Congress authorizes a unit of new public housing, it must include all future mortgage payments, running decades ahead. In authorizing a housing voucher, Congress pledges money for only five years—the lifetime of the voucher.

In addition, vouchers provide the same housing at only half the price. A unit of public housing costs the federal government $8,000 a year, while a voucher costs only $4,000. Thus, twice as many people can be reached with the same amount of money. This is why HUD has been able to extend housing aid to more low-income people without an equivalent increase in spending.

But if the liberal argument about "spending cuts" is based largely on a misunderstanding of the budgetary process, the conservative argument that homelessness has not really increased at all seems equally ill-founded.

There were indeed homeless people long before 1980, and their numbers have always been difficult to count. But it is hard to ignore the almost unanimous reports from shelter providers (many of them old-line conservative church groups) that the problem has been getting steadily worse since 1980. The anecdotal evidence is also abundant. Anyone who has walked the streets of New York or Washington over the last decade knows that there are more beggars sitting on the sidewalks and sleeping on park benches than there were ten years ago.

Although many of the homeless are obviously alcoholics, drug addicts, and people who are clinically insane, large numbers appear only to be down on their luck. The most widely accepted statistical breakdown was first proposed in a 1988 Urban Institute paper: "Feeding the Homeless: Does the Prepared Meals Provision Help?" According to authors Martha Burt and Barbara Cohen, one-third of the homeless can be categorized as released mental patients, one-third as alcoholics and drug abusers, and one-third as people who are homeless for purely economic reasons.

Thus the component of homeless people who are not affected by personal pathologies is large. It should also be noted that being a chronic alcoholic or drug addict does not condemn a person to living in the streets. Even "winos" or "stumblebums" were able to find minimal housing in the past.

And so paradoxes remain. How can we have such a large homeless population at a time when rental vacancy rates are near postwar highs? How can there be plenty of housing but not enough "affordable housing"? In short, how can there be scarcity in the housing market when so much housing is still available?

VARIATIONS AMONG HOUSING MARKETS

These paradoxes can be resolved when we recognize that the housing market is not a national market but is instead the sum of many regional and local markets. Rental vacancy rates probably serve as the best measure of the availability of affordable housing, since most poor people rent. These rates vary widely from city to city. During the 1980s, rental vacancy rates in Dallas and Houston were rarely below 12 percent—a figure that is about twice what is considered a normal vacancy rate. At the same time, housing has been absurdly scarce in other cities. New York has not had vacancy rates over 3 percent since 1972. San Francisco had normal vacancy rates during the 1970s, but they plunged to 2 percent during the 1980s, where they remain today.

Since the poor tend to be limited in their mobility, vacancy rates significantly affect their ability to find housing. Although southern and southwestern cities claim to receive a regular seasonal migration of homeless people during the winter months, there is little evidence that people are moving from city to city to find housing. Other factors, like work opportunities, proximity to family members, and sheer inertia, seem to dominate people's choice of locale.

What should be far more mobile is the capital that builds housing and has created such a superabundance in specific cities. If it is difficult to find tenants for new apartments in Dallas and Phoenix, why don't builders shift to Boston or San Francisco, where housing is desperately needed?

Once we start asking this question, the impediments in the housing market suddenly become visible. It is obviously not equally easy to build housing in all cities. In particular, the local regulatory climate has a tremendous impact on the housing supply. Dallas and Houston are free-wheeling, market-oriented cities with lit-tle or no zoning regulation and negligible antigrowth sentiment. They have been able to keep abreast of housing demand even as their populations grew rapidly. Boston and San Francisco, on the other hand, have highly regulated housing markets. Both are surrounded by tight rings of exclusionary suburbs, where zoning and growth-control sentiment make new construction extremely difficult. In addition, both have adopted rent control as a way of "solving" local housing shortages. As a result, both have extremely high housing prices and extremely tight rental markets. The median home price in each approaches $200,000, while in Dallas and Phoenix the median price is below the national median of $88,000.

Thus it makes little sense to talk about a national housing market's effect on homelessness. Local markets vary widely, and municipal regulation seems to be the deciding factor.

This is what has misled both liberals and conservatives. Conservatives look at the national superabundance of housing and conclude that local problems do not exist. Liberals look at local shortages and conclude that there is a national housing problem. In fact, housing shortages are a local problem created by local regulation, which is the work of local municipal governments.

It is not surprising, then, to find that homelessness varies widely from city to city, with local housing policies once again the decisive factor. These conclusions are supported by research that I conducted in 1988: I calculated comparative rates of per-capita homelessness for various cities, using the homelessness figures for the largest thirty-five cities investigated in the 1984 *Report to the Secretary of Housing and Urban Development on the Homeless and Emergency Shelters.* I also added fifteen other large cities that were not included in the initial HUD survey. I then subjected the comparative rates of homelessness to regression analysis, in order to look for possible associations with other factors.

Among the independent variables that I considered were the local unemployment rate, the poverty rate, city size, the availability of public housing, the median rent, annual mean temperature, annual rainfall, the size of the minority population, population growth over the past fifteen years, the rental vacancy rate, the presence or absence of rent control, and the median home price in the metropolitan area surrounding each city.

Of all these variables, only four showed a significant correlation: the median home price, the rental vacancy rate, the presence of rent control, and the size of the minority population. The first three formed an overlapping cluster, with the median home price being the strongest predictor (accounting for around 42 percent of the variation, with a chance of error of less than .001 percent). The size of the minority population added about another 10 percent. The total predictive value for both factors was 51 percent, with a margin of error below .00001 percent.

When combined on a single graph (see [graph]), the figures for the forty cities for which all of the relevant data are available show a strong trendline for median home prices; the cities with rent control are predominantly clustered in the top right-hand quadrant. Of the four major cities with minority populations of more than 60 percent, the two with rent control (Newark and Washington) are right on the trendline, while the two without it (Miami and Detroit) are the sole "outliers"—cities whose rates of homelessness do not seem to correspond with their positions in correlation with median home prices.

Altogether, these data suggest that housing variables are a better indicator of homelessness than are the traditional measures of unemployment, poverty, and the relative size of a city's public housing stock. High median home prices are usually found in cities with strict zoning ordinances and a strong no-growth effort. Cities with a tight ring of exclusionary suburbs (such as Boston, New York, Washington, San Francisco, and Los Angeles) have high home prices. Strangely enough, most have also adopted rent control.

At the same time, rent control is closely correlated with low rental vacancy rates. Every city in the country with rent control (except Los Angeles) has a vacancy rate below 4 percent, while the average for cities without rent control is over 8 percent.

When viewed historically, these low vacancy rates are obviously the result of rent control rather than its cause. When most of these cities adopted rent control in the 1970s, all had vacancy rates around the norm of 6 percent. Rather than being spurred by low vacancies, the rent-control ordinances that swept the East and West Coasts during the 1970s were advertised as a response to inflation. The housing shortages came later. (New York, on the other hand, has had rent control since 1943, when it was imposed as part of World War II price controls. Vacancy rates stood at 10 percent in 1940, but have never been above 5 percent since the war ended; they have been below 3 percent since the late 1960s.)

Given these facts, the most plausible explanation of the relation of homelessness to high median home prices, low

Homelessness in Forty American Cities, Correlated with Rent Control, Size of Minority Population, and Median Home Price

(R = .649 P < .0001)

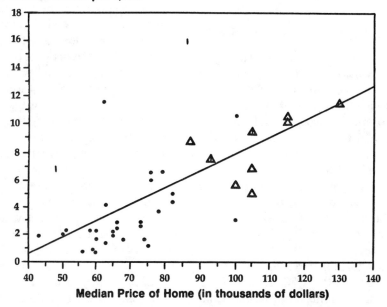

Homelessness per 1,000

Median Price of Home (in thousands of dollars)

ı Cities with Minority Populations > 60 percent △ Cities with Rent Control

• All Other Cities

rental vacancies, and the presence of rent control seems to be what might be called "intense housing regulation." Many cities, such as San Francisco, Berkeley, and Santa Monica, have adopted rent control as part of municipal efforts to slow growth and stop development. These efforts are often aimed against new housing construction, particularly of apartments and rentals.

Since most communities that adopt no-growth ordinances usually like to think of themselves as liberal-minded, they do not like to admit to limiting housing opportunities for low-income people. So they try to compensate by imposing rent control, which they claim "protects" tenants from rising rents.

But of course rent control makes things only worse, by causing vacancy rates to decline and apartments to become much harder to find. The words of Assa Lindbeck, the Swedish socialist (and now chairman of the Nobel Prize Committee for Economics) can hardly be improved upon:

The effects of rent control have in fact been exactly what can be predicted from the simplest type of supply-and-demand analysis—"housing shortage" (excess demand for housing), black markets, privileges for those who happen to have a contract for a rent-controlled apartment, nepotism in the distribution of the available apartments, difficulties in getting apartments for families with children, and, in many places, deterioration of the housing stock. In fact, next to bombing, rent control seems in many cases to be the most efficient technique so far known for destroying cities.

ATTACKS ON GROWTH AND SRO's

Perhaps the best place to see this syndrome at work is in the San Francisco area, which has some of the country's most intense and innovative housing regulation and is also generally considered to be the center of some of the nation's worst homelessness.

It may be hard to believe, but housing prices in California in 1970 were no higher than the national average—even though the state experienced astonishing population growth during the 1950s and 1960s. It was not until the wave of environmental regulation and no-growth sentiment emerged in the 1970s that housing prices began to climb. Throughout California, the increase in home prices has consistently outpaced the national average over the last two decades. By 1988, the median price for a home stood at $158,000 there, in contrast to the nationwide figure of $88,000. In the highly regulated San Francisco Bay area, the median was $178,000, more than twice the national median.

California also experienced a wave of rent-control ordinances in the 1970s. Berkeley adopted rent control in 1971, shortly after imposing a "neighborhood preservation ordinance" that all but prohibited new development. The ordinance was eventually overturned in the California courts in 1975. Then in 1978, Howard Jarvis made an ill-fated promise that Proposition 13 would lower rents by reducing property taxes. When rent reductions failed to materialize, angry tenants

in more than a dozen cities retaliated by adopting rent control.

As a result, housing in highly regulated metropolitan regions around San Francisco, San Jose, and Los Angeles has become very scarce. At the same time, homelessness has become a pronounced problem. Santa Monica, which imposed rent control in 1979 as part of an intense antidevelopment campaign, has become the homelessness capital of the West Coast.

Once growth control, tight zoning, and rent control are in place, even middle-class people may have trouble finding housing. A municipality in effect becomes a closed community, open only to its current residents (who either experience remarkable run-ups in the value of their homes or live at rents far below market) and people with strong inside connections. Mark Kann's 1986 book *Middle Class Radicalism in Santa Monica*, which generally praised the city's housing policies, speaks of a "woman who tried to get a Santa Monica apartment for more than a year without success[;] . . . she broke into the city, finally, by marrying someone who already had an apartment there."

No-growth ordinances and rent control have not, of course, been embraced everywhere; but city administrations have often produced comparable results through intense housing-code enforcement, designed to drive "undesirable" housing (and the people who live in it) out of their jurisdictions.

In *New Homeless and Old: Community and the Skid Row Hotel*, Charles Hoch and Robert Slayton have traced the disappearance of the single-room occupancy (SRO) and "cubicle" hotels that once provided cheap housing to thousands of marginal tenants in downtown Chicago. Over 8,000 of these hotel rooms—still available to Chicago's low-income transients in 1963—have disappeared, leaving barely 2,000 today. These lost accommodations were all supplied by the private market. Although remarkably inexpensive (often costing only $2 a night), these rooms offered residents exactly what they wanted—security and privacy. Most of the hotels had elaborate security systems, with desk clerks screening visitors and protecting residents from unwanted ones. In addition, the cheap hotels were usually convenient to stores and public transportation, allowing low-income residents with few family connections to lead frugal but relatively dignified lives.

What happened to these old SRO hotels? Almost without exception, they became the target of urban-renewal efforts and municipal campaigns to "clean up downtown." Intense building-code enforcement and outright condemnation drove most of them out of business. Strict zoning ordinances have since made it virtually impossible to build replacements. Hoch and Slayton conclude:

> We do not believe that the demise of Skid Row and the SRO hotels was the inevitable result of market forces, or that Skid Row residents embodied peculiar social and psychological characteristics that produced deviant and pathological social behavior. . . . [Instead,] this loss was the result of decades of antagonism from civic and business leaders, legitimated from the 1950s on by social scientists, and incorporated into dramatic change-oriented programs like urban renewal.

Nor have these policies abated today. Despite the hue and cry over the loss of SRO hotels, their replacement is still generally forbidden by zoning ordinances. In

Los Angeles, there is a movement afoot to close down SRO hotels—even those subsidized by the city government—because they are not built to withstand earthquakes. Peter Smith, president of the New York City Partnership for the Homeless, comments: "It's essentially illegal for private developers to build SRO hotels in New York anymore."

RESTRICTING DEVELOPMENT

What is causing homelessness, then, is the familiar phenomenon of government regulation. This regulation tends to escape the attention of the public and the enthusiasts of deregulation, because it is done at the local rather than the state or national level.

The truth is that cities and towns do not always welcome new development. At bottom, even the most enthusiastic advocates of progress would often prefer to see their own neighborhoods remain just as they are. People will usually settle for higher-priced housing, because it raises the value of their own homes; but few want tenements, rentals, or other forms of "low-income" housing.

Through regulation, most cities and towns hold a tight rein on their housing markets. Suburbs are particularly exclusionary, zoning out everything but high-priced single-family homes (which require large lot sizes), and prohibiting the rental of rooms or apartments. Cities themselves, although sometimes offering rhetorical welcomes, often play the same exclusionary games.

An example can be seen in Takoma Park, Maryland, a nineteenth-century "streetcar suburb" of Washington, D.C., which until recently had a long history of tolerant housing policies. Takoma Park is a hodgepodge of two-, three-, and four-family homes within easy commuting distance of Washington. During World War II, homeowners rented attics and spare bedrooms to wartime officials who could not find housing in Washington. This tradition continued after the war, when many returning GI's sought housing while attending nearby Columbia Union College. Many homeowners permanently converted their homes to two- and three-family units.

During the 1970s, however, a group of homeowners living in a recently constructed, more suburban part of the city asked Montgomery County to enforce a sixty-year-old zoning ordinance that prohibited rentals in single-family zones. (Zoning is controlled by county governments in Maryland.) After a long dispute, the city council adopted a compromise in 1978, which permitted anyone who was renting before 1954 to continue to do so for another ten years. In 1988 the reprieve expired, however, and evictions began. More than six hundred tenants were forced to leave their homes.

THE APPEAL OF UTOPIANISM

It is important to realize that housing regulations are to blame for a lot of homelessness. But at the same time, we must acknowledge the impulses that make people want to intervene in the housing marketplace.

About a year ago, I spent a few days in San Francisco's Market Street district, a notorious skid row. Although not particularly dangerous, the surroundings were decidedly unpleasant. Weather-beaten young men, each of whom seemed to have his entire worldly belongings wrapped in a sleeping bag, lounged along the sidewalks. Ragged holdovers from the sixties perched on public monuments, performing drunken imitations of rock singers. Veterans of motorcycle gangs weaved past timid pedestrians, carrying on garrulous arguments with their equally disheveled girlfriends. Along the side streets, tattoo parlors jostled with cheap cafeterias, pornography shops, and the inevitable flophouse hotels.

It is easy enough to imagine some ambitious politician surveying the scene and deciding that it was time to "clean up Market Street." Such campaigns have occurred all over the country and have inevitably produced the disjuncture that we now find between the supply of housing and the price that poor people can afford to pay for it.

Yet distasteful as it may seem, skid rows play a crucial role in providing the poor and near-poor with cheap housing. Not everyone can live in suburban subdivisions or high-rise condominiums. To provide for everyone, we also need rooms for rent, fleabag hotels, tenements, trailer parks—and the "slumlords" who often run them. Although usually imagined to be rich and powerful, these bottom-rung entrepreneurs almost always turn out to be only slightly more affluent than the people for whom they are providing housing.

In the utopian dreams of regulators and "housing activists," such landlords are always eliminated. They are inevitably replaced by the federal government and the "non-profits," orchestrated by the city planners and visionary architects who would "tear down the slums" and replace them with "model tenements" and the "garden cities of tomorrow."

It is not wrong to have such visions. But let us do things in stages. Let us build the new housing *first*—and only then tear down the old "substandard" housing that is no longer needed. If we let the best become the enemy of the good—or even the barely adequate—the homeless will have nothing more substantial to live in than the dreams of the housing visionaries themselves.

POSTSCRIPT

Helping the Homeless: Do We Need More Government Regulation?

Tucker states that "the local regulatory climate has a tremendous impact on the housing supply." Cities with heavily regulated housing markets have an acute shortage of housing and many homeless, whereas cities with unregulated housing markets have a surplus of housing and fewer homeless. Rent control in particular causes homelessness, as his data seem to show. His answer is to deregulate, and if the poor need help, give them vouchers. Dreier and Appelbaum approve of vouchers but say that they would not recommend increasing the supply of inexpensive housing. They argue that the private sector will provide plenty of housing but not plenty of inexpensive housing. Obviously the government must provide or subsidize the provision of this type of housing. They recommend nonprofit housing builders and housing subsidies. Whose policies would you follow? Would these policies solve the structural problems that cause homelessness?

The first problem in addressing homelessness is to find out the number and type of homeless persons. Much research to make an accurate estimate of the number of homeless persons has been undertaken, but the research so far has not resolved the issue. Two articles on how these estimates are done are Peter H. Rossi, "The Urban Homeless: Estimating Size and Composition," *Science* (March 13, 1987), and Constance Holden, "Homelessness: Experts Differ on Root Causes, *Science* (May 2, 1986). For a rough estimate of the types of people who are homeless, Martha Burt and Barbara Cohen's "Feeding the Homeless: Does the Prepared Meals Provision Help?" Urban Institute Paper (1988) provides a breakdown of the homeless into three relatively equal groups: the mentally ill, alcoholics and drug users, and those who are homeless for primarily economic reasons.

Some of the major efforts to explain the causes of homelessness are provided by Peter H. Rossi in *Down and Out in America: The Origins of Homelessness* (University of Chicago Press, 1988); James D. Wright in *Address Unknown: The Homeless in America* (Aldine de Gruyter, 1989); Karin Ringheim in *At Risk of Homelessness: The Role of Income and Rent* (Praeger, 1990); and

Richard P. Appelbaum in "The Affordability Gap," *Social Policy* (May/June 1989). Charles Hoch and Robert A. Slayton carefully examine the differences between homelessness today and homelessness in the 1960s in *New Homelessness and Old: Community and the Skid Row Hotel* (Temple University Press, 1989). Useful collections of articles that analyze homelessness are Carol L. M. Catton, ed., *Homelessness in America* (Oxford University Press, 1990), and Jamsid A. Momeni, ed., *Homelessness in the United States, Vol. 2: Data and Issues* (Greenwood Press, 1990). For two useful discussions of solutions, see Peter Dreier and John Atlas, "Grassroots Strategies for the Housing Crisis: A National Agenda," *Social Policy* (Winter 1989), and Congressional Budget Office, "Current Housing Problems and Possible Federal Responses" (December 1988). For an argument against Tucker's rent control thesis, see John Atlas and Peter Dreier, "The Phony Case Against Rent Control," *The Progressive* (April 1989). For a sensitive examination of the ambivalent feelings that Americans have against the homeless, see Peter Marin, "Helping and Hating the Homeless," *Harper's* (January 1987). Finally, for a deeply moving portrayal of the lives of the homeless, see the award-winning *Rachel and Her Children: Homeless Families in America*, by Jonathan Kozol (Anchor Press, 1985).

PART 4

Political Economy

Are political power and economic power merged within a "power elite" that dominates the U.S. political system? The first issue in this part explores that debate. The next debate concerns public policy: How should we assess the impact and efficacy of welfare programs? Finally, in the last issue in this part, we examine the political economy from a global perspective: Does the breakup of communism prove that capitalism is the dominant economic institution?

Is Government Dominated by Big
    Business?

Does Welfare Do More Harm Than
    Good?

Does the Breakup of Communism
    Show the Success of Capitalism?

ISSUE 13

Is Government Dominated by Big Business?

YES: Thomas Byrne Edsall, from *The New Politics of Inequality: How Political Power Shapes Economic Policy* (W. W. Norton, 1984)

NO: David Vogel, from *Fluctuating Fortunes: The Political Power of Business in America* (Basic Books, 1989)

ISSUE SUMMARY

YES: Political reporter Thomas Byrne Edsall argues that the power of big business is stronger than ever because of the increasing political sophistication of big business coupled with the breakdown of political parties.

NO: Professor of business administration David Vogel contends that the power of business fluctuates with the times and is currently being kept in check by other forces in U.S. society.

Since the framing of the U.S. Constitution in 1787, there have been periodic charges that America is unduly influenced by wealthy financial interests. Richard Henry Lee, a signer of the Declaration of Independence, spoke for many Anti-Federalists, those who opposed ratification of the Constitution, when he warned that the proposed charter shifted power away from the people and into the hands of the "aristocrats" and "moneyites," those who "avariciously grasp at all power and property." Before the Civil War, Jacksonian Democrats denounced the eastern merchants and bankers who, they charged, were usurping the power of the people. After the Civil War, a number of radical parties and movements revived this theme of antielitism. The ferment—which was brought about by the rise of industrial monopolies, government corruption, and economic hardship for western farmers—culminated in the founding of the People's party at the beginning of the 1890s. The Populists, as they were more commonly called, wanted economic and political reforms aimed at transferring power away from the rich and back to "the plain people."

By the early 1900s the People's party had disintegrated, but many writers and activists have continued to echo the Populists' central thesis: that the U.S. democratic political system is in fact dominated by business elites. Socialists, Communists, those on the political left, and some on the political right have all argued it or made it the premise of other arguments.

Yet the thesis has not gone unchallenged. During the 1950s and the early 1960s, many social scientists subscribed to the *pluralist* view of America. Pluralists admit that there are many influential elites in our society, and that is precisely their point: Because America contains so many groups, the pluralists argue, each group has a tendency to counterbalance the power of the others. Labor groups are often opposed to business groups; conservative interests challenge liberal interests, and vice versa; organized civil libertarians sometimes fight with groups that seek government-imposed bans on pornography or groups that demand tougher criminal laws. No single group can dominate the political system or have a monopoly on power in our pluralist system. Pluralists were not comfortable with calling America a *democracy*, a word that has become invested with emotional connotations, but they did think that rule in America emanates from many centers, so they favored the word *polyarchy* (literally, "rule by many") to describe the operation of the American system.

Among the leading pluralists of the 1950s was Charles E. Lindblom, an economist and political scientist. But Lindblom altered his views considerably over the course of the years, and in *Politics and Markets*, published in 1977 to considerable attention, Lindblom contended that corporate influence in all capitalist countries is so disproportionate that the political and social systems in those countries are *not* truly pluralist. This general argument, with particular reference to the United States, is developed in the following selection by Thomas Byrne Edsall. Opposing this view is David Vogel, who contends that the political clout of business has fluctuated in recent decades and is now fragmented and defensive.

YES

Thomas Byrne Edsall

THE NEW POLITICS OF INEQUALITY

In the United States in recent years there has been a significant erosion of the power of those on the bottom half of the economic spectrum, an erosion of the power not only of the poor but of those in the working and middle classes. At the same time, there has been a sharp increase in the power of economic elites, of those who fall in the top 15 percent of the income distribution.

This transfer of power has coincided with an economic crisis: productivity growth, which for the three decades following the Second World War had been the source of a continuing rise in the standard of living, slowed to zero by the end of the 1970s; the median family income, which had doubled in real, uninflated dollars from 1950 to 1973, declined during the next ten years, paralleling a decline in the average factory worker's weekly earnings; and inflation and unemployment, instead of acting as counterbalancing forces, rose simultaneously.

This mounting economic crisis provided an opportunity for newly ascendant representatives of the interests of the business community and of the affluent to win approval of a sea change in economic policy. For nearly fifty years, since the formation of the New Deal coalition in the 1930s, there had been a sustained base of support for both social spending programs and a tax system that modestly redistributed income and restricted the concentration of wealth in the hands of the few. These deeply rooted liberal traditions were abandoned during the late 1970s in favor of policies calling for a major reduction of the tax burden on income derived from capital, and for reductions in domestic spending programs directed toward the poor and the working poor. These shifts in tax and spending policies, in combination with inflation, have had enormous distributional consequences, resulting, for the period from 1980 through 1984, in losses for every income group except the very affluent.

Although the election of Ronald Reagan to the presidency has been the catalyst for much of this alteration of policy, its roots run far deeper. The delicate balance of power between elites and larger groups seeking represen-

From Thomas Byrne Edsall, *The New Politics of Inequality: How Political Power Shapes Economic Policy* (W. W. Norton, 1984). Copyright © 1984 by W. W. Norton & Company, Inc. Reprinted by permission. Notes omitted.

tation in the political process has been changing in almost all quarters, including the Democratic party, the Republican party, the business lobbying community, organized labor, and the intellectual establishment. These changes have been both accelerated and exacerbated throughout the entire electorate by increasingly class-skewed voting patterns. In each of these areas, the changes are resulting in a diminution of the representation of the majority in the development of economic policy, and in the growing leverage of the well-to-do.

Underlying this shift in the balance of political power among economic groups is a changed economic environment that has forced fundamental revisions in political strategies for both political parties. The economic crisis of the past decade has cut to the heart of a tradition in American politics, particularly in Democratic politics, playing havoc with that party's tradition of capitalizing on a growing and thriving economy in order to finance a continuing expansion of benefits for those toward the bottom of the income distribution. Past economic growth had provided the federal government with a fiscal dividend in additional tax revenues with which to finance growth in such broad-based programs as Social Security and Medicare, while simultaneously maintaining popular support, as all wage earners benefited from rising real incomes.

Altered economic circumstances have turned politics into what Lester Thurow has termed a zero-sum process. The balance of power in the competition for the benefits of government has shifted increasingly in favor of those in the top third of the income distribution. In many respects these shifts have pushed the national debate well to the right of its locus ten or twenty years ago. In 1964, the Republican presidential nominee, Senator Barry Goldwater, was decisively defeated while advocating a major reduction in domestic federal spending and a sharp increase in military spending; sixteen years later, Ronald Reagan, one of Goldwater's most ardent supporters, was elected to the presidency on a platform remarkably similar to Goldwater's and succeeded in persuading Congress, including a Democratic House of Representatives, to act into law legislation that would have been politically inconceivable at any time during the previous fifty years.

The roots of this shift to the right are by now deeply imbedded in the political system, severely restricting the scope of choices available to either party, particularly to the Democratic party. Just as the shift to the left in public policy in the early 1960s resulted from fundamental alterations in the balance of power—ranging from rapid postwar economic growth, to the cohesiveness of the liberal-labor coalition, to the political vitality of the civil rights movement—the shift to the right over the past decade has resulted from complex, systemic alterations in the terms of the political and economic debate and in the power of those participating in the debate.

The election of a Democrat to the White House would inevitably slow the conservative initiative; forces pushing the national agenda to the right, however, will retain what amounts to veto power both over the scope of issues admitted to national political discourse and over congressional legislation likely to achieve victory. These conservative forces, as this book will explore, are not only within the Republican party, the right-wing ideological groups, and the business community but within the Democratic party itself. Not only are these forces present in all major elements of the political system; even with economic recovery, lowered inflation, declining unemployment, and growth in the gross national product, the shape of economic and political pressures on the electorate at large would appear to preclude, for at least the near future, the emergence of a consensus in support of a revived liberal agenda. . . .

During the 1970s, the political wing of the nation's corporate sector staged one of the most remarkable campaigns in the pursuit of political power in recent history. By the late 1970s and the early 1980s, business, and Washington's corporate lobbying community in particular, had gained a level of influence and leverage approaching that of the boom days of the 1920s. What made the acquisition of power in the 1970s remarkable was that business achieved its goals without any broad public-political mandate such as that of the 1920s, when probusiness values were affirmed in the elections of 1920, 1924, and 1928. Rather, business in the 1970s developed the ability to dominate the legislative process under adverse, if not hostile, circumstances. Corporate leaders had been closely associated with Watergate and its related scandals, and a reform-minded Democratic party with strong ties to the consumer and environmental movements had gained increasingly large majorities in Congress.

Despite these devastating odds, the political stature of business rose steadily from the early 1970s, one of its lowest points in the nation's history, until, by the end of the decade, the business community had achieved virtual dominance of the legislative process in Congress. The rise of the corporate sector is a case study in the ability of an economic elite to gain power by capitalizing on changes in the political system. In the case of the Democratic party, the shift in the balance of power toward the affluent, the erosion of the labor union movement, and the vastly increased importance of money in campaigns all combined to make Democratic politicians more vulnerable to pressures from the right. In the case of the Republican party, a de facto alliance has emerged between the GOP and much of the business community, a relationship paralleling the ties between the Democratic party and labor but lacking the inherent conflicts characteristic of that liaison. The political ascendancy of the business community, furthermore, has coincided with a sustained and largely successful attack upon organized labor, an attack conducted both in private-sector union representation fights and in legislative battles on Capitol Hill.

In 1978, in the midst of the corporate political revival, R. Heath Larry, president of the National Association of Manufacturers, contended that the single most important factor behind the resurgence of business was "the decline in the role of the party, yielding a new spirit of independence among congressmen—independent of each other, of the president, of the party caucus." Larry's perception of the role of the decline in political parties in the revival of the stature of business was accurate, but his contention that this decline produced increased independence is wrong. In fact, the collapse of political parties and of traditional political organizations, especially those at the local level that formerly had the power to assure or to deny reelection, has been a key factor in a network of forces and developments undermining the independence of politicians and aug menting the strength of the business community.

WEAKENING OF PARTIES

The decline of political organizations, rather than increasing independence, has eliminated a fundamental base of support for those elected to public office, functioning to intensify the elective anxieties of public officials, particularly members of the House and Senate. For a member of Congress, a healthy local political organization traditionally both provided a secure source of backing at election time and served as a conduit, transmitting to the congressman or senator spending the majority of his or her time in Washington the assessment of the local party leadership of public opinion—or the lack of it—on a cross-section of issues. Without this source of information, and without the security provided by the support of a strong local political organization, a House representative or senator becomes highly vulnerable, not only to incessant reelection anxiety but to orchestrated public pressure. Many of the toughest battles in Congress in recent years—legislation to create a consumer protection agency; labor law reform; regulation of used-car dealers and funeral directors; major tax legislation, including the $749 billion tax reduction in 1981, and the 1983 struggle over legislation mandating 10 percent withholding on interest and dividend income—have been fought on this terrain: the organized creation of seemingly spontaneous outpourings of public opinion for or against specific legislative proposals, voiced through coordinated letter writing, telegram, and telephone campaigns—all deluging members of Congress.

This form of lobbying, although centralized, is known as "grass-roots lobbying" and has always been a weapon in the political arsenal, becoming, during the late 1960s and early 1970s, an essential mechanism in strategies to influence congressional decisions in the hands of the environmental movements and of such organizations as Common Cause and Ralph Nader's Congress Watch, organizations that coordinated citizens' grass-roots lobbying campaigns in the successful pressuring of Congress to enact political reforms, health and safety legislation, consumer protection legislation, and environmental conservation legislation. A similar but substantially different form of lobbying has characterized congressional procedures since the days of George Washington: pressure on individual members from local contractors, unions, bankers, chambers of commerce, and developers, to obtain defense, road, dam, and other pork-barrel benefits from the federal government. Pork-barrel lobbying and grass-roots lobbying differ, however, in that pork-barrel lobbying traditionally seeks specific benefits for a congressman's district or state—jobs, buildings, construction products, contract awards—while grass-roots lobbying is an attempt to seek to influence congressional votes on legislation of national importance, legislation that is seen or thought to transcend parochial boundaries.

In the mid-1970s, key leaders of the nation's corporate and trade association network perceived that their institutions and structures were far better suited to grass-roots lobbying than the liberal-reform groups that seemed to have a corner on these tactics. The interest of the constituencies of the liberal-reform organizations in the political process is fluid, rising when issues have high visibility—such as President Nixon's highly controversial Supreme Court nomination of G. Harrold Carswell, the southern judge with a segregationist background whose appointment was opposed by groups ranging from the American Bar Association to the NAACP; or the post-Watergate campaign to enact election reform—and falling when issues are no longer unambiguous.

In contrast, the nation's corporate and trade association communities have a sustained economic interest in the outcome of the legislative and elective process, day in and day out. The basic function of Washington's corporate and trade association lobbying community, a network of well over 150,000 professionals, is not only the defeat or passage of major bills but, in a much more complex process, the shaping of the precise language of legislation and of the committee reports that accompany legislation. This process involves the addition, deletion, and alteration of individual words, paragraphs, and sections of bills as they wend their way from House committee, to House floor, to Senate committee, to the full Senate and then to a House-Senate conference committee. One seemingly minor provision in the 1982 tax bill retroactively legalized corporate sales of investment tax credits from January 1, 1981, to October 20, 1981. This provision, which occupied nine lines out of a 465-page report, in fact sanctioned a controversial $20 million tax deal between Chris Craft Corp. and International Harvester.

Economically driven, sustained interest in the legislative process does not stop with the passage or defeat of legislation. A battle lost on legislation to create a program can be partially redeemed when entirely separate legislation setting the dollar appropriation for the program is later taken up by Congress. An agency empowered to enforce workplace health and safety regulation, without money for an inspection staff, in effect has little or no power. Finally, the way in which a law mandating certain general health and safety requirements will be specifically applied on the production line and on the office floor is determined by the detailed rules and regulations written in the executive branch, and subject in turn to pressure and counterpressure from the White House, Congress, the industry, and the enforcing agency itself.

Just as important as the sustained interest of business in all aspects of the legislative process is the compatibility of the structure of corporations and trade associations with the mechanics of orchestrated grass-roots lobbying. Such diverse major United States companies as General Motors, American Express, Caterpillar Tractor, PepsiCo, Westinghouse Electric Corp., Standard Oil Co. of Ohio, U.S. Steel, Raytheon Company, Squibb Corp., American Airlines, and Allied Chemical Corp. each have networks of plants, suppliers, retailer outlets, subcontractors, salesmen, and distributors in every congressional district in the nation, as well as thousands of dispersed stockholders.

The scope of this leverage was demonstrated during the 1979 debate over legislation to provide federal loan guarantees to the Chrysler Corporation. In the attempt to convince conservative Congressman Elwood R. Hillis, Republican of the Fifth District of Indiana, to vote for the legislation, Chrysler produced for Hillis, as it did for all other members of Congress, a list of all Chrysler suppliers in his district. The list runs to three and a quarter single-spaced pages and includes the names of 436 companies in Hillis's district whose sales to Chrysler totaled $29.52 million, ranging from $6.67 million from the GTR Fiberglass Products Company in Marion to $90 from Leck's Radiator Repair Shop in Hillis's home town of Kokomo. . . .

THE CORPORATE MOBILIZATION

The revival of the political power of business began in 1973 and 1974, initiated in large part by a small group of Washington's most influential corporate lobbyists who began to meet privately to discuss the darkening storm clouds everywhere on the political horizon. Watergate had not only damaged the Republican party, but the taint of corruption had sharply altered the public perception of corporate America. The secret financing for President Nixon's Committee to Re-elect the President in 1972; the case for what was known as the "Townhouse Operation"; channeling unreported money to Republican House and Senate candidates in 1970; the bribes to foreign officials in charge of government contracts—all had come from business executives and from corporate treasuries. Furthermore, American corporations providing weaponry and material for the Vietnam War, ranging from Dow Chemical to the Raytheon Company, had been targeted with extensive and effective negative publicity by the anti-war movement. Public confidence in the chief executives of major corporations fell like a stone from the mid-1960s to the mid-1970s. The percentage of the public describing themselves as having a great deal of confidence in corporate leaders dropped from 51 percent in the 1966–67 period to an average of 20 percent in the 1974–76 period. The rate of decline in confidence was sharper

than for any other major institution in the United States, public or private, including the executive branch, the press, organized labor, and educators—excepting only Congress, which fell from a favorability rating of 42 percent to 20 percent during the same period.

At the same time, Watergate had revived the Democratic party, particularly that wing of the Democratic party supporting the environmental and consumer movements. After losing the 1972 presidential election under the leadership of George S. McGovern, by a 61–39 margin and by 17.9 million votes, the Democrats in 1974 would gain forty-nine House seats and five Senate seats. Before these Democratic gains, and despite the presence of a Republican in the White House, Congress by 1974 had already enacted into law the Environmental Protection Agency (1970), the Occupational Safety and Health Administration (1970), the Consumer Product Safety Commission (1972), the National Traffic Safety Commission (1970), the Mine Safety and Health Administration (1973), increased food stamp funding (1970), a 20 percent Social Security increase (1974), Supplemental Security Income (1972), and the Employee Retirement Income Security Act.

"The danger had suddenly escalated," Bryce Harlow, senior Washington representative for Procter & Gamble and one of the most respected members of the old-line corporate lobbying community, commented later. "We had to prevent business from being rolled up and put in the trash can by that Congress," he said, referring to the Ninety-fourth Congress elected in 1974. The mobilization of business in this critical period, the early and mid-1970s, began at the top. Harlow worked most actively with the elite

Washington lobbyists, men like William Whyte of the United States Steel Corporation; Albert D. Bourland, Jr., of General Motors; Don A. Goodall of American Cyanamid Company; and Wayne H. Smithey of Ford Motor Co. These men were an integral pat of the Washington establishment, not only representing some of the largest American corporations but conducting their business in such exclusive downtown facilities as the Metropolitan and University clubs. Their roots, however, were in a style of lobbying that no longer worked on Capitol Hill—the cultivation, largely behind closed doors, of a few key holders of power: committee chairmen who could determine with the tap of a gavel or a nod to the staff the content of legislation; cabinet secretaries who could be persuaded over lunch that their employees were pressing a regulatory mandate with too much vigor; and key White House aides whose political currency was the provision of favors for the influential.

By the mid-1970s, however, the decline of party loyalties, congressional reforms weakening the power of committee chairmen, and the diffusion of power to junior members of Congress forced a major alteration in lobbying strategies. "As long as you could go and get the cooperation of the committee chairman and the ranking members, and maybe a few others, you didn't have to have the vast network we are talking about now," Smithey noted. Smithey's reference to a "vast network" describes both the development of grass-roots lobbying as a legislative tactic and a much more pervasive effort to set the terms of the legislative debate in the nation's capital. Not only have the targets of lobbyists changed over the past generation, but the tech-

nology of public opinion molding has undergone changes of unprecedented magnitude, producing computerized direct-mail communications in which much of the nation's adult population has been broken down into demographic and "psychographic" profiles. A group or institution seeking to mobilize support or opposition on any issue can seek out ready-made lists of allies in the general public from computer specialists who can then communicate almost instantaneously with any selected constituency via letters produced on high-speed laser printers. If lobbying during the 1950s, in the words of one of the most eminent Washington lobbyists, Charles E. Walker, consisted of personal access to four natives of Texas—President Dwight Eisenhower, House Speaker Sam Rayburn, Senate Majority Leader Lyndon Baines Johnson, and Treasury Secretary Robert Anderson—it currently involves minimally the ability to recognize the interests of 535 members of the House and Senate, an acute sensitivity to potential malleability in public opinion, the cultivation of both print and electronic media, the use of sophisticated technologies both to create and to convey an impression of public sentiment, and the marshaling on Capitol Hill and across the country of legions of newly enlisted corporate personnel.

The effort on the part of the business community to shape the legislative debate has taken place on a number of fronts, one of the most important of which has been the politicization of employees and stockholders. Atlantic Richfield (Arco), for example, spends about $1 million annually on a program in which 15,000 employees are members of politically active local committees. In addition, the nearly 80,000 Arco stockholders, suppliers, and distributors are on a mailing list for company newsletters and publications focusing on political and public policy issues. W. Dean Cannon, Jr., executive vice-president of the California Savings and Loan League, suggested in 1978 to savings and loan firms that they give employees "specific assignments to work in politics" and that an employee's raises "might well be tied directly to his involvement in the political assignment you have given him." During the debate over the 1978 tax bill, officials of a single, mid-sized firm, the Barry Wright Corporation in Watertown, Mass, generated 3,800 letters from its stockholders to members of Congress in favor of a reduction in capital gains taxation.

The politicization of management-level employees is a critical element in achieving effective grass-roots lobbying: an employee who sees a direct economic interest in the outcome of legislative battles will be a far more effective and persistent advocate than an employee who is acting in response only to orders or implied orders from superiors. Stockholders, in turn, represent an ideal target for political mobilization. Only 15 percent of American citizens hold stock, according to liberal estimates by the Securities Industry Association, and those who do are, on average, in the upper-income brackets. They have little or no direct interest in the expansion or maintenance of domestic spending programs, although they have considerable interest in lowering tax rates. In this sense, the economic interests of affluent individuals and of corporations are sharply intertwined. Both stockholders and corporations, for example, share a direct interest in either lowering the capital gains rate or shortening the minimum holding pe-

riod to qualify for the more favorable capital gains rate. . . .

An equally, if not more, effective use of business money in altering the terms of the policy debate has been in the total or partial financing of such private institutions engaged in research and scholarship as the American Enterprise Institute; the Heritage Foundation; the Hoover Institution on War, Revolution and Peace; the National Bureau of Economic Research; the Center for the Study of American Business at Washington University in St.Louis, and the American Council for Capital Formation. In a decade during which economic stagnation contributed to the undermining of the intellectual basis of traditional Democratic economic and political strategies, these organizations, among others, have functioned to lay the scholarly and theoretical groundwork for a major shift in public policy favoring business and the higher-bracket taxpayers. . . .

BUSINESS AND ECONOMIC POLICY

The rising political power of business has been associated with the general increase in the number of political action committees [PACs] and with the growing volume of money channeled through them. This line of thinking, in turn, has given rise to charges that Congress, overwhelmed by the flow of cash from the PACs, has become the puppet of special interests, a forum in which every organized group, from doctors to dairymen, can, in return for campaign contributions, receive special antitrust exemption from competition or from taxpayer-financed price supports, or special insulation from the federal regulatory process. The most vocal critic of the system has been Common Cause, the principal reform lobby. "Our system of representative government is under siege because of the destructive role that political action committees or PACs are now playing in our political process," Fred Wertheimer, president of Common Cause, declared in 1983. . . .

These analyses, while both accurate and timely, fail to take into account a number of less frequently reported factors adding to the complexity and subtlety of the current political situation on Capitol Hill. For one, Common Cause and the press have become increasingly effective watchdogs over the legislative process, preventing many of the attempts by special-interest groups to slip through favorable legislation. More important, however, while these analyses, particularly [New Yorker correspondent Elizabeth] Drew's detailed description of the overwhelming concern with fundraising in Congress, accurately portray an essential element of the political process, neither recognizes what has been a major ideological shift in Congress. Business has played a key role in this shift, using not just PAC contributions but increasingly sophisticated grass-roots lobbying mechanisms, the financing of a sympathetic intellectual community, and the expenditure of somewhere in the neighborhood of $1 billion annually on institutional advertising.

This ideological shift in the nation's capital has been pervasive, alerting basic tax, spending, and regulatory policies and moving both political parties well to the right over the past decade. Of the various elites that have gained strength in recent years, business has been among the most effective. Not only has it gained from highly favorable tax treatment and from a major reduction in regulation, but government action has increased the bar-

gaining leverage of management in its relations with organized labor. This increased leverage grows out of reductions in unemployment compensation and out of the elimination of the public service job programs, and through the appointment of promanagement officials at such key agencies as the Occupational Safety and Health Administration and at the National Labor Relations Board. The end result is a labor movement that has lost much of its clout at the negotiating table and in the polling booth. . . .

THE WAGES OF INEQUALITY

In the late 1970s, a set of political and intellectual forces began to converge and to gain momentum, joining together in a direction that substantially altered economic policy in the United States. While the forces involved were by no means in agreement as to the specific goals to be achieved, they shared an interest in seeking to change the basic assumptions that have dominated taxation and spending policies in the United States. For nearly fifty years, since the administration of Franklin Delano Roosevelt, two dominant themes of taxation and spending policy have been equity and the moderate redistribution of income. The forces gaining ascendancy in the late 1970s sought to replace such liberal goals with a drive to slow the rate of growth in federal spending in order to increase the availability of money for private capital formation; with a reduction of corporate and individual tax rates, particularly of those rates in the top brackets, in order to provide predicted incentives for work, savings, and investment; and with the paring down of government regulation to facilitate a more productive marketplace. In short, the goal became to influence government policy so as to supplant, in an economic sense, equity with efficiency.

The inherent contradictions between equity, efficiency, redistribution, and investment go to the heart of the conflict in developing economic policy in advanced capitalist democracies. The political resolution of such contradictions determines the balance between competing claims on government: that is, whether government is granted the authority to intervene in the private marketplace in order to correct or to modify inequities inherent in the market system, through a progressive tax rate schedule and through the payment of benefits to the poor; whether it is the role of government to subsidize, encourage, and direct marketplace forces with tax incentives and loan subsidies targeted toward specific industries; or whether government should reduce to a minimum its role in the economy, remaining as remote from and as disengaged as possible from the private sector.

The period from 1977 through the first months of 1982, however, marked a rare moment in American history, when the disparate forces supporting the conservative coalition on these basic economic questions all simultaneously became politically ascendant. Forces coalescing on the political right included a politically revitalized business community; increasing sophistication and centrality among leaders of the ideological new right; the sudden explosion of wealth in the domestic oil community following the 1973 OPEC embargo; the emergence within the academic community and within the major economic research institutions of proponents of tax cuts and of sharp reductions in the tax rate on capital income; a Republican party whose financial resources were exponentially increased by computerized direct-mail and other new political technologies, providing often decisive access to television, to polling, and to highly sophisticated voter targeting tactics; and the rise of politically conservative evangelical Christian organizations. The emergence of these forces coincided with a series of developments and trends giving conservatism new strength. The business and the new, or ideological, right-wing communities developed a shared interest in the candidates of the Republican party, as such organizations as the Chamber of Commerce and the National Conservative Political Action Committee became de facto arms of the GOP. Voting patterns increased the class bias of voter turnout, as the affluent became a stronger force both within the electorate as a whole and within the Republican party.

Conversely, the forces making up the liberal coalition, represented in large part by major segments of the Democratic party—organized labor, civil rights and civil liberties organizations, political reformers, environmental groups, and feminists—were experiencing increasing disunity. The power of organized labor, essential to any coalition of the left, had been steadily declining. Even more damaging was the emergence of growing inflation and unemployment, a continued decline in the rate of productivity growth, and a drop in the take-home pay of the average worker. This economic deterioration not only splintered the fragile coalition of Democrats that had supported policies of equity and redistribution over the previous forty years but created a growing belief that the nation was caught in an economic crisis that the Democratic party could not resolve, a belief compounded by Democratic disarray.

It was this combination of trends, all favoring the right, that provided the opportunity for a major alteration in public policy. The election in 1980 of Ronald Reagan to the presidency and the takeover of the Senate by the Republican party created the political opportunity for this fundamental realignment, but the groundwork had already been carefully laid. This groundwork included an increasingly sophisticated political strategy capitalizing on the conflicts within the fragile Democratic majority, the careful nurturing and financing of intellectual support both in academia and within a growing network of think tanks financed by corporations and conservative foundations, and the advance preparation of specific legislative proposals, particularly of tax legislation. . . .

The power shift that produced the fundamental policy realignment of the past decade did not result from a conservative or Republican realignment of the voters; nor did it produce such a realignment after the tax and spending legislation of 1981 was enacted. Rather, these policy changes have grown out of pervasive distortions in this country's democratic political process. These distortions have created a system of political decision making in which fundamental issues—the distribution of the tax burden, the degree to which the government sanctions the accumulation of wealth, the role of federal regulation, the level of publicly tolerated poverty, and the relative strength of labor and management—are resolved by an increasingly unrepresentative economic elite. To a large extent, these changes have turned the Republican party, in terms of the public policies it advocates, into a party of the elite. For the Democratic party, the

political changes of the past decade have distorted the distribution of power and weakened the capacity of the party to represent the interests of its numerous less affluent constituents. Even if the Democrats are victorious in capturing the presidency, there is no evidence that the Democratic party is in any way prepared to set an agenda economically benefiting its core constituents in the same way that the Republican-conservative movement has been able to define the political debate in recent years to the advantage of its most loyal supporters. As long as the balance of political power remains so heavily weighted toward those with economic power, national economic policy will remain distorted, regardless of which party is in control of the federal government.

NO

David Vogel

FLUCTUATING FORTUNES

THE IMPORTANCE OF TIME

The purpose of this book is not to continue the debate between those who argue that the political position of business is privileged and those who assert that it is not. It is rather to move us beyond it. I offer a new way of looking at the political power of business in contemporary American politics. My central argument is that both perspectives are flawed because they mistakenly assume that the power of business is relatively stable. The pluralists contend that the political power of business is usually countervailed by other interest groups, while the critics of pluralism assert that it rarely is. Both contentions are incomplete. The political power of business can and does vary. Furthermore, these variations follow a discernible pattern, which can in turn be explained.

The power of business in American national politics has changed substantially since 1960. The political position of business was relatively secure during the first half of the 1960s, declined significantly between the mid-1960s and mid-1970s, increased between the mid-1970s and early 1980s, and has since slightly eroded. These changes are not unprecedented: the political power of significant segments of American business also declined during both the Progressive Era and the New Deal. This book describes and explains the third major set of fluctuations in the political fortunes of business since the turn of the century.

There is no need to choose between the depictions of business power offered by the pluralists and their critics. The accuracy of each perspective depends on the period in which one is interested. In a number of respects, the political position of business in America could be accurately characterized as "privileged" during the 1950s and through the first half of the 1960s. Few issues appeared on the political agenda that threatened business prerogatives, and business exercised virtual power over the resolution of those few issues that did. Correspondingly, American politics between the

From David Vogel, *Fluctuating Fortunes: The Political Power of Business in America* (Basic Books, 1989). Copyright © 1989 by Basic Books, Inc. Reprinted by permission of Basic Books, a division of HarperCollins Publishers. Notes omitted.

mid-1960s and mid-1970s more closely resembled the pluralists' description of interest-group competition. The power of business was challenged by both the public-interest movement and organized labor, while public confidence in business dropped dramatically; between 1968 and 1977, the percentage of Americans who believed that "business tries to strike a fair balance between profits and the interests of the public" declined from 70 percent to 15 percent. . . .

It is possible to interpret the ten-year period during which business found itself on the political and ideological defensive as a brief interlude in a political system normally characterized by business dominance. Similarly, the relative resurgence of the influence of business during the next fifteen years, rather than representing a return to the status quo, could instead be viewed as a temporary phenomenon—one shortly to be followed by a backlash from nonbusiness constituencies. My position is that neither period constitutes the norm. While it is true that during this century the years when business has been relatively powerful have been more numerous than those when it has not, it does not necessarily follow that the former state of affairs is the normal one. Rather, as in the case of the business cycle, each "phase" is temporary. Which state of affairs is preferable I leave to the readers' judgment.

POLITICAL POWER AND ECONOMIC CONDITIONS

Because both the pluralists and their critics tend to ignore the extent to which the political influence of business changes over time, they have also overlooked the relationship between political development and changing economic conditions. . . . These omissions are crucial. The political influence of business has been significantly affected by the long-term performance of the American economy. Over the last three decades, the two have been inversely related. Paradoxically, business has tended to lose political influence when the economy was performing relatively well and has become more influential when the performance of the economy deteriorated.

The relative political power of business is *not* a function of the business cycle. Otherwise, the political power of business would be more unstable than it actually has been. Rather, what *is* critical is the public's perception of the long-term strength of the American economy. The unprecedented increases in both government regulation of corporate social performance and in social-welfare expenditures from the mid-1960s through the early 1970s was made possible by the equally unprecedented economic growth rates of the 1960s. The economy grew at an average rate of 4.5 percent between 1961 and 1968, and between 1965 and 1969 the after-tax rate of return of nonfinancial corporations averaged 9 percent—its highest level since the Second World War. As a result, significant segments of the American middle class began to take both their own prosperity and the success of business for granted. They believed that business could afford to rebuild the inner cities, hire the chronically unemployed, make safer products, clean up air and water pollution, provide all Americans with a healthy and safe working environment and, at the same time, still further improve their own living standards. Politicians from both parties competed with each other to propose policies based on this assumption.

However, during the second half of the 1970s, the American public's perception of the American economy and the continued profitability of the business corporation began to change. The recession of 1974–75 was not simply another downturn in the business cycle. It marked a major discontinuity in the postwar development of American capitalism: rates of economic growth, investment, growth in productivity, and growth in wages and family incomes were all significantly lower in the decade after 1973 than they had been during the preceding one. Between 1975 and 1978, corporate profit rates averaged 5.9 percent, their lowest level since the Second World War. Persistent double-digit inflation, declining real wages and stagnant family income, increased dependence on imported oil, and a dramatic growth in imports in highly visible sectors of the American economy all made the American business corporation, and consequently America itself, suddenly appear economically vulnerable. General Motors, the epitome of arrogant and omnipotent big business during the 1960s, now found itself pleading for government to protect it from Japanese imports; Chrysler, the nation's ninth largest corporation, was on the verge of bankruptcy.

Consequently, the political and social climate became transformed. . . . "Baby boomers," who had played a critical role in organizing and supporting the public-interest movement during the first half of the 1970s, discovered "bracket creep" and became preoccupied with finding well-paying jobs in the private sector or in starting their own companies. The "new class" of college-educated professionals, now worried about their own economic prospects, became more sympathetic to the demands of business to reduce taxes, to slow down the growth of government spending and regulation, and to weaken the power of unions. As a result, the political pendulum shifted. The political position of business once again became relatively privileged: the second half of the 1970s and the early 1980s witnessed a substantial increase in the ability of business to define the terms of political debate and affect governmental decisions.

The economy performed relatively well after 1982. And this in part explains why the political influence of business did not continue to increase throughout the decade: the Reagan administration was unable to deliver on its promises to provide business with significant regulatory relief, and corporate taxes were increased in both 1982 and 1986. But both the rate at which new regulations have been imposed on business and the growth in social welfare expenditures were far less during the 1980s than they were during the 1960s. Politicians from both parties were also more willing to support increased government assistance to industry than they were fifteen years earlier. And these developments in turn can be attributed to the public's continued concern about the apparent ability of American industry to compete successfully in the global economy—particularly vis-à-vis Japanese firms. A poll taken in January 1987 reported that "88 percent of all Americans say that they are concerned that this country is losing its competitive edge and cannot remain the world's preeminent economic power." The globalization of the American economy may have created severe economic difficulties for substantial segments of American business, but politically it has been something of a boon.

BUSINESS AND THE POLITICAL SYSTEM

Both pluralists and their critics have also paid insufficient attention to the relationship between the political influence and strategies of business and the changing structure of American politics. Between the mid-1960s and mid-1970s, the American political system changed substantially. One reason why business suffered so many political defeats during this period is that business lobbyists failed to appreciate the extent to which public policy was no longer being made in private negotiations between Washington insiders and a handful of strategically placed representatives and senators. Power within Congress had become more decentralized, the number of interest groups represented in Washington had increased, the role of the media in defining the political agenda and the terms of political debate had expanded, the importance of political parties had declined, and the courts had begun to play a much more active role in making regulatory policy. In a remarkably short period of time, consumer and environmental organizations were able to take advantage of these changes to move from a peripheral position in American politics to become active and effective participants in the making of public policies in the nation's capital.

It took business about seven years to rediscover how to win in Washington. Significantly, when business did become more politically active, it did so in ways that recognized how fundamentally the American political system had changed: it proceeded to imitate the political strategies that had previously been responsible for so many of its defeats. The sponsorship of research studies to influence elite opinion, the attention to the media as a way of changing public attitudes, the development of techniques of grass-roots organizing to mobilize supporters in congressional districts, and the use of ad hoc coalitions to maximize political influence had all been successfully employed, and in some cases even developed, by the public-interest movement. Campaign finance reform, by legalizing the formation of political action committees (PACs), opened another path for business participation in politics. Just as the decentralization of power within Congress during the second half of the 1960s and early 1970s helped reduce the political influence of business, the dramatic growth of business PACs during the second half of the 1970s helped increase it. . . .

MY APPROACH

. . . The interests of business are not monolithic: firms can use politics either to compete with each other or advance their collective interests. Among the most important factors affecting the relative political influence of business since the early 1960s has been the extent to which firms of different sizes and in different industries have been able to work together politically. When business has been unified, its political power has often been extremely impressive. But the degree of business unity also varies over time. With the exception of a relatively brief period between 1977 and 1981, business tended to function as a "community" in name only. Particularly during the 1980s, American business lacked effective leadership. And this, in turn, enabled both politicians and nonbusiness constituencies to play off different segments of business against each other.

This book assumes that it is legitimate to generalize about the political fortunes of business. Admittedly, just as the profit rates of all firms or industries are not affected equally by variations in the business cycle, the political influence of all firms does not vary uniformly. At any given time, some firms or industries have more influence over the decisions of government than others. Nevertheless, the efforts of particular industries and firms to achieve their political objectives do not take place in isolation; they are affected by and in turn affect changes in the relative political influence of other segments of the business community. Thus, the passage of the National Traffic and Motor Vehicle Safety Act in 1966 was not simply a political defeat for the automobile industry: by revealing the political ineptness and the vulnerability of the nation's largest industrial corporation, as well as the political popularity of consumerism, it opened the floodgates for the enactment of scores of additional regulatory statutes over the next decade. Similarly, the defeat of legislation legalizing common situs picketing by the House of Representatives in 1977 was not simply an unexpected political victory for the construction industry and a demoralizing defeat for the building-trade unions: by exposing the political vulnerability of organized labor and the responsiveness of a Congress dominated by liberal Democrats to intensive and sophisticated business lobbying, it encouraged business to become much more politically aggressive.

Momentum is important in politics. Many of the business community's most important political setbacks and gains over the last two decades have come in waves. From 1969 through 1972, Congress enacted the most progressive tax bill in the postwar period, reduced the oil-depletion allowance, imposed price controls on oil, transferred the primary authority for the regulation of both pollution and occupational health and safety from the states to the federal government, established the Consumer Product Safety Commission, and banned the advertising of cigarettes from radio and television. In a comparable span of four years—1978 through 1981—Congress defeated labor-law reform, voted against the establishment of a Consumer Protection Agency, restricted the power of the Federal Trade Commission, deregulated oil prices, delayed the imposition of automobile-emission standards, reduced price controls on natural gas, and enacted two tax bills, the first of which primarily benefited the wealthy and a second which reduced corporate taxes to their lowest level since the Second World War.

It is also characteristic of periods when business finds itself on the defensive that an unusually large proportion of public policies affects relatively large segments of the business community, though not necessarily in an identical manner. Among the most distinctive features of the regulatory statutes enacted during the first half of the 1970s was precisely that they were not directed toward specific industries. Rather, they sought to change the behavior of companies in a wide variety of different industries. This made many business executives much more conscious of their common or class interests, which in turn led to both the formation and revival of political organizations that represented firms in many different industries, such as the Business Roundtable, the United States Chamber of Commerce, and the National Federation of Independent Business.

The history of government intervention is also replete with examples of industry's inability to recognize its self-interest. It is now clear that the business community seriously underestimated the economic consequences of both the Occupational Safety and Health Act and the National Environmental Policy Act. And, in retrospect, the enormous resources the energy industry devoted to the phasing out of federal price controls was ill-advised, since the subsequent decline in the price of oil would have made them obsolete in any event. A similar analysis can be made of the political strategies of other interest groups. The Campaign Reform Act of 1971, which was initiated by organized labor, legalized the use of political action committees—which in turn enhanced the ability of business to participate in the electoral process. In addition, many of the regulatory statutes and rules for which public-interest groups fought so strongly have failed to accomplish their objectives. Indeed, some appear to have made the constituencies in whose name they were enacted actually worse off. . . .

What was the impact of the Reagan administration on the political fortunes of business?

While the business community's influence on public policy during the Reagan administration fell substantially below its expectations, in one respect its relative influence did increase: throughout the 1980s, the political and economic influence of organized labor continued to decline. The cumulative effect of the administration's free trade policies, its disbanding of the air traffic controllers' union, its support for economic deregulation, its unwillingness to restrict hostile takeovers and leveraged buyouts, and its tight monetary policies, as well as its appointments to the NLRB [National Labor Relations Board], was to weaken the bargaining power of both trade unions and unorganized workers. Real wages declined during the 1980s, and the percentage of workers belonging to unions reached a postwar low of 17.5 percent in 1987—a reduction of 6.5 percent since 1979. There were fewer work stoppages in 1987 than in any year since the Department of Labor started to keep records. Thus the Reagan administration helped business accomplish an objective for which it had been striving since the early 1970s, namely, to reduce labor's claims on its resources. The overall wage share, after increasing by a rate of 0.5 percent between 1966 and 1973, rose by only 0.1 percent between 1973 and 1979. But between 1979 and 1986, it actually declined by 0.4 percent.

The administration also dramatically slowed down the trend toward increased government regulation of corporate social conduct. While it was not able to repeal any of the statutes—or even modify many of the rules—enacted during the previous fifteen years, it certainly affected the rate at which new rules and regulations were promulgated. With a handful of exceptions, the regulatory statutes enacted during the 1980s were virtually all reauthorizations of the laws that had been initially approved during the 1970s: the scope of government controls over corporate social conduct was only marginally greater in 1988 than it had been in 1980. And while enforcement tended to be stricter during Reagan's second term than during his first, in a number of cases it still was less strict than it had been during the 1970s. On balance, the relationship between business and the new social regulatory agencies was much less contentious during the Reagan administration than it had been under its three predecessors.

Third, the 1981 Revenue Act contained the most significant cut in corporate taxes in history. While corporate taxes were increased in 1982, they were significantly lower through 1986 than they had been when Ronald Reagan took office. At the same time, because of the administration's increases in both defense spending and farm subsidies, the amount of direct government assistance to business was far greater under Reagan than it had been under his four predecessors.

On the other hand, the Reagan administration was clearly unable to fulfill its commitment to roll back the increases in government regulation of corporate social conduct that had occurred during the previous four administrations: the "regulatory time bomb" that David Stockman had committed himself to defuse was ticking as loudly in 1988 as it had in 1980. The administration may have succeeded in making significant segments of the American public more skeptical of the virtues of government intervention in a number of policy areas, but its highly visible failure to provide business with "regulatory relief" ironically helped make the government's responsibility to protect the public's health and safety a part of the national consensus. In addition, the 1986 tax reform legislation represented a major political defeat for significant segments of the business community. Finally, much to the frustration of business, the federal budget deficit continued to expand throughout the 1980s; indeed, by 1987, the national debt was more than twice as large as when President Reagan was inaugurated. Why, then, given the popularity of President Reagan, Republican control of the Senate through 1986, a much more probusiness House of Repre-

sentatives, and a politically sophisticated and active business community, was business not more politically influential during the Reagan years? . . .

When the priorities of the administration and business were similar, business did well. Thus, both corporate taxes and nondefense spending were significantly cut in 1981, and the federal government was unresponsive to the demands of organized labor and its liberal allies that the government intervene to ameliorate the impact of the 1981–82 recession, either by establishing a jobs program or restricting imports. Both the administration and the business community agreed on the need to reduce the economic power and political influence of organized labor; as a result, trade unions experienced major setbacks in both areas throughout the 1980s. And the president's desire to reduce the size of government helped reduce the rate at which new rules and regulations were enacted, and in many cases made their enforcement less strict. Finally, both placed major priority during the first half of the 1980s on reducing inflation—an objective whose achievement represented one of the administration's most important accomplishments in the area of economic policy.

But business and the Reagan administration were able to work extremely well together only in 1981. Afterward, their priorities and interests diverged. In 1982, the president decided that a tax increase was needed, and after his reelection in 1984 he committed his administration to a sweeping reform of the nation's tax laws. The result of both decisions was to increase the effective corporate tax rate. In the area of social regulation, business depended on the Reagan administration to take the initiative in proposing major statutory changes. But the administration had other priorities: in 1981 and 1982, it was more concerned about the budget and taxes, and in 1983 and 1984, it was preoccupied with preventing the Democrats from making a campaign issue out of its disastrous management of the EPA [Environmental Protection Agency]. In a sense, the administration undermined the position of business twice, initially through its zealotry in attempting to change the direction of regulatory policy and then by moving in the opposite direction to defuse the political fallout that resulted. The business community remained, on the whole, strongly committed to reducing the federal deficit. But this flew in the face of the administration's firm commitment to increase defense spending substantially and to keep individual tax rates low. As a result, the deficit continued to increase.

Many of the president's disagreements with business stemmed from a tension between his own conservative ideology and the economic interests of the private sector. The president was persuaded that a substantial increase in defense spending was necessary if the United States was to reassert its preeminence in world affairs; business, on the other hand, was more interested in reducing the size of the budget deficit. Likewise, it was precisely the president's desire to strengthen the role of the market in allocating capital that led him to support a major reduction in the granting of tax preferences to business in 1986. The administration's resistance to virtually all of the pleas of particular industries for protection from imports as well as its unwillingness to restrict hostile takeovers also stemmed from the president's free-market orientation. In many respects, Reagan was not so much probusiness as he was anti-government.

A second factor had to do with the performance of the economy. Although Reagan did preside over the worst recession in the postwar period shortly after he took office, the economy recovered strongly after 1982. Between 1983 and 1987, economic growth averaged 3.4 percent and inflation averaged only 3.8 percent. Equally significant, the recovery was a continual one. By the fall of 1988, the economy had begun to approach the previous postwar record for consecutive months of growth set in the 1960s. This performance was not impressive enough to rekindle the economic euphoria of the 1960s or early 1970s. Real family income increased only modestly, and the magnitude of the trade deficit created considerable public anxiety about the long-term competitiveness of American industry. Nonetheless, the success of Reaganomics was sufficient to make politicians less deferential to the demands of business. It is unlikely that Congress would have increased the size of the superfund or raised corporate taxes so significantly in 1986 had the economy not recovered from both the stagflation in the late 1970s and the recession of the early 1980s.

A third factor contributing to the limited political effectiveness of business after 1981 was its own political division. The business community was unable to sustain the degree of unity and political cohesion that had served it so well between 1977 and 1981. With only a handful of exceptions, business lobbying after 1981 was not characterized by the kind of broad coalitions that had proved so effective in the late 1970s. To be sure, corporations and trade associations continued to form alliances; indeed, more than one hundred distinctive business coalitions were established during the 1980s. But more frequently than not, these new coalitions found themselves opposed by coalitions formed by other companies and trade associations. They also frequently sought to enlist nonbusiness constituencies as members in order to enhance their own legitimacy and effectiveness. In addition, 1980 and 1982 marked the high point of business political unity with respect to campaign contributions. In 1984 and 1986, a significant share of corporate spending was directed less at changing either the partisan or ideological composition of Congress than at securing advantages for particular segments of the business community. In 1986, nearly fifty percent of corporate and trade association PAC contributions went to Democrats.

In short, the focus of business political activity changed during the 1980s. Compared to the 1970s, a relatively small share of the political efforts of business was devoted to defending the interests of business as a whole or of particular industries from challenges from either the public-interest movement or organized labor. Rather, more of it was directed at advancing the economic interests of particular segments of the business community—often at the expense of other firms. In effect, the Washington office became another profit center; government relations became an integral component of economic competition. Companies originally came to Washington in the early 1970s primarily to defend themselves. But, once having invested so much in learning how the political process works, many decided to use their political skills to help them gain advantages over their competitors, domestic as well as foreign. As a result, the political agenda became increasingly dominated by the requests

of particular firms and industries for changes in public policies that would enhance their competitive positions. . . .

THE DYNAMICS OF BUSINESS POLITICAL INFLUENCE

How powerful is American business? The question itself is misconceived. There is little point in continuing to debate whether the managers and owners of American enterprises exercise political influence disproportionate to their share of the American population. Rather than analyzing the power of business in the abstract, we need to understand its exercise in dynamic terms: What, in fact, makes business as a whole, or segments of business, more or less powerful?

One of the most crucial factors that has affected the relative political influence of business is the public's perception of the long-term strength of the American economy. The relative political influence of business—particularly vis-à-vis public-interest groups—declined as a result of the strong performance of the American economy from the early 1960s through 1973. The 1974–75 recession did not immediately reverse this decline. This was due both to the scandals associated with Watergate that allowed the Democrats to make substantial gains in the 1974 congressional elections and the depth of public hostility to the oil industry following OPEC's oil embargo. But by 1978, business had regained the political initiative. Not only was it able to block the major legislative proposals of both organized labor and the public-interest movement but it began to make significant progress in achieving its own legislative goals. The perennial shortage of energy was now attributed in part to price controls, and in 1978, Congress began to phase them out, while the sluggish growth of business investment, coupled with stagflation, helped persuade Congress to reduce the capital-gains tax in 1978 and corporate income taxes three years later. The continued stagnation of the economy also gave credibility to the complaints of business about the cost of government regulation. Significantly, the high point of business's political influence during the last two decades coincided with the most severe postwar recession.

In turn, the relatively strong performance of the economy following the 1981–82 recession helped make it more difficult for business to further the political gains it had achieved between 1978 and 1981. It is unlikely that the Tax Reform Act of 1986 would have been enacted had the economy experienced another downturn in the mid-1980s, and a third energy crisis might well have made it more difficult for the environmental movement to continue to occupy the moral high ground following the Gorsuch-Watt scandals. On the other hand, the dramatic growth in foreign competition during the 1980s placed the issue of competitiveness on the political agenda and facilitated the efforts of some sectors of American business to secure government assistance in order to compete more effectively with foreign companies and countries.

A second critical factor that affects the relative political influence of business is the degree of cooperation among different firms and industries. One reason so many industries suffered so many political setbacks between the mid-1960s and early 1970s is that they received no assistance from other sectors of the business community. The automobile industry in 1966 and again in 1970, the textile industry and the meat packers in 1967, the cigarette companies in 1970, and the manufacturers of pesticides in 1972 each fought more or less alone. The only industries that were politically active were those whose members were directly affected by regulatory legislation. Likewise, many of the major political victories experienced by business between 1977 and 1981 can be attributed to the ability of a large number of firms, trade associations, and business organizations to work closely together—an effort that reached its climax with the passage of the Revenue Act of 1981. However, after 1981, the business community was less effective than it otherwise might have been because of divisions both within and among industries.

When business is both mobilized and unified, its political power can be formidable. But while the former is now the norm, the latter occurs relatively infrequently. Large numbers of firms were able to work together effectively only for approximately five years. The class consciousness of American business, like that of the American working class, is limited: companies generally tend to become aware of their common interests only when they are faced with a common enemy. In a number of respects, the 1970s were an unusual decade: a significant proportion of political issues affected the interests of business as a whole. As a result, by the end of the decade, companies and trade associations had learned the importance of cooperating with one another. But during the 1980s, as during the 1960s, relatively few issues united the business community. Instead, companies and industries generally pursued relatively narrow goals: corporate public affairs became another form of economic competition. In short, business is not a monolith: the extent of its political unity, like the extent of its political influence, fluctuates.

The political influence of business is also affected by the dynamics of the American political system. Prior to the mid-1960s, business did not need to become politically active to remain influential in Washington. The centralized structure of congressional decision making, along with the prevailing ideological consensus regarding the appropriate role of the federal government, effectively limited any expansion of government controls over the private sector. Over the next decade, both the institutional and the ideological barriers to increased government intervention were eroded, requiring business to play the game of interest-group politics in order to regain its influence. The political resurgence of business was in turn facilitated by a change in the laws governing campaign spending, the increased fragmentation of decision making in Congress, and an increase in public hostility to government.

However, politicians do not simply react passively to either changing economic conditions or interest-group pressures. They also have their own priorities and preferences, which are in turn shaped by both their ideology and their desire to be reelected. The Democratic senators who played a critical role in enacting consumer and environmental legislation during the 1960s and early 1970s, and who challenged the oil industry in the mid-1970s, were responding less to lobbying by public-interest groups than to their perception of the changing preferences of their constituents. President Johnson viewed consumer and environmental regulation as a way of maintaining the momentum of the Great Society without increasing government expenditures, and President Nixon's support for both occupational safety and health legislation and the strengthening of the Clean Air Act Amendments of 1970 was dictated by electoral considerations. In 1983, Ronald Reagan, motivated by the same considerations as Richard Nixon in 1970, hastily abandoned his effort to provide business with regulatory relief, lest the Democrats use the scandals at EPA to challenge his reelection bid. On occasion, politicians can transform the political agenda on their own. There was virtually no public interest in the issue of tax reform during the mid-1980s. It was placed on the political agenda because Ronald Reagan, supported by a handful of key congressional leaders from both parties, decided to make it the major political priority of his second term.

To paraphrase Karl Marx, business does make its own political history, but it does so in circumstances that are largely beyond its control. Since the mid-1960s, business has tended to be politically effective when its resources have been highly mobilized, when companies share similar objectives, when the public is critical of government, when the economy is performing relatively poorly, and when its preferences coincide with those of powerful politicians. But with the exception of the first, the ability of business to influence each of these contingencies is limited. There are many important issues on which it is simply impossible for substantial numbers of firms and business associations to agree. Business investment decisions are only one of the number of factors that affect the performance of the economy and, in any event, managers and owners are hardly likely to deliberately slow down the economy or reduce their company's profits so that their lobbyists can become more effective. Business certainly can, through both its campaign spending and influence over the climate of public and elite opinion, affect the preferences of politicians. But politicians' calculations are influenced by many considerations other than the desire to placate business. On balance, business is more affected by broad political and economic trends than it is able to affect them.

POSTSCRIPT

Is Government Dominated by Big Business?

Vogel's brand of pluralism is a linear kind: he says that the power of business ebbs and flows in American history. Business was dominant in the 1950s, in retreat during the 1960s and early 1970s, dominant again in the early 1980s, and is now once again on the defensive. The only change Edsall sees is the increasing political sophistication of business and a corresponding breakdown in countervailing forces. Perhaps the only way to see who is right is to examine contemporary political developments: to what extent does American business seem to be unified, confident, and successful today?

Social science literature contains a number of works discussing the issues of pluralism and corporate power. As noted in the introduction to this issue, Charles E. Lindblom was one of those early pluralists who made the journey all the way over to elite theory. His earlier book, written with political scientist Robert A. Dahl, was *Politics, Economics, and Welfare* (Harper, 1953). His repudiation of pluralism was complete by the time he published *Politics and Markets: The World's Political-Economic Systems* (Basic Books, 1977). Lindblom may have been influenced by some of the critiques of pluralism that appeared in the 1960s, including Peter Bachrach, *The Theory of Democratic Elitism* (Little, Brown, 1967), and Theodore Lowi, *The End of Liberalism* (W. W. Norton, 1969). Recent works arguing that corporate elites possess inordinate power in American society include Michael Schwartz, ed., *The Structure of Power in America* (Holmes & Meier, 1987), and G. William Domhoff, *The Power Elite and the State* (Aldine de Gruyter, 1990).

Other important studies of corporate elite dominance include Domhoff's earlier *Who Rules America Now?* (Prentice Hall, 1983); Michael Useem, *The Inner Circle* (Oxford University Press, 1984); Beth Mintz and Michael Schwartz, *The Power Structure of American Business* (University of Chicago Press, 1985); and Robert R. Alford and Roger Friedland, *Powers of Theory: Capitalism, the State, and Democracy* (Cambridge University Press, 1985).

Today, pluralism has few defenders, though Vogel's book may help it gain back some of the ground it has lost.

ISSUE 14

Does Welfare Do More Harm Than Good?

YES: Murray Weidenbaum, from "Beyond Handouts," *Across the Board* (April 1991)

NO: Theodore R. Marmor, Jerry L. Mashaw, and Philip L. Harvey, from *America's Misunderstood Welfare State: Persistent Myths, Enduring Realities* (Basic Books, 1990)

ISSUE SUMMARY

YES: Economist Murray Weidenbaum argues that the extensive system of welfare set up during the 1960s and early 1970s has mired the poor in dependency, making their condition worse, not better.
NO: Social analysts Theodore R. Marmor, Jerry L. Mashaw, and Philip L. Harvey contend that the American welfare state has been widely misunderstood by its critics and that conservative "reforms" will only increase the misery of the poor.

Long before Ronald Reagan's campaign for the presidency in 1980, the welfare problem had become a national issue. As far back as the Nixon administration, plans had been made to reform the system by various means, including the institution of modest cash payments based upon a negative income tax in place of the crazy quilt pattern of services, commodities, checks, and in-kind payments provided by the existing welfare system. The Carter administration also tried to interest Congress in a reform plan that would simplify, though probably not reduce, welfare.

There is a backlash against welfare recipients, often voiced in mean-spirited jibes such as "make the loafers work" and "I'm tired of paying them to breed." Such slogans ignore the fact that most people on welfare are not professional loafers, but women with dependent children or old or disabled persons. Petty fraud may not be uncommon, but "welfare queens" who cheat the system for spectacular sums are extremely rare. The overwhelming majority of people on welfare are those whose condition would become desperate if payments were cut off. Finally, to reassure those who worry that women on welfare commonly bear children in order to increase their benefits, there is no conclusive evidence that child support payments have anything to do with conception; the costs of raising children far exceed the payments.

This does not mean that all objections to welfare can be dismissed. There does seem to be evidence that welfare can in some cases promote work disincentives (welfare makes it possible for a recipient to stay home instead of looking for a job, for example). Benefits available in some states exceed what some recipients would earn after taxes if they did work, and the high rate at which welfare benefits are reduced as other income increases—the so-called notches in the payment scale—may mean that an additional dollar in earnings can result in more than a dollar loss in total income. Nor is it only in the economic sphere that the welfare system produces unintended effects. Of particular concern to sociologists were the experiments conducted during the 1970s in Seattle and Denver, in which poor families were supplied with guaranteed annual incomes. Breakups among these families then began to increase. The reasons for this phenomenon were not clear from the experiments, but some critics of welfare have hypothesized that guaranteed income may undermine the traditional "provider role" of husbands. There are also some severe social costs of welfare that must be borne by the recipients themselves. In addition to the stigma of being on welfare, there is the constant threat of intrusion by government agents. The social workers charged with administering the program have a great deal of power over those who receive the benefits, and some of the provisions of the program can add more strain to an already shaky family situation.

What is to be done about welfare? Broadly speaking, the suggestions fall into three categories: (1) Some say to *trim* the program. (2) Others advocate *monitoring* it carefully to make sure the truly needy are receiving a fair share of it and that work incentives are not lost. (3) Others favor outright *abolition* of welfare, except for the aged and the physically handicapped.

The *trim* approach was a central tenet in the philosophy of the Reagan administration. When Reagan first campaigned for the presidency in 1980, he promised to "get government off our backs." His contention was that government welfare programs tend to stifle initiative, depress the economy, and do the poor more harm than good. After eight years in office, Reagan's conservative critics claimed that he had not really fulfilled his promises to trim welfare; his liberal critics claimed that he had indeed carried out his promises, albeit with disastrous results.

The radical approach of abolishing welfare is advocated by writer Charles Murray in his 1984 book *Losing Ground*, which was extremely influential. Conservatives hailed it as a masterful critique and even writers on the left paid it a kind of backhanded homage by refuting it at length. In the following selections, Murray Weidenbaum takes Murray's side in denouncing the welfare state, while Theodore R. Marmor, Jerry L. Mashaw, and Philip L. Harvey criticize Murray in supporting welfare programs for the nation's poor.

YES

Murray Weidenbaum

BEYOND HANDOUTS

In 1935, President Franklin D. Roosevelt declared: "I can now see the end of public assistance in America." FDR's forecast did not come true despite the expenditure of what were then unparalleled amounts of Federal funds for a variety of programs to benefit the poor. The Administrations of Harry S. Truman and John F. Kennedy experienced the same frustration.

In 1964, President Lyndon B. Johnson announced: "The days of the dole in our country are numbered." Both the number of Americans in poverty and the size of the anti-poverty efforts expanded under the four Administrations that followed. Federal spending designed to achieve the Roosevelt-Johnson goal has totaled hundreds of billions of dollars during this period. Over the past 25 years, Federal spending for income support to individuals multiplied more than five times in constant dollars. Any way you measure it, the outlay of public funds to end poverty has been expanding faster than inflation and population combined or the number of poor people.

It is inaccurate for Americans to castigate themselves as a heartless society. In recent Presidential Administrations—whether that of Jimmy Carter or Ronald Reagan—a far larger share of the nation's resources has been devoted to social welfare programs than during the years when Roosevelt or Johnson served in the Oval Office. The problem is that these expensive efforts, while producing some gains, did not bring about the promised results.

There is virtually universal agreement in the United States that those who are physically or mentally unable to support themselves should be helped by society, and that such assistance should be provided in adequate amounts and with a minimum of hassle.

But over the years, a subtle yet profound broadening has occurred in the qualification for such aid. Low or no income has become the only basis necessary to qualify for the receipt of welfare, food stamps, and many other types of assistance. The governmental fiscal payments that the public earlier had referred to as "handouts," "charity," or the "dole" have become transformed into "transfer payments" and, more recently, "entitlements."

And what has been the effect of these entitlements? According to economic researchers, they reduce people's willingness to work. If that sounds

From Murray Weidenbaum, "Beyond Handouts," *Across the Board* (April 1991). Copyright © 1991 by Murray Weidenbaum. Reprinted by permission.

too jarring, let me resort to economic jargon. Researchers support "significant net negative impacts on labor supply." As would be expected, different researchers report different numerical results, but the overall negative impact of welfare on work effort is clear.

The realization is growing that many long-term welfare "clients" are families or individuals beset by a multiplicity of personal and social problems that are deeply rooted and that do not yield to simple economic approaches such as payment of cash. You needn't be a right-wing zealot to conclude that there is a powerful connection between the health of the family as an institution and the depth and pervasiveness of the poverty problem: Less than one out of every 10 married-couple families is poor. Men living alone consistently have unemployment rates that are more than double those of family men. Nine out of every 10 families on welfare are headed by women.

WITHOUT JUDGING THE MORAL BASES OF alternative life styles, it is apparent that there are very substantial economic consequences of such actions as having a child out of wedlock, getting divorced, or living with a partner without getting married. Much of the cost of such actions is not borne by the individuals making these decisions, but by society as a whole.

A persuasive argument can be made that in the case of poverty—and in many other areas of human conduct—individuals no longer bear the full consequences of their own actions or inactions. In olden times "a man who deserted his children pretty much insured that they would starve, or near to it, if he was not brought back, and that he would be horse-whipped if he were," said Senator

Daniel Patrick Moynihan nearly two decades ago. "The poor in the United States today enjoy a quite unprecedented de facto freedom to abandon their children in the certain knowledge that society will care for them and, what is more, in a state such as New York, to care for them by quite decent standards."

The freedom Moynihan speaks about is in large part a result of a number of Supreme Court decisions that have invalidated efforts to focus welfare benefits on the family:

• In the Court's 1968 ruling on King v. Smith, an Alabama law denying welfare to households that have "substitute fathers" (adult males unrelated to the mother by blood or marriage) was struck down. The decision, in effect, made cohabitation profitable in most states.

• In its 1972 decision of Weber v. Aetna Casualty and Surety Company, the Court ruled that worker's compensation benefits cannot be limited to legitimate children.

• In New Jersey Welfare Rights Organization v. Cahill, the Court's 1973 decision forbid state government preference for marriage over cohabitation in welfare programs.

• In 1973 the Court ruling on USDA v. Moreno invalidated a provision of the food stamp program basing household eligibility on ties of blood, marriage, or adoption.

In dealing with the problem of poverty, we need to recognize that it is not primarily a matter of how much money the government should spend on poor people. The basic issue is how to deal with poverty's root causes. To begin with, we must recognize that growth of the nation's economy is a necessary but by no means sufficient condition for eliminating poverty. An expanding economy creates new employment opportunities and makes it politically feasible to fund anti-poverty programs. But economic growth alone cannot cure the problem of chronic poverty. Many of the long-term poor have developed attitudes toward work that make it difficult for them to escape poverty.

As *The New Consensus on Family and Welfare*, a recent report issued by a panel of both liberal and conservative analysts, concluded, climbing out of poverty is not something that government can do for an individual. Rather, eliminating poverty is something that the individual must undertake, albeit with some help from society. More often than not it takes just three things for a person to move out of poverty: completing high school; getting and staying married, even if not on the first try; and staying employed, even if at modest wages, such as the statutory minimum wage.

Very few Americans, of any race, who are heads of households are even near poverty—if they have a high school education. In 1986, less than 5 percent of black males and less than 10 percent of black females who met this requirement were in poverty. Of adult black males who were high school graduates in 1986, 86 percent had family incomes more than twice the poverty level.

Welfare (technically aid for dependent children) has come a long way from the original justification—to help widows or divorced women make the difficult transition to a new status. In 1937–38, the father had died or was incapacitated in 71 percent of the welfare cases. Since then, public assistance has in large measure become a program that finances out-of-wedlock births. In 1983, 46 percent of the children receiving welfare benefits were born out of wedlock.

Not only does welfare finance illegitimate births, it also seems to promote them. A *Los Angeles Times* poll in 1985 reported that 70 percent of poor women say it is "almost always" or "often" true that "poor young women have babies so they can collect welfare." Two thirds say that welfare "almost always" or "often" encourages fathers to avoid family responsibilities.

Several specific ways have been suggested to reinforce the responsibility of parents for the support of their children. They include allowing lawyers to accept child-support cases on a contingency fee basis, instituting mandatory paternity findings to identify fathers of out-of-wedlock children receiving welfare, holding all fathers accountable for meeting child-support obligations and making strong efforts to collect from them, requiring young mothers on welfare to complete high school and then seek work, and not paying welfare benefits to mothers under 18 who are living in "independent households."

The third key to solving the poverty problem is work experience itself. It is counterproductive to advise people on welfare to hold out for "good" jobs rather than to leave welfare status for "dead-end" work. It seems obvious that if you stay on welfare, you'll never get any work experience.

Often negative attitudes rather than insufficient work opportunities keep people unemployed. Studies show that poor people do not keep the jobs that they find simply because they cannot get to work on time, will not work a full work schedule, and will not pay attention on the job. When out of work, the typical inner-city youngster is more likely to spend his time "hanging out or watching TV" than engaging in activities likely to help in getting a job, says Richard Freeman, the Harvard economist.

It is becoming apparent that much of what used to be the conventional wisdom about a sound public-assistance program is no longer widely endorsed; particularly unpopular is the keeping of able-bodied people on welfare rolls for long periods of time. A new consensus is emerging in favor of encouraging welfare recipients to get steady work.

THE WORKING SEMINAR ON FAMILY AND American Welfare Policy, which brought together researchers from a variety of policy institutes such as Brookings Institution and the Heritage Foundation, concludes that it is essential that all able recipients of welfare either be working or be enrolled—for just a limited period of time, they stress—in education and training programs. Furthermore, the seminar members urge that "the overriding emphasis" be placed on personal responsibility for finding jobs in the private sector rather than on government job-placement efforts. Work is seen as more than a way to cut welfare costs and promote self-sufficiency. It confers emotional and psychological benefits on the recipients and is an opportunity for them to join the nation's mainstream.

Many proponents of making welfare recipients work want *all* recipients to hold a job—even those with young children. This does not seem unreasonable. In 1986, 61 percent of all mothers worked (including 53 percent of mothers with children under the age of six), but only 9 percent of mothers on welfare.

When a woman on welfare takes a full-time job, the odds are overwhelming that she is lifting herself out of poverty. In every state, a woman holding a full-time job at the minimum wage—plus the remaining welfare benefits that she is still eligible for—provides enough income to lift the average welfare family (one mother and two children) above the poverty level. And few women working steadily earn only the minimum wage, even without a high school degree.

Most states have not given work requirements a high priority. Saying you tried to get a job by registering with the employment service is usually sufficient to meet the regulatory requirements. West Virginia is an exception. Here, workfare (jobs provided by the state government) is seen as a way of providing public services that the state government cannot otherwise afford. Surveys of work-site supervision indicate that people taking part in the workfare program are, on average, about as productive as regular employees.

Some scholars, such as the sociologists Francis Fox Piven and Barbara Ehrenreich, have criticized the workfare approach as a new form of "mass peonage," contending that forcing millions of poor Americans into an already overcrowded, underpaid labor force will not cure their poverty. These scholars' answer is to raise welfare benefits "at least to the poverty level."

Many researchers, however, assert that trying to increase government transfer payments to the poor sufficiently to eliminate poverty would place in jeopardy the willingness of many other workers to take a host of low and moderately paid jobs. In addition, there is solid evidence to support the widely held belief that welfare recipients migrate to states where they receive the best benefits package.

The new consensus among researchers on welfare policy is that it has been a mistake to offer welfare benefits without imposing on the recipients the same obligations that are assumed by other citizens—to try to become self-sufficient through education, responsible family behavior, and work.

It is unlikely, though, that wholesale changes in life styles, attitudes, and other characteristics of large numbers of low-income individuals can be achieved quickly. The uneven experience with work requirements and other efforts to reform welfare suggest that changes should not be introduced on a massive scale or designed for swift results, but should be made in the spirit of experimentation. It is probable that the financial burden of maintaining large social welfare programs will continue to take a major share of the Federal budget. Any improvements are likely to occur at the margins, but they surely are a worthwhile undertaking.

NO

Theodore R. Marmor,
Jerry L. Mashaw, and
Philip L. Harvey

AMERICA'S MISUNDERSTOOD WELFARE STATE

We believe that claims of social, political, and economic crisis attributable to the welfare state are either demonstrably false or wildly exaggerated. . . .

A . . . positive view of our social welfare efforts is justified. The public has shown that it supports the programs constituting the American welfare state. It deserves to feel better about that support. There is no dearth of problems in the administration of individual programs; obvious gaps exist in the protection they afford; and practical achievements fall short of our aspirations. Still, claims that these programs actually harm the economy do not withstand close scrutiny. Nagging concerns that the welfare state may be responsible for sluggish economic growth, that it is unaffordable, and that its growth is beyond our control deserve to be dismissed.

THE (ECONOMICALLY) UNDESIRABLE WELFARE STATE

Before we begin, we want to make it clear that we are not here discussing the morally most controversial elements of the American welfare state, in particular, cash assistance to the able-bodied poor. "Welfare" is a perennial topic of controversy, but it is of very little significance to the fiscal difficulties of the modern welfare state. Because cash assistance programs for the able-bodied poor are so small, whatever "perverse incentives" they provide, they can have no significant impact on general economic productivity. We will document and elaborate these points [later]. For now, we only want to avoid confusing the "crisis of the welfare state" with the "problems of welfare." The vast majority of welfare state expenditures are for social insurance programs that provide cash and in-kind assistance to persons who are not expected to work and who have earned their entitlement to welfare state support through prior contributions to social insurance. It is these large,

From Theodore R. Marmor, Jerry L. Mashaw, and Philip L. Harvey, *America's Misunderstood Welfare State: Persistent Myths, Enduring Realities* (Basic Books, 1990). Copyright © 1990 by Basic Books, Inc. Reprinted by permission of Basic Books, a division of HarperCollins Publishers. Notes omitted.

politically popular social insurance programs that are at issue in debates over the economic effects of the welfare state. . . .

The weakness of the claim that welfare state spending hurts economic growth is also demonstrated by comparative data. If growing social welfare expenditures depress growth rates, one would expect countries that spend more on social welfare programs to suffer from lower rates of economic growth. However, . . . data from the Organization for Economic Cooperation and Development (OECD) shows that over the period in which American economic growth has been recognized to be a problem, social welfare expenditures in Western industrial nations have had no consistent relationship to rates of economic growth. Neither the percentage of GNP [gross national product] spent on social welfare programs nor the rate of growth of social welfare expenditures has a consistent relationship with overall growth rates. The great variability of growth rates among both big social welfare spenders and small social welfare spenders suggests that other factors must play a decisive role in determining economic growth rates. . . .

THE UNAFFORDABLE WELFARE STATE

There is some difficulty in understanding what is meant by the claim that social welfare expenditures are unaffordable. In one sense the idea is synonymous with the claim that social welfare spending limits economic growth: We can't afford the welfare state because it steadily shrinks the economic base from which it is financed. We have already explained why it is misguided to believe that social welfare expenditures are operating to limit economic growth either by their effects on the savings rate or their effects on work effort and labor mobility.

From another perspective, the "affordability" of the welfare state depends on our willingness to pay for it. In the ordinary private household, when we say we "can't afford" something, we normally mean that we don't have the cash or cannot finance it in a way that allows us to carry the capital costs of acquisition while maintaining other expenditures at desired levels. Translated to the public realm, this would be a claim that there are not sufficient tax revenues to finance current expenditures for social welfare programs and that the public is unwilling to pay sufficient taxes for their current support or for the debt retirement necessary to bring these accounts back into balance. As such, the claim is transparently false. The major American programs of social insurance are in current balance—indeed headed toward mammoth surpluses—and the public reports itself willing to pay more to maintain them at current levels. There is no deficit here of either fiscal capacity or fiscal will. Public willingness to support the smaller, noninsurance portions of the welfare state is not as strong as the support for social insurance, and its continued support is, therefore, not so certain should the economy worsen. But if we declared AFDC [Aid to Families with Dependent Children] and Food Stamps "unaffordable" tomorrow and reduced their expenditures to zero, we would have erased only 10 percent of the overall budget deficit. These programs are simply too small to have much bearing on the affordability of the welfare state. . . .

There is no reason to believe that the current size or character of the American welfare state is a serious impediment to economic growth, threatens us with imminent public bankruptcy, or makes adjustment and "steering" of social policy and expenditure impossible. For all the talk of "crisis" in the welfare state, there is precious little evidence to bolster that claim. The institutions of the welfare state have not reflected—either in their programmatic actions or by their inability to adjust—the sense of critical disjuncture that hostile intellectuals have managed, with the help of some politicians, to popularize. . . .

[T]here exists something like a set of standard beliefs among well-educated adults concerning welfare, poverty, and the welfare state.

The standard belief goes something like this: First, by "welfare," most people mean cash assistance for needy families provided by the Aid to Families with Dependent Children program (AFDC). Second, "welfare," so defined, is viewed as a substantial and growing component of American social welfare expenditures. Third, AFDC in particular, and means-tested programs in general, are viewed as the government's primary weapons in combating poverty. Finally, there is, if not a conviction, at least a concern that these massive expenditures have failed to turn the tide in the war against poverty. Many people adopt the even more pessimistic view that welfare actually has contributed to the incidence of poverty. "Welfare," in short, is seen as having failed in its essential goals. . . .

THE SIZE, GROWTH, AND CHARACTER OF "WELFARE"

. . . [T]he belief that the American welfare state has grown dramatically over the past two decades is surely correct.

Total federal spending has risen spectacularly since the 1960s, whether measured in terms of total dollars spent or as a percentage of either total federal spending or gross national product. But "welfare" is not "the welfare state." Indeed, once we begin to dig into the numbers, we discover that social welfare spending and welfare spending have followed radically different paths.

First, take a look at spending for AFDC, the program that most people equate with welfare. . . . The facts are startling, given the common view that welfare expenditures constitute a substantial and growing component of the American welfare state. In real terms, AFDC spending was lower in 1987 than it was in 1971. As a percentage of total federal social welfare expenditures, of total federal outlays, and of GNP, it has also shrunk. Nor is this shrinkage trivial. In relation to total spending by the federal government, AFDC has been cut to less than a third of its former relative size. At less than 4 percent of total federal social welfare spending, AFDC is fiscally an insubstantial part of the American welfare state. At less than two-fifths of one percent of GNP, this program's contribution, if any, to our current fiscal strain is vanishingly small.

Why are popular impressions of the size of welfare programs so wide of the mark? There are several answers to this question, and all are important for understanding the American welfare state and the quite different public assistance system for low-income persons that we actually have constructed. There is a tendency to equate "welfare" with AFDC, to equate both with the "welfare state," and to regard the latter as synonymous with "antipoverty" programs. As a comparison of the welfare state's growth with

AFDC's relative decline makes clear, some of these equivalencies are wildly wrong-headed. Welfare is a minuscule fraction of the American welfare state. . . .

A Brief Recapitulation. We now know a fair amount about the state of welfare and poverty in the American welfare state. Cash assistance to the poor has never been a large part of our welfare state and is literally dwarfed by social insurance expenditures. This pattern of expenditure fits our preferences for pooling common risks and the creation of opportunity as the primary functions of the welfare state. The American public may care about the elimination of poverty, but it is not keen on addressing income poverty through the simple expedient of cash transfers to the poor. Fortunately, however, our large and growing welfare state, particularly its social insurance component, does prevent much poverty. As the American welfare state has grown over the last three decades, the rate of poverty has declined by nearly 40 percent. . . .

WELFARE AND DEPENDENCY

Why did progress against poverty stagnate in the early 1970s? Why did the incidence of poverty actually grow in the early 1980s? Why did both of these results occur while overall welfare state expenditures were steadily increasing? Charles Murray provided a widely publicized answer to these questions that captured the imaginations of many in his 1984 book, appropriately entitled, *Losing Ground*. The welfare state must spend more and more to do less and less, said Murray, because it actually aggravates the problem it is ostensibly designed to solve. Welfare generates rather than reduces dependency.

The World According to Murray. From this perspective the substantial success story we have been telling is instead a story of failure. We should be looking not at how many are poor *after* welfare state transfers, but how many are poor *before* those payments are made. The welfare state should be viewed as a success only if the pretransfer or "latent" poor are declining. The numbers show that this is not the case. The latent poor are in fact increasing. Why? Murray claims that it is because the welfare state encourages dependency. It gives people money and other support for taking up positions in society for which transfers are available. We are now simply spending more and more to support the dependents that we have created and continue to create. The only solution is to stop making the payments. . . .

A basic failing in Murray's argument is one we have already encountered. His approach is enormously overgeneral. Does he really mean that income transfers and other supports are causing people to get old, to become blind or disabled, to need medical care? Not really. In fact, of the welfare state's major support programs, Murray is really only concerned with "welfare," principally AFDC. And since we know that the major growth areas of the welfare state have been elsewhere, the image that Murray conjures up of massive expenditures on antipoverty efforts to no, or to detrimental, effect is just that—image, not reality. Taking "welfare" in its broadest sense of means-tested programs, he could be talking about somewhere between 14 percent and 23 percent of welfare state expenditures. Yet, throughout *Losing Ground* he often seems to be talking about much, much more.

To put the point slightly differently, Murray's idea of increasing "latent poverty" or "dependency" suffers from a seriously misleading lack of focus. "Dependency" sounds like a bad thing, but that is because we tend to associate it with particular subgroups of the "latent poor," those whom we believe should be supporting themselves. Does Murray really think, for example, that the very substantial reduction of poverty among the aged over the past twenty-five years has been a bad thing? Would he argue that Social Security pensions should be viewed as having created a group of "dependents" who represent a serious social welfare policy failure? Again, clearly not. He has simply used a technical term, "latent poverty," interchangeably with a pejorative label, "dependency," to justify a massive and unnecessary sense of disquiet about our social welfare arrangements.

What then is Murray really concerned about? The answer is straightforward: young, unemployed males and young, unmarried females with illegitimate children, especially among blacks. Now let us get one thing straight at the outset. We agree with Murray that these are people who deserve our concern. Youth unemployment, illegitimacy, and the formation of female-headed households are indeed serious problems. They are highly associated with poverty, and they are particularly concentrated in poor black communities. The question, however, is what the relationship is between these problems and welfare. . . .

If Murray is correct about incentive effects, we should expect to find that the illegitimacy rates in states with very high AFDC payments would be greater than the illegitimacy rates in states with lower payments. But careful research fails to reveal any significant effect of AFDC levels on illegitimacy. . . .

In short, researchers have not been able to find any substantial evidence to support Murray's thesis that links increased illegitimacy to welfare changes. But what about unemployment or labor force participation? According to Murray's thesis, as the real value of AFDC benefits rises, more Harolds live off of more Phyllises' AFDC checks and become unemployed or drop out of the labor force. The reverse should also be the case—as AFDC benefits go down in real terms, the number of unemployed Harolds should decrease as well. [In *Losing Ground*, Murray examines the question of the relationship between youth unemployment, illegitimacy, and the formation of female-headed households in terms of a hypothetical couple named Harold and Phyllis. They represent young, poorly educated, unmarried, prospective parents considering the benefits and disadvantages of getting married and getting jobs—Eds. Note.]

Testing this thesis is not as easy as one might think. The unemployment figures do not identify which of the unemployed are Harolds with a Phyllis to support them and which are the Homers who haven't a romantic prospect in sight. About the best that can be done is to look at the unemployment rates for young black men. Because black women receive about one-half of all AFDC payments, we are here in something like the right ballpark. But as the charts and tables in Murray's own book attest, the numbers moved in exactly the opposite direction from the one he would have predicted. As AFDC benefits went up in the late 1960s, the unemployment of young black men fell. As the real value of AFDC benefits declined over the whole of the

1970s, the unemployment rates for young black men rose. . . .

Our point is that Murray's story of the dynamics of welfare and dependency is wildly exaggerated. The change in economic incentives produced by the welfare "reforms" of the 1960s were quite modest, and the effects of those incentives on behavior were so small that serious social scientists have been unable to detect them after assiduous effort.

But if Murray is right that the latent poverty rate was going up during the 1970s and 1980s, and if we are right that this increase in "dependency" cannot be ascribed to American welfare policy, then what was happening? The answer is quite straightforward. First, pretransfer poverty is highly sensitive to the unemployment rate. . . . The poverty rate for most periods parallels the unemployment rate. Indeed, serious attempts to estimate the impact of unemployment on poverty rates find that an increase in the unemployment rate of 1 percent increases pretransfer poverty by 0.7 percent.

Second, demographic trends also affect the poverty rate. Certain groups—the aged, children, female-headed households, and nonwhites—have always been at greater risk of poverty in the United States. If the percentage of residents having these characteristics was increasing over the period from the mid-1960s to the mid-1980s, one would expect the poverty rate before transfers to be increasing as well. This has indeed been the case. When the poverty rate for all persons is adjusted for changes in demographics, it falls nearly $1\frac{1}{2}$ percentage points below the official poverty rate reported by the Census Bureau.

Finally, a trend toward increasing inequality in earned income has been at work in the United States for the past several decades. Through the mid-1970s this trend was counterbalanced by the equalizing effect of rapidly rising income transfer benefits. But as the growth in social welfare spending slowed, the underlying tendency toward increasing inequality began to predominate. The causes of this trend are not well-understood, but it has been very broad-based, affecting virtually all population groups, occupations, and industries. It has not been limited to the poor but instead appears to reflect a trend towards inequality in the distribution of market income generally.

These three factors—rising average unemployment rates, an increase in the percentage of the population in high-risk groups, and a long-term trend toward inequality in the distribution of market income—explain virtually all of the change in pretransfer poverty rates which has occurred in the United States from the beginning of the War on Poverty to the publication of *Losing Ground*. There is little cause for comfort in the identification of these trends. They pose a series of daunting challenges to policymakers. But we can at least feel confident that our efforts to relieve poverty have not been causing it to grow.

Welfare is not causing poverty, illegitimacy, and a flight from work. But overall poverty rates are as high now as they were in the late 1960s; illegitimacy is increasing; and the employment rates of some subgroups, particularly of young black men, lag far behind the general population. . . .

Unemployment and Poverty. The principal determinant of poverty is unemployment, and of long-term poverty, long-term unemployment. This is true not only in the United States; it is what our Western European allies have found as well. Most of the developed Western nations have seen their levels of poverty creep up over the last decade along with their levels of unemployment. In the United Kingdom, France, Germany, and elsewhere, there is increasing talk of a permanent class of persons left out of the labor market. Many factors contribute to this emerging problem, but in every case analysts have found high unemployment rates to be the principal cause. . . .

THE STATE OF WELFARE

"Welfare" (meaning the major means-tested programs of the American welfare state) has changed rapidly in the United States over the past two decades. In the late 1960s and early 1970s, welfare grew, both programmatically, adding Medicaid, Food Stamps, and SSI [Supplementary Security Income] to long-standing public assistance programs, and fiscally, as Congress and state legislatures beefed up their attack on poverty. Since the mid-1970s, "welfare" funding has varied from program to program and within discrete periods, but the overall total has remained roughly constant. Meanwhile, economic conditions have worsened and eligibility requirements have become increasingly stringent. Welfare expenditures are a modest part of the welfare state, but the one most sensitive to the general economic health of the country. This sensitivity constrains the antipoverty effectiveness of means-tested programs. As poverty increases in bad times, welfare expenditures are unlikely to fill the gap.

But welfare cannot in any event be expected to eliminate poverty in the United States. Our welfare programs are not designed for that purpose. They are designed instead to support particular populations subject to risks beyond their control, and to provide certain basic goods and services necessary to health and potential productivity. We seek to protect the "deserving poor" and to provide the means for achieving economic self-sufficiency. It is both unnecessary and inaccurate to explain the failure of welfare to eliminate poverty by asserting that welfare *causes* poverty. The purpose, structure, and fiscal dynamics of welfare are explanation enough.

To evaluate welfare by its capacity to solve the pretransfer poverty problem borders on the absurd. Welfare's success or failure can be appreciated only in terms of its real aims—to help those who cannot help themselves and to promote family independence and self-support. Where those two aims are not perceived to be in conflict, as with support of the aged and the disabled poor, we have made real progress in reducing the incidence of posttransfer poverty. This progress is due, in part, to the greater fiscal stability of the welfare programs that target these groups (SSI and Medicaid), but more importantly to our relatively generous and nearly universal social insurance programs. On the other hand, where a conflict is thought to exist between the goal of relieving material distress and that of encouraging self-sufficiency, as in AFDC, we are prone to failure. We want to protect dependent children, but we do not want to encourage their able-bodied parents to abandon their responsibility to support either their children or themselves. The result has been a program with low payments and stringent, often degrading, eligibility conditions, a program that seems to serve neither of the purposes of welfare very well.

POSTSCRIPT

Does Welfare Do More Harm Than Good?

The welfare debate in this issue has been argued in rational terms. In the public arena, however, it is entangled in emotional language, and rational discussion seems impossible. One side accuses the other of being heartless. The other side responds with anecdotes about "welfare queens." The only way a genuine public dialogue can begin is to de-escalate the rhetoric.

A little candor on both sides might help. Surely all rational Americans accept the fact that there are genuinely needy people. In many cases, these people do not have families to help them, and private charity is limited. They need public assistance. At the same time, we have to recognize that public assistance carries with it a cost—not merely the immediate dollar cost of the programs, but cost in terms of its effect on self-respect and work incentives.

After analyzing its history and structure, Sar A. Levitan and Clifford M. Johnson conclude that the current welfare system is a rational and necessary response to emerging societal needs in *Beyond the Safety Net: Reviving the Promise of Opportunity in America* (Ballinger, 1984). Michael B. Katz, *The Undeserving Poor: From the War on Poverty to the War on Welfare* (Pantheon Books, 1989), traces the evolution of welfare policies in the United States from the 1960s through the 1980s. Michael K. Brown, ed., *Remaking the Welfare State: Retrenchment and Social Policy in America and Europe* (Temple University Press, 1988), is a collection of 14 essays pondering the present and future of the welfare state. Among the more thoughtful (and troubling) essays is that of political scientist Andrew Hacker, who contends that "providing for citizens who are not self-supporting may well become the nation's foremost activity."

Writers who criticize the welfare program for going too far include Martin Anderson, *Welfare* (Hoover Institution, 1977), Charles Hobbs, *The Welfare Industry* (Heritage Foundation, 1978), and Jack D. Douglas, *The Myth of the Welfare State* (Transaction, 1989). Neil Gilbert acknowledges in *Capitalism and the Welfare State* (Yale University Press, 1983) that the welfare system is overextended, but he points out that this is largely because much of the money goes into the pockets of middle-class service providers and middle-class recipients. An excellent review of some of the debates on the welfare system from several viewpoints is presented in the January/February 1986 issue of *Society*. A work that should be examined to understand the psychology of the recipients of welfare is Leonard Goodwin's *Causes and Cures of Welfare: New Evidence on the Social Psychology of the Poor* (Lexington, 1983). He explodes the myth that welfare recipients do not want to work and argues that welfare creates less dependency than is commonly supposed.

ISSUE 15

Does the Breakup of Communism Show the Success of Capitalism?

YES: Milton Friedman, from "Four Steps to Freedom," *National Review* (May 14, 1990)

NO: Robert Pollin and Alexander Cockburn, from "The World, the Free Market and the Left," *The Nation* (February 25, 1991)

ISSUE SUMMARY

YES: Economist Milton Friedman contends that the countries newly liberated from communist dictatorships can emerge from economic ruin by adopting laissez-faire capitalism.

NO: Economist Robert Pollin and Alexander Cockburn, columnist for *The Nation*, argue that the collapse of Soviet communism does not invalidate the role of socialist planning as an essential tool for broadening democracy and making the economy serve human needs.

In November 1917, one month after the birth of the Soviet Union, a visiting American journalist named John Reed predicted that "this proletarian government will last . . . in history, a pillar of fire for mankind forever." The Soviet "pillar of fire" lasted 74 years, and when what was left of it was extinguished in December 1991, another visiting American journalist, Serge Schemann of the *New York Times*, offered this assessment of the first communist nation-state.

> It had promised no less than the creation of a "Soviet new man," imbued with selfless devotion to the common good, and it ended up all but crushing the initiative and spirit of the people, making many devoted only to vodka. It had proclaimed a new humanitarian ideology, and in its name butchered 10 million of its own. It envisioned a planned economy in which nothing was left to chance, and it created an elephantine bureaucracy that finally smothered the economy. Promising peace and freedom, it created the world's most militarized and ruthless police state.

At the time of its founding, however, and for nearly the first three decades of its existence, the Soviet Union was regarded by many Western reformers as a model socialist system. They claimed that the new Soviet republic had put an end to exploitation, eliminated class differences, instituted a highly rational system of distribution, reformed the educational system, infused the masses with a new cooperative spirit, and was well on its way to abolishing poverty altogether. Ironically, most of these observations were made during the darkest years of Soviet totalitarianism, when the masses of people lived in poverty and fear or died in concentration camps.

Today, few socialists attempt to defend the practices of the former Soviet Union. Some even deny that it deserved to be called socialist. This brings us to definitions. In general terms, *socialism* stands for public ownership of the major means of production and distribution. Under *capitalism*, goods are produced and distributed under private control; this is also called a *market economy*, because it relies upon buying and selling to determine prices and wages. As socialists view it, capitalism leads inevitably to distortions—to huge economic differences between rich and poor, poverty in the midst of plenty, chronic unemployment and exploitation of workers, periodic economic depression and inflation, and a culture that glorifies consumption and greed. Socialism aims to replace competition for profit with cooperation and social responsibility.

The dispute between proponents of socialism and capitalism is sometimes seen as a clash between the ideals of equality and liberty. Socialists have a passion for equality; what bothers them is not merely poverty but poverty side by side with great wealth. For promoters of capitalism, on the other hand, the theme of freedom seems to predominate: freedom to buy and sell, to change what you please, and to contract over terms and conditions of work. The keynote is economic freedom. Yet both sides to the dispute would probably insist that they support *both* equality and freedom. Socialists often claim that capitalism, not socialism, is the real enemy of freedom. What kind of freedom do you have if you cannot feed yourself? What kind of freedom does a worker have to leave a job if there is no other work available? For their part, the promoters of capitalism say that they are the true friends of equality—equality of opportunity. Pure capitalism is not interested in anyone's skin color, family background, or political connections. It is interested in performance. Build a better car, do a better job, charge a lower price, and you will be rewarded. Under socialism, they add, rewards are handed out arbitrarily, by bureaucrats and apparatchiks, who make sure they reward themselves amply.

This brings us to the future of socialism and capitalism. At the present period, the collapse of Soviet socialism and the retreat from socialism and quasi-socialism in other countries have put socialists on the defensive. But it would be premature for capitalists to proclaim victory. If socialism has not worked very well, how is capitalism going to work? Now that the people of the former Soviet Union and Eastern Europe are experiencing a market economy, they are getting a taste of its less pleasant features: unemployment, hyperinflation, and the diminution of state assistance to those in need. How long the people will endure these hardships remains to be seen. In the following selections, Milton Friedman expresses the hope that they will stay the course until prosperity comes, while Robert Pollin and Alexander Cockburn insist that human needs can be served only through socialist planning.

YES

Milton Friedman

FOUR STEPS TO FREEDOM

The political revolutions in Eastern Europe have raised in an acute form questions about the relation among four different sorts of freedom (civil, personal, economic, and political) that have troubled economists, political scientists, and philosophers for centuries.

It is a historical fact that 1) free and prosperous societies have been rare in world history, very much the exception; 2) all such exceptional societies have organized the bulk of their economic activities through free private markets—competitive private capitalism; 3) the converse is not true: not all societies that have organized the bulk of their activities through free private markets have enjoyed civil, personal, and political freedom (Classical Greece and the pre–Civil War U.S. with their slaves are ancient examples; Portugal under Salazar and Chile under Pinochet are more recent examples); 4) political freedom is neither necessary nor sufficient for economic, civil, and personal freedom (re necessary, Hong Kong has been one of the freest societies in the world in these respects, yet it has had no political freedom: it has been ruled by Britain; re sufficient, India has had a large measure of political freedom, yet it has little economic freedom and only limited civil and personal freedom); 5) political freedom has often led to the limitation and destruction of economic and civil freedom and to its own demise (the former British colonies "liberated" after World War II are striking examples).

These historical facts make it evident that economic, civil, personal, and political freedoms are not the mutually reinforcing quartet that would so neatly satisfy the value most of us attach to all four components.

A full discussion of the complex relation among the several freedoms—and of their connection with economic prosperity—is the subject for a treatise. At the moment, the vital issue is the implications of the political upheaval in Eastern Europe.

The collapse of totalitarian governments has produced understandable rejoicing in all the countries involved and in the Western world as a whole. But that collapse has also raised unreasonable expectations of economic improvement as a prompt result of the political change. Those expectations

From Milton Friedman, "Four Steps to Freedom," *National Review* (May 14, 1990). Copyright © 1990 by National Review, Inc., 150 East 35th Street, New York, NY 10016. Reprinted by permission.

are bound to be frustrated, endangering the new and fragile political structures.

Some authoritarian societies have moved fairly rapidly toward economic and civil freedom—most recently, Spain after Franco and Chile after Pinochet. But so far no totalitarian society has achieved a large degree of economic and civil freedom. When I was in China over a year ago, I had high hopes that it might prove the first. Tiananmen Square shattered that hope. Will Poland, Hungary, Czechoslovakia, Bulgaria, or Rumania provide the first example? (I omit East Germany because its prospective unification with West Germany makes it a special case.)

MAKING A START

The transition to freedom cannot be accomplished overnight. The formerly totalitarian societies have developed institutions, public attitudes, and vested interests that are wholly antithetical to the rapid creation of the basic economic requisites for freedom and prosperity.

These requisites are easy to state, but far from easy to achieve.

1. First and most important: the bulk of wealth (including means of production) must be privately owned to the fullest sense, so that the private owner has wide discretion in its use and can transfer it to other private individuals or groups of private individuals on mutually agreeable terms. This condition implicitly includes the right of any individual to exchange any services or products with others on any terms that are mutually agreeable: i.e., no control over wages or prices, including foreign-exchange rates; no restrictions on imports or exports.

This stark statement conceals many complexities in the words "bulk" and "privately owned." "Private property" cannot be defined *a priori* because of possible conflicts between the rights of different individuals; and it cannot be complete, because of the necessity of financing and carrying out essential government functions such as defense. Nonetheless, it states the most important single condition for achieving freedom and prosperity.

2. Security of private property is implicit in the first condition. If governments can and frequently do expropriate property, property owners will have no incentive to take a long view—to preserve their property and enhance its economic value.

3. In order for private property to be secure, government must be narrowly limited to its essential functions of maintaining law and order, including enforcing private contracts; of providing a judicial system to adjudicate differences in the interpretation of contracts and to assure that laws against theft, murder, and the like are applied justly; of establishing the rules of the game, including the definition of private property.

4. I list a relatively stable monetary system as a separate item rather than as part of item 3 for two reasons: a) As a theoretical matter, a stable money can exist without governmental involvement (other than to enforce private contracts). That was largely the case when gold or silver or some other commodity was the base of the monetary system. b) As a practical matter, the major immediate threat to successful reform in most of the countries in question is inflation and the danger of hyperinflation. So monetary reform is a particularly urgent task.

No advanced Western society possesses these requisites in anything like full measure, though all possessed them in far greater measure when they achieved rapid growth and attained prosperity. I would contend that if they had then departed from the ideal as much as they do now, they would not today be "advanced." The countries seeking to imitate the success of the West will make a great mistake if they pattern their policies on the current situation in the West rather than on what the situation was when the Western countries were at the stage the Eastern European countries are at now. Only our attained wealth enables us to support such wasteful, overblown government sectors. Hong Kong is a far better model for these than the U.S., Great Britain, or Sweden.

None of these requisites is easy to achieve. The one thing that is common to all of them is a drastic reduction in the size and role of the government. Such a reduction threatens almost every powerful vested interest in the current society. Indeed, it will be attainable, I believe, only under conditions of extreme crisis and only if done rapidly. Macbeth's words about the assassination of Duncan, "if it were done when 'tis done, then 'twere well it were done quickly," are equally applicable to the assassination of a totalitarian government.

A detailed blueprint specifying how to achieve these requisites is not possible. The specific details will depend on the circumstances of the separate countries, which differ widely with respect to economic arrangements, public attitudes, social structure, and political conditions. But a number of general remarks are possible.

1. With respect to the first requisite—widespread private property—some parts of the transfer of government-owned property to private individuals can be done readily: for example, the transfer by sale of current government-owned housing units to those existing tenants willing to buy them (for cash or credit) at a price that corresponds to a reasonable capitalization of a private market rental (the qualification is necessary because present rents are often nominal). A similar process is possible for relatively small enterprises: government-owned retail and service shops, small manufacturing enterprises, and the like. The most difficult problem is raised by larger-scale enterprises—steel mills, automobile plants, shipyards, coal mines, railroads, and so on. . . . One much-bruited solution must be avoided: selling the enterprises at bargain-basement prices to foreigners. That is equally true of another proposed solution: transferring plants to their employees. The property has been accumulated at the expense of all the citizens; no favored group should get something for nothing. Liabilities as well as assets should be transferred to private individuals—not transferring assets to individuals while leaving liabilities to the government.

Foreigners should be free to invest and engage in economic activity on the same terms as private citizens; no specially favorable conditions should be granted to them.

2. With respect to security of private property, it can only be attained over a long period as a middle class grows up that is independent of the government and can provide a climate of respect for private property and ownership.

3. With respect to a stable monetary system and, indirectly, the free-price system required to make private property meaningful, two steps are essential: first, a sharp reduction in government spending so that the government is not forced to print money to finance its expenditures; second, a prompt elimination of all

controls over foreign-exchange transactions and the prices of foreign currencies "Convertibility" can and should be achieved overnight simply by removing all restrictions on the terms on which individuals can exchange domestic currency for foreign currencies. Governmentally fixed exchange rates are, in my opinion, the most pernicious of all price controls, inevitably generating other internal price controls and assuring widespread corruption. The truth about the real value of the country's currency will hurt—but also be curative.

Even though many required measures can and should be taken quickly, the transition to a stable and prosperous competitive capitalist society will inevitably take years, not months. It will require patience on the part of the populace and faith that matters are moving in the right direction. Inevitably, some people and groups will suffer in the process. However, the talk about "the enormous costs of moving to a free-market economy" is much too gloomy. There is no reason why total output cannot start expanding rapidly almost immediately after the totalitarian restrictions on people's activities are removed. That certainly was the case in the agricultural sector of China after the major reforms of the late 1970s. Removing the controls on wages, prices, and exchange rates, and eliminating the compulsory allocations of labor, could produce the same results in Eastern Europe.

One final note: the widespread talk of the need for major financial assistance from Western governments to the emerging democratic governments of Eastern Europe is, in my opinion, not only wrong but dangerous. Such aid would do far more harm than good (as most foreign aid has done in the past). It would retard the transition, not speed it up. The transition requires above all reducing the size and scope of government so that the private sector can expand and take over basic productive and other activities. Aid to governments strengthens them, and encourages them to continue their counterproductive interventions in the economy and to postpone taking the necessary steps toward a free and viable economy.

The unprecedented political upheavals that believers in human freedom have welcomed with so much joy can be the prelude to comparable economic miracles, but that is far from inevitable. They can equally be the prelude to a continuation of collectivism under a different set of rulers. Everything depends on the political will of the people, the economic understanding of their leaders, and the ability of those leaders to persuade the public to support the radical measures that are necessary.

NO

**Robert Pollin and
Alexander Cockburn**

THE WORLD, THE FREE MARKET
AND THE LEFT

A year ago the capitalist future appeared, in the auguries of its toastmasters, as rosy as the old Socialist Realist posters once were in their visions of the shining path. Eastern Europe was commencing its economic renewal, along lines administered by crusading theorists of the free market and kept under critical review by the World Bank and the International Monetary Fund [I.M.F.]. In the Soviet Union itself the outlines of Gorbachev's nebulous *perestroika* were firming satisfactorily into a profile of capitalist reform, against a backdrop of economic disintegration advertised most vividly by appeals for food baskets from the West. . . .

So the economic idiom of the free-marketeers is now one of prolonged sacrifice, and the presumptive rewards of free-market capitalism promise to be outstripped by its penalties as the real living standards for peoples supposedly basking in its blessings continue to fall. It is therefore a good moment to examine the fundamental claims of the free-marketeers. Does the present situation signal merely an uncomfortable detour along a path that is sound, following a model essentially impregnable in its assumptions? Is the socialist path forever a cul-de-sac, one of history's false turns in the road?

THE MARKET LOVE FEAST

With a few variations to account for local conditions, the formulas being advanced throughout the world are the same: in the short term, rapid and deep cuts in wages, social spending and subsidies to control inflation and provide a climate of stability for business; in the long term, fundamental restructuring, involving the deregulation of business, wholesale sell-offs of public-sector enterprises, elimination of tariffs and other barriers to international trade, and inducements to foreign multinational corporations.

This passion for the free market has been nourished from many sources, beginning with the ideological premise of Adam Smith that through markets

From Robert Pollin and Alexander Cockburn, "The World, the Free Market and the Left," *The Nation* (February 25, 1991). Copyright © 1991 by Alexander Cockburn. Reprinted by permission.

each individual's free and selfish pursuit of gain will be transformed "as if by an invisible hand" to a socially optimal result. The ideological appeal is greatest in Eastern Europe, where the discrediting of communism has encouraged the embrace of whatever seems most contrary to the old order. Elsewhere the role of ideology has been less important than other factors—primarily, slow growth or even actual decline in real incomes, ossified institutions, crippling levels of indebtedness. Whether in Sweden, Jamaica, Poland, Brazil, Mozambique or any other stricken economy, governments faced crisis and had to change. But how? Many have sought enlightenment from the economies they regard as successful: those of the United States, Britain, Japan, South Korea and recently even Chile, all supposedly splendid advertisements for free-market capitalism. . . .

Do the celebration of the market and the rejection of large-scale government intervention find justification in the recent historical record? Is it true that governments that regulate and redistribute are the cause of the indisputable crises faced by so many of the world's economies, and that free-market capitalism can resolve those crises? In fact, such conclusions are entirely unwarranted, based on myths and fallacies which, shiny with use by mainstream economists and regnant economic powers, have achieved the status of certitude.

MYTH #1: SOCIALIST CENTRAL PLANNING HAS BEEN A DISASTER

The failures of central planning under what were the "actually existing" socialist governments are now universally understood—chief among them, the way in which the lack of democracy engendered an all-powerful, stifling bureaucracy. Central premises of socialism were, time and again, debauched. But substantial successes should not be forgotten. During the early phases of central planning the Soviet Union and China recorded stunning growth. In the period of the first two five-year plans, from 1928 to 1937, while the West was suffering through its worst depression, Soviet industrial growth as measured by conservative Western analysts averaged more than 12 percent. Under the duress of war mobilization and Stalinist purges, growth fell during the third five-year plan, but it took off again after World War II. C.I.A. estimates place industrial growth at an average of 9.3 percent during the 1950s, more than twice the rate in the United States over the same period. . . .

Cuba has also attained remarkable achievements through the egalitarian ethos underlying its planning apparatus. By any health or social indicator, Cuba stands well ahead of all other Latin American countries. For example, life expectancy in Cuba in 1988 was 76 years, while the average for Mexico, Brazil and Argentina—Latin America's three largest economies—was 69, 65 and 71 years, respectively. Cuba has also virtually eliminated illiteracy, and its rate of infant mortality of twelve per thousand live births is comparable to the U.S. figure of ten per thousand.

Relative to those of other countries in the Caribbean and in Central America, Cuba's economy has also been successful in producing a wide range of commodities both for domestic consumption and for export. Most impressive has been its development of a capital goods industry, the silver lining of the devastating thirty-one-year U.S. embargo. Andrew Zimbalist, an economist at Smith College and an expert on the Cuban economy, reports that "approximately one-quarter of investment spending on capital goods in the 1980s was on machinery and equipment produced in Cuba, a level no other third world economy the size of Cuba has attained." Items being manufactured for domestic use now include irrigation equipment, air-conditioning and refrigeration equipment, sugarcane harvesting machinery, semiconductors, batteries and railroad cars. Among its nontraditional exports Cuba counts shellfish, citrus fruit, medicine, iron and steel products, non-electrical machinery and the cowhide baseball.

It is popular to attribute the present crisis in the Cuban economy to some inherent failure of socialism, to inefficiency and moribund central planning, and to credit any of its successes to past infusions of Soviet aid. Of course, there have been errors and inefficiencies, but the problems plaguing the economy can be explained mainly by Cuba's status as a Third World island in a straitened international climate: the dissolution of favorable trade relations with Eastern Europe, higher oil prices, falling sugar prices and hard currency in desperately short supply. As for Soviet aid, while it has been essential, its effects have been overstated. When properly measured, Soviet aid accounted for 6 to 7 percent of Cuba's national income. . . .

Even in Eastern Europe, where the official rejection of central planning has been most intense, the picture is not one-sided. Take agriculture, a favorable experience almost never acknowledged in the West. Communist governments did force collectivization onto the peasantry in most Eastern European countries. Nevertheless, agricultural output and incomes rose sharply from the early 1960s to the 1980.

More important, the insecurity and heavy work burdens traditionally attached to individual farming have been mitigated through collective farming. . . .

At the same time, the socialist central planning system had been building toward a crisis since the early 1970s. For the Soviet Union especially, the costs of competition with the West were draining its resources. The attempts to stimulate the socialist economies by opening trade relations with the West were largely failures, leaving Poland, among others, in a Third World-style debt crisis.

But central planning also faced more fundamental difficulties. Over time, it showed itself to be much more capable of mobilizing unutilized resources than managing an economy of increasing complexity. Workers, meanwhile, did lack motivation. This is not, however, a natural byproduct of guaranteed full employment, the once vaunted but now maligned feature of labor conditions under central planning. The problem with authoritarian central planning is that it creates no affirmative work incentives to replace hunger and insecurity, the traditional prods to labor effort associated with capitalism. Material incentives in the socialist countries were too weak because of consumer goods shortages, and moral exhortation failed so long as workers had no control over workplace conditions, production decisions or labor organizations. Repression became the only remaining motivator, and this proved insufficient unless applied with a vehemence worthy of Stalin.

MYTH #2: GOVERNMENT INTERVENTION UNDER CAPITALISM HAS ALSO BEEN A FAILURE

Let's look first at Latin America, where statist policies are blamed for that region's continued underdevelopment and, in particular, for the debt crisis and "lost decade" of the 1980s. Beginning in the mid-1930s, most governments of Latin America embarked on heavily interventionist policies. Their main idea was to encourage domestic manufacturing, a policy rooted in the nationalist/populist movements led by such figures as Cárdenas in Mexico, Vargas in Brazil and Perón in Argentina. Through a plan of "import substitution" local industries would develop the capacity to supply manufactured goods that would otherwise be imported, thus providing the motor for Latin industrialization. These policies presented no challenge to existing internal class relations, but they did reject the free-market doctrines of free trade and minimal government. High tariffs discouraged imports while subsidies and public enterprises, which sold their products locally at below-market prices, supported domestic manufacturers.

The model was largely successful for a while. Mexico, Argentina and Brazil did attain their most immediate goal of producing domestic substitutes for nonluxury consumer goods. They all began to develop machine-building capacity as well during the 1960s, and by the early 1970s the industrialized sectors of those economies started to export on the world market. The growth of per capita income was also generally high over the 1950s and 1960s.

In the end the strategy proved unsustainable not because it violated the tenets of free-market capitalism but because other features of capitalism obtruded. Income distribution remained highly unequal, so domestic purchasing power never widened sufficiently to absorb the goods generated by the new industrial capacity. Even more damaging, the Latin economies were never able to break their chronic and debilitating dependence on foreign capital, though this was the explicit aim of the strategy.

Thus, despite the nationalist rhetoric that accompanied import substitution policies, implementation of the strategy relied both on imports of equipment and technology and on investment by multinationals. In Brazil, multinational firms accounted for 44 percent of all domestic sales in 1965, while private domestic firms and state enterprises accounted for 28 percent each. By 1972 multinationals controlled 50 percent of total manufacturing assets in both Brazil and Mexico. This led to chronic financial difficulties, particularly balance of payments deficits, as foreign multinationals remitted profits to the head office back home. By the early 1970s, the model was exhausted. And like well-heeled drug pushers, international bankers moved in, enticing Latin governments, which, strapped for funds and bereft of fresh development ideas, succumbed. International debt thus reactivated the old protectionist/interventionist model, but on an unsustainable foundation of debt. This was the background to the debt crisis of 1982 and the subsequent lost decade of punishing austerity. . . .

MYTH #3: THE PARAGONS OF FREE-MARKETEERISM ARE THE 'MIRACLE' ECONOMIES OF EAST ASIA

With typical hyperbole, Ronald Reagan said in his 1985 State of the Union Message: "Many countries in East Asia and the Pacific have few resources other than the enterprise of their own people. But through . . . free markets they've soared ahead of centralized economies." The problem here is that the Asian economies, especially those of Japan and South Korea, the region's greatest success stories, are not now nor have they ever been free-market economies.

In both planning and strategic financing, the state is dominant. It provides business with export subsidies, protection and cheap money. According to the development economist Aiden Foster-Carter, the South Korean agricultural system is virtually "a single gigantic state farm, with the state setting prices, providing inputs and credit, and buying the crop." By any measure, then, the state has been at least as active as in Latin America. So why have Japan and South Korea succeeded over the long term, in contrast to their Latin counterparts? Free markets can take little credit. In the 1950s, the United States saw both Japan and South Korea as bulwarks against communist expansion and gave them tremendous support. It is often forgotten that besides postwar reconstruction grants, Japan received nearly $2.2 billion in U.S. military procurement orders from 1950 to 1953 (equal to $10 billion in 1989 dollars). Such orders accounted for about 65 percent of Japanese exports over those years. Military Keynesianism, the declared U.S. policy in Paul Nitze's famous planning document N.S.C. 68 was not confined to the United States.

Outright aid to South Korea was even greater. More than 80 percent of Korean imports in the 1950s were financed by U.S. economic assistance. And in a parallel to Japan's experience during the Korean War, South Korea flourished with procurement contracts during the Vietnam War years. By 1975 such contracts accounted for no less than one-fifth of South Korea's exports of goods and services.

State intervention in East Asia was also more effective than in Latin America. States that subsidize and protect business always risk the misappropriation of resources. That happened in Japan and South Korea, but to an unusual extent the governments there were able to discipline the corporations they protected and subsidized, forcing them to meet product and quality standards necessary to penetrate export markets. In both cases the state's power over the capitalist class was partly the result of a sweeping U.S.-directed land reform in the years immediately following World War II. The United States backed these reforms in hopes of weakening left peasant insurgencies, but their impact—even given erosion over time—was to break the control of landed elites and their mercantile capitalist allies.

Finally, as a matter of conscious policy Japan and South Korea restricted intervention by foreign multinationals, especially during their phases of most rapid growth. While the state aggressively promoted the appropriation of modern technologies by domestic firms, it was not willing to allow foreign firms much purchase on the economy. The United States tolerated such violations of the free-market canon in the interests of the overall anticommunist alliance.

Japan and South Korea are by no means unqualified successes. Wages were low and working conditions harsh during the main period of development and they remain unacceptable today. At least with Japan, this fact contradicts the image of a country of guaranteed employment, high wages and egalitarian labor practices. In reality, the Japanese labor market is highly segmented between a minority of privileged workers in the core corporations and a majority who work long hours at low pay with little security. There is much to oppose in the East Asian model even while its basic lesson—that given favorable circumstances intelligent and aggressive government planning can produce remarkable results—remains compelling. . . .

POST-FORDISTS AND THEIR HOT-AIR FACTORY

The adoption of free-market, open-border policies by governments throughout the world coincides with probably the single most important trend in the world economy today: the increased integration of national economies in trade, finance and investment. To some degree the internationalization of capital is inevitable given that new technologies in communications and transportation allow products, ideas and people to traverse the globe at an unprecedented rate. But the driving force, certainly with respect to production if less so in trade and finance, has been the stagnation of corporate profits in the advanced capitalist economies since the early 1970s. The result: widescale corporate restructuring to cut costs. And the swiftest and most assured method of cutting costs is to lower wages and taxes, hence the increasing mobility of capital, placing workers and governments throughout the world in internecine competition to attract private investment.

Many on the left have argued that there are natural limits to capital's mobility—that firms must always place a high premium on proximity to their equipment producers, repair technicians, suppliers of inventory and spare parts, and major markets; and that high-tech production requires skilled workers who can be found in sufficient supply only in advanced countries. Indeed, by pushing the logic of this position, some have concluded that gains in high technology will lead to the demise of "Fordism"— the large-scale, mass-production corporate form—and its displacement by a "post-Fordist" model in which highly skilled, well-educated workers can be spread among small-scale, clean-producing and relatively autonomous high-tech cottage industries. In other words, in the post-Fordist world, technology itself could bring an end to alienating work, the goal for which socialists have traditionally fought but never attained.

The flaw in this reasoning was recently demonstrated by the labor economist Harley Shaiken, who examined the operations of two engine-assembly plants of a major, unnamed U.S. auto maker: one in the United States and one in Mexico. Only the newer of the two plants, in Mexico, utilized cutting-edge production technologies. Yet it did not rely on experienced workers with sophisticated training. Rather, almost all of the workers in the Mexican plant were in their early 20s, recent graduates of a local vocational school. Nevertheless, the plant operated spectacularly, achieving, according to Shaiken, "comparable machine efficiency, labor productivity and quality to the U.S. plant within its first two and one-half years of operation." At the same time, wage costs were less than 10 percent of what they were at the U.S. plant. As Shaiken recognizes, one cannot thus generalize that multinationals are essentially free to move anywhere with any set of production technologies, regardless of local conditions. The point is that the most advanced technological operations *can* be successfully operated by a minimally trained, inexperienced and low-paid work force. And if this can be accomplished in one place, it surely can be repeated elsewhere. Just in the past month Ford announced it would invest $700 million to expand an engine-assembly plant in northern Mexico; meanwhile it has been retrenching operations and selling assets in the United States.

The opening of national economies to trade and investment via free-market policies will only accentuate capital's clout in confrontations with labor and government. Thus, as governments throughout the world continue to clamor for free-market capitalism, pressure will mount for more wage concessions, less unionization, more austerity and less government regulation of business—i.e., an increasing surrender to the dictates of the capitalist class. . . .

SHINING PATHS

Alternatives to this bleak prospect can come only from the imagination and assertion of renewed left movements around the world. The left needs, at a minimum, to be confident in its fundamental economic positions. In plain terms this means it must not be afraid to be socialist, to counter free-market celebration and to defend economic planning and an activist state as a necessary brake on the assertions of capital.

The reasoning behind such positions is straightforward. First, an export-led and multinational-led investment strategy cannot work for everyone. It is logically impossible for all countries to run trade surpluses, since the surpluses of some countries must be exactly balanced by deficits in others. Similarly, an investment inflow to some countries will be exactly matched by an outflow—a "capital flight"—from others. Thus, even on its own terms, the model will have to fail

in at least as many countries as it succeeds. This underscores the destructive downward spiral in which countries compete for multinational investment by pushing wages and taxes as low as possible. Any alternative to the export-led open economy, wherever it may be pursued, will require active state intervention. One strategy is to strengthen local markets for domestically produced goods by increasing wages and reducing income inequality—a variation on some of the features of the populist import substitution strategy. However, any effort to raise wages significantly without concurrently increasing productivity in domestic industry will encourage hyperinflation, as occurred in Peru under the government of Alan García. Thus state planning becomes necessary to coordinate all the activities that can raise both productivity and wages: investment in industrial plant and equipment; the improvement of infrastructure and marketing arrangements; and, especially over the long term, the raising of education, health and housing standards so that people's lives can become more productive, as well as more secure and perhaps enjoyable.

Planning of this sort does not imply the eradication of markets or the suppression of democracy. Quite the opposite. In the right context, markets are the most efficient, indeed the only effective tools for establishing some prices and transmitting some information as well as rewarding people fairly for differences in ability and effort. The experience in the socialist countries has made clear that government planners should not squander their energy on inevitably ineffective efforts at controlling the production and marketing of soap, fresh fruit or blue jeans.

However, the planning system does need to unshackle from the market's grasp the functions that historical experience shows it performs badly—the setting of an economy's overall development strategy, the guarantee of a minimum level of economic security, the generation of a fair distribution of income, wealth and economic power, the control over the destructive side effects of profit-seeking activity in the workplace, the environment and elsewhere. The challenge, as Diane Elson has written in *New Left Review*, is to strike a balance by utilizing markets extensively but in a framework in which the markets themselves are socialized. As Elson has discussed, such "socialization of the market" would entail, at a minimum, the following:

• *Social control of investment.* Investment decisions are the primary determinant of an economy's overall development trajectory. The consequences of relying almost entirely on profit incentives in guiding investment activity are evident now in the United States and Britain, where for a decade the obsessive and debt-dependent drive for short-term gain has wasted these economies' financial and entrepreneurial resources. Through the public allocation of credit, public ownership of key firms and industries or other mechanisms, public institutions must at least set a framework to channel the energies of private profit-seeking. All governments already participate in investment decisions to some extent, but their customary role is mainly to act as public agents of private capital. The goal of democratic investment planning would be to represent the popular will as against the drive for profitability, especially in the realm of large-scale investment decisions. In other words, the commanding heights of the economy must be gov-erned democratically, not through the dictatorship of private capital. . . .

• *Socialize the labor market.* Labor markets cannot constitute a fair voluntary exchange as long as capitalists control the means of livelihood and workers must sell their labor to subsist. A government's commitment to meeting people's basic needs in health, education and housing reduces workers' insecurity and increases their productivity, thereby strengthening their relative position in the labor market. But workers must rely on their own united efforts to attain even this minimum degree of labor market leverage as well as to push beyond, toward higher living standards, more security and better working conditions. Unionism is in eclipse in Western countries and under attack virtually everywhere. Union strength will continue to erode as long as multinational firms are increasingly able to pit workers in one region or country against those in others. Thus, in the contemporary world more than ever, Marx's call for workers of the world to unite is no mere slogan; it is practical necessity.

• *Socialize information.* Marx wrote that capitalism "fetishizes" commodities—meaning that in market arrangements the social conditions under which commodities are produced are obscured as consumers attach interest only to the commodities themselves and their price. As Elson stresses, a socialized market would require democratic institutions to lift the market's informational shroud: to disseminate systematically information about the processes that shape our lives and environment and that produce and distribute commodities. People who eat Perdue chickens, for example, not only should know the chicken's price; they should know that the price reflects Perdue's antilabor practices—a high proportion of workers receiving minimum wages, no benefits and suffering from repetitive-motion illnesses due to speedups—as well as brutishness toward animals. Similarly, corporations' lying campaigns portraying their ecological commitment can be opposed successfully only through increased public consciousness of the effects of how we produce and consume.

To the extent that capitalists can suppress this sort of information, they can manipulate our decisionmaking as consumers, gutting the idea, so appreciated by free-market economists, of "consumer sovereignty." In the context of a vibrant left movement, access to heretofore hidden information can be a powerful tool for restraining the market's destructive tendencies. . . .

Considered in themselves, the ideas of socializing investment, the labor market and information are hardly earth shattering. All have been practiced with varying degrees of commitment and success in virtually every country. In a capitalist context, Japan and South Korea have become economic icons through their governments' strong involvement in major investment decisions. The boycott and sanctions movement against apartheid shows what an informed and aroused citizenry can effect; so, for that matter, does the dramatic change in attitudes toward smoking. The conditions enjoyed by workers in Sweden demonstrate what a highly organized and persistent labor movement can win.

The necessary fusion of labor and environmental struggles points to a deeper truth. The essence of the socialist challenge, as André Gorz writes, is "the striving after a society in which the rationality of the maximization of productivity and profit is locked into a total social framework in such a way that it is subordinated to non-quantifiable values and goals, where economically rational labor no longer plays the principal role in the life of society or of the individual." Hence a left-labor movement today in strategic coalitions can seize the time only if it leads the debate on the social and political implications of new and old technologies and how they affect the natural, that is to say, social environment.

Only socialism can challenge the capitalist rationality of hunger amid opulence and growth via natural destruction. Socialism can also confront the emergent capitalist rationality of casualized labor, half-time labor, semi-employed labor, and translate this into a social opportunity: less-alienating, productive jobs and a shorter working day. Capitalism can define itself only with the parameters of market rationality, whether in the "industries" of work or leisure. Socialism puts economic rationality at the service of individual and social autonomy.

It is in pursuit of this autonomy that economic planning and an activist state should be seen as our indispensable tools: tools for defending and broadening democracy, for raising mass living standards rather than acquiescing in the imposition of mass austerity, for protecting ourselves against the brutalities of an unfettered free market and for recapturing socialism's great life-affirming vision.

POSTSCRIPT
Does the Breakup of Communism Show the Success of Capitalism?

Pollin and Cockburn deny that they want to do away with free markets: "In the right context, markets are the most efficient, indeed the only tools for establishing some prices . . . as well as rewarding people fairly for differences in ability and effort." Having said this, they then go on to insist that every good economic system requires government planning, a minimum wage, "the generation of a fair distribution of income," government control of investment, socialization of the labor market, and, in general, "socialized markets." The obvious question is whether all this government intervention is compatible with any kind of market economy. Perhaps it is, but the challenge for believers in "socialized markets" is to explain more fully how the terms "socialized" and "markets" can be put together without contradiction.

The writings of America's preeminent spokesman for democratic socialism, the late Michael Harrington, parallel some of the historic ups and downs of socialism. His first book, *The Other America* (Macmillan, 1962), was his most popular and influential. During the next two decades Harrington became increasingly convinced that socialism was at hand. In *The Accidental Century* (Macmillan, 1965) he wrote that we were "on [the] eve of its fulfillment," and in *The Twilight of Capitalism* (Simon & Schuster, 1976) he was sure that America had entered the "contradictory, crisis-prone, last stage of capitalism." But by the time of *Decade of Decision* (Simon & Schuster, 1980), Harrington seemed less confident. "The very existence of systemic unfairness," he wrote, ought to be enough to make people demand socialism, but "that, alas is a leftist fairy tale." An older advocate of socialism, Irving Howe, records some of his earlier disillusionments but remains faithful to the core of his socialist beliefs in *Socialism in America* (Harcourt Brace Jovanovich, 1985). Recent defenses of capitalism include Peter Berger, *The Capitalist Revolution* (Basic Books, 1988), and Michael Novak, *The Spirit of Democratic Capitalism* (Madison Books, 1991), but one of the classic defenses is still in print: Milton Friedman's *Capitalism and Freedom* (University of Chicago Press, 1963).

As far as nation-states are concerned, there are no perfect specimens of capitalism or socialism. Every capitalist nation contains at least some elements of state economic intervention, and the socialist regimes that have clearly failed were ones in the Stalinist mold, which most socialists today would consider a distortion of their doctrine. Pure capitalism and pure socialism live only in the minds of theorists. In the real world there are enough variables to enable either side to say, "this regime succeeded (or failed) only because it contained elements of socialism (or capitalism)." The debate will continue.

EPA Documerica

PART 5

Crime and Social Control

The social costs of crime are often weighed against the public funds expended for crime prevention. Inevitably, this leads to debates over degrees of crime, as society struggles to match funds and punishment with the severity of the transgressions that occur. Does street crime pose more of a threat to the public well-being than white-collar crime? Billions of dollars have been spent in the "War on Drugs," but who is winning? Would legalizing some drugs free up money that could be directed to other types of social welfare programs, such as the rehabilitation of addicts? Does imprisonment serve as an effective means of reducing crime by removing criminals from the streets? Or is it, in the long run, costly and inhumane?

Is Street Crime More Harmful Than
  White-Collar Crime?

Should Drugs Be Legalized?

Is Incapacitation the Answer to the
  Crime Problem?

ISSUE 16

Is Street Crime More Harmful Than White-Collar Crime?

YES: John J. DiIulio, Jr., from "The Impact of Inner-City Crime," *The Public Interest* (Summer 1989)

NO: Jeffrey H. Reiman, from *The Rich Get Richer and the Poor Get Prison* (Macmillan, 1984)

ISSUE SUMMARY

YES: Associate professor of politics and public affairs John J. DiIulio, Jr., analyzes the enormous harm done—especially to the urban poor and, by extension, to all of society—by street criminals and their activities.
NO: Professor of criminal justice Jeffrey H. Reiman suggests that the dangers visited on society by corporations and white-collar criminals are a great menace, and he reviews how some of those dangers threaten society.

The word *crime* entered the English language (from the Old French) in about A.D. 1250, when it was identified with "sinfulness." Later, the meaning of the word was modified: crime became the kind of sinfulness that was rightly punishable by law. Even medieval writers, who did not distinguish very sharply between church and state, recognized that there were some sins for which punishment was best left to God; the laws should punish only those that cause harm to the community. Of course, their concept of harm was a very broad one, embracing such offenses as witchcraft and blasphemy. Modern jurists, even those who deplore such practices, would say that the state has no business punishing the perpetrators of these types of offenses.

What, then, should the laws punish? The answer depends in part on our notion of harm. We usually limit the term to the kind of harm that is tangible and obvious: taking a life, causing bodily injury (or extreme psychological trauma, as in the case of rape, for example), and destruction or loss of property. For most Americans today, particularly those who live in cities, the word *crime* is practically synonymous with street crime. Anyone who has ever been robbed or beaten by street criminals will never forget the experience, and there are few people living in urban slums today who have not been victimized or threatened by street criminals. The harm that these criminals cause is tangible, and the connection between the harm and the perpetrator is very direct, even intimate: A hits B on the head; A points a pistol at B and demands money; A rapes B.

But suppose the connection is not so intimate. Suppose, for example, that A hires B to shoot C. Is that any less a crime? B is the actual shooter, but is A any less guilty? Of course not, we say; he may even be more guilty, since he is the ultimate mover behind the crime. A would be guilty even if the chain of command were much longer, involving A's orders to B, and B's to C, then on to D, E, and F to kill G. Organized crime kingpins go to jail even when they are far removed from the people who carry out their orders. High officials of the Nixon administration, even though they were not directly involved in the burglary attempt at the Democratic National Committee headquarters at the Watergate Hotel complex in 1972, were imprisoned.

This brings us to the topic of white-collar crime. The actual burglars at the Watergate Hotel were acting on orders that trickled down from the highest reaches of power in the United States. Their orders were issued by men who wore well-tailored suits and did not carry burglar's tools. Other white-collar criminals are as varied as the occupations from which they come. They include stockbrokers who make millions, as Ivan Boesky did, through insider trading; members of Congress who take payoffs; and people who cheat on their income tax, like hotel owner and billionaire Leona Helmsley. Some, like Mrs. Helmsley, get stiff prison sentences when convicted, though many others (like most of the officials in the Watergate scandal) do little or no time in prison. Do they deserve stiffer punishment, or do their crimes seem less harmful than the crimes of street thugs?

White-collar criminals do not put guns to people's heads or beat them. They do not directly cause physical harm or relieve people of their wallets. You can walk to the bus stop tonight with the certain knowledge that you will not be assaulted by the likes of Leona Helmsley or Ivan Boesky. Still, white-collar crime can end up doing considerable harm. The harm done by Nixon's aides threatened the integrity of the U.S. electoral system. Every embezzler, bad check writer, corrupt politician, and tax cheat exacts a toll on our society. Individuals can also be hurt in more tangible ways by decisions made in corporate boardrooms. Auto executives have approved design features that have caused fatalities. Managers of chemical companies have given the go-ahead to practices that have polluted the environment with cancer-causing agents. Heads of corporations have presided over industries wherein workers have been needlessly killed and maimed.

Whether these decisions should be considered crimes is debatable. As we noted at the beginning, the English word *crime* originally meant sin, and there is some trace of that meaning left. A crime must always involve "malicious intent," what jurists call *mens rea*. This certainly applies to street crime—the mugger obviously has sinister designs—but does it apply to every decision made in a boardroom that ends up causing harm? And does that harm match or exceed the harm caused by street criminals? In the following selections, John J. DiIulio, Jr., focuses on the enormous harm done—especially to the poor—by street criminals, while Jeffrey H. Reiman suggests that white-collar criminals are a greater menace.

YES

John J. DiIulio, Jr.

THE IMPACT OF INNER-CITY CRIME

My grandmother, an Italian immigrant, lived in the same Philadelphia row house from 1921 till her death in 1986. When she moved there, and for the four decades thereafter, most of her neighbors were Irish and Italian. When she died, virtually all of her neighbors were black. Like the whites who fled, the first blacks who moved in were mostly working-class people living just above the poverty level.

Until around 1970, the neighborhood changed little. The houses were well-maintained. The children played in the streets and were polite. The teenagers hung out on the street corners in the evenings, sometimes doing mischief, but rarely—if ever—doing anything worse. The local grocers and other small businesspeople (both blacks and the few remaining whites) stayed open well past dark. Day or night, my grandmother journeyed the streets just as she had during the days of the Great Depression, taking the bus to visit her friends and relatives, going shopping, attending church, and so on.

She was a conspicuous and popular figure in this black community. She was conspicuous for her race, accent, and advanced age; she was popular for the homespun advice (and home-baked goods) she dispensed freely to the teenagers hanging out on the corners, to the youngsters playing ball in the street in front of her house, and to their parents (many of them mothers living without a husband).

Like the generations of ethnics who had lived there before them, these people were near the bottom of the socioeconomic ladder. I often heard my grandmother say that her new neighbors were "just like us," by which she meant that they were honest, decent, law-abiding people working hard to advance themselves and to make a better life for their children.

But in the early 1970s, the neighborhood began to change. Some, though by no means all, of the black families my grandmother had come to know moved out of the neighborhood. The new neighbors kept to themselves. The exteriors of the houses started to look ratty. The streets grew dirty. The grocery and variety stores closed or did business only during daylight hours. The children played in the schoolyard but not in front of their homes. The

From John J. DiIulio, Jr., "The Impact of Inner-City Crime," *The Public Interest*, no. 96 (Summer 1989), pp. 28-46. Copyright © 1989 by National Affairs, Inc. Reprinted with permission of *The Public Interest* and the author.

teenagers on the corners were replaced by adult drug dealers and their "runners." Vandalism and graffiti became commonplace. My grandmother was mugged twice, both times by black teenagers; once she was severely beaten in broad daylight.

In the few years before she died at age eighty-four, and after years of pleading by her children and dozens of grandchildren, she stopped going out and kept her doors and windows locked at all times. On drives to visit her, when I got within four blocks of her home, I instinctively checked to make sure that my car doors were locked. Her house, where I myself had been raised, was in a "bad neighborhood," and it did not make sense to take any chances. I have not returned to the area since the day of her funeral.

My old ethnic and ghetto neighborhood had become an underclass neighborhood. Why is it that most readers of this article avoid, and advise their friends and relatives to avoid, walking or driving through such neighborhoods? Obviously we are not worried about being infected somehow by the extremely high levels of poverty, joblessness, illiteracy, welfare dependency, or drug abuse that characterize these places. Instead we shun these places because we suppose them to contain exceedingly high numbers of predatory street criminals, who hit, rape, rob, deal drugs, burglarize, and murder.

This supposition is absolutely correct. The underclass problem, contrary to the leading academic and journalistic understandings, is mainly a crime problem. It is a crime problem, moreover, that can be reduced dramatically (although not eliminated) with the human and financial resources already at hand.

Only two things are required: common sense and compassion. Once we understand the underclass problem as a crime problem, neither of those two qualities should be scarce. Until we understand the underclass problem as a crime problem, policymakers and others will continue to fiddle while the underclass ghettos of Philadelphia, Newark, Chicago, Los Angeles, Miami, Washington, D.C., and other cities burn. . . .

THE TRULY DEVIANT

Liberals . . . have understood the worsening of ghetto conditions mainly as the by-product of a complex process of economic and social change. One of the latest and most influential statements of this view is William Julius Wilson's *The Truly Disadvantaged: The Inner City, the Underclass, and Public Policy* (1987).

Wilson argues that over the last two decades a new and socially destructive class structure has emerged in the ghetto. As he sees it, the main culprit is deindustrialization. As plants have closed, urban areas, especially black urban areas, have lost entry-level jobs. To survive economically, or to enjoy their material success, ghetto residents in a position to do so have moved out, leaving behind them an immobilized "underclass." . . .

Wilson has focused our attention on the socioeconomic straits of the truly disadvantaged with an elegance and rhetorical force that is truly admirable.[1] But despite its many strengths, his often subtle analysis of the underclass problem wrongly deemphasizes one obvious possibility: "The truly disadvantaged" exist mainly because of the activities of "the truly deviant"—the large numbers of chronic and predatory street criminals—in their midst. One in every nine adult black males in this country is under some form of correctional supervision (prison, jail, probation, or parole).[2] Criminals come disproportionately from underclass neighborhoods. They victimize their neighbors directly through crime, and indirectly by creating or worsening the multiple social and economic ills that define the sad lot of today's ghetto dwellers.

PREDATORY GHETTO CRIMINALS

I propose [another] way of thinking about the underclass problem. The members of the underclass are, overwhelmingly, decent and law-abiding residents of America's most distressed inner cities. Fundamentally, what makes them different from the rest of us is not only their higher than normal levels of welfare dependency and the like, but their far higher than normal levels of victimization by predatory criminals.

This victimization by criminals takes several forms. There is *direct victimization*—being mugged, raped, or murdered; being threatened and extorted; living in fear about whether you can send your children to school or let them go out and play without their being bothered by dope dealers, pressured by gang members, or even struck by a stray bullet. And there is *indirect victimization*—dampened neighborhood economic development, loss of a sizable fraction of the neighborhood's male population to prison or jail, the undue influence on young people exercised by criminal "role models" like the cash-rich drug lords who rule the streets, and so on.

Baldly stated, my hypothesis is that this victimization causes and perpetuates the other ills of our underclass neighborhoods. Schools in these neighborhoods are unable to function effectively because of their disorderly atmosphere and because of the violent behavior of the criminals (especially gang members) who hang around their classrooms. The truly deviant are responsible for a high percentage of teen pregnancies, rapes, and sexual assaults. Similarly, many of the chronically welfare-dependent, female-headed households in these neighborhoods owe their plights to the fact that the men involved are either unable (because they are under some form of correctional supervision) or unwilling (because it does not jibe well with their criminal lifestyles) to seek and secure gainful employment and live with their families. And much of the poverty and joblessness in these neighborhoods can be laid at the door of criminals whose presence deters local business activity, including the development of residential real estate.

Blacks are victims of violent crimes at much higher rates than whites. Most lone-offender crime against blacks is committed by blacks, while most such crimes against whites are committed by whites; in 1986, for instance, 83.5 percent of violent crimes against blacks were committed by blacks, while 80.3 percent of violent crimes against whites were committed by whites. This monochrome picture of victim-offender relationships also holds for multiple-offender crimes. In 1986, for example, 79.6 percent of multiple-offender violent crimes against blacks were committed by blacks; the "white-on-white" figure was 59.4 percent.

Criminals are most likely to commit crimes against people of their own race. The main reason is presumably their physical proximity to potential victims. If so, then it is not hard to understand why underclass neighborhoods, which have more than their share of would-be criminals, have more than their share of crime.

Prison is the most costly form of correctional supervision, and it is normally reserved for the most dangerous felons—violent or repeat offenders. Most of my readers do not personally know anyone in prison; most ghetto dwellers of a decade or two ago probably would not have known anyone in prison either. But most of today's underclass citizens do; the convicted felons were their relatives and neighbors—and often their victimizers.

For example, in 1980 Newark was the street-crime capital of New Jersey. In the Newark area, there were more than 920 violent crimes (murders, non-negligent manslaughters, forcible rapes, robberies, and aggravated assaults) per 100,000 residents; in the rest of the state the figure was under 500, and in affluent towns like Princeton it was virtually nil. In the same year, New Jersey prisons held 5,866 criminals, 2,697 of them from the Newark area.[3] In virtually all of the most distressed parts of this distressed city, at least one of every two hundred residents was an imprisoned felon.[4] The same basic picture holds for other big cities.[5]

Correlation, however, is not causation, and we could extend and refine this sort of crude, exploratory analysis of the relationship between crime rates, concentrations of correctional supervisees, and the underclass neighborhoods from which they disproportionately come. But except to satisfy curiosity, I see no commanding need for such studies. For much the same picture emerges from the anecdotal accounts of people who have actually spent years wrestling with—as opposed to merely researching—the problem.

For example, in 1988 the nation's capital became its murder capital. Washington, D.C., had 372 killings, 82 percent of them committed on the streets by young black males against other young black males. The city vied with Detroit for the highest juvenile homicide rate in America. Here is part of the eloquent testimony on this development given by Isaac Fulwood, a native Washingtonian and the city's police-chief designate:

> The murder statistics don't capture what these people are doing. We've had in excess of 1,260 drug-related shootings. . . . People are scared of these kids. Someone can get shot in broad daylight, and nobody saw anything. . . . Nobody talks. And that's so different from the way it was in my childhood.

The same thing can be said about the underclass neighborhoods of other major cities. In Detroit, for instance, most of the hundreds of ghetto residents murdered over the last six years were killed within blocks of their homes by their truly deviant neighbors.

To devise meaningful law-enforcement and correctional responses to the underclass problem, we need to understand why concentrations of crime and criminals are so high in these neighborhoods, and to change our government's criminal-justice policies and practices accordingly.

UNDERSTANDING THE PROBLEM

We begin with a chicken-and-egg question: Does urban decay cause crime, or does crime cause urban decay?

In conventional criminology, which derives mainly from sociology, ghettos are portrayed as "breeding grounds" for predatory street crime. Poverty, joblessness, broken homes, single-parent families, and similar factors are identified as the "underlying causes" of crime.[6] These conditions cause crime, the argument goes; as they worsen—as the ghetto community becomes the underclass neighborhood—crime worsens. This remains the dominant academic perspective on the subject, one that is shared implicitly by most public officials who are close to the problem.

Beginning in the mid-1970s, however, a number of influential studies appeared that challenged this conventional criminological wisdom.[7] Almost without exception, these studies have cast grave doubts on the classic sociological explanation of crime, suggesting that the actual relationships between such variables as poverty, illiteracy, and unemployment, on the one hand, and criminality, on the other, are far more ambiguous than most analysts freely assumed only a decade or so ago. . . .

LOCKS, COPS, AND STUDIES

Camden, New Jersey, is directly across the bridge from Philadelphia. Once-decent areas have become just like my grandmother's old neighborhood: isolated, crime-torn urban war zones. In February 1989 a priest doing social work in Camden was ordered off the streets by drug dealers and threatened with death if he did not obey. The police chief of Camden sent some extra men into the area, but the violent drug dealers remained the real rulers of the city's streets.

The month before the incident in Camden, the Rockefeller Foundation announced that it was going to devote some of its annual budget (which exceeds $100 million) to researching the underclass problem. Other foundations,

big and small, have already spent (or misspent) much money on the problem. But Rockefeller's president was quoted as follows: "Nobody knows who they are, what they do. . . . The underclass is not a topic to pursue from the library. You get out and look for them."

His statement was heartening, but it revealed a deep misunderstanding of the problem. Rather than intimating that the underclass was somehow hard to locate, he would have done better to declare that his charity would purchase deadbolt locks for the homes of ghetto dwellers in New York City who lacked them, and subsidize policing and private-security services in the easily identifiable neighborhoods where these poor people are concentrated.

More street-level research would be nice, especially for the networks of policy intellectuals (liberal and conservative) who benefit directly from such endeavors. But more locks, cops, and corrections officers would make a more positive, tangible, and lasting difference in the lives of today's ghetto dwellers.

NOTES

1. In addition, he has canvassed competing academic perspectives on the underclass; see William Julius Wilson, ed., "The Ghetto Underclass: Social Science Perspectives," *Annals of the American Academy of Political and Social Science* (January 1989). It should also be noted that he is directing a $2.7 million research project on poverty in Chicago that promises to be the most comprehensive study of its kind yet undertaken.

2. According to the Bureau of Justice Statistics, in 1986 there were 234,430 adult black males in prison, 101,000 in jail, an estimated 512,000 on probation, and 133,300 on parole. There were 8,985,000 adult black males in the national residential population. I am grateful to Larry Greenfeld for his assistance in compiling these figures.

3. I am grateful to Hank Pierre, Stan Repko, and Commissioner William H. Fauver of the New Jersey Department of Corrections for granting me access to these figures and to related data on

density of prisoner residence; to Andy Ripps for his heroic efforts in organizing them; and to my Princeton colleague Mark Alan Hughes for his expert help in analyzing the data.

4. Ten of the thirteen most distressed Newark census tracts were places where the density of prisoner residence was that high. In other words, 76.9 percent of the worst underclass areas of Newark had such extremely high concentrations of hardcore offenders. In most of the rest of Newark, and throughout the rest of the state, such concentrations were virtually nonexistent.

5. In 1980 in the Chicago area, for example, in 182 of the 1,521 census tracts at least one of every two hundred residents was an imprisoned felon.

Fully twenty of the thirty-five worst underclass tracts had such extraordinary concentrations of serious criminals; in several of them, more than one of every hundred residents was behind prison bars. I am grateful to Wayne Carroll and Commissioner Michael Lane of the Illinois Department of Corrections for helping me with these data.

6. For example, see the classic statement by Edwin H. Sutherland and Donald R. Cressey, *Principles of Criminology*, 7th rev. ed. (Philadelphia: J. P. Lippincott, 1966).

7. See, for example, James Q. Wilson, *Thinking About Crime* (New York: Basic Books, 1975), especially the third chapter.

NO

Jeffrey H. Reiman

A CRIME BY ANY OTHER NAME

WHAT'S IN A NAME?

If it takes you an hour to read this chapter, by the time you reach the last page, two of your fellow citizens will have been murdered. *During that same time, at least 4 Americans will die as a result of unhealthy or unsafe conditions in the workplace!* Although these work-related deaths could have been prevented, they are not called murders. Why not? Doesn't a crime by any other name still cause misery and suffering? What's in a name?

The fact is that the label "crime" is not used in America to name all or the worst of the actions that cause misery and suffering to Americans. It is primarily reserved for the dangerous actions of the poor.

In the March 14, 1976 edition of the *Washington Star*, a front-page article appeared with the headline: "Mine Is Closed 26 Deaths Late." The article read in part:

> Why, the relatives [of the 26 dead miners] ask, did the mine ventilation fail and allow pockets of methane gas to build up in a shaft 2,300 feet below the surface? . . .
>
> [I]nvestigators of the Senate Labor and Welfare Committee . . . found that there have been 1,250 safety violations at the 13-year-old mine since 1970. Fifty-seven of those violations were serious enough for federal inspectors to order the mine closed and 21 of those were in cases where federal inspectors felt there was imminent danger to the lives of the miners working there. . . .

Next to the continuation of this story was another, headlined: "Mass Murder Claims Six in Pennsylvania." It described the shooting death of a husband and wife, their three children, and a friend in a Philadelphia suburb. This was murder, maybe even mass murder. My only question is, why wasn't the deaths of the miners also murder?

Why do 26 dead miners amount to a "disaster" and 6 dead suburbanites a "mass murder"? "Murder" suggests a murderer, while "disaster" suggests the work of impersonal forces. But if over 1000 safety violations had been found in the mine—three the day before the first explosion—was no one

From Jeffrey H. Reiman, *The Rich Get Richer and the Poor Get Prison* (Macmillan, 1984). Copyright © 1984 by Jeffrey H. Reiman. Reprinted by permission of Macmillan Publishing Company. Notes omitted.

responsible for failing to eliminate the hazards? Was no one responsible for preventing the hazards? And if someone could have prevented the hazards and did not, does that person not bear responsibility for the deaths of 26 men? Is he less evil because he did not want them to die although he chose to leave them in jeopardy? Is he not a murderer, perhaps even a mass murderer?

These questions are at this point rhetorical. My aim is not to discuss this case but rather to point to the blinders we wear when we look at such a "disaster." Perhaps there will be an investigation. Perhaps someone will be held responsible. Perhaps he will be fined. But will he be tried for *murder*? Will anyone think of him as a murderer? *And if not, why not?* Would the miners not be safer if such people were treated as murderers? Might they not still be alive? . . . didn't those miners have a right to protection from the violence that took their lives? *And if not, why not?*

Once we are ready to ask this question seriously, we are in a position to see that the reality of crime—that is, the acts we label crime, the acts we think of as crime, the actors and actions we treat as criminal—is *created*: It is an image shaped by decisions as to *what* will be called crime and *who* will be treated as a criminal.

THE CARNIVAL MIRROR

It is sometimes coyly observed that the quickest and cheapest way to eliminate crime would be to throw out all the criminal laws. There is a thin sliver of truth to this view. Without criminal laws, there would indeed be no "crimes." There would, however, still be dangerous acts. And this is why we cannot

really solve our crime problem quite so simply. The criminal law *labels* some acts "crimes." In doing this, it identifies those acts as so dangerous that we must use the extreme methods of criminal justice to protect ourselves against them. But this does not mean that the criminal law *creates* crime—it simply "mirrors" real dangers that threaten us. And what is true of the criminal law is true of the whole justice system. If police did not arrest or prosecutors charge or juries convict, there would be no "criminals." But this does not mean that police or prosecutors or juries create criminals any more than legislators do. They *react* to real dangers in society. The criminal justice system—from lawmakers to law enforcers—is just a mirror of the real dangers that lurk in our midst. *Or so we are told.*

How accurate is this mirror? We need to answer this in order to know whether or how well the criminal justice system is protecting us against the real threats to our well-being. The more accurate a mirror, the more the image it shows is created by the reality it reflects. The more misshapen a mirror is, the more the distorted image it shows is created by the mirror, not by the reality reflected. It is in this sense that I will argue that the image of crime is created: The American criminal justice system is a mirror that shows a distorted image of the dangers that threaten us—an image created more by the shape of the mirror than by the reality reflected. What do we see when we look in the criminal justice mirror?

On the morning of September 16, 1975, the *Washington Post* carried an article in its local news section headlined "Arrest Data Reveals Profile of a Suspect." The article reported the results of a study of crime in Prince George's County, a suburb of Washington, D.C. It read in part that

The typical suspect in serious crime in Prince George's County is a black male, aged 14 to 19. . . .

This is the Typical Criminal feared by most law-abiding Americans. His crime, according to former Attorney General John Mitchell (who is by no means a typical criminal), is forcing us "to change the fabric of our society," "forcing us, a free people, to alter our pattern of life," "to withdraw from our neighbors, to fear all strangers and to limit our activities to 'safe' areas." These poor, young, urban (disproportionately) black males comprise the core of the enemy forces in the war against crime. They are the heart of a vicious, unorganized guerrilla army, threatening the lives, limbs, and possessions of the law-abiding members of society—necessitating recourse to the ultimate weapons of force and detention in our common defense. They are the "career criminals" President Reagan had in mind when he told the International Association of Chiefs of Police, assuring them of the tough stance that the Federal Government would take in the fight against crime, that "a small number of criminals are responsible for an enormous amount of the crime in American society." . . .

The acts of the Typical Criminal are not the only acts that endanger us, nor are they the acts that endanger us the most. We have a greater chance (as I show below) of being killed or disabled, for example, by an occupational injury or disease, by unnecessary surgery, by shoddy emergency medical services than by aggravated assault or even homicide! Yet even though these threats to our well being are graver than that posed by our

poor, young, urban, black males, they do not show up in the FBI's Index of serious crimes. And the individuals who are responsible for them do not turn up in arrest records or prison statistics. *They never become part of the reality reflected in the criminal justice mirror, although the danger they pose is at least as great and often greater than those who do!*

Similarly the general public loses more money *by far* . . . from price-fixing and monopolistic practices, and from consumer deception and embezzlement, than from all the property crimes in the FBI's Index combined. Yet these far more costly acts are either not criminal, or if technically criminal, not prosecuted, or if prosecuted, not punished, or if punished, only mildly. . . . *Their faces rarely appear in the criminal justice mirror, although the danger they pose is at least as great and often greater than those who do. . . .*

A CRIME BY ANY OTHER NAME . . .

Think of a crime, any crime. Picture the first "crime" that comes into your mind. What do you see? The odds are you are not imagining a mining company executive sitting at his desk, calculating the costs of proper safety precautions, and deciding not to invest in them. Probably what you see with your mind's eye is one person physically attacking another or robbing something from another on the threat of physical attack. Look more closely. What does the attacker look like? It's a safe bet he (and it is a *he*, of course) is not wearing a suit and tie. In fact, my hunch is that you—like me, like almost anyone in America—picture a young, tough, lower-class male when the thought of crime first pops into your head. You (we) picture someone like the Typical Criminal described above. And the crime itself is one in which the Typical Criminal sets out to attack or rob some specific person.

This last point is important. What it indicates is that we have a mental image not only of the Typical Criminal, but also of the Typical Crime. If the Typical Criminal is a young lower-class male, the Typical Crime is *one-on-one harm*—where harm means either physical injury or loss of something valuable or both. . . .

It is important to identify this model of the Typical Crime because it functions like a set of blinders. It keeps us from calling a mine disaster a mass murder even if 26 men are killed, even if someone is responsible for the unsafe conditions in which they worked and died. In fact, I argue that this particular piece of mental furniture so blocks our view that it keeps us from using the criminal justice system to protect ourselves from the greatest threats to our persons and possessions.

What keeps a mine disaster from being a mass murder in our eyes is the fact that it is not one-on-one harm. What is important here is not the numbers but the *intent to harm someone.* An attack by a gang on one or more persons or an attack by one individual on several fits the model of one-on-one harm. That is, for each person harmed there is at least one individual who wanted to harm that person. Once he selects his victim, the rapist, the mugger, the murderer, all want this person they have selected to suffer. A mine executive, on the other hand, does not want his employees to be harmed. He would truly prefer that there be no accident, no injured or dead miners. What he does want is something legitimate. It is what he has been hired to get: maximum profits at minimum costs. If he cuts corners to save a buck, he is just doing his job. If 26 men die because he cut corners on safety, we may think him crude or callous but not a killer. He is, at most, responsible for an *indirect harm*, not a one-on-one harm. For this, he may even be criminally indictable for violating safety regulations—but not for murder. The 26 men are dead as an unwanted consequence of his (perhaps overzealous or undercautious) pursuit of a legitimate goal. And so, unlike the Typical Criminal, he has not committed the Typical Crime. Or so we generally believe. As a result, 26 men are dead who might be alive now if cutting corners of the kind that leads to loss of life, whether suffering is specifically intended or not, were treated as murder.

This is my point. Because we accept the belief . . . that the model for crime is one person specifically intending to harm another, we accept a legal system that leaves us unprotected against much greater dangers to our lives and well-being than those threatened by the Typical Criminal. . . .

WORK MAY BE DANGEROUS TO YOUR HEALTH

Since the publication of *The President's Report on Occupational Safety and Health* in 1972, numerous studies have documented both the astounding incidence of disease, injury, and death due to hazards in the workplace *and* the fact that much or most of this carnage is the consequence of the refusal of management to pay for safety measures and of government to enforce safety standards.

In that 1972 report, the government estimated the number of job-related illnesses at 390,000 per year and the number of annual deaths from industrial disease at 100,000. In *The Report of the President to the Congress on Occupational Safety and Health* for 1980, these estimates were rather sharply reduced to 148,900 job-related illnesses and 4950 work-related deaths. Note that the latter figure is not limited to death from occupational disease but includes all work-related deaths including those resulting from accidents on the job.

Before considering the significance of these figures, it should be mentioned that all sources including the just-mentioned report as well as the U.S. Department of Labor's *Interim Report to Congress on Occupational Diseases* indicate that occupational diseases are seriously underreported. *The Report of the President* states that "recording and reporting of illnesses continue to present measurement problems, since employers (and doctors) are often unable to recognize some illnesses as work-related." The annual survey includes data only on the visible illnesses of workers. To the extent that occupational illnesses are unrecognized and, therefore, not recorded or reported, the illness survey estimates may understate their occurrence. . . .

For these reasons, plus the fact that OSHA's* figures on work-related deaths are only for workplaces with 11 or more employees, we must supplement the OSHA figures with other reported figures. One study conservatively estimates the number of annual cancer deaths attributable to occupational factors at 17,000. Richard Schweiker, U.S. Secretary of Health and Human Services, states that "current estimates for overall workplace-associated cancer mortality

*[Occupational Health and Safety Administration.—ED.]

vary within a range of five to fifteen percent." With annual cancer deaths at 400,000, that translates into between 20,000 and 60,000 cancer deaths per year associated with the workplace. A report for the American Lung Association estimates 25,000 deaths a year from job caused respiratory diseases. None of these figures include deaths from heart disease, America's number one killer, a substantial portion of which are likely caused by stress and strain on the job. Thus even if we discount the OSHA's 1972 estimate of 100,000 deaths a year due to occupational disease, we would surely be erring in the other direction to accept the figure of 4950. We can hardly be overestimating the actual toll if we set it at 25,000 deaths a year resulting from occupational disease.

As for the OSHA estimate of 148,000 job-related illnesses, here too there is reason to assume that the figure considerably underestimates the real situation. One study suggests that it may represent no more than half of the actual number. However, since this figure is probably less inaccurate than the figure for job-related deaths, it will suffice for our purposes. Let us assume, then, that there are annually in the United States approximately 150,000 job-related illnesses and 25,000 deaths from occupational diseases. How does this compare to the threat posed by crime? Before jumping to any conclusions, note that the risk of occupational disease and death falls only on members of the labor force, while the risk of crime falls on the whole population, from infants to the elderly. Since the labor force is less than half the total population (96,800,000 in 1980, out of a total population approaching 230,000,000), to get a true picture of the *relative* threat posed by occupational diseases compared to that posed by crime we should *halve* the crime statistics when comparing them to the figures for industrial disease and death. Using the 1980 statistics, this means that the *comparable* figures would be:

	Occupational Disease	Crime (halved)
Death	25,000	11,500
Other physical harm	150,000	325,000

. . . It should be noted further that the statistics given so far are *only* for occupational *diseases* and deaths from those diseases. They do not include death and disability from work-related injuries. Here too, the statistics are gruesome. The National Safety Council reported that in 1980, work-related accidents caused 13,000 deaths and 2.2 million disabling work injuries; 245 million man-days lost during that year because of work accidents, plus another 120 million man-days that will be lost in future years because of these accidents; and a total cost to the economy of $30 billion. This brings the number of occupation-related deaths to 38,000 a year. If, on the basis of these additional figures, we recalculated our chart comparing occupational to criminal dangers, it would look like this:

	Occupational Hazard	Crime (halved)
Death	38,000	11,500
Other physical harm	2,350,000	325,000

Can there be any doubt that workers are more likely to stay alive and healthy in the face of the danger from the underworld than in the face of what their employers have in store for them on the job? . . .

To blame the workers for occupational disease and deaths is simply to ignore the history of governmental attempts to compel industrial firms to meet safety standards that would keep dangers (such as chemicals or fibers or dust particles in the air) that are outside of the worker's control down to a safe level. This has been a continual struggle, with firms using everything from their own "independent" research institutes to more direct and often questionable forms of political pressure to influence government in the direction of loose standards and lax enforcement. . . .

Over and over again, the same story appears. Workers begin to sicken and die at a plant. They call on their employer to lower the level of hazardous material in the air, and their employer responds first by denying that a hazard exists. As the corpses pile up, the firm's scientists "discover" that some danger does exist but that it can be removed by reducing the hazardous material to a "safe" level—which is still above what independent and government researchers think is really safe. At this point, government and industry spar about "safe" levels and usually compromise at a level in between—something less dangerous than industry wants but still dangerous. This does not mean that the new levels are met, even if written into the law. So government inspectors and compliance officers must come in, and when (and if) they do, their efforts are too little and too late:

• Federal officials cited the Beryllium Corporation for 26 safety violations and 5 "serious violations" for "excessive beryllium concentration in work place areas."

Fine: $928. The corporation's net sales for 1970 were $61,400,000.

• On request from the Oil, Chemical and Atomic Workers Union, OSHA officials inspected the Mobil Oil plant at Plausboro, New Jersey. Result: citations for 354 violations of the Occupational Health and Safety Act of 1970. Fine: $7350 (about $20 a violation).

• In 1972, a fire and explosion at the same Mobil plant killed a worker. Fine: $1215. . . .

• "In 1981, a Labor Department study found nearly 2 million Americans were severely or partially disabled from an occupational disease; the lost income is estimated at $11.4 billion. Yet, the study found, only 5 percent of the severely disabled received workers' compensation." . . .

Is a person who kills another in a bar brawl a greater threat to society than a business executive who refuses to cut into his profits in order to make his plant a safe place to work? By any measure of death and suffering the latter is by far a greater danger than the former. But because he wishes his workers no harm, because he is only indirectly responsible for death and disability while pursuing legitimate economic goals, his acts are not called *crimes*. . . .

HEALTH CARE MAY BE DANGEROUS TO YOUR HEALTH

. . . On July 15, 1975, Dr. Sidney Wolfe of Ralph Nader's Public Interest Health Research Group testified before the House Commerce Oversight and Investigations Subcommittee that there "were 3.2 million cases of unnecessary surgery performed each year in the United States." These unneeded operations, Dr. Wolfe added, "cost close to $5 billion a year and killed as many as 16,000 Americans." . . .

A congressional committee earlier this year [1976] estimated that more than 2 million of the elective operations performed in 1974 were not only unnecessary—but also killed about 12,000 patients and cost nearly $4 billion.

WAGING CHEMICAL WARFARE AGAINST AMERICA

. . . Based on the knowledge we have, there can be no doubt that air pollution, tobacco, and food additives amount to a chemical war that makes the crime wave look like a football scrimmage. Quite conservatively, I think we can estimate the death toll in this war as at least a quarter of a million lives a year—*more than ten times the number killed by criminal homicide!*

POVERTY KILLS

. . . We are prone to think that the consequences of poverty are fairly straightforward: Less money equals less things. And so poor people have fewer clothes or cars or appliances, go to the theater less often, and live in smaller homes with less or cheaper furniture. And this is true and sad, but perhaps not intolerable. I will argue that one of the things poor people have less of is *good health*. Less money means less nutritious food, less heat in the winter, less fresh air in summer, less distance from other sick people, less knowledge about illness or medicine, fewer doctor visits, fewer dental visits, less preventive health care, and above all, less first-quality medical attention when all these other deprivations take their toll and a poor person finds himself seriously ill. What this means is that the poor suffer more from poor health and die earlier than do those who are well off. Poverty robs them of their days while they are alive and then kills them before their time. A prosperous society that allows poverty in its midst is guilty of murder. . . .

ONCE AGAIN, OUR INVESTIGATION LEADS to the same result. The criminal justice system does not protect us against the gravest threats to life, limb, or possessions. Its definitions of crime are not simply a reflection of the objective dangers that threaten us. The workplace, the medical profession, the air we breathe, and the poverty we refuse to rectify lead to far more human suffering, far more death and disability, and take far more dollars from our pockets than the murders, aggravated assaults, and thefts reported annually by the FBI. And what is more, this human suffering is preventable. A government really intent on protecting our well-being could enforce work safety regulations, police the medical profession, require that clean air standards be met, and funnel sufficient money to the poor to alleviate the major disabilities of poverty. But it does not. Instead we hear a lot of cant about law and order and a lot of rant about crime in the streets. It is as if our leaders were not only refusing to protect us from the major threats to our well-being but trying to cover up this refusal by diverting our attention to crime—as if this were the only real threat. But as we have seen, the criminal justice system is a carnival mirror that presents a distorted image of what threatens us. . . . All the mechanisms by which the criminal justice system comes down more frequently and more harshly on the poor criminal than on the well-off criminal take place *after* most of the dangerous acts of the well-to-do have been excluded from the definition of crime itself.

POSTSCRIPT

Is Street Crime More Harmful Than White-Collar Crime?

DiIulio implies that much of the social misery of America, including the persistence of poverty, can be traced to the "truly depraved" street criminals in our central cities. Is this focus too narrow? Surely there are many other sources of the social crisis that afflicts our central cities. Reiman's focus, on the other hand, may be overly broad. He claims that more people are killed and injured by "occupational injury or disease, by unnecessary surgery, and by shoddy emergency medical services than by aggravated assault or even homicide!" Though we may say it rhetorically, can we really categorize shoddy medical services as a crime? And could Reiman ever convince residents of city ghettos, where most of the violent crime occurs, that they face a greater risk from occupational injury or disease than from street criminals?

A set of readings that support Reiman's viewpoint is *Corporate Violence: Injury and Death for Profit*, edited by Stuart L. Hills (Rowman & Littlefield, 1987). Further support is provided by Marshall B. Clinard, *Corporate Corruption: The Abuse of Power* (Praeger, 1990). *White-Collar Crime*, edited by Gilbert Geis and Robert F. Meier (Free Press, 1977), is a useful compilation of essays on corporate and political crime, as is Gary Green's *Occupational Crime* (Nelson-Hall, 1990). Four other books that focus on crime in high places are J. Douglas and J. M. Johnson, *Official Deviance* (Lippincott, 1977); J. Anthony Lukas, *Nightmare: The Underside of the Nixon Years* (Viking Press, 1976); Marshall B. Clinard, *Corporate Elites and Crime* (Sage Publications, 1983); and David R. Simon and Stanley Eitzen, *Elite Deviance* (Allyn and Bacon, 1982). A work that deals with the prevalence and fear of street crime is Elliott Currie, *Confronting Crime: An American Challenge* (Pantheon Books, 1985). One interesting aspect of many corporate or white-collar crimes is that they involve crimes of obedience, as pointed out by Herman C. Kelman and V. Lee Hamilton in *Crimes of Obedience: Toward a Social Psychology of Authority and Responsibility* (Yale University Press, 1989).

ISSUE 17

Should Drugs Be Legalized?

YES: Claudia Mills, from "The War on Drugs: Is It Time to Surrender?" *QQ: Report from the Institute for Philosophy and Public Policy* (Spring/Summer 1989)

NO: James Q. Wilson and John J. DiIulio, Jr., from "Crackdown," *The New Republic* (July 10, 1989)

ISSUE SUMMARY

YES: Claudia Mills, a writer and student of philosophy, concludes that the cost of fighting drugs—in financial and human terms—outweighs any benefits obtained from waging the battle against drugs, and she argues that they should therefore be legalized.

NO: Political scientists James Q. Wilson and John J. DiIulio, Jr., argue that drug legalization would vastly increase dangerous drug use and the social ills that are created by such usage.

A century ago, drugs of every kind were freely available to Americans. Laudanum, a mixture of opium and alcohol, was popularly used as a painkiller. One drug company even claimed that it was a very useful substance for calming hyperactive children, and they called it Mother's Helper. Morphine came into common use during the Civil War. Heroin, developed as a supposedly less addictive substitute for morphine, began to be marketed at the end of the nineteenth century. By that time, drug paraphernalia could be ordered through Sears and Roebuck catalogues, and Coca-Cola, which contained small quantities of cocaine, had become a popular drink.

Public concerns about addiction and dangerous patent medicines, and an active campaign for drug laws waged by Dr. Harvey Wiley, a chemist in the U.S. Department of Agriculture, led Congress to pass the first national drug regulation act in 1906. The Pure Food and Drug Act required that medicines containing certain drugs, such as opium, must say so on their labels. Later amendments to the Act required that the labels must also state the quantity of each drug and affirm that the drug met official standards of purity. The Harrison Narcotic Act of 1914 went much further and cut off completely the supply of legal opiates to addicts. Since then, ever stricter drug laws have been passed by Congress and by state legislatures.

Drug abuse in America again came to the forefront of public discourse during the 1960s, when heroin addiction started growing rapidly in inner-city neighborhoods. Also, by the end of the decade, drug experimentation had spread to the middle-class, affluent baby boomers who were then attending college. (The name "baby boom" generation has been given to Americans born during the late 1940s through 1960, whose cohort history has been widely analyzed and widely publicized because they are far more numerous than were older generations.) Indeed, certain types of drugs began to be celebrated by some of the leaders of the counterculture. Heroin was still taboo, but other drugs, notably marijuana and LSD (a psychedelic drug), were regarded as harmless and even spiritually transforming. At music festivals like Woodstock in 1969, marijuana and LSD were used openly and associated with love, peace, and heightened sensitivity. Much of this enthusiasm cooled over the next 20 years as baby boomers entered the work force full-time and began their careers. But even among the careerists, certain types of drugs enjoyed high status. Cocaine, noted for its highly stimulating effects, became the drug of choice for many hard-driving young lawyers, TV writers, and Wall Street bond traders.

The high price of cocaine put it out of reach for many people, but by the early 1980s, cheap substitutes began to appear on the streets and to overtake poor urban communities. Crack cocaine, a potent, highly addictive, smokable form of cocaine, came into widespread use. More recently a new drug known as "ice," or as it is called on the West Coast, "L.A. glass," a smokable form of amphetamine, hit the streets. These stimulants tend to produce very violent, disorderly behavior. Moreover, the street gangs who sell it are frequently at war with one another and are well armed. Not only gang members but also many innocent people have become victims of contract killings, street battles, and drive-by shootings.

This new drug epidemic prompted President Bush to declare a "war on drugs," and he asked Congress to appropriate $10.6 billion for the fight. Reaction has been mixed. Some support it in its entirety; others think that more money is needed, or that spending priorities should be shifted more toward treatment than law enforcement. Still, the vast majority of Americans seem ready to support some version of a major national campaign to fight drugs. Others, however, see the whole effort as doomed to failure, and they argue that the best solution to the drug problem would be to legalize, tax, and control drugs, as has been done with alcohol.

The drug legalization issue is especially interesting to sociologists because it raises basic questions about what should be socially sanctioned or approved, what is illegal or legal, and what is immoral or moral. An aspect of the basic value system of America is under review. The process of value change may be taking place in front of our eyes. As part of this debate, Claudia Mills makes a case for the legalization of drugs, and James Q. Wilson and John J. DiIulio, Jr., argue against it.

YES

Claudia Mills

THE WAR ON DRUGS:
IS IT TIME TO SURRENDER?

Two decades after the doomed and undeclared war in Vietnam, America has declared itself at war with drugs. Recent polls have blasted illegal drugs as public enemy number one; in an era of budget retrenchments and hands-off government, the crusade against drugs has become a central priority for federal action and funding. All told, expenditures on all aspects of drug enforcement, from drug eradication in foreign countries to imprisonment of drug users and dealers in the United States, totaled in 1987 over ten billion dollars. Convicted drug offenders crowd our prisons: nationwide in 1987, 75,000 people were arrested for violating drug laws, and many faced stiff mandatory sentences. Drug "czar" William Bennett has called for capital punishment for drug dealers and remarked that "morally" he doesn't "have any problem" with beheading as the method of execution. In unison schoolchildren shout "Just say no!" and everyone knows what it is they're saying no to. Even legal drug use—the consumption of alcohol and tobacco—is declining steadily, as we strive toward the goal of drug-free schools, drug-free neighborhoods, a drug-free America.

Yet few think this is a war we are winning. Despite accelerated enforcement efforts, the black market in cocaine has grown to record size. Crack, the most lethal cocaine derivative, was all but unheard of five years ago; today 15 percent of infants born in the nation's capitol suffer brain damage from exposure to crack in the womb. Drug-related murder rates soar; drug-related violence holds our inner cities hostage to fear; drug-related civil war rages in Colombia. Is the drug war one we can possibly win?

Indeed, the drug war itself has come to be more deadly than the enemy it is waged against. The greatest costs are incurred, it can be claimed, not by drugs per se, but as a direct or indirect by-product of their criminalization. While 90 percent of Americans appear to be opposed to the legalization of drugs, decriminalization measures are gaining support across the political spectrum; advocates of legalization range from conservative William F. Buckley to the liberal, black mayor of Baltimore, Kurt Schmoke.

From Claudia Mills, "The War on Drugs: Is It Time to Surrender?" *QQ: Report from the Institute for Philosophy and Public Policy* (Spring/Summer 1989), pp. 1-5. Copyright © 1989 by the Institute for Philosophy and Public Policy, School of Public Affairs, University of Maryland. Reprinted by permission.

Are there moral considerations that tell in favor of legalization? Can we draw parallels between how we treat legal drugs such as tobacco and alcohol and how we should treat illegal drugs such as heroin, marijuana, and cocaine? Should we legalize drugs as a way of respecting individual autonomy against government paternalism, or as a way of showing compassion to the victims of addiction? Most important, do the consequences of legalization promise to be less terrible than those we now face?

THE ARGUMENT FROM CONSISTENCY

A first argument offered for legalization is that currently illegal drugs are in no relevant way morally different from the most popular legal drugs—alcohol and tobacco—and so consistency demands that if beer and cigarettes are legal, marijuana, heroin, and cocaine should be legal as well. There is certainly nothing particularly distinctive, nothing inherently *worse*, about the drugs that through historical accident happen to find themselves on the "illegal" list. After all, narcotics were legal in this country only a century ago, with a wide choice of hypodermic kits available for purchase from the Sears, Roebuck Catalog. Many doctors at the turn of the century prescribed opium as a treatment for alcoholism, viewing opiate addiction as the lesser of two evils. And cocaine, of course, gave its name to Coca-Cola, of which it was long an ingredient.

If anything, illegal drugs are far less harmful than the legal ones. The federal data for 1985 documented 2177 deaths from the most popular illicit drugs: heroin, cocaine (including crack), PCP, and marijuana. Disease related to alcohol and tobacco, on the other hand, kill close to half a million Americans every year. No illegal drug is more clearly linked to drug-induced violence than alcohol; nicotine and alcohol are both powerfully addictive. Ethan A. Nadelman, assistant professor of politics and public affairs at Princeton University, suggests that "if degrees of immorality were measured by the levels of harm caused by one's products, the 'traffickers' in tobacco and alcohol would be vilified as the most evil of all substance purveyors."

But parallels between legal and illegal drugs can cut both ways. While Prohibition produced a level of crime and gang violence eerily prescient of today's drug-related crime and violence, it also slashed alcohol consumption in half, with all the attendant benefits to human health and family stability. Legal drugs may take a greater toll on health and happiness precisely as a result of their legality—and so of their widespread use and cultural entrenchment. Sue Rusche, director of the National Drug Information Center of Families in Action, claims that "illegal drugs kill fewer people only because fewer people use them." Why on earth, one might ask, would we want to encourage the use of cocaine and heroin on a par with today's levels of smoking and drinking?

But in any case, the argument from consistency is a weak one. Robert Fullinwider, research scholar at the Institute for Philosophy and Public Policy, regards the argument that if we tolerate alcohol and tobacco, we are somehow logically bound to tolerate crack in the same way, as the kind of foolish consistency that is the hobgoblin of small minds. We make our laws not only on the basis of logic, but of history; we have an entrenched cultural history with some drugs that we need not repeat with others. Thus Fullinwider, who is inclined toward drug legalization, notes that we could treat cocaine and heroin, if legalized, very differently from alcohol and tobacco. It would be insane, for example, to allow advertising of such drugs; we needn't permit a whole new array of billboards extolling their pleasures.

THE ARGUMENT AGAINST PATERNALISM

A second argument against criminal penalties for drug use is essentially an argument against the exercise of state power to coerce citizens' private and personal choices regarding what they do with their own "free" time. Steven Wisotsky, professor of law at Nova University, argues that "zero tolerance" of drug use is simply an inappropriate goal for a liberal society. "The overwhelming majority of incidents of drug use," Wisotsky claims, "are without lasting personal or societal consequence, just as the overwhelming majority of drinking causes no harm to the drinker or to society." For Wisotsky, "The . . . goal of a drug-free America, except for children, is both ridiculous—as absurd as a liquor-free America—and wrong in principle. This is not a fundamentalist Ayatollah land after all. A democratic society must respect the decisions made by its adult citizens, even those perceived to be foolish or risky."

David A. J. Richards, in his book *Sex, Drugs, Death, and the Law*, also argues that we must respect "the individual's ability to determine, evaluate, and revise the meaning of his or her own life." Drug experience, Richards suggests, "is merely one means by which the already existing interests of the person may be explored or realized." While it may seem strange to claim that the drug *addict* is voluntarily pursuing his or her own possibly quite reasonable goals, Richards sees the whole concept of addiction as complex and highly confused: talk of "addiction" conflates the *physiological* features of tolerance (the progressive need for higher doses of a drug to secure the same effect) and physical dependence (the incidence of withdrawal symptoms when drug use is stopped), with the *psychological* centrality of the drug in the user's system of ends, and, most important, with a *moral* judgment that drug use is intrinsically degrading or debasing. These features have no necessary connection to one another. Moreover, the moral condemnation of certain drug use as drug "abuse," according to Richards, involves importing middle-class values into judgments about others' lifestyle choices. He writes, "The psychological centrality of drug use for many young addicts in the United States may, from the perspective of their own circumstances, not unreasonably organize their lives and ends."

But it hardly takes a set of stuffy "middle-class values" to argue that involvement with a highly addictive drug such as crack counts as a form of slavery. The insatiable craving for crack leads people to neglect and abuse their children, to live in unspeakable filth and foulness, to commit any crime to service one all-encompassing obsession. No crack mother, it is safe to say, views crack addiction as a future she would choose for her children. John Kaplan, professor of law at Stanford University, observes that the anti-paternalistic principle of letting each person decide for himself "seems singularly inappropriate when it is applied to a habit-forming psychoactive drug that alters the user's perspective as to postponement of gratification and his desire for the drug itself." Kaplan cites research showing that cocaine scores by far the highest "pleasure" score in laboratory experiments on drug use and is also the most "reinforcing" of drugs known to man: in animal studies, monkeys, if permitted, will perform a given task again and again to gain a reward of cocaine, neglecting food or rest until they die of debilitation.

The anti-paternalistic argument for legalization of drugs is most persuasive for benign and non-addictive drugs like marijuana—but marijuana is the least of our drug problems today. When the drugs to be legalized are dangerous and highly addictive drugs like crack, the argument fails. If paternalism is justifiable anywhere, it is justifiable here. Paternalistic prohibitions against highly addictive drugs are legitimate in principle; the central issue, as we shall see shortly, is how they work in practice.

THE ARGUMENT FOR COMPASSION

By contrast, a third argument for the legalization of drugs starts from a very different assumption: that drug abuse is a serious health problem, a condition to be addressed with compassionate medical aid rather than stigmatizing criminal sanctions. While the argument against paternalism downplays the addictiveness of many drugs, the argument from compassion fastens on this as its starting point. As Baltimore's Mayor Schmoke, a leading advocate of this position, argues, "Addiction is a disease, and whether we want to admit it or not, addicts need medical care." Decriminalization, for Schmoke, is a means of reassigning responsibility for the epidemic of drug abuse away from the overburdened criminal justice system to the public health system, where it properly belongs.

Given the fundamental nature of drug addiction, Schmoke points out that "we cannot hope to solve addiction through punishment. . . . Even after prolonged periods of incarceration, during which they have no physical access to heroin, most addicts are still defeated by their physical dependence and return to drugs. . . . The sad truth is that heroin and morphine addiction is, for most users, a lifetime affliction that is impervious to any punishment that the criminal justice system could reasonably mete out."

While the anti-paternalism argument would justify a relatively free market in drugs on the analogy to current arrange-

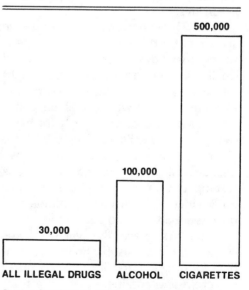

Number of Americans Killed by Illegal Drugs
(Bars Represent Thousands of Users)

Number of Americans Killed by Legal Drugs
(Bars Represent Thousands of Users)

500,000

100,000

30,000

ALL ILLEGAL DRUGS   ALCOHOL   CIGARETTES

Source: Sue Rusche, Testimony before the House Select Committee on Narcotics Abuse

ments for alcohol and tobacco, the argument from addiction would point to a prescription system as we have today for tranquilizers and other drugs under the control of the medical establishment. A prescription system, however, would fail to eradicate the worst problems accompanying the criminalization of drug use, for it is likely we would continue to see a booming black market in the controlled substances.

THE ARGUMENT FROM CONSEQUENCES

However tolerant and compassionate our attitudes and policies may be toward drug users, we may take a very different and far dimmer view of drug pushers. How can we sanction the terrible harms wrought by those who purvey drugs such as crack and PCP to children and to other vulnerable groups? By taking steps toward legalizing drugs it seems that we implicitly condone and legitimate a market in misery.

But the most powerful and persuasive argument for the legalization of drugs is simply that however morally distasteful legalization of crack and PCP might intrinsically be, in practical terms the alternative is far worse. A sane policy analysis must consider not only the harm caused by using illegal drugs, but also the harm caused by the measures we take against them. The war on drugs is turning out to be a holocaust for our inner cities, and on these grounds it is unconscionable not to surrender.

In the first place, the war on drugs creates all-but irresistible financial incentives for drug dealers. Black market prices of heroin and cocaine are about a hundred times greater than their pharmaceutical prices: on one estimate, for example, $625 worth of coca leaves has a street value in the United States of $560,000. Such hyper-inflated prices mean hyper-inflated profits. As James Ostrowski, former chairman of the New York County Lawyers Association Committee on Law Reform, explains, "Failure [of the war on drugs] is guaranteed because the black market thrives on the war on drugs and benefits from any intensification of it. At best, increased enforcement simply boosts the black market price of drugs, encouraging more drug suppliers to supply more drugs. The publicized conviction of a drug dealer, by instantly creating a vacancy in the lucrative drug market, has the same effect as hanging up a help-wanted sign saying, 'Drug dealer needed—$5,000 a week to start—exciting work.' "

Given this kind of financial incentive to deal in illegal drugs (an industry boasting an estimated $200 billion in annual sales), Fullinwider suggests that no criminal sanction can work to dissuade the dealer. The necessary cost-benefit calculations are easily performed: given that the rewards are enormous and certain, no penalty, even Bennett's favorite beheading, can act as a countervailing consideration, unless the penalty can be made equally certain. And it cannot, even if all the resources of all our police forces and all our courts were to be devoted exclusively to the war on drugs.

Furthermore, the circumstances of criminalization worsen the consequences of the drugs themselves on users. As drug interdiction efforts have increased, drug traffickers have turned to smuggling purer forms of their product; for example, the average purity of cocaine has soared. More potent law enforcement leads to the development of more potent drugs. Schmoke is one who argues that "crack is almost entirely a result of prohibition." Illegal drugs keep getting stronger, even as legal drugs are becoming weaker, with health pressures for low-tar cigarettes, light beer, and wine coolers. There is no Food and Drug Administration regulating the content and purity of illegal drugs, so users buy drugs of uncertain strength, adulterated with various poisons. The illegal status of drugs hastens the spread of AIDS by posing obstacles to needle exchange programs; it inhibits drug users from seeking needed medical attention.

The most serious negative consequence threatened by decriminalization of drugs is a possible increase in use. Opponents of legalization argue that drug-prohibition laws succeed in deterring many people from trying drugs and reduce their availability. But while the lessons of Prohibition lend some support for worries about increased drug use following the repeal of drug laws, decriminalization of marijuana by about a dozen states in the 1970s did not lead to increases in marijuana consumption; in the Netherlands, which decriminalized pot during the 1970s, consumption has actually declined significantly. Culture seems more important than law in determining patterns of drug use. One may doubt that most Americans would inject cocaine or heroin into their veins even if given the chance to do so legally. And, finally, usage could double or triple without tipping the balance in favor of any escalation in the war on drugs, given the scale of the devastation from that war.

One last danger of the war on drugs, and in some ways the most troubling, is the threat that it poses to our civil rights. In a state of war, ordinary protections of civil liberties may give way to an all-out effort to combat the enemy. The same is true in the war on drugs. Wisotksy expresses concern about what he sees as two dangerous and related phenomena: "(1) the government's sustained attack, motivated by the imperatives of drug enforcement, on traditional protections afforded to criminal defendants under the Bill of Rights [such as more permissive use of illegally seized evidence, relaxation of search and seizure requirements, and draconian mandatory sentences], and (2) the gradual but perceptible rise of "Big Brotherism" against the public at large in the form of drug testing, investigative detention, eavesdropping, surveillance, monitoring, and other intrusive enforcement methods. "He concludes, "Since the early 1980s, the prevailing attitude, both within government and in the broader society, has been that the crackdown on drugs is so imperative that extraordinary measures are justified. The end has come to justify the means. The result is that Americans have significantly less freedom than they did only five or six years ago"—all in the waging of a war we cannot win.

CONCLUSION

Whatever the strength of any other arguments for the legalization of drugs, a sober cost-benefit analysis that pays heed to the terrible costs brought by our national war on drugs seems to support some degree of decriminalization. In the end, the best war on drugs may be to revive and overhaul our old war on poverty: to take the resources and energy marshaled in the war on drugs and direct them instead to programs designed to combat the entrenched hopelessness that makes drug use and abuse so tragically appealing.

The sources quoted in this article are: Ethan A. Nadelman, "The Case for Legalization" *The Pub-*

lic Interest, vol. 92 (1988); Sue Rusche, testimony before the House Select Committee on Narcotics Abuse and Control, September 29, 1988; Robert Fullinwider, interview; Steven Wisotsky, testimony before the House Select Committee; David A. J. Richards, *Sex, Drugs, Death, and the Law* (Totowa, N.J.: Rowman and Littlefield, 1982);

John Kaplan, "Taking Drugs Seriously," *The Public Interest*, vol. 92 (1988); Kurt Schmoke, testimony before the House Select Committee; and James Ostrowski, "Thinking about Drug Legalization," *Cato Institute Policy Analysis*, No. 121 (May 25, 1989).

NO

James Q. Wilson
and John J. DiIulio, Jr.

CRACKDOWN

According to the projections, crime was supposed to be under control by now. The postwar baby-boom generation, which moved into its crime-prone years during the early 1960s, has grown up, yielding its place to the (proportionately) less numerous baby-bust generation. With relatively fewer 18-year-olds around, we should all be walking safer streets.

And in fact for most people crime *has* gone down. The Census Bureau's victimization surveys tell us that between 1980 and 1987 the burglary rate declined by 27 percent, the robbery rate by 21 percent. Despite what we hear, 3,000 fewer murders were committed in 1987 than in 1980. Even in some big cities that are in the news for the frequency with which their residents kill each other, the homicide rate has decreased. Take Los Angeles: despite freeway shootings and gang warfare, there were 261 fewer murders in 1987 than in 1980, a drop of more than 20 percent.

But in specific enclaves the horror stories are all too true. In south central Los Angeles, in much of Newark, in and around the housing projects of Chicago, in the South Bronx and Bedford-Stuyvesant sections of New York, and in parts of Washington, D.C., conditions are not much better than they are in Beirut on a bad day. Drugs, especially crack, are sold openly on street corners; rival gangs shoot at each other from moving automobiles; automatic weapons are carried by teenagers onto school playgrounds; innocent people hide behind double-locked doors and shuttered windows. In Los Angeles there is at least one gang murder every day, Sundays included. A ten-foot-high concrete wall is being built around the junior high school one of us attended, in order, the principal explained, to keep stray bullets from hitting children on the playground.

The problem is drugs and the brutal struggles among competing gangs for control of the lucrative drug markets. The drug of choice is crack (except in Washington, where it is PCP). The crack craze has led to conditions far worse than were found in these same neighborhoods a decade or so ago, when

From James Q. Wilson and John J. DiIulio, Jr., "Crackdown," *The New Republic* (July 10, 1989). Copyright © 1989 by The New Republic, Inc. Reprinted by permission of *The New Republic*.

heroin was the preferred drug. The reasons for the change are not reassuring.

Crack is a stimulant; heroin is a sedative. Crack produces exceptional euphoria; heroin produces, after a quick "rush," oblivion. Crack (and PCP) addicts are often stimulated to acts of violence and daring that make them dangerous to themselves as well as to others; heroin addicts are rarely violent when high—the drug even depresses the sexual drive.

Crack is marketed by competitive distribution systems, some of whose members are fighting—literally—to establish monopoly control. Heroin (at least on the East Coast) was marketed in a criminal environment dominated by established monopolies that were well equipped, in muscle and in political connections, to protect their market shares with a minimum of random violence.

Crack users have no attractive chemical alternative. The drug is far more rewarding than any substitute. Heroin users who had progressed to the point where they wanted nothing but relief from the pains of withdrawal and the disease caused by intravenous injection could take oral methadone. The heroin substitute, though addictive, required no injections, prevented withdrawal pains, and (in the correct dosages) produced little or no "high."

In short, certain neighborhoods of our larger cities are being ravaged by a drug that consumers find more alluring than heroin, that stimulates rather than sedates its users, that suppliers must use violence to sell, and that therapists are at a loss to manage by chemical means.

Attempting to suppress the use of drugs is very costly. Some people therefore conclude that we must eliminate all the costs of law enforcement by repealing the laws that are being enforced. The result would be less crime, fewer and weaker gangs, and an opportunity to address the public health problems in a straightforward manner.

But legalizing drugs would also entail costs. Those costs are hard to measure, in part because they are to a large degree moral and in part because we have so little experience with legalized drugs.

There is an obvious moral reason for attempting to discourage drug use: the heavy consumption of certain drugs ravages human character. These drugs—principally heroin, cocaine, and crack—are for many people powerfully reinforcing. The pleasure or oblivion they produce leads many users to devote their lives to seeking pleasure or oblivion, and to do so regardless of the cost in ordinary human virtues, such as temperance, duty, and sympathy. The dignity, autonomy, and productivity of users is at best impaired, at worst destroyed.

SOME PEOPLE THINK SOCIETY HAS NO obligation to form and sustain the character of individuals. Libertarians would leave all adults free to choose their own habits and seek their own destiny so long as their behavior did not cause any direct harm to others. But most people, however willing they may be to tolerate human eccentricities and support civil liberties, act as if they believe that government, as the agent for society, is responsible for helping to instill certain qualities in the citizenry. This was the original reason for mandatory schooling. We not only want to train children to be useful, we want to train them to be decent. It is also the reason that virtually every nation that has been confronted by a sharp increase in addiction to any psychoactive substance, including alcohol, has enacted laws designed to regulate or suppress its use.

Great Britain once allowed physicians to prescribe opiates for addicts. The system worked reasonably well so long as the addicts were middle-class people who had become hooked as a consequence of receiving pain-killers in hospitals. But when thrill-seeking youth discovered heroin, the number of addicts increased *40-fold*, and so Britain ended the prescription system. It was replaced at first with a system of controlled dispensation from government clinics, and then with a system of substituting methadone for heroin coupled with the stringent enforcement of the laws against the latter.

Even if we were to decide that the government had no responsibility for character formation and should regulate only behavior that hurts other people, we would still have to figure out what to do about drug-dependent people—because such dependency does hurt other people. A heroin addict dreamily enjoying his euphoria, a crack smoker looking for the next high, a cocaine snorter eager for relief from his depression—these users are not likely to be healthy people, productive workers, good parents, reliable neighbors, attentive students, or safe drivers. Moreover, some people are harmed by drugs that they have not chosen to use. The babies of drug-dependent women suffer because of their mothers' habits. We all pay for drug abuse in lowered productivity, more accidents, higher insurance premiums, bigger welfare costs, and less effective classrooms.

The question is whether the costs of drug use are likely to be higher when the drug is illegal or when it is legal. In both cases society must pay the bill. When the drug is illegal, the cost consists of the law enforcement costs (crime, corruption, extensive and intrusive policing), the welfare costs (poorer health, lost wages, higher unemployment benefits, more aid to families with dependent children, and various treatment and prevention programs), and the moral costs (debased and degraded people). If the drug were legal, the bill would consist primarily of the welfare costs and the moral costs. And there would still be the law enforcement costs: the costs of enforcing tax collection if the drugs were sold, or of preventing diversion if the drugs were distributed through the health care system, and the costs in either case of keeping the drugs out of the hands, lungs, and veins of minors. Legalization without some form of regulation is inconceivable; the more stringent the regulation, the higher the law enforcement bill.

WHICH SCENARIO WILL BE COSTLIER? THE answer chiefly depends on how many people will use the drug. We have a rough idea of how many people regularly use heroin and cocaine despite its illegality. How many will regularly use it under the legal scenario?

No one really knows, but it will almost surely be many more than now. The free market price of cocaine is probably no more than five percent of its present black market price. Even allowing for heavy taxes, Stanford's John Kaplan has estimated that the free market price would be no more than 20 percent of what it now costs. The consumption of a widely desired, pleasure-inducing substance without question will increase dramatically if the price is cut by 80 percent to 95 percent.

Moreover, the true price of the drug is the monetary cost plus the difficulty and inconvenience of the search for it and the risk associated with consuming a product of unknown quality. Though drugs are sold openly on the streets of some communities, for most people—especially for novice, middle-class users—they are hard to come by and often found only in threatening surroundings. Legalization will make the drug more attractive, even if the price actually rises, by reducing the costs of searching for it, negotiating a transaction, and running the risk of ingesting a dangerous substance. The combined effect of lowered market prices and lowered transaction costs will be very great.

Just how great cannot be known without trying it. And one cannot try it experimentally, for there is no way to run a meaningful experiment. The increase in use that would occur if people in one neighborhood or patients at one clinic were allowed to buy the drug at its market cost can give us no reliable information on how many people would use the drug if it were generally available. And the experiment would have irreversible effects. Moreover, as the British experience showed, there is no such thing as "controlled distribution." Inevitably there will be massive leaks of government-supplied drugs into the black market.

We already have the "benefits" of one quasi-experiment. So long as cocaine was available only in its relatively expensive powdered form, its use was pretty much concentrated among more affluent people. But with the invention of crack, which can be sold in single low-priced doses rather than by the high-priced gram, cocaine use increased sharply.

We believe that the moral and welfare costs of heavy drug use are so large that society should continue to enforce the laws against its use for the sake of keeping the number of users as small as possible. But we recognize that by adopting this position, we are placing a heavy burden on those poor communities where drug use is endemic. We are allowing these neighborhoods to be more violent than they would be if the drug were legal. Since we do not live in such communities, we must ask ourselves whether our preferences can be justified to people who do.

The answer to that question is given by the testimony of those who live in the midst of the problem. They want drugs kept illegal. They say so and their representatives in Congress say so. We hope that our libertarian critics will not accuse the people of Watts, Anacostia, and the South Bronx of suffering from false consciousness on this matter. These people know what drug use is and they don't like it.

But if drugs are to be kept illegal, we have a special responsibility to prevent the streets of inner-city neighborhoods from being controlled by those who seek to profit from the trade. We have not done a very good job of this.

In some places there may not be enough police. In others the cops are just badly used, as when the focus is on making a case against "Mr. Big," the local drug kingpin. There are two things wrong with this. First, nothing is easier than replacing Mr. Big; indeed, often the police get evidence on him from tips supplied by his would-be replacement. Meanwhile the distribution of drugs goes on unabated. Second, arresting Mr. Big does nothing to improve the lives of the decent people in the neighborhood who want the drug dealers off the street.

MANY CITIES, NOTABLY NEW YORK, HAVE recognized this and are concentrating on street-level dealers. The NYPD has wrested control from the drug dealers in parts of the Lower East Side, all of Washington Square Park, much of West 107th Street, and other places. But they have done so at a cost, what Aric Press of *Newsweek* calls the criminal justice equivalent of bulimia. The police go on an arrest binge, and then, "overwhelmed and overfed, the rest of the system—prosecutors, defenders, judges, and jailers—has spent its days in an endless purge, desperately trying to find ways to move its population before it gets hit with another wave tomorrow." The purgatives included granting early release to some inmates and trying to shift other city prisoners to state penitentiaries; pressuring the governor to authorize the appointment of more judges while encouraging faster plea bargaining to clear the crowded dockets; and building "temporary" holding facilities for new arrestees.

The District of Columbia has begun to enter the bulimia phase. The number of people going through the criminal justice system on drug charges has exploded. Between 1983 and 1987 drug arrests increased by 45 percent, drug prosecutions by over 500 percent, drug convictions by over 700 percent. Clearly judges and prosecutors were starting to get tough. But until very recently, the toughness stopped at the jailhouse door. As recently as 1986, only seven percent of the adults arrested on drug charges—and only 20 percent of those convicted on such charges—were sent to the city's principal correctional facility at Lorton. Then, suddenly, the system lurched into overdrive. Between 1986 and 1987 the number of drug incarcerations more than doubled, so that by the end of the year an adult arrested on a drug charge had a one-in-five chance of going to jail, and one convicted on such a charge had a one-in-two chance of winding up at Lorton.

This means that, until very recently, the price of drug dealing in Washington has been quite low. Those who say that "law enforcement has failed" should remember that until the last two years it was barely tried. Police Chief-designate Isaac Fulwood says that the same dealer may be arrested eight or nine times in the space of a few weeks. The city has been operating a revolving-door criminal justice system.

One reason for the speed with which the door revolves is that in Washington, as in most parts of the country, the prisons are jammed full. Another factor is that professional drug dealers know they can get a favorable plea bargain if they threaten to make the system give them a full trial, replete with every conceivable motion. The mere threat of such a demand is ordinarily enough to ensure that an attractive bargain is offered.

HOW CAN AN OVERTAXED SYSTEM HELP protect people in the drug-ridden neighborhoods? Building more conventional prisons is part of the answer, but that takes a lot of time, and no one wants them in their back yard. The goal is to take drug dealers off the streets for a longer period than the time it takes to be booked and released. One step is to ensure that no good arrest is washed out for want of prosecution because of a shortage of judges, prosecutors, and public defenders. These are not cheap, but candidates for these posts are more readily available than vacant lots on which to build jails.

Nevertheless, prisons are still needed and can be had, provided we are willing to think of alternatives to conventional holding tanks. One is to reserve regular prison space for major traffickers and to use parts of present (or all of former) military camps as boot camps for lower-level dealers. At these minimum-security camps, inmates would receive physical training, military discipline, and drug-abuse treatment, all under the direction of military personnel and with the aim of preparing them for a life that would combine, to the extent possible, the requirement of regular drug tests and the opportunity for gainful employment.

Meanwhile, the chances of released inmates rejoining old gangs can perhaps be reduced by enforcing a law, such as the one recently passed in California, that makes mere membership in certain gangs illegal and attaches civil or criminal penalties to parents who knowingly allow their children to join them. . . .

AT THIS STAGE, WE ARE NOT TRYING TO deter drug sales or reduce drug use. All we wish to do is to reassert lawful public control over public spaces. Everything else we may wish to achieve—reducing the demand for drugs, curing the users of drugs, deterring the sale of drugs—can only be done after the public and the police, not the dealers and the gangs, are in charge of the neighborhoods. In the short run, this can be done by repeatedly arresting every suspected dealer and user and sending them through the revolving door. If we cannot increase the severity of the penalties they face, we can at least increase the frequency with which they bear them. In police terms, we want to roust the bad guys.

After the bad guys find they are making repeated trips to the same prison camps, the decent people of the neighborhood must form organizations willing and able to work with the police to keep the bad guys from regaining control of the streets. The Kenilworth-Parkside area of Washington shows what can be done. A few years ago this neighborhood, the site of a public housing project, was an open-air drug market that spawned all manner of crime. In 1982 a tenants' committee led by Kimi Gray formed a corporation and assumed control of the housing project. Though the residents were primarily unwed mothers living on welfare, over the next five years their association collected the rents, ran the buildings, enforced school attendance on the children, and got rid of the addicts. In 1988 the association signed a contract to purchase the project from the government. . . .

THE DRUGS-CRIME PROBLEM ULTIMATELY will be solved only when the demand for drugs is dramatically reduced. Though it is necessary to make major investments in overseas crop eradication, the interdiction of international drug shipments, and the control of our borders, there is scarcely an experienced law enforcement officer in the country who does not believe that controlling the sources of supply is much more than a holding operation.

How do we reduce demand? We do not know. Realizing that is the beginning of wisdom. The greatest mischief is to assume that the demand for drugs will decline only when there is less racism and poverty, better schools and more jobs, more religion, and better-quality television.

Recall how the heroin epidemic finally ended. At one time the number of new addicts seemed to be rising exponentially despite the ending of the Turkish supply of illicit opium and the breaking up of the French processing laboratories. Now we have a fairly stable number of confirmed addicts whose ranks seem not to be increasing and may be decreasing. This was accomplished by three things: death, testing, and methadone.

Youngsters who were ready to ignore the lectures of their teachers or the blandishments of public-service television commercials were not so ready to ignore the testimony of their everyday experiences. Heroin addicts were dying from drug overdoses, dirty needles, and personal neglect. Doing heroin no longer seemed as glamorous as it did when one first heard about it from jazz musicians and big-time crooks.

The military began a rigorous program of testing, which continues to this day. There were sanctions attached to being found out—often a delay in being returned home, possibly military punishment, and probably a dishonorable discharge. Drug use in the military dropped dramatically and has stayed low.

Heroin addicts who were burned out by their long and increasingly unsatisfying bout with the drug often turned to methadone as a way of easing the pain and stabilizing their lives. If they stayed with it, they had a good chance of benefiting from the counseling and training programs made available to them.

These three prevention measures were not likely to be as effective with cocaine and crack addicts. Some users were dying from these drugs, but smoking crack still seems to many users to be far more exciting and much less dangerous than injecting heroin. In time, enough people will ruin their lives so that even the fantastic high that crack produces will begin to seem unattractive to potential users. But that time is not here yet.

Testing works but only if it is done rigorously and with real consequences, ranging from immediate counseling to discharge or punishment. As yet few civilian institutions seem prepared (or able) to do what the armed forces did. It is hard enough for private employers to test, and they are not subject to the search-and-seizure provisions of the Fourth Amendment. Opposition from employee groups and civil libertarians shows little sign of abating. Some government agencies are testing, but they are doing so gingerly, usually by limiting tests to workers such as prison guards and customs agents who are in obviously sensitive positions. It is hard to imagine many schools adopting a testing program, though some are trying.

And there is no cocaine equivalent for methadone, though science may yet find one.

That doesn't leave much: some school-based drug-education programs that look promising but have not (as yet) proved their efficacy and many treatment programs that can have some success—provided the patient is willing to stay in them.

"WILLING": THAT IS THE KEY. HEAVY drug use is an addiction about which we have in other contexts already learned a great deal. Fifty years ago we knew as little about dealing with alcoholism as we now know about cocaine abuse. Today we know enough about alcoholism to realize the key steps to coping with it.

First and foremost: addicts will not get better until they first confront the fact that they are addicts. Alcoholics Anonymous knows this full well, making it the cornerstone of its Twelve Steps. The families of alcoholics are taught that they did not cause and can neither control nor cure the addictive behavior—the disease—of the alcoholic. The deaths of others and an inescapable testing program can help provoke among drug users what the destruction of the lives of alcoholics sometimes stimulates—a recognition that they are powerless in the face of the drug and that they need the help of others like themselves. . . .

We must begin with the facts, not with theories. The facts are these: some parts of our cities are being destroyed by gangs competing for the right to destroy lives by selling drugs. Those gangs have to be defeated, even if it means hiring more judges and building more correctional facilities. After that we can help communities reorganize themselves so that the good people control the streets and the teachers, doctors and scientists have a chance to find out what will prevent another addictive epidemic from breaking out when some chemist discovers a drug that is even cheaper and more euphoria-inducing than crack. And that last event, we can be certain, will happen.

POSTSCRIPT

Should Drugs Be Legalized?

The analogy often cited by proponents of drug legalization is the ill-fated attempt to ban the sale of liquor in the United States, which lasted from 1919 to 1933. Prohibition has been called "an experiment noble in purpose," but it was an experiment that greatly contributed to the rise of organized crime. The repeal of Prohibition brought about an increase in liquor consumption and alcoholism, but it also deprived organized crime of an important source of income. Would drug decriminalization similarly strike a blow at the drug dealers? Possibly, and such a prospect is obviously appealing. But would drug decriminalization also exacerbate some of the ills associated with drugs? Would there be more violence, more severe addiction, more crack babies born to addicted mothers? Here, there is clearly a choice between evils. How should society go about answering questions like these? What role should the social sciences play?

David F. Musto's *The American Disease* (Yale University Press, 1973) is a classic discussion of the drug problem in America. Sidney Cohen reviews the problems of alcoholism in *The Alcoholism Problem* (Haworth, 1983). Erich Goode, *Drugs in American Society* (McGraw-Hill, 1988), provides a sociological perspective on drugs. H. Wayne Morgan's *Drugs in America: A Social History, 1800–1900* (Syracuse University Press, 1981) also gives a historical background on the drug problem. Larry Sloman's book *Reefer Madness: The History of Marijuana in America* (Grove Press, 1983) describes changing attitudes and laws regarding marijuana, while Lester Brinspoon and James B. Bakalar do the same for cocaine in *Cocaine: A Drug and Its Social Evolution* (Basic Books, 1985). James A. Inciardi, *The War on Drugs: Heroin, Cocaine, Crime and Public Policy* (Mayfield, 1986) gives a close-up look at the cocaine and crime scene. A book by Edward M. Brecher and the editors of *Consumer Reports*, entitled *Licit and Illicit Drugs* (Consumers Union, 1972), argues for the decriminalization of marijuana, heroin maintenance programs, and lenient treatment of other drug offenders. Thomas S. Szasz, *Ceremonial Chemistry: The Ritual Persecution of Drugs, Addicts, and Pushers* (Learning Publications, 1985), criticizes our current antidrug crusades. The connection between drugs and crime is explored in *Drugs and Crime*, edited by Michael Toney and James Q. Wilson (University of Chicago Press, 1990). A work on the legalization debate, biased toward the legalization side, is *The Drug Legalization Debate*, edited by James A. Inciardi (Sage Publications, 1991).

ISSUE 18

Is Incapacitation the Answer to the Crime Problem?

YES: James Q. Wilson, from *Thinking About Crime* (Basic Books, 1975)

NO: David L. Bazelon, from "Solving the Nightmare of Street Crime," *USA Today Magazine*, a publication of the Society for the Advancement of Education (January 1982)

ISSUE SUMMARY

YES: Criminologist and sociologist James Q. Wilson argues that imprisoning everyone convicted of a serious offense for several years would greatly reduce these crimes. He contends that incapacitation is the one policy that works.

NO: Judge David L. Bazelon discusses the moral and financial costs of the incapacitation approach and argues that society must attack the brutal social and economic conditions that are the root causes of street crime.

Not a day passes in America without reports of murders, rapes, or other violent crimes. As crime has increasingly captured the headlines, public indignation has intensified—particularly when spectacular cases have been brought to light about paroled convicts committing new felonies, light sentences being handed down for serious crimes, and cases being thrown out of court on legal technicalities. The perception that Michael Dukakis was soft on criminals seriously hurt his bid for the presidency in 1988. (As governor of Massachusetts, Dukakis approved a prison furlough program that released a convict named Willie Horton, who subsequently went on to commit a widely publicized, horribly violent crime in another state.) Over the past three decades, there has been a dramatic increase in the number of Americans who think that the authorities should be tougher on criminals. To take one prominent example: While a majority of Americans in the 1960s favored the abolition of the death penalty, today more than 70 percent favor its use in some cases.

Even in the intellectual community, there has been a turnaround. When George Wallace, the Southern Democrat and presidential candidate, and other politicians raised the issue of "law and order" at the end of the 1960s, the term was called "a code word for racism" in academic and literary circles.

This is understandable because Wallace *had* previously identified himself with white racism. The attitude toward crime that was popular in academic circles during the 1960s might be briefly summarized under two headings: the prevention of crime and the treatment of criminals.

To prevent crime, some academics argued, government must do more than rely upon police, courts, and jails. It must do something about the underlying social roots of crime, especially poverty and racism. It was assumed that, once these roots were severed, crime would begin to fade away, or at least cease to be a major social problem.

The prescription for treating criminals followed much the same logic. The word *punishment* was avoided in favor of *treatment* or *rehabilitation*, for the purpose was not to inflict pain or to "pay back" the criminal but to bring about a change in his behavior. If that could be done by lenient treatment—short prison terms, education, counseling, and above all by understanding—then so much the better.

By the late 1970s, the intellectual community itself showed signs that it was reassessing its outlook toward crime. Professor James Q. Wilson's views on crime became widely respected in universities and in the mass media—he was teaching at Harvard University at the time. Wilson stresses the need for "realism." It may be that some day all poverty and social injustice will cease to exist, says Wilson, but until that day arrives we had better keep criminals off the streets. He maintains that crime can be significantly reduced here and now simply by incapacitating (incarcerating) dangerous offenders. Wilson also takes a dim view of the prospects for rehabilitating criminals in prison. In his view, statistics prove that the question of whether a criminal goes back to crime after release does not depend upon what kind of prison he has gone to but rather on his own personal characteristics. In other words, Wilson believes, it is unlikely that even the most enlightened prison system can rehabilitate a hardened criminal.

David L. Bazelon admits that incapacitation is a short-term solution to street crime that delivers some results. He points out, however, that it has high financial and moral costs, explaining that the United States already imprisons a larger proportion of its citizens than do all other developed nations. A threefold increase in the prison population will not make a significant dent in the rate of serious crimes, maintains Bazelon, and the new prisons needed to house those increased numbers will cost many billions of dollars. More importantly, he says, the incapacitation approach assumes that convicted offenders will continue to commit crimes and in effect punishes them for future misdeeds. Bazelon's approach raises serious questions concerning individual justice. He believes the only satisfactory answer is to attack the social and economic conditions that are the root causes of street crime.

YES

James Q. Wilson

THINKING ABOUT CRIME

I argue for a sober view of man and his institutions that would permit reasonable things to be accomplished, foolish things abandoned, and utopian things forgotten. A sober view of man requires a modest definition of progress. A 20 percent reduction in robbery would still leave us with the highest robbery rate of almost any Western nation but would prevent about sixty thousand robberies. A small gain for society, a large one for the would-be victims. Yet a 20 percent reduction is unlikely if we concentrate our efforts on dealing with the causes of crime or even if we concentrate on improving police efficiency. Were we to devote those resources to a strategy that is well within our abilities—namely, to incapacitating a larger fraction of the convicted serious robbers—then not only is a 20 percent reduction possible, but even larger ones are conceivable.

Most serious crime is committed by repeaters. What we do with first offenders is probably far less important than what we do with habitual offenders. A genuine first offender (and not merely a habitual offender caught for the first time) is in all likelihood a young person who, in the majority of cases, will stop stealing when he gets older. This is not to say we should forgive first offenses, for that would be to license the offense and erode the moral judgments that must underlie any society's attitude toward crime. The gravity of the offense must be appropriately impressed on the first offender, but the effort to devise ways of reeducating or uplifting him in order to insure that he does not steal again is likely to be wasted—both because we do not know how to reeducate or uplift and because most young delinquents seem to reeducate themselves no matter what society does.

After tracing the history of nearly ten thousand Philadelphia boys born in 1945, Marvin Wolfgang and his colleagues at the University of Pennsylvania found that over one-third were picked up by the police for something more serious than a traffic offense, but that 46 percent of these delinquents had no further police contact after their first offense. Though a third started on crime, nearly half seemed to stop spontaneously—a good thing, because the criminal justice system in that city, already sorely taxed, would in all

From James Q. Wilson, *Thinking About Crime* (Basic Books, 1975). Copyright © 1975 by Basic Books, Inc. Reprinted by permission of Basic Books, Inc., Publishers, New York.

likelihood have collapsed. Out of the ten thousand boys, however, there were six hundred twenty-seven—only 6 percent—who committed five or more offenses before they were eighteen. Yet these few chronic offenders accounted for *over half* of these recorded delinquencies and about *two-thirds* of all the violent crimes committed by the entire cohort.

Only a tiny fraction of all serious crimes lead immediately to an arrest, and only a slightly larger fraction are ultimately "cleared" by an arrest, but this does not mean that the police function is meaningless. Because most serious crime is committed by repeaters, most criminals eventually get arrested. The Wolfgang findings and other studies suggest that the chances of a persistent burglar or robber living out his life, or even going a year, with no arrest are quite small. Yet a large proportion of repeat offenders suffer little or no loss of freedom. Whether or not one believes that such penalties, if inflicted, would act as a deterrent, it is obvious that they could serve to incapacitate these offenders and thus, for the period of the incapacitation, prevent them from committing additional crimes.

We have a limited (and declining) supply of detention facilities, and many of those that exist are decrepit, unsafe, and overcrowded. But as important as expanding the supply and improving the decency of the facilities is the need to think seriously about how we wish to allocate those spaces that exist. At present, that allocation is hit or miss. A 1966 survey of over fifteen juvenile correctional institutions revealed that about 30 percent of the inmates were young persons who had been committed for conduct that would not have been judged criminal were it committed by adults. They were runaways, "stubborn children," or chronic truants—problem children, to be sure, but scarcely major threats to society. Using scarce detention space for them when in Los Angeles over 90 percent of burglars with a major prior record receive no state prison sentence seems, to put it mildly, anomalous.

Shlomo and Reuel Shinnar have estimated the effect on crime rates in New York State of a judicial policy other than that followed during the last decade or so. Given the present level of police efficiency and making some assumptions about how many crimes each offender commits per year, they conclude that the rate of serious crime would be only *one-third* what it is today if every person convicted of a serious offense were imprisoned for three years. This reduction would be less if it turned out (as seems unlikely) that most serious crime is committed by first time offenders, and it would be much greater if the proportion of crimes resulting in an arrest and conviction were increased (as also seems unlikely). The reduction, it should be noted, would be solely the result of incapacitation, making no allowance for such additional reductions as might result from enhanced deterrence or rehabilitation.

The Shinnar estimates are based on uncertain data and involve assumptions that can be challenged. But even assuming they are overly optimistic by a factor of two, a sizable reduction in crime would still ensue. In other countries such a policy of greater incapacitation is in fact followed. A robber arrested in England, for example, is more than three times as likely as one arrested in New York to go to prison. That difference in sentencing does not account for all the difference between English and American crime rates, but it may well account for a substantial fraction of it.

That these gains are possible does not mean that society should adopt such a policy. One would first want to know the costs, in additional prison space and judicial resources, of greater use of incapacitation. One would want to debate the propriety and humanity of a mandatory three-year term; perhaps, in order to accommodate differences in the character of criminals and their crimes, one would want to have a range of sentences from, say, one to five years. One would want to know what is likely to happen to the process of charging and pleading if every person arrested for a serious crime faced a mandatory minimum sentence, however mild. These and other difficult and important questions must first be confronted. But the central fact is that *these are reasonable questions* around which facts can be gathered and intelligent arguments mustered. To discuss them requires us to make few optimistic assumptions about the malleability of human nature, the skills of officials who operate complex institutions, or the capacity of society to improve the fundamental aspects of familial and communal life.

Persons who criticize an emphasis on changing the police and courts to cope with crime are fond of saying that such measures cannot work so long as unemployment and poverty exist. We must acknowledge that we have not done very well at inducting young persons, especially but not only blacks, into the work force. Teenage unemployment rates continue to exceed 20 percent; though the rate of growth in the youthful component of the population has slowed, their unemployment shows little sign of abating. To a degree, anticrime policies may be frustrated by the failure of employment policies, but it would be equally correct to say that so long as the criminal justice system does not impede crime, efforts to reduce unemployment will not work. If legitimate opportunities for work are unavailable, many young persons will turn to crime; but if criminal opportunities are profitable, many young persons will not take those legitimate jobs that exist. The benefits of work and the costs of crime must be increased simultaneously; to increase one but not the other makes sense only if one assumes that young people are irrational.

One rejoinder to this view is the argument that if legitimate jobs are made absolutely more attractive than stealing, stealing will decline even without any increase in penalties for it. That may be true provided there is no practical limit on the amount that can be paid in wages. Since the average "take" from a burglary or mugging is quite small, it would seem easy to make the income from a job exceed the income from crime. But this neglects the advantages of a criminal income: One works at crime at one's convenience, enjoys the esteem of colleagues who think a "straight" job is stupid and skill at stealing is commendable, looks forward to the occasional "big score" that may make further work unnecessary for weeks, and relishes the risk and adventure associated with theft. The money value of all these benefits—that is, what one who is not shocked by crime would want in cash to forego crime—is hard to estimate, but is almost certainly far larger than what either public or private employers could offer to unskilled or semiskilled young workers. The only alternative for society is to so increase the risks of theft that its value is depreciated below what society can afford to pay in legal wages, and then take whatever steps are necessary to insure that those legal wages are available.

Another rejoinder to the "attack poverty" approach to crime is this: The desire to reduce crime is the worst possible reason for reducing poverty. Most poor persons are not criminals; many are either retired or have regular jobs and lead conventional family lives. The elderly, the working poor, and the willing-to-work poor could benefit greatly from economic conditions and government programs that enhance their incomes without there being the slightest reduction in crime—indeed, if the experience of the 1960s is any guide, there might well be, through no fault of most beneficiaries, an increase in crime. Reducing poverty and breaking up the ghettoes are desirable policies in their own right, whatever their effects on crime. It is the duty of government to devise other measures to cope with crime, not only to permit antipoverty programs to succeed without unfair competition from criminal opportunities, but also to insure that such programs do not inadvertently shift the costs of progress, in terms of higher crime rates, onto innocent parties, not the least of whom are the poor themselves.

One cannot press this economic reasoning too far. Some persons will commit crimes whatever the risks; indeed, for some, the greater the risk the greater the thrill, while others—the alcoholic wife beater, for example—are only dimly aware that there are any risks. But more important than the insensitivity of certain criminal activities to changes in risks and benefits is the impropriety of casting the crime problem wholly in terms of a utilitarian calculus. The most serious offenses are crimes not simply because society finds them inconvenient, but because it regards them with moral horror. To steal, to rape, to rob, to assault—these acts are destructive of the very possibility of society and affronts to the humanity of their victims. It is my experience that parents do not instruct their children to be law abiding merely by pointing to the risks of being caught, but by explaining that these acts are wrong whether or not one is caught. I conjecture that those parents who simply warn their offspring about the risks of crime produce a disproportionate number of young persons willing to take those risks.

Even the deterrent capacity of the criminal justice system depends in no small part on its ability to evoke sentiments of shame in the accused. If all it evoked were a sense of being unlucky, crime rates would be even higher. James Fitzjames Stephens makes the point by analogy. To what extent, he asks, would a man be deterred from theft by the knowledge that by committing it he was exposing himself to one chance in fifty of catching a serious but not fatal illness—say, a bad fever? Rather little, we would imagine—indeed, all of us regularly take risks as great or greater than that; when we drive after drinking, when we smoke cigarettes, when we go hunting in the woods. The criminal sanction, Stephens concludes, "operates not only on the fears of criminals, but upon the habitual sentiments of those who are not criminals. [A] great part of the general detestation of crime . . . arises from the fact that the commission of offenses is associated . . . with the solemn and deliberate infliction of punishment wherever crime is proved."

Much is made today of the fact that the criminal justice system "stigmatizes" those caught up in it, and thus unfairly marks such persons and perhaps even furthers their criminal careers by having "labeled" them as criminals. Whether the labeling process operates in this way is as yet unproved, but it would indeed be unfortunate if society treated a convicted offender in such a way that he had no reasonable alternative but to make crime a career. To prevent this, society ought to insure that one can "pay one's debt" without suffering permanent loss of civil rights, the continuing and pointless indignity of parole supervision, and frustration in being unable to find a job. But doing these things is very different from eliminating the "stigma" from crime. To destigmatize crime would be to lift from it the weight of moral judgment and to make crime simply a particular occupation or avocation which society has chosen to reward less (or perhaps more!) than other pursuits. If there is not stigma attached to an activity, then society has no business making it a crime. Indeed, before the invention of the prison in the late eighteenth and early nineteenth centuries, the stigma attached to criminals was the major deterrent to and principal form of protection from criminal activity. The purpose of the criminal justice system is not to expose would-be criminals to a lottery in which they either win or lose, but to expose them in addition and more importantly to the solemn condemnation of the community should they yield to temptation. . . .

One wonders whether the stigma properly associated with crime retains much deterrent or educative value. My strong inclination is to resist explanations for rising crime that are based on the alleged moral breakdown of society, the community, or the family. I resist in part because most of the families and communities I know have not broken down, and in part because, had they broken down, I cannot imagine any collective action we could take consistent with our civil liberties that would restore a moral consensus, and yet the facts are hard to ignore. Take the family: Over one-third of all black children and one in fourteen of all white children live in single-parent families. Over two million children live in single-parent (usually father absent) households, almost *double* the number of ten years ago. In 1950, 18 percent of black families were female-headed; in 1969 the proportion had risen to 27 percent; by 1973 it exceeded 35 percent. The average income for a single-parent family with children under six years of age was, in 1970, only $3,100, well below the official "poverty line."

Studies done in the late 1950s and the early 1960s showed that children from broken homes were more likely than others to become delinquent. In New York State, 58 percent of the variation in pupil achievement in three hundred schools could be predicted by but three variables—broken homes, overcrowded housing, and parental educational level. Family disorganization, writes Urie Bronfenbrenner, has been shown in thousands of studies to be an "omnipresent overriding factor" in behavior disorders and social pathology. And that disorganization is increasing.

These facts may explain some elements of the rising crime rate that cannot be attributed to the increased number of young persons, high teenage unemployment, or changed judicial policies. The age of persons arrested has been declining for more than fifteen years and the median age of convicted defendants (in jurisdictions for which data are available) has been declining for the last six years. Apparently, the age at which persons begin to commit serious crime has been falling. For some young people, thus, whatever forces weaken their resistance to criminal activity have been increasing in magnitude, and these forces may well include the continued disorganization of the family and the continued deterioration of the social structure of inner city communities.

One wants to be objective, if not optimistic. Perhaps single-parent families today are less disorganized or have a different significance than such families in the past. Perhaps the relationship between family structure and social pathology will change. After all, there now seem to be good grounds for believing that, at least on the East Coast, the heroin epidemic of the 1960s has run its course; though there are still thousands of addicts, the rate of formation of new addicts has slowed and the rate of heroin use by older addicts has dropped. Perhaps other aspects of the relationship among family, personality, and crime will change. Perhaps.

No one can say how much of crime results from its increased profitability and how much from its decreased shamefulness. But one or both factors must be at work, for population changes alone simply cannot account for the increases. Crime in our cities has increased far faster than the number of young people, or poor people, or black people, or just plain people who live in those cities. In short, objective conditions alone, whether demographic or economic, cannot account for the crime increases, though they no doubt contributed to it. Subjective forces—ideas, attitudes, values— played a great part, though in ways hard to define and impossible to measure. An assessment of the effect of these changes on crime would provide a partial under-standing of changes in the moral structure of our society.

But to understand is not to change. If few of the demographic factors contributing to crime are subject to planned change, virtually none of the subjective ones are. Though intellectually rewarding, from a practical point of view it is a mistake to think about crime in terms of its "causes" and then to search for ways to alleviate those causes. We must think instead of what it is feasible for a government or a community to do, and then try to discover, by experimentation and observation, which of those things will produce, at acceptable costs, desirable changes in the level of criminal victimization.

There are, we now know, certain things we can change in accordance with our intentions, and certain ones we cannot. We cannot alter the number of juveniles who first experiment with minor crimes. We cannot lower the recidivism rate, though within reason we should keep trying. We are not yet certain whether we can increase significantly the police apprehension rate. We may be able to change the teenage unemployment rate, though we have learned by painful trial and error that doing this is much more difficult than once supposed. We can probably reduce the time it takes to bring an arrested person to trial, even though we have as yet made few serious efforts to do so. We can certainly reduce the arbitrary and socially irrational exercise of prosecutorial discretion over whom to charge and whom to release, and we can most definitely stop pretending that judges know, any better than the rest of us, how to provide "individualized justice." We can confine a larger proportion of the serious and repeat offenders and fewer of the common drunks and truant children. We know that confining criminals prevents them from harming society, and we have grounds for suspecting that some would-be criminals can be deterred by the confinement of others.

Above all, we can try to learn more about what works, and in the process abandon our ideological preconceptions about what *ought* to work. Nearly ten years ago I wrote that the billions of dollars the federal government was then preparing to spend on crime control would be wasted, and indeed might even make matters worse if they were merely pumped into the existing criminal justice system. They were, and they have. In the next ten years I hope we can learn to experiment rather than simply spend, to test our theories rather than fund our fears. This is advice, not simply or even primarily to government—for governments are run by men and women who are under irresistible pressures to pretend they know more than they do—but to my colleagues: academics, theoreticians, writers, advisers. We may feel ourselves under pressure to pretend we know things, but we are also under a positive obligation to admit what we do not know and to avoid cant and sloganizing. The government agency, the Law Enforcement Assistance Administration, that has futilely spent those billions was created in consequence of an act passed by Congress on the advice of a presidential commission staffed by academics, myself included.

It is easy and popular to criticize yesterday's empty hopes and mistaken beliefs, especially if they seemed supportive of law enforcement. It is harder, and certainly most unpopular, to criticize today's pieties and pretensions, especially if they are uttered in the name of progress and humanity. But if we were wrong in thinking that more money spent on the police would bring down crime rates, we are equally wrong in supposing that closing our prisons, emptying our jails, and supporting "community-based" programs will do any better. Indeed, there is some evidence that these steps will make matters worse, and we ignore it at our peril.

Since the days of the crime commission we have learned a great deal, more than we are prepared to admit. Perhaps we fear to admit it because of a new-found modesty about the foundations of our knowledge, but perhaps also because the implications of that knowledge suggest an unflattering view of man. Intellectuals, although they often dislike the common person as an individual, do not wish to be caught saying uncomplimentary things about humankind. Nevertheless, some persons will shun crime even if we do nothing to deter them, while others will seek it out even if we do everything to reform them. Wicked people exist. Nothing avails except to set them apart from innocent people. And many people neither wicked nor innocent, but watchful, dissembling, and calculating of their opportunities, ponder our reaction to wickedness as a cue to what they might profitably do. We have trifled with the wicked, made sport of the innocent, and encouraged the calculators. Justice suffers, and so do we all.

NO

David L. Bazelon

SOLVING THE NIGHTMARE
OF STREET CRIME

The nightmare of street crime is slowly paralyzing American society. Across the nation, terrified people have altered their lifestyles, purchasing guns and doubling locks to protect their families against the rampant violence outside their doors. After seething for years, public anxiety is now boiling over in a desperate search for answers. Our leaders are reacting to these public demands. In New York, Gov. Hugh Carey proposed the hiring of more police officers and prosecutors; in California, Attorney General Deukmejian has asked the legislature for immediate adoption of a package of new law enforcement bills.

A recent address by the Chief Justice of the United States has helped to place this crisis high on the public agenda. Speaking before the American Bar Association in February, Chief Justice Warren Burger described ours as an "impotent society," suffering a "reign of terror" in its streets and homes. The time has come, he declared, to commit vast social resources to the attack on crime—a priority comparable to the national defense.

Some have questioned whether a sitting Chief Justice should advocate sweeping changes in the criminal justice system and others have challenged his particular prescriptions, but I believe the prestige of his office has focused the nation's attention on issues critical to our future. We should welcome this opportunity to begin a thoughtful and constructive debate about our national nightmare.

In this debate, public concern is sure to generate facile sloganeering by politicians and professionals alike. It would be easy to convert this new urgency into a mandate for a "quick fix." The far-harder task is to marshall that energy toward examining the painful realities and agonizing choices we face. Criminologists can help make our choices the product of an informed, rational, and morally sensitive strategy. As citizens and as human beings, they have a special responsibility to contribute their skills, experience, and knowledge to keep the debate about crime as free of polemics and unexamined assumptions as possible.

I would like to outline some avenues of inquiry worthy of exploration. I offer no programs, no answers. After 31 years on the bench, I can say with

From David L. Bazelon, "Solving the Nightmare of Street Crime," *USA Today Magazine* (January 1982). Copyright © 1982 by the Society for the Advancement of Education. Reprinted by permission.

confidence that we can never deal intelligently and humanely with crime until we face the realities behind it. First, we must carefully identify the problem that so terrorizes America. Second, we should seek to understand the conditions that breed those crimes of violence. Finally, we should take a close look at both the short- and long-term alternatives for dealing with the problem.

TYPES OF CRIMES AND WHO COMMITS THEM

A reasoned analysis must begin by asking: What is it that has our society in such a state of fear? Politicians, journalists, and criminal justice professionals who should know better speak rather generally about "crime in America" without specifying exactly what they mean. There are, in fact, several distinct types of crimes and people who commit them.

Consider white-collar crime. This category embraces activities ranging from shoplifting to tax fraud to political corruption. It is undoubtedly a phenomenon of the gravest concern, costing society untold billions of dollars—far more than street crime. To the extent that such crimes appear to go unpunished, they breed disrespect for law and cynicism about our criminal justice institutions. Yet, as costly and corrosive as such crimes are, they do not instill the kind of fear reflected in the recent explosion of public concern. White-collar crimes, after all, are committed by the middle and upper classes, by "[p]eople who look like one's next-door neighbor," as sociologist Charles Silberman puts it. These people do not, by and large, threaten our physical safety or the sanctity of our homes.

Nor do the perpetrators of organized crime. After all, hired guns largely kill each other. The average citizen need not lock his doors in fear that he may be the object of gang warfare. Organized crime unquestionably does contribute to street crime—the most obvious connection is drugs—but organized crime has certainly not produced the recent hysteria.

Nor do crimes of passion cause us to bolt our doors so firmly at night. That would be like locking the fox *inside* the chicken coop. Clearly, it is the random assault of *street* crime—the muggings, rapes, purse snatchings, and knifings that plague city life—which puts us all in such mortal fear for our property and lives.

Once we focus on the kind of crime we fear, the second step in a constructive analysis is to identify those people who commit it. This is no pleasant task. The real roots of crime are associated with a constellation of suffering so hideous that, as a society, we can not bear to look it in the face. Yet, we can never hope to understand street crime unless we summon the courage to look at the ugly realities behind it. Nobody questions that street criminals typically come from the bottom of the socioeconomic ladder —from among the ignorant, the ill-educated, and the unemployed, and the unemployable. A recent National Institute of Justice study confirms that our prison population is disproportionately black and young. The offenders that give city dwellers nightmares come from an underclass of brutal social and economic deprivation. Urban League president Vernon Jordan calls them America's "boat people without boats."

It is no great mystery why some of these people turn to crime. They are born into families struggling to survive, if they have families at all. They are raised in deteriorating, overcrowded housing. They lack adequate nutrition and health care. They are subjected to prejudice and educated in unresponsive schools. They are denied the sense of order, purpose, and self-esteem that makes law-abiding citizens. With nothing to preserve and nothing to lose, they turn to crime for economic survival, a sense of excitement and accomplishment, and an outlet for frustration, desperation, and rage.

Listen to the words of a 15-year-old ghetto youth:

> In Brooklyn you fall into one of two categories when you start growing up.... First, there's the minority of the minority, the "ducks" or suckers. These are the kids who go to school every day. They even want to go to college. Imagine that! School after high school! . . . They're wasting their lives waiting for a dream that won't come true.
>
> The ducks are usually the ones getting beat up on by the majority group— the "hard rocks." If you're a real hard rock you have no worries, no cares. Getting high is as easy as breathing. You just rip off some duck. You don't bother going to school, it's not necessary. You just live with your mom until you get a job—that should be any time a job comes looking for you. Why should you bother to go looking for it? Even your parents can't find work.
>
> Hard rocks do what they want to do when they want to do it. When a hard rock goes to prison it builds up his reputation. He develops a bravado that's like a long sad joke. But it's all lies and excuses. It's a hustle to keep ahead of the fact that he's going nowhere. . . .

This, then, is the face behind the mask we call "the crime problem."

Having identified the kind of crime that causes public anxiety and the kind of people who commit it, we can now consider some alternative responses. For purpose of analysis, we can divide the alternatives into two types. The first set, which enjoys the greatest currency in the political arena today, consists of short-term proposals. They proceed from our universally acknowledged need to protect ourselves *immediately* from the menace of crime. These kinds of prescriptions are endorsed by many good people in high places, including the Chief Justice of the United States and the Mayor of New York. The short-term proposals rely principally on deterrence and incapacitation as means of controlling the symptoms of our national disease. The second, more long-term proposals seek to attack the root causes of crime. Both of these approaches have great costs as well as benefits that must be carefully understood and weighed before we set our course.

DETERRENCE

Let us first examine the short-run proposals. Deterrence has always been intuitively attractive. The recent spate of prescriptions underscores the popularity of this theory and has taken many forms. The Chief Justice says we must provide "swift and certain consequences" for criminal behavior. The California Attorney General advocates mandatory prison terms for certain kinds of crimes. New York Mayor Edward Koch favors harsher sentences including the death penalty. Former U.S. Attorney Whitney North Seymour, Jr., contends that tougher prosecution is necessary. Each of these proposals is premised on Harvard University Prof. James Q. Wilson's theory that, "if the expected cost of crime goes up without a corresponding increase in the expected benefits, then the would-be criminal—unless he or she is among that small fraction of criminals who are utterly irrational—engages in less crime." To the same effect, Wayne State Prof. Ralph Slovenko wrote in a letter to the editor of *The New York Times* that, since "[p]rofits are tax-free and penalties are minimal," those who violate the law are "criminals by choice."

This "rational man" theory of crime is quite plausible with respect to certain kinds of criminals. I can believe that those who have alternatives to crime can indeed be dissuaded from choosing the lawless path if the price is made high enough. If the Abscam episode accomplished nothing else, it induced some potentially corrupt politicians to forbear from taking bribes—at least where there might be cameras around. In fact, white-collar offenders may be so susceptible to deterrence that punishment is superfluous. The fellow country-club members of a corporate embezzler whose life is ruined in a storm of publicity may not need to actually see him go to jail in order to be deterred.

However, the white-collar criminal is *not* the object of these deterrence proposals. Seymour says his proposals are aimed at "the hoodlums and ruffians who are making life in our cit[ies] a nightmare for many citizens"; in other words, at the "hard rocks." Can *these* kinds of criminals be effectively deterred? Diana Gordon, Executive Vice Pres. of the National Council on Crime and Delinquency, points out that the threat of prison may be a meaningless deterrent to one whose urban environment is itself a prison; and as our 15-year-old ghetto resident informs us, "[w]hen a hard rock goes to prison it builds up his reputation."

Common sense is confirmed by experience. New York's highly touted Rockefeller drug law did not produce a decrease in heroin use. In fact, it was actually followed by an increase in property crimes associated with heroin users. Nor is the New York situation unique. Since 1965, the average time served in Federal prison has *risen* from 18 to 30 months. Yet, crime continues to rise unabated.

Even the high priest of deterrence, Prof. Wilson, recognizes the limits of this theory. Although many bandy about his name in support of get-tough proposals, Wilson suggests that the *severity* of punishment has little deterrent effect. Indeed, "the more severe the penalty, the more unlikely that it will be imposed." The benefits of deterrence, according to Wilson, lie only in *certainty* of punishment.

How can we increase that certainty? The *Miranda* rule, the right to seek collateral review, and even the time to prepare for trial have all come under attack in the name of "swift and certain" punishment. These trial and appellate safeguards reflect our fundamental commitment to the presumption of innocence. Before we trade them away, we must know what we are getting in return. From an exhaustive review of the evidence, Silberman concluded that "criminal courts generally *do* an effective job of separating the innocent from the guilty; most of those who should be convicted are convicted, and most of those who should be punished are punished." Today, we prosecute, convict, and incarcerate a larger proportion of those arrested for felonies than we did 50 years ago; yet, the crime rate continues to rise. Clearly, the uncertainty about punishment derives from the great unlikelihood of *arrest*. For every 100 crimes committed, only six persons will be arrested. Thus, sacrificing the constitutional protections of those charged with crime will do little to deter the "hard rocks."

What must we do to achieve certainty of arrest sufficient to have an impact on crime? I asked my good friend, Maurice Cullinane, the former Chief of Police of the District of Columbia, about this. He presided over a force with far more policemen per capita than any other in the country, and that is aside from the several thousand park, Capitol, and other Federal police visible all over Washington. Chief Cullinane told me that, in order to deter street crime to any significant degree, he would have to amass an enormous concentration of patrolmen in one particular area. Only then might the physical presence of a policeman on virtually every block possibly keep crime under control. Of course, crime suppressed in one neighborhood would burgeon in other, unguarded parts of the city. Before we can endorse certainty of arrest as an effective deterrent, we must consider whether we could tolerate the kind of police state it might require.

We need to know much more about the precise costs of an effective program of deterrence before we can dismiss the recent proposals. At the present time, however, the case for deterrence has not been convincingly made. After a comprehensive review of the literature, a panel of the National Academy of Sciences concluded:

> Despite the intensity of the research effort, the empirical evidence is still not sufficient for providing a rigorous confirmation of the existence of a deterrent effect. . . . Policy makers in the criminal justice system are done a disservice if they are left with the impression that the empirical evidence, which they themselves are frequently unable to evaluate, strongly supports the deterrence hypothesis.

INCAPACITATION

A more realistic rationale put forth for short-term proposals, in my opinion, is incapacitation. This politely named theory has become the new aim of corrections. No one who has been in an American prison can seriously adhere to the ideal of rehabilitation, and more and more of us have come to suspect the futility of deterrence. The new theory of incapacitation essentially translates as lock the bastards up. At least then they will pose no threat to us while incarcerated. Incapacitation takes many forms: preventive detention, isolation of "career criminals," and stricter parole release requirements.

This notion has something to be said for it. We *must* do something to protect ourselves immediately so that we may "live to fight another day." Thus, the swift and tough route is appealing—get the attackers off the street forthwith; put them away fast and long so that the threat they pose to our daily lives can be neutralized.

A thorough commitment to this policy might indeed make our streets somewhat safer, but at what price? Consider first the cost in dollars. Today, even without an avowed commitment to incapacitation, we already imprison a larger proportion of our citizens than any other industrialized nation in the world, except Russia and South Africa. This dubious honor has cost us dearly. A soon-to-be published survey by the Department of Justice's National Institute of Justice reports that the 1972-78 period saw a 54 percent increase in the population of state prisons. The survey predicts that demand for prison space will continue to outstrip capacity. It has been conservatively estimated that we need

$8–10,000,000,000 immediately for construction just to close the gap that exists *now*.

Embarking on a national policy of incapacitation would require much more than closing the gap. One study has estimated that, in New York, a 264 percent increase in state imprisonment would be required to reduce serious crime by only 10 percent! Diana Gordon has worked out the financial requirements for this kind of incapacitation program. In New York alone, it would cost about $3,000,000,000 just to construct the additional cells necessary and probably another $1,000,000,000 each year to operate them. The public must be made aware of the extraordinary financial costs of a genuine incapacitation policy.

In addition, there are significant nonmonetary costs. Incapacitation rests on the assumption that convicted offenders would continue to commit crimes if not kept in prison, but can we determine in advance which offenders would in fact repeat and which would not? We simply do not know enough about the "hard rocks" to decide who to warehouse, and for how long. It has been estimated that, to be sure of identifying one potential criminal, we would have to include as many as eight people who would not offend. Thus, to obtain the benefits of incapacitation, we might have to incarcerate a substantial number of people who would have led a blameless life if released. A policy of sentencing individuals based on crimes not yet committed would therefore raise serious doubts about our dedication to the presumption of innocence. The thought of having to choose between immediate safety and sacred constitutional values is frightening.

Nor can there be any comfort that the grave moral and financial costs of incapacitation will only be temporary. Even as we put one generation of offenders behind bars, another set of "hard rocks" will emerge from the hopeless subculture of our ghettos, ready to follow the model set by their fathers and brothers. Unless we intend to keep every criminal and potential criminal in prison *forever*, we must acknowledge the futility of expecting them to behave when they get out. As journalist Tom Wicker recently observed, "to send them to the overcrowded, underfunded, inadequately staffed and policed prisons of America would negate [the] purpose; because more, and more frightening, criminals come out of these schools of crime and violence than go into them." Merely providing inmates with educational and counseling services would do little good "when they return to a society largely unwilling to hire them." We should not fool ourselves that the "hard rocks" will emerge from the cesspools of American prisons willing or able to conduct law-abiding lives.

Incapacitation, then, must be recognized as an extraordinarily costly and risky policy. To meaningfully affect crime, it might require a garrison state. This is not to deny that our "clear and present danger" must be addressed immediately. Still, reason and good faith require us to consider alternatives to a program of endlessly warehousing succeeding generations of human beings.

ATTACKING THE ROOT CAUSES OF CRIME

A more long-term response to crime is to attack its root causes. This approach also offers no decisive balance of costs and benefits. The unique advantage of a successful attack on the roots of crime would be the promise of *enduring* social tranquility. If we can first break the cycle of suffering which breeds crime, we could turn it to our advantage. We would achieve more than "damage control." Our nation could begin to tap the resources of those we now fear. Instead of a police or garrison state, ours would then be a social order rooted in the will and hearts of our people. We would achieve criminal justice by pursuing social justice.

However, like the short-term solutions, this path would involve substantial risks and uncertainties. The root causes of crime are, of course, far more complex and insidious than simple poverty. After all, the vast majority of the poor commit no crime. Our existing knowledge suggests that the roots of street crime lie in poverty *plus*—plus prejudice, plus poor housing, plus inadequate education, plus insufficient food and medical care, and, perhaps most importantly, plus a bad family environment or no family at all.

Accepting the full implications of what we know about street crime might require us to provide every family with the means to create the kind of home all human beings need. It might require us to afford the job opportunities that pose for some the only meaningful alternatives to violence. It would assure all children a constructive education, a decent place to live, and proper pre- and postnatal nutrition. It would seek to provide those children of inadequate family environments with proper day care or foster care. More fundamentally, it would seek to eradicate racism and prejudice.

Such an attack on the roots of crime would obviously be an extremely long and expensive process. Before we can determine which programs offer the greatest promise, we must face what we know about crime and build on previous efforts to attack its root causes.

More importantly, a genuine commitment to attacking the roots of crime might force us to reconsider our entire social and economic structure. Like the short-term approach, this might conflict with other deeply held values. Can we break the cycle at crime's roots without invading the social sphere of the ghetto? Would this require the state to impose its values on the young? If we really want a lasting solution to crime, can we afford not to?

In short, any approach we take to crime presents attractive benefits and frightening risks. None of our choices offers a cheap or easy solution. Analysis takes us this far. As I have repeatedly emphasized, we can not choose which difficult path to take without facing the realities of street crime. Obviously, we can not deter those whom we do not understand. Nor can we make a rational assessment of incapacitation without knowing how many we will have to incapacitate and for how long. Finally, of course, we can not evaluate the longterm approach without some idea of its specific strategies and their various costs.

A constructive and fruitful debate about the best means of solving the nightmare of street crime is long overdue. The public's fear of crime cries out for a response and our leaders have made it a national priority, but we can never hope to achieve a just and lasting solution to crime without first facing the realities that underlie it. Emerson said, "God offers to every mind its choice between truth and repose." Truth will not come easy. It will take patience and the strength to put aside emotional reactions. If we do not strive for truth, this nation and all it stands for is bound to enjoy only a brief, false, and dangerous repose.

POSTSCRIPT

Is Incapacitation the Answer to the Crime Problem?

If realism is the criterion for choosing policy options, Wilson's case is the stronger. Bazelon himself allows that incapacitation is a realistic short-term solution, though he argues that it is too costly and produces unsatisfactory long-term results. Bazelon's major argument is a moral one. He criticizes the incapacitation approach as inhumane, dangerous to civil liberties, and hypocritical. Criminals may be errant humans, he says, but they are humans and should be treated with compassion. He sees the incapacitation approach as expressing a revengeful attitude of "lock the low-lifes up" and believes this attitude is unbecoming to a civilized society. The rehabilitation of criminals—not their punishment—should be our goal, even if its accomplishment is very difficult, maintains Bazelon, adding that the incapacitation approach also threatens the civil liberties upon which this society stands. He believes that it is unfortunate that our civil liberties, which are among our proudest possessions, increase the difficulty of putting criminals behind bars. But he emphasizes that we must not weaken these rights in trying to solve the crime problem. Finally, Bazelon contends that the incapacitation approach treats the criminal as the only guilty party and that a more enlightened view recognizes the contributions of blocked opportunities, slum environments, broken families, and social pressures that are in conflict with legitimate values.

It should be pointed out that Wilson shares many of Bazelon's concerns but still sees the incapacitation approach as necessary under present circumstances. On this issue, as on many other issues, hard choices must be made between conflicting values.

In *Crime in America* (Simon & Schuster, 1971) former attorney general Ramsey Clark takes a position in many ways similar to Bazelon's. Hans Zeisel, in *The Limits of Law Enforcement* (University of Chicago Press, 1983), argues that the criminal justice system can do little to effectively reduce crime. His emphasis is on increasing protection from crime and attacking its root causes in the conditions of poverty. On the other side, Andrew Von Hirsch's *Doing Justice* (Hill & Wang, 1976) is critical of the Bazelon philosophy.

The issue of deterrence is hotly debated by authors Ernest van den Haag and John P. Conrad in their book on the ultimate in deterrence punishment, *The Death Penalty: A Debate* (Plenum Press, 1983). Graeme Newman presents an extreme position on punishment in advocating electric shocks and whippings in *Just and Painful: A Case for the Corporal Punishment of Criminals* (Macmillan, 1983). A history of punishment choices other than prison is presented in *Alternatives to Prison: Punishment, Custody and the Community* (Sage Publications, 1990).

A revival of biological explanations of crime is occurring along with some shocking proposals such as sterilization and abortion when the wrong genes are detected in adults or fetuses, as discussed in Lawrence Taylor, *Born to Crime: The Genetic Causes of Criminal Behavior* (Greenwood Press, 1984). A more sophisticated and less shocking discussion is presented by James Q. Wilson and Richard Harstein in *Crime and Human Nature* (Simon & Schuster, 1985). Strong support for Wilson's position on deterrence and incapacitation is provided by Morgan O. Reynolds with recent data in "Crime Pays, But so Does Imprisonment," *The Journal of Social, Political and Economic Studies* (Fall 1990).

PART 6

The Future: Population/ Environment/Society

Can a world with limited resources support an unlimited population? This question has taken on new dimensions as we approach the start of a new century. Technology has increased enormously in the last 100 years, as have new forms of pollution that threaten to undermine the world's fragile ecological support system. Will technology itself be the key to controlling or accommodating an increased population growth? All nations have a stake in the health of the planet and the world economy. Is America in a political and economic position to meet these global challenges?

Does Population Growth Threaten Humanity?

Is America's Socioeconomic System Breaking Down?

UN PHOTO 153428/JOHN ISAAC

ISSUE 19

Does Population Growth Threaten Humanity?

YES: Lester R. Brown, from "The New World Order," in Lester R. Brown et al., *State of the World 1991* (W. W. Norton, 1991)

NO: Julian L. Simon, from "Population Growth Is Not Bad for Humanity," *National Forum: The Phi Kappa Phi Journal* (Winter 1990)

ISSUE SUMMARY

YES: Lester R. Brown, president of the Worldwatch Institute, describes the major ways in which the environment is deteriorating due to economic and population growth.
NO: Professor of economics and business administration Julian L. Simon challenges the factual correctness of the negative effects of population growth that are cited by environmentalists.

Much of the literature on socioeconomic development in the 1960s was premised on the assumption of inevitable material progress for all. It largely ignored the impacts of development on the environment and presumed that the availability of raw materials would not be a problem. The belief was that all societies would get richer, because all societies were investing in new equipment and technologies that would increase productivity and wealth. It recognized that some poor countries were having trouble developing, but blamed those problems on the deficiencies of their values and attitudes and on inefficient organizations. Nevertheless, progress was thought possible even in the most difficult of places. If certain social and psychological defects could be overcome by a modernizing elite, and 10 percent of the gross national product could be devoted to capital formation for at least three decades, then poor countries would take off into self-sustained growth, just as industrial societies had done decades earlier. See Walt W. Rostow, *The Stages of Economic Growth* (Cambridge University Press, 1960) for a review of this. After take-off, growth would be self-sustaining and continue for the foreseeable future.

In the late 1960s and early 1970s an intellectual revolution occurred. Environmentalists had criticized the growth paradigm throughout the 1960s, but they were not taken very seriously at first. By the end of the 1960s, however, Rachel Carson's *Silent Spring* (Alfred A. Knopf, 1962) had worked its way into the public's consciousness. Carson's book traced the noticeable loss of birds to the use of pesticides. Her book made the middle and upper classes in the United States realize that pollution affected complex ecological systems in ways that put even the wealthy at risk.

In 1968 Paul Ehrlich wrote *The Population Bomb* (Ballantine Books), which stated that overpopulation was the major problem facing mankind and that population had to be controlled or the human race might cause the collapse of the global ecosystem and its own destruction. Ehrlich explained why he thought the death of the world was imminent.

> Because the human population of the planet is about five times too large, and we're managing to support all these people—at today's level of misery—only by spending our capital, burning our fossil fuels, dispersing our mineral resources and turning our fresh water into salt water. We have not only overpopulated but overstretched our environment. We are poisoning the ecological systems of the earth—systems upon which we are ultimately dependent for all of our food, for all of our oxygen and for all of our waste disposal.

In 1973 *The Limits to Growth* (Universe), by Donella H. Meadows et al., was published and presented a dynamic systems computer model for world economic, demographic, and environmental trends. When the computer model projected trends into the future, it predicted that the world would experience ecological collapse and population die-off unless population growth and economic activity were greatly reduced. This study was both attacked and defended, and the debate about the health of the world has been heated ever since.

Let us review the population growth rates past, present, and future. At about A.D. 0, the world had about one-quarter billion people. It took about 1,650 years to double this number to one-half billion and two hundred years to double the world population again to 1 billion by 1850. The next doubling took only about 80 years, and the last doubling time took about 45 years (from 2 billion in 1930 to about 4 billion in 1975). The world population may double again to 8 billion sometime between 2010 and 2020. Is population growth and the increased economic activity that it requires diminishing the carrying capacity of the planet and jeopardizing the prospects for future generations?

Currently, the major proponent of the optimistic view of further economic development without serious environmental consequences is Julian L. Simon. In the article that follows, he argues that the environment is becoming more beneficent for human beings because pollution is decreasing, resources are becoming more available and inexpensive, people are living longer, and population growth has largely positive economic and social impacts. Lester R. Brown argues for the need to control population growth and quickly reverse the dangerous deterioration of the environment that is occurring throughout the world.

YES

Lester R. Brown

THE NEW WORLD ORDER

As the nineties begin, the world is on the edge of a new age. The cold war that dominated international affairs for four decades and led to an unprecedented militarization of the world economy is over. With its end comes an end to the world order it spawned.

The East-West ideological conflict was so intense that it dictated the shape of the world order for more than a generation. It provided a clear organizing principle for the foreign policies of the two superpowers and, to a lesser degree, of other governments as well. But with old priorities and military alliances becoming irrelevant, we are now at one of those rare points in history—a time of great change, a time when change is as unpredictable as it is inevitable.

No one can say with certainty what the new order will look like. But if we are to fashion a promising future for the next generation, then the enormous effort required to reverse the environmental degradation of the planet will dominate world affairs for decades to come. In effect, the battle to save the planet will replace the battle over ideology as the organizing theme of the new world order.

As the dust from the cold war settles, both the extent of the environmental damage to the planet and the inadequacy of efforts to cope with it are becoming all too apparent. During the 20 years since the first Earth Day, in 1970, the world lost nearly 200 million hectares of tree cover, an area roughly the size of the United States east of the Mississippi River. Deserts expanded by some 120 million hectares, claiming more land than is currently planted to crops in China. Thousands of plant and animal species with which we shared the planet in 1970 no longer exist. Over two decades, some 1.6 billion people were added to the world's population—more than inhabited the planet in 1900. And the world's farmers lost an estimated 480 billion tons of topsoil, roughly equivalent to the amount on India's cropland.

This planetary degradation proceeded despite the environmental protection efforts of national governments over the past 20 years. During this time nearly all countries created environmental agencies. National legislatures

From Lester R. Brown, "The New World Order," in Lester R. Brown et al., *State of the World 1991* (W. W. Norton, 1991). Copyright © 1991 by the Worldwatch Institute. Reprinted by permission. Notes omitted.

passed thousands of laws to protect the environment. Tens of thousands of grass-roots environmental groups sprung up in response to locally destructive activities. Membership in national environmental organizations soared. But as Earth Day 1990 chairman Denis Hayes asks, "How could we have fought so hard, and won so many battles, only to find ourselves now on the verge of losing the war?"

One reason for this failure is that although governments have professed concern with environmental deterioration, few have been willing to make the basic changes needed to reverse it. Stabilizing climate, for example, depends on restructuring national energy economies. Getting the brakes on population growth requires massive changes in human reproductive behavior. But public understanding of the consequences of continuously rising global temperatures or rapid population growth is not yet sufficient to support effective policy responses.

The battle to save the earth's environmental support systems will differ from the battle for ideological supremacy in some important ways. The cold war was largely an abstraction, a campaign waged by strategic planners. Except for bearing the economic costs, which were very real, most people in the United States and the Soviet Union did not directly take part. In the new struggle, however, people everywhere will need to be involved: individuals trying to recycle their garbage, couples trying to decide whether to have a second child, and energy ministers trying to fashion an environmentally sustainable energy system. The goal of the cold war was to get others to change their values and behavior, but winning the battle to save the planet depends on changing our own values and behavior. . . .

TWO VIEWS OF THE WORLD

Anyone who regularly reads the financial papers or business weeklies would conclude that the world is in reasonably good shape and that long-term economic trends are promising. Obviously there are still problems—the U.S. budget deficit, Third World debt, and the unsettling effect of rising oil prices—but to an economist, things appear manageable. Even those predicting a severe global recession in 1991 are bullish about the longer term economic prospects for the nineties.

Yet on the environmental front, the situation could hardly be worse. Anyone who regularly reads scientific journals has to be concerned with the earth's changing physical condition. Every major indicator shows a deterioration in natural systems: forests are shrinking, deserts are expanding, croplands are losing topsoil, the stratospheric ozone layer continues to thin, greenhouse gases are accumulating, the number of plant and animal species is diminishing, air pollution has reached health-threatening levels in hundreds of cities, and damage from acid rain can be seen on every continent.

These contrasting views of the state of the world have their roots in economics and ecology—two disciplines with intellectual frameworks so different that their practitioners often have difficulty talking to each other. Economists interpret and analyze trends in terms of savings, investment, and growth. They are guided largely by economic theory and indicators, seeing the future more or less as an extrapolation of the recent past. From their vantage point, there is little reason to worry about natural constraints on human economic activity; rare is the economic text that mentions the carrying capacity principle that is so fundamental to ecology. Advancing technology, economists believe, can push back any limits. Their view prevails in the worlds of industry and finance, and in national governments and international development agencies.

In contrast, ecologists study the relationship of living things with each other and their environments. They see growth in terms of S-shaped curves, a concept commonly illustrated in high school biology classes by introducing a few algae into a petri dish. Carefully cultured at optimum temperature and with unlimited supplies of food, the algae multiply slowly at first, and then more rapidly, until growth eventually slows and then stops, usually because of waste accumulation. Charting this process over time yields the familiar S-shaped curve to which all biological growth processes in a finite environment conform.

Ecologists think in terms of closed cycles—the hydrological cycle, the carbon cycle, and the nitrogen cycle, to name a few. For them, all growth processes are limited, confined within the natural parameters of the earth's ecosystem. They see more clearly than others the damage to natural systems and resources from expanding economic activity. . . .

The contrast between . . . basic global economic indicators and those measuring the earth's environmental health could not be greater. While . . . economic measurements are overwhelmingly positive, all the principal environmental indicators are consistently negative. As the need for cropland led to the clearing of forests, for example, and as the demand for firewood, lumber, and paper soared, deforestation gained momentum. By the end of the decade, the world's forests were shrinking by an estimated 17 million hectares each year. Some countries, such as Mauritania and Ethiopia, have lost nearly all their tree cover.

Closely paralleling this is the loss of topsoil from wind and water erosion, and the associated degradation of land. Deforestation and overgrazing, both widespread throughout the Third World, have also led to wholesale land degradation. Each year, some 6 million hectares of land are so severely degraded that they lose their productive capacity, becoming wasteland.

During the eighties, the amount of carbon pumped into the atmosphere from the burning of fossil fuels climbed to a new high, reaching nearly 6 billion tons in 1990. In a decade in which stock prices climbed to record highs, so too did the mean temperature, making the eighties the warmest decade since recordkeeping began more than a century ago. The temperature rise was most pronounced in western North America and western Siberia. Preliminary climate data for 1990 indicate it will be the hottest year on record, with snow cover in the northern hemisphere the lightest since the satellite record began in 1970.

Air and water pollution also worsened in most of the world during the last 10 years. By 1990, the air in hundreds of cities contained health-threatening levels of pollutants. In large areas of North America, Europe, and Asia, crops were being damaged as well. And despite widespread reduction in water pollution in the United States, the Environmental Protection Agency reported in 1988 that groundwater in 39 states contained pesticides. In Poland, at least half the river water was too polluted even for industrial use.

These changes in the earth's physical condition are having a devastating effect on the biological diversity of the planet.

Although no one knows how many plant and animal species were lost during the eighties, leading biologists estimate that one fifth of the species on earth may well disappear during this century's last two decades. What they cannot estimate is how long such a rate of extinction can continue without leading to the wholesale collapse of ecosystems.

How can one set of widely used indicators be so consistently positive and another so consistently negative? One reason the economic measures are so encouraging is that national accounting systems—which produce figures on gross national product—miss entirely the environmental debts the world is incurring. The result is a disguised form of deficit financing. In sector after sector, we are consuming our natural capital at an alarming rate—the opposite of an environmentally sustainable economy, one that satisfies current needs without jeopardizing the prospects of future generations. As economist Herman Daly so aptly puts it, "there is something fundamentally wrong in treating the earth as if it were a business in liquidation."

To extend this analogy, it is as though a vast industrial corporation quietly sold off a few of its factories each year, using an incomplete accounting system that did not reflect these sales. As a result, its cash flow would be strong and profits would rise. Stockholders would be pleased with the annual reports, not realizing that the profits were coming at the expense of the corporation's assets. But once all the factories were sold off, corporate officers would have to inform stockholders that their shares were worthless.

In effect, this is what we are doing with the earth. Relying on a similarly incomplete accounting system, we are depleting our productive assets, satisfying our needs today at the expense of our children. . . .

WHAT FOOD INDICATORS SAY

Of all the sectors in the world economy, it is agriculture where the contrast between the economic and environmental indicators is most obvious. It is in the relentless push to produce more food that several decades of borrowing from the future are beginning to take a toll. In many countries, growth in the farm sector is pressing against the limits of land and water supplies. And in some, the backlog of technology available for farmers to raise food output is shrinking.

By traditional measures, world agriculture appears to be doing well. Western Europe worries about surpluses, particularly of dairy products, and the United States still idles cropland to control production. Grain-exporting countries use subsidies to compete for markets that never seem large enough. For an economist, there may be distribution problems in the world food economy, but not a production problem.

To an ecologist who sees a substantial fraction of current world food output being produced on highly erodible land that will soon be abandoned or by overpumping groundwater, which cannot continue indefinitely, the prospect is far less promising. As world agriculture presses against natural limits imposed by the area of productive land, by the amount of fresh water produced by the hydrological cycle, and by the geophysical processes that produce soil, growth in output is beginning to slow. Modest new additions to the cropland base are offset by the conversion of land to nonfarm uses and by the abandonment of severely degraded land.

The scarcity of fresh water is imposing limits on crop production in many agricultural regions. Competition among countries for the water from internationally shared rivers, such as the Tigris-Euphrates, Jordan, and Nile in the Middle East, is a source of growing political tension. In Soviet central Asia, the Amu Darya, the source of most of the region's irrigation water, now runs dry long before it reaches the Aral Sea. Falling water tables are now commonplace in heavily populated countries such as India and China, which are overpumping aquifers in their effort to satisfy the growing need for irrigation water. Under parts of the North China Plain, water tables are dropping up to a meter per year. And the vast Ogallala aquifer, which supplies irrigation water to U.S. farmers and ranchers from central Nebraska to the Texas panhandle, is gradually being depleted. Cities such as Denver and Phoenix are outbidding farmers in the intensifying competition for water.

In addition to the degradation of land by farming practices, outside forces are also beginning to take a little-acknowledged toll on agriculture. Air pollution is reducing U.S. crop production by an officially estimated 5–10 percent, and is probably having a similar effect in the coal-burning economies of Eastern Europe and China. As deforestation progresses in the mountainous areas of the world, the term "flood-damaged harvests" appears with increasing frequency in world crop reports.

Even as these environmental and resource constraints slow world food output growth, the backlog of unused agricultural technology is diminishing.

In Asia, for example, the highest yielding rice varieties available to farmers were released in 1966, a quarter-century ago. The International Rice Research Institute, the world's premier research facility in this field, observed in a strategy paper released for 1990 that "during the past five years, growth in rice yields has virtually ceased."

One way of assessing the technological prospect for boosting food output during the nineties is to look at trends in fertilizer use, since the phenomenal growth in world food output from 1950 to 1984 was due largely to the ninefold growth in fertilizer use. In large measure, other major advances in agriculture, such as the near-tripling of irrigated area and the adoption of ever higher yielding varieties, greatly enhanced the potential to use more fertilizer profitably. But as the nineties begin many countries have reached the point where using additional fertilizer does little to boost food output. . . .

For the world as a whole, the annual growth in grain production from 1984 to 1990 was 1 percent, while that of population was nearly 2. The diminishing crop response to the additional use of fertilizer, the negative effect of environmental degradation on harvests, and the lack of any new technology to replace fertilizer as the engine of agricultural growth are each contributing to a potentially hungry future for much of humanity. In both 1984 and 1990, per hectare yields of the three grains that dominate the world diet—wheat, rice, and corn—set new records, indicating unusually favorable growing conditions in all the major grain-growing regions. If these two years are broadly comparable weatherwise, as they appear to be, then this slower growth in world grain output may indeed be a new trend. . . .

POPULATION: THE NEGLECTED ISSUE

Nowhere is the conceptual contrast between economists and ecologists more evident than in the way they view population growth. In assessing its effect, economists typically have not seen it as a particularly serious threat. In their view, if a nation's economy is growing at 5 percent per year and its population at 3 percent, this leads to a steady 2-percent gain in living standards. Relying on economic variables alone, this situation seemed to be tenable, one that could be extrapolated indefinitely into the future.

Ecologists looking at biological indicators in the same situation see rising human demand, driven by population growth and rising affluence, surpassing the carrying capacity of local forests, grasslands, and soils in country after country. They see sustainable yield thresholds of the economy's natural support systems being breached throughout the Third World. And as a result, they see the natural resource base diminishing even as population growth is expanding.

Against this backdrop, biologists find recent population trends profoundly disturbing. Accelerating sharply during the recovery period after World War II, the annual growth of world population peaked at about 1.9 percent in 1970. It then slowed gradually, declining to 1.7 percent in the early eighties. But during the late eighties it again began to accelerate, reaching 1.8 percent, largely because of a modest rise of the birth rate in China and a decrease in the death rate in India. With fertility turning upward in the late eighties instead of declining, as some had expected and many had hoped, the world is projected to add at least 960 million people during this decade, up from 840 million in the eighties and 750 million in the seventies.

Concern with the effects of population growth is not new. Nearly two centuries have passed since [economic theorist Thomas Robert] Malthus published his famous treatise in which he argued that population tends to grow exponentially while food production grows arithmetically. He argued that unless profligate childbearing was checked, preferably through abstinence, famine and hunger would be inevitable. Malthus was wrong in the sense that he did not anticipate the enormous potential of advancing technology to raise land productivity. He was writing before [Austrian botanist Gregor Johann] Mendel formulated the basic principles of genetics and before [Justus] Von Leibeg demonstrated that all the nutrients taken from the soil by plants could be returned in mineral form.

Malthus was correct, however, in anticipating the difficulty of expanding food output as fast as population growth. Today, hundreds of millions of the earth's inhabitants are hungry, partly because of inequitable distribution, but increasingly because of falling per capita food production. And as the nineties begin, the ranks of the hungry are swelling.

Malthus was concerned with the relationship between population growth and the earth's food-producing capacity. We now know that increasing numbers and economic activity affect many other natural capacities, such as the earth's ability to absorb waste. At any given level of per capita pollution, more people means more pollution. As the discharge of various industrial and agricultural wastes overwhelms the waste-absorptive capacity of natural systems, the cumulative effects of toxic materials in the environment begins to affect human health.

Another consequence of continuing population growth in much of the Third World is a shortage of firewood, the primary fuel. As the local demand for firewood for cooking exceeds the sustainable yield of local woodlands, the forests recede from the villages. Women, who gather most of the firewood, often find themselves trekking long distances to find enough to prepare meals. In some situations, families are reduced to only one hot meal a day. Malthus worried about whether there would be enough food, but he never reckoned that finding the fuel to prepare it would become part of the daily struggle for survival.

The record population growth projected for the nineties means the per capita availability of key resources such as land, water, and wood will also shrink at an unprecedented rate. (See Table 1.) Since the total cropland area is not expected to change during the decade, the land available per person to produce our basic staples will shrink by 1.7 percent a year. This means that grainland per person, averaging 0.13 hectares in 1990, will be reduced by one sixth during the nineties. And with a projected growth in overall irrigated land of less than 1 percent per year, the irrigated area per person will decline by nearly a tenth.

Forested area per person, reduced both by the overall loss in forests and by population growth, is likely to decline by one fifth or more during this decade. The 0.61 hectares per person of grazing land, which produces much of our milk, meat, and cheese, is also projected to drop by one fifth by the year 2000 as population grows and desertification spreads. Maintaining an improvement in living conditions with this reduction in per capita natural resources will not be easy. . . .

Table 1

Availability of Basic Natural Resources Per Person in 1990 and 2000

Resource	1990	2000
	(hectares)	
Grain land	0.13	0.11
Irrigated land	0.045	0.04
Forest land	0.79	0.64
Grazing land	0.61	0.50

Source: Based on U.S. Department of Agriculture, Economic Research Service, *World Grain Database* (unpublished printouts) (Washington, D.C.: 1990); U.N. Food and Agriculture Organization, *Production Yearbook* (Rome: various years); and U.N. Department of International Economic and Social Affairs, *World Population Prospects 1988* (New York: 1989).

A NEW AGENDA, A NEW ORDER

With the end of the ideological conflict that dominated a generation of international affairs, a new world order, shaped by a new agenda, will emerge. If the physical degradation of the planet becomes the principal preoccupation of the global community, then environmental sustainability will become the organizing principle of this new order. (For a discussion of the rough outline of an environmentally sustainable global economy, see Chapter 10 in *State of the World 1990.*) The world's agenda will be more ecological than ideological, dominated less by relationships among nations and more by the relationship between nations and nature. For the first time since the emergence of the nation-state, all countries can unite around a common theme. All societies have an interest in satisfying the needs of the current generation without compromising the ability of future generations to meet their needs. It is in the interest of everyone to protect the earth's life-support systems, for we all have a stake in the future habitability of the planet. . . .

Although it is premature to describe the shape of the post–cold war world order, its determining characteristics can now be identified. A commitment to the long-term improvement in the human condition is contingent on substituting environmental sustainability for growth as the overriding goal of national economic policymaking and international development. Political influence will derive more from environmental and economic strength than from military strength. And in the new order, the political stresses between East and West are likely to be replaced by the economic stresses between North and South, including such issues as the need to reduce Third World debt, access to markets in the industrial North, and how the costs of environmental protection initiatives are allocated between rich and poor.

In the emerging order, the United Nations seems certain to figure much more prominently in world affairs, particularly in peacekeeping, where its role is likely to be closer to that envisaged by its founders. Evidence of this new capacity emerged in 1990 as the United Nations took a leading and decisive role in the international response to Iraq's invasion of Kuwait. It was also evident in the U.N.-negotiated Kampuchean peace settlement of mid-1990. If the United Nations can effectively play the envisaged peacekeeping role, it will speed demilitarization and the shift of resources to environmental security.

Another indication of the expanding U.N. role was the June 1990 international agreement on a rapid phaseout of CFCs [chlorofluorocarbons] to minimize further losses from the stratospheric ozone layer. Some 93 countries agreed to halt CFC production by the end of the nineties, going far beyond the 1987 Montreal Accord that called for a 50-percent cut by 1998. This essential advance hinged on the establishment of an international fund that will provide $240 million of technical assistance over the next three years to help the Third World obtain CFC substitutes. The funding mechanism was essential to broadening support for the phaseout among developing countries, importantly India and China, the world's two most populous countries.

Reaching international agreement on a plan to stabilize climate, which in effect requires a restructuring of the world energy economy, will be far more difficult. . . . The current schedule, designed to produce a draft agreement for the U.N. Conference on Environment and Development in June 1992, will be the first major test of the new world order.

Environmental alliances to deal with specific transnational threats are likely to become commonplace and far more numerous than the military alliances that have featured so prominently since World War II. To cite a few examples, European countries could work together to save the region's deteriorating forests, nations bordering the Baltic Sea could join together to reverse its degradation, and countries in the Indian subcontinent could combine forces to reforest the Himalayas and reduce the frequency of crop-damaging floods. New North-South alliances to save migratory birds, whether songbirds within the western hemisphere or waterfowl that migrate from Europe to Africa, are increasingly probable.

As noted earlier, leadership in the new order is likely to derive less from military power and more from success in building environmentally sustainable economies.

The United States and the Soviet Union, the traditional military superpowers, are lagging badly in this effort and are thus likely to lose ground to those governments that can provide leadership in such a shift. For example, the path-breaking June 1990 decision by the West German cabinet to reduce carbon emissions 25 percent by 2005, along with other ambitious environmental initiatives in material reuse and recycling, . . . may cast the newly unified Germany in a leadership role.

With time running out in the effort to reverse the environmental destruction of the earth, there is an obvious need for initiatives that will quickly convert our environmentally unsustainable global economy into one that is sustainable. The many means of achieving this transformation range from voluntary life-style changes, such as limiting family size or reducing waste, to regulated changes such as laws boosting the fuel efficiencies of automobiles and household appliances. But the most effective instrument of all promises to be tax policy—specifically, the partial replacement of income taxes with those that discourage environmentally destructive activities. Prominent among the activities to tax are carbon emissions, the use of virgin materials, and the generation of toxic waste.

We can see what environmentally unsustainable growth does to the earth. And we know what the outlines of an environmentally sustainable economy look like. If the move toward the latter is not speeded up, we risk being overwhelmed by the economic and social consequences of planetary degradation. This in turn depends on more of us becoming environmental activists, working on behalf of the future of the planet and our children. Unless we can reverse quickly some of the environmental trends that are undermining our economy, our dream of a better life for our children and grandchildren will remain just that.

NO

Julian L. Simon

POPULATION GROWTH IS NOT BAD FOR HUMANITY

The prospectus for this issue of *National Forum* that came to us authors included this: "Is the situation as desperate as Lester Brown [who edits the annual *State of the World* volume] says, 'by the end of the next decade . . . The community of nations either will have rallied and turned back threatening trends, or environmental deterioration and social disintegration will be feeding on each other'?"

This question is wholly miscast. The trends are *not* threatening. Rather, all the trends important to humanity point to benign directions, and have for centuries and perhaps millennia.

The prospectus also included a list of "ecological issues" to be discussed in this issue such as "soil erosion," "deforestation," "depletion of the U.S. wheat harvest," "poisoning the food supply," "the price of pesticides," and many more such descriptions which imply that conditions are getting worse.

Each of these issues is misstated. There are no data showing that the soil in the world is becoming more eroded than less eroded. The U.S. wheat harvest is one of the great success stories of all time and continues to be so. And so it is with other issues.

All of the other issues are supposedly related to the subject about which I am to write, "the consequences of overpopulation," insofar as the purported bad trends are supposedly the result of human beings, and therefore fewer human beings are supposed to alleviate the negative trends. But if the trends really are not negative—and the scientific evidence shows them not to be—then it does not make sense to ask whether population is growing too fast or too slow in the context of these issues.

Yet once again there is hysteria about there being too many people and too many babies being born. Television presents notables ranging from the late Andrei Sakharov to Dan Rather repeating that more people on earth mean poorer lives now and worse prospects for the future. The newspapers chime in. A typical editorial in the 3 June 1989 *Washington Post* says that "in the developing world . . . fertility rates impede advances in economic growth,

From Julian L. Simon, "Population Growth Is Not Bad for Humanity," *National Forum: The Phi Kappa Phi Journal*, vol. 70, no. 1 (Winter 1990). Copyright © 1990 by The Honor Society of Phi Kappa Phi. Reprinted by permission of *National Forum: The Phi Kappa Phi Journal*.

health, and educational opportunities."
Nobel-winner Leon Lederman says in
his statement as candidate for the president of the American Association for the
Advancement of Science that "overpopulation" is one of our "present crises"
(2 June 1989 announcement). The president of NOW [National Organization for
Women] warns that continued population growth would be a "catastrophe"
(Nat Hentoff in the *Washington Post*, 29
July 1989). The head of the Worcester
Foundation for Experimental Biology
calls for more funding for contraceptive
research because of "overpopulation together with continuing deterioration of
the environment" (The *Wall Street Journal*, 14 August 1989). And this is just a
tiny sample of one summer.

Erroneous belief about population
growth has cost dearly. It has directed
attention away from the factor that we
now know is central in a country's economic development, its economic and
political system. Economic reforms away
from totalitarianism and central economic planning in poor countries probably would have been faster and more
widespread if slow growth was not
explained by recourse to population
growth. And in rich countries, misdirected attention to population growth
and the supposed consequence of natural resource shortage has caused waste
through such programs as synthetic fuel
promotion and the development of air-
planes that would be appropriate for an
age of greater scarcity. Our antinatalist
foreign policy is dangerous politically because it risks our being labeled racist, as
happened when [India's prime minister]
Indira Ghandi was overthrown because
of her sterilization program. Furthermore, misplaced belief that population
growth slows economic development

provides support for inhumane programs of coercion and the denial of personal liberty in one of the most sacred
and valued choices a family can make—
the number of children that it wishes to
bear and raise—in such countries as
China, Indonesia, and Vietnam. . . .

[I]t is now well-established scientifically that population growth is not the
bogey that conventional opinion and the
press believe it to be. In the 1980s a
revolution occurred in scientific views
toward the role of population growth in
economic development. By now the economic profession has turned almost completely away from the previous view that
population growth is a crucial negative
factor in economic development. There is
still controversy about whether population growth is even a minor negative
factor in some cases, or whether it is
beneficial in the long run. But there is no
longer any scientific support for the earlier view which was the basis for the U.S.
policy and then the policy of other
countries. . . .

The "official" turning point came in
1986 with the publication of a report by
the National Research Council and the
National Academy of Sciences (NRC-NAS),
entitled *Population Growth and Economic Development*, which almost completely reversed a 1971 report on the same subject
from the same institution. On the specific
issue of raw materials that has been the
subject of so much alarm, NRC-NAS concluded: "The scarcity of exhaustible resources is at most a minor constraint on
economic growth. . . . the concern about
the impact of rapid population growth on
resource exhaustion has often been exaggerated." And the general conclusion goes
only as far as "On balance, we reach the
qualitative conclusion that slower population growth would be beneficial to eco-

nomic development for most developing countries . . ." That is, NRC-NAS found forces operating in both positive and negative directions, its conclusion does not apply to all countries, and the size of the effect is not known even where it is believed to be present. This is a major break from the past monolithic characterization of additional people as a major drag upon development across the board. This revolution in thought has not been reported in the press, however, and therefore had had no effect on public thought on the subject.

There now exist perhaps two dozen competent statistical studies covering the few countries for which data are available over the past century, and also of the many countries for which data are available since World War II. The basic method is to gather data on each country's rate of population growth and its rate of economic growth, and then to examine whether—looking at all the data in the sample together—the countries with high population growth rates have economic growth rates lower than average, and countries with low population growth rates have economic growth rates higher than average.

The clear-cut consensus of this body of work is that faster population growth is *not* associated with slower economic growth. On average, countries whose populations grew faster did not grow slower economically. That is, there is no basis in the statistics for the belief that faster population growth causes slower economic growth.

Additional powerful evidence comes from pairs of countries that have the same culture and history, and had much the same standard of living when they split apart after World War II—East and West Germany, North and South Korea, and China and Taiwan. In each case the centrally planned communist country began with less population "pressure," as measured by density per square kilometer, than did the market-directed noncommunist country. And the communist and noncommunist countries in each pair also started with much the same birth rates and population growth rates.

The market-directed economies have performed much better economically than the centrally planned countries. Income per person is higher. Wages have grown faster. Key indicators of infrastructure such as telephones per person show a much higher level of development. And indicators of individual wealth and personal consumption, such as autos and newsprint, show enormous advantages for the market-directed enterprise economies compared to the centrally planned, centrally controlled economies. Furthermore, birth rates fell at least as early and as fast in the market-directed countries as in the centrally planned countries.

These data provide solid evidence that an enterprise system works better than does a planned economy. This powerful explanation of economic development cuts the ground from under population growth as a likely explanation. And under conditions of freedom, population growth poses less of a problem in the short run, and brings many more benefits in the long run, than under conditions of government planning of the economy.

One inevitably wonders: How can the persuasive common sense embodied in the Malthusian theory be wrong? To be sure, in the short run an additional person—baby or immigrant—inevitably means a lower standard of living for everyone; every parent knows that. More consumers mean less of the fixed available stock of goods to be divided among more people. And more workers laboring with the same fixed current stock of capital means that there will be less output per worker. The latter effect, known as "the law of diminishing return," is the essence of Malthus's theory as he first set it out.

But if the resources with which people work are not fixed over the period being analyzed, then the Malthusian logic of diminishing returns does not apply. And the plain fact is that, given some time to adjust to shortages, the resource base does not remain fixed. People create more resources of all kinds. When horse-powered transportation became a major problem, the railroad and the motor car were developed. When schoolhouses become crowded, we build new schools—more modern and better than the old ones.

As with man-made production capital, so it is with natural resources. When a shortage of elephant tusks for ivory billiard balls threatened in the last century, and a prize was offered for a substitute, celluloid was invented, followed by the rest of our plastics. Englishmen learned to use coal when trees became scarce in the sixteenth century. Satellites and fiber-optics (derived from sand) replace expensive copper for telephone transmission. And the new resources wind up cheaper than the old ones were. Such has been the entire course of civilization.

Extraordinary as it seems, natural-resource scarcity—that is, the cost of raw materials, which is the relevant economic measure of scarcity—has tended to decrease rather than to increase over the entire sweep of history. This trend is at least as reliable as any other trend observed in human history; the prices of all natural resources, measured in the wages necessary to pay for given quantities of them, have been falling as far back as data exist. A pound of copper—typical of

all metals and other natural resources—now costs an American only a twentieth of what it cost in hourly wages two centuries ago, and perhaps a thousandth of what it cost three thousand years ago. . . . And the price of natural resources has fallen even relative to consumer goods. . . .

The most extraordinary part of the resource-creation process is that temporary or expected shortages—whether due to population growth, income growth, or other causes—tend to leave us even better off than if the shortages had never arisen, because of the continuing benefit of the intellectual and physical capital created to meet the shortage. It has been true in the past, and therefore it is likely to be true in the future, that we not only need to solve our problems, but we need the problems imposed upon us by the growth of population and income.

The idea that scarcity is diminishing is mind-boggling because it defies the common-sense reasoning that when one starts with a fixed stock of resources and uses some up, there is less left. But for all practical purposes there are no resources until we find them, identify their possible uses, and develop ways to obtain and process them. We perform these tasks with increasing skill as technology develops. Hence, scarcity diminishes.

The general trend is toward natural resources becoming less and less important with economic development. Extractive industries are only a very small part of a modern economy, say a twentieth or less, whereas they constitute the lion's share of poor economies. Japan and Hong Kong are not at all troubled by the lack of natural resources, whereas such independence was impossible in earlier centuries. And though agriculture is thought to be a very important part of the American economy, if all of our agricultural land passed out of our ownership tomorrow, we would be the poorer by only about a ninth of one year's Gross National Product. This is additional evidence that natural resources are less of a brake upon economic development with the passage of time, rather than an increasing constraint.

There is, however, one crucial "natural" resource which is becoming more scarce—human beings. Yes, there are more people on earth now than in the past. But if we measure the scarcity of people the same way we measure the scarcity of economic goods—by the market price—then people are indeed becoming more scarce, because the price of labor time has been rising almost everywhere in the world. Agricultural wages in Egypt have soared, for example, and people complain of a labor shortage because of the demand for labor in the Persian Gulf, just a few years after there was said to be a labor surplus in Egypt.

Nor does it make sense to reduce population growth because of the supposedly increasing pollution of our air and water. In fact, our air and water are becoming cleaner rather than dirtier, . . . wholly the opposite of conventional belief.

The most important and amazing demographic fact—the greatest human achievement in history, in my view—is the "recent" decrease in the world's death rate. It took *thousands of years* to increase life expectancy at birth from just over twenty years to the high twenties. Then in just the last *two centuries*, life expectancy at birth in the advanced countries jumped from *less than thirty years* to perhaps seventy-five years. What greater event has humanity witnessed?

Then starting well after World War II, life expectancy in the poor countries has leaped upwards by perhaps *fifteen or even twenty years* since the 1950s, caused by advances in agriculture, sanitation, and medicine. Is this not an astounding triumph for humankind? It is this decrease in the death rate that is the cause of their being a larger world population nowadays than in former times.

Let's put it differently. In the 19th century the planet Earth could sustain only one billion people. Ten thousand years ago, only four *million* could keep themselves alive. Now, *five billion* people are living longer and more healthily than ever before, on average. The increase in the world's population represents our victory over death.

One would expect lovers of humanity to jump with joy at this triumph of human mind and organization over the raw forces of nature. Instead, many lament that there are so many people alive to enjoy the gift of life because they worry that population growth creates difficulties for development. And it is this misplaced concern that leads them to approve the inhumane programs of coercion and denial of personal liberty in one of the most precious choices a family can make—the number of children that it wishes to bear and raise.

Then there is the war-and-violence bugaboo. A typical recent headline is "Excessive Population Growth a Security Threat to U.S.," invoking the fear of "wars that have their roots in the unrestrained growth of population." This is reminiscent of the Hitlerian cry for "lebensraum" ["living space"] and the Japanese belief before World War II that their population density demanded additional land.

There is little scientific literature on the relation of population to war. But to the extent that there has been systematic analysis—notably the great study of war through the ages by Quincy Wright (1968), the work on recent wars by Nazli Choucri (1974), and a study of Europe between 1870 and 1913 by Gary Zuk (1985)—the data do not show a connection between population growth and political instability due to the struggle for economic resources. The purported connection is another of those notions that everyone (especially the CIA and the Defense Department) "knows" is true, and that seems quite logical, but has no basis in factual evidence.

The most important benefit of population size and growth is the increase it brings to the stock of useful knowledge. Minds matter economically as much as, or more than, hands or mouths. Progress is limited largely by the availability of trained workers. The main fuel to speed the world's progress is the stock of human knowledge. And the ultimate resource is skilled, spirited, hopeful people, exerting their wills and imaginations to provide for themselves and their families, thereby inevitably contributing to the benefit of everyone.

Even the most skilled persons require, however, an appropriate social and economic framework that provides incentives for working hard and taking risks, enabling their talents to flower and come to fruition. The key elements of such a framework are respect for property, fair and sensible rules of the market that are enforced equally for all, and the personal liberty that is particularly compatible with economic freedom. There is justice in such an approach, and wisdom, and the promise of unlimited economic and human development.

Which should be our vision? The doomsayers of the population control movement offer a vision of limits, decreasing resources, a zero-sum game, conservation, deterioration, fear, and conflict, calling for more governmental intervention in markets and family affairs. Or should our vision be that of those who look optimistically upon people as a resource rather than as a burden—a vision of receding limits, increasing resources and possibilities, a game in which everyone can win, creation, building excitement, and the belief that persons and firms, acting spontaneously in the search of their individual welfare, regulated only by rules of a fair game, will produce enough to maintain and increase economic progress and promote liberty.

And what should our mood be? The population restrictionists say we should be sad and worry. I and many others believe that the trends suggest joy and celebration at our newfound capacity to support human life—healthily, and with fast-increasing access to education and opportunity all over the world. I believe that the population restrictionists' hand-wringing view leads to despair and resignation. Our view leads to hope and progress, in the reasonable expectation that the energetic efforts of humankind will prevail in the future, as they have in the past, to increase worldwide our numbers, our health, our wealth, and our opportunities.

REFERENCES

Additional references may be found in my *The Ultimate Resource* (Princeton: PUP, 1981), and "Population Growth, Economic Growth, and Foreign Aid" in *The Cato Journal* 7 (Spring-Summer, 1987).

Choucri, Nazli. (1974) *Population Dynamics and International Violence.* Lexington, MA: Lexington Books.

Zuk, Gary. (1985) "National Growth and International Conflict: A Reevaluation of Choucri and North's Thesis," *Journal of Politics* 47: 269–281.

POSTSCRIPT

Does Population Growth Threaten Humanity?

This debate cannot be resolved because the future is indeterminate. The key issue of the debate is whether future technological improvements can continue to overcome the law of diminishing returns on investments and increasing costs for nonrenewable resources and environmentally benign waste disposal. Brown argues that the environment cannot be properly assessed in strictly economic terms. He points out the difference between economics and ecology. Economics gives little recognition to limits except as obstacles to overcome, whereas limits and carrying capacity are central concepts of ecology. Furthermore, ecosystems are complex and are tampered with at great risk. Unintended consequences of major development activities often cause unintended environmental disasters. Simon points out that the pessimists always underestimate humankind's ability to adapt to environmental problems. Though the pessimists can cite a long list of environmental problems, Simon is confident that they will be taken care of by human effort and inventiveness. He expects necessity to give birth to inventions, because technological developments will reap substantial economic rewards as resources become scarce. Simon's problem-solving thesis is supported by Charles Maurice and Charles W. Smith with 10 major historical examples in *The Doomsday Myth: Ten Thousand Years of Economic Crisis* (Hoover Institution Press, 1985).

Some of the prominent optimists on the issues of the availability of resources and health of the environment include Herman Kahn, *World Economic Development 1979 and Beyond* (Westville Press, 1979); Christopher Freeman and Marie Jahoda, eds., *World Futures: The Great Debate* (Universe Books, 1978); Julian L. Simon, *The Ultimate Resource* (Princeton University Press, 1981); and Julian L. Simon and Herman Kahn, eds., *The Resourceful Earth: A Response to Global 2000* (Basil Blackwell, 1984). Some of the prominent pessimists include Ferdinand E. Banks, *Scarcity, Energy, and Economic Progress* (Lexington Books, 1977); W. Jackson Davis, *The Seventh Year: Industrial Civilization in Transition* (W. W. Norton, 1979); S. R. Eye, *The Real Wealth of Nations* (St. Martin's Press, 1978); *The Global 2000 Report to the President* (Government Printing Office, 1980); and William Catton, *Overshoot* (University of Illinois Press, 1980).

For a balanced review of both sides of the debate, see Barry B. Hughes, *World Futures: A Critical Analysis of Alternatives* (Johns Hopkins University Press, 1985).

ISSUE 20

Is America's Socioeconomic System Breaking Down?

YES: Werner Meyer-Larsen, from "America's Century Will End With a Whimper," *World Press Review* (January 1991)

NO: Herbert Stein, from "The U.S. Economy: A Visitors' Guide," *The American Enterprise* (July/August 1990)

ISSUE SUMMARY

YES: Journalist Werner Meyer-Larsen describes the many problems of the American economy and society and concludes that the United States has declined considerably from its economic preeminence of three decades ago. **NO:** Economist Herbert Stein puts America's economic problems in comparative perspective and concludes that the United States is still the richest country in the world. He argues that problems like the national debt are relatively small and quite manageable.

Is the United States a great nation with some problems or a declining nation with great problems? This question has been hotly debated ever since Paul Kennedy published *The Rise and Fall of the Great Powers: Economic Change and Military Conflict from 1500 to 2000* (Random House, 1987). He maintained that all empires decline because they overextend themselves, and the United States is following suit. With the demise of the Soviet empire, the United States will remain the great political superpower for quite some time, but the decline thesis could still be relevant to America's economic difficulties. Accordingly, the two articles in this section focus on the economic prowess of the United States.

The United States emerged after World War II as the most powerful nation in the world. In part this was the result of the cumulative economic costs of World Wars I and II for England, Germany, the Soviet Union, and Japan. America escaped the physical devastation of the wars that these nations suffered, and America's economy boomed during the war years and continued to grow in the postwar periods. Having become the most prosperous and powerful of nations, the United States assumed international leadership in armaments, investments, and aid.

Critics such as Kennedy now argue that the costs of maintaining this leadership role have surpassed the nation's willingness to pay. In the last decade, the national debt has tripled. A nation that was long the world's greatest creditor is now the largest debtor nation in history.

Kennedy summarized his thesis: "The historical record suggests that there is a very clear connection *in the long run* between an individual Great Power's economic rise and fall and its growth and decline as an important military power (or world empire)." Nations must spend to create the armies and navies that protect their wealth and security; but if they spend too much, they weaken their economic competitiveness. "Imperial overstretch" is Kennedy's term for the tendency of great powers to commit too much wealth to overseas commitments and too little to domestic economic growth. This sociological law (probabilistic) is at the heart of Kennedy's analysis.

Kennedy identifies the loss of power with the decline of economic competitiveness. In his account, the most powerful nations in the last five centuries—successively, Spain, the Netherlands, France, and England—were unable or unwilling to tax themselves sufficiently to pay for their armed forces and empires, and the United States now finds itself in a comparable position. The greater the power of a state, the greater the expenditure that must be made to support it.

The question about superpower decline is background to the question about the economic position and direction of the United States, because the political and the economic positions strongly affect each other. In addition, economic conditions are related to the social conditions. As a result, social problems ramify during times of economic stress, and some types of social progress occur in times of economic prosperity. In the readings that follow, Werner Meyer-Larsen criticizes the United States for an indulgence that has contributed to the current economic and social crises. For him it is time for the United States to awaken from its greed and complacency and make the necessary sacrifices to revive socially, economically, and politically. In contrast, Herbert Stein tries to show that there is no economic crisis in the United States and that it will be easy to strengthen the economy and then take care of other matters of deep concern.

YES

AMERICA'S CENTURY WILL END
WITH A WHIMPER

In 1941, Henry Luce, the editor of *Time*, decided that the era now ending should be known as "the American century." He was right. Almost 50 years later, the West—above all, its ruling power—has won the cold war. "Countless people all over the world," brags Alvin Toffler, author of the best-selling book *Future Shock*, "are eager to embrace the Western, meaning the American, way of life."

And American protection. When Iraqi dictator Saddam Hussein invaded Kuwait last summer, there was only one land that the emirate's neighbors could call upon for emergency assistance: the U.S. But at home in America, everything looks very different. The American century is dragging inexorably to a close, and not a single cry of triumph can be heard. "There is a groundswell of opinion in this land," says John Chancellor, the respected television commentator, "that in recent years something has gone terribly wrong here."

The decline of America is an idea that was discussed in the U.S. for several years and then rejected. But now it seems that the great majority of Americans no longer have any confidence. . . .

The American people show signs of wanting to stop their country's economic, social, and political erosion. But to do so will require resolve and changes in almost every sector of the country: industry, finance, education, and government. The problems facing the country are daunting.

Superpower America can no longer pay for what it undertakes, can no longer develop what it will need in the future, can no longer produce what it needs. The nation's finances are overextended. The Gulf crisis may cost up to $100 billion, causing the federal budget deficit to zoom up to $250 billion or $300 billion. Interest must be paid on more than $3 trillion of government debt, including the cost of the savings-and-loan collapse.

As a result, President George Bush must go begging for money to pay for his expeditionary corps. The U.S., the world's policeman, is trying to sell itself as a security-guard company.

From Werner Meyer-Larsen, "America's Century Will End with a Whimper," *World Press Review* (January 1991). This article first appeared in *Der Spiegel*, a news magazine of Hamburg, Germany. Copyright © 1990 by *Der Spiegel*. Distributed by and reprinted by permission of The New York Times Special Features.

The world power is exhausted, a nation at the end of its rope. The 40 years of cold-war militarization, superpower status, and the role of world policeman have gravely wounded the nation's economy and society. They have turned the U.S., in spite of its wealth and human capital, into a land that increasingly exhibits Third World symptoms:

• Every year, 2 million Americans leave school without having learned to read and write;

• 37 million Americans do not have health insurance;

• Almost a fourth of all children younger than six, and about half of all black children younger than six, live beneath the official poverty line. In the cities, infant mortality rates resemble those in traditionally agrarian lands.

Critics of America have fixed on a single guilty party when it comes to explaining the nation's decline: former President Ronald Reagan. But the decline began long before he took office. Only the extent of the damage is a result of the years of illusion under the Great Communicator. Reagan, with a clear grasp of what the great majority wanted, fed the nation a powerfully addictive drug: He built up the most expensive and powerful military machine in the history of the world—while pumping up endless consumption, financed through tax cuts and foreign capital. It is true that the military buildup forced the Soviet Union into an arms race that it eventually had to abandon. But domestically, the president and his California mafia opened the gates for a replay of the robber-baron years of yearly American capitalism.

The wartime economy unleashed by Reagan created boom and bust zones, distorting the country's industrial structure in ways as dramatic as they were dangerous. Research money was followed by streams of capital going to the military-industrial complex, and both captured the nation's top scientific talent. This slowly but surely ate away at America's industrial competitiveness. The per capita investment in civilian research and development in America has been far lower, for many years, than in Japan and Western Europe. The result: American business, with the exception of perhaps space and satellite technology, is no longer leading the world as it did 20 years ago. For example, in 1975, the first 15 places on the *Fortune* 500 list of the world's largest companies included 11 American corporations. Now there are only seven. Further, in the early 1970s, America's computer industry controlled 90 percent of the U.S. market. By 1990, Japan had surpassed it in many areas.

"THE JAPANESE ARE EATING THEIR WAY UP the electronics food chain," says a representative of the American Electronics Association, a trade group. Hans Wiesendanger, who works on patents at Stanford University, says that American companies are often unwilling to pay the costs of turning basic patents into production technology. This has already cost America its photo, audio, and video industries.

For almost a century, America had a balance-of-trade surplus. In 1971, the deficits returned—$2.7 billion worth. Since 1985, the trade deficit has been at that level every week. Direct American investment overseas also has not kept pace. As late as 1970, Americans invested $75.5 billion in foreign lands, while non-American companies pumped only $13.3 billion into the U.S. economy. In 1989, Americans invested $374.4 billion overseas, while foreigners brought $400.8 billion into the U.S. Because the Japanese have invested heavily in high-visibility projects, Americans are especially unnerved by Japanese investments. A Japanese car, the Honda Accord, is the most popular car in the U.S.

The fact that the Accord, produced in America, has achieved the highest quality rating in the country contradicts the popular notion that American industrial workers are careless, unwilling to work, and stupid. It is not their fault that so many defective products emerge from the assembly line—the problem is with management.

Corporate America follows different rules from those of Japanese or European firms. U.S. executives look only at quarterly financial results and pay more attention to stock prices than to investment or market share. Meanwhile, Americans save less than 6 percent of their incomes, only a third the Japanese rate and less than half of what Germans save. Further, Americans are consuming 3–4 percent more than they create in wealth.

The heads of the country's savings-and-loan institutions used the slackening of government regulation during the Reagan administration to increase their profits, legally and illegally. The losses incurred during this spree, which could rise as high as $1 trillion, will be borne by the taxpayers. On top of the disaster at the savings and loans came the blows to the commercial banks. They have been hurt by the S&L crisis, uncollectible Third World loans, and risky domestic lending. The government estimates that 35 major banks may collapse.

Along with Wall Street investment banks, the commercial banks allowed themselves to be drawn into another variant of the great American money-instead-of-productivity spectacle—the so-called Rebuilding of Corporate America.

This "reconstruction" was invented by a clique, centered around financial magician Michael Milken, that bought companies with borrowed money. To secure their loans, they offered as collateral not their own fortunes, but the net worth of the company they wanted to buy. The entire deal hinged on short-term financing, which was taken care of by so-called junk bonds. The takeover artists, once successful, had two alternatives when it came to making their big profits. They could let the company they had taken over assume the debts run up during the takeover and install a management that would make Draconian cuts, or they could sell off parts of the firm.

These takeover artists tricked the public by claiming that they were forcing American industry to become more efficient. In fact, though, the companies often were forced to pay off the debts incurred by their buyers and had to sell off their major assets.

Once stagnation set in, the whole takeover game collapsed, leaving behind billions in losses. The winners were the takeover artists, stockholders, and lawyers. Even Milken, who has been sentenced to prison, still has millions of dollars from his maneuvers.

Financial adventures, the debt mentality, and the quest for quick profits have brought American industry to ruin. Banks and corporations are not able to keep up with Japanese or European competitors.

The situation for the U.S. has been made worse by the internationalization of competition. According to Jean-Claude Derian, an economic adviser to the French government, 1970 was the year "of the historical turning point when world economic competition began. . . . As the world's largest market for high-tech goods and the most open market in the world, the U.S. was condemned to be the arena in which the new trade war was fought."

But the American system reacted exceptionally passively to the country's loss of competitiveness. Instead of expanding internationally, many American banks closed their branches overseas. Instead of throwing themselves into new investments to yield higher productivity, entire industries in the U.S. simply gave up. Henry Luce's successor, Henry Grunwald, wrote recently, "In many ways, American business has let America down."

While finance and business have faltered, the social structure of America has been thrown into disarray. New York vividly exemplifies what the entire nation is going through. One in 100 New Yorkers is homeless; one in 300 has AIDS. Every four-and-a-half hours, someone is murdered; every six minutes, someone is robbed; every four minutes, a car disappears. To restore the city to a state of relative health, almost the entire gross national product (GNP) of the U.S. would be required: Lewis Rudin, chairman of the Association for a Better New York, estimates the cost of reconstruction at $5 trillion.

America's 50 states and thousands of counties form social islands, comprise ethnic niches, and represent particular interests. So the nation has moved toward the arithmetic average of its many identities: No new taxes, and no social redistribution, are what the broad, conservative middle class demands, thwarting any attempt even to maintain the status quo.

Twenty-five years ago, all of this was quite different. It was then that President Lyndon B. Johnson promised his citizens the Great Society: first-class schools, social support for the elderly, decent housing for the poor, health services and safeguards against disaster for everyone. But the money disappeared in the Vietnam war and its aftermath and seeped away during the economic emergency caused by the oil crisis of the 1970s. Social programs, infrastructure maintenance, and school reforms could no longer be financed and were dealt with piecemeal. Thus the rift between the rich and the poor has been widening. Nearly 13 percent of the population—31.5 million Americans—lives below the official poverty line of $12,675 annually for a household of four. Minorities are particularly affected: More than 30 percent of blacks and 26 percent of Hispanics—but only 10 percent of whites—earn less than this amount. And many of them are working at full-time jobs; about 7 million Americans do not earn enough from their jobs to lift themselves above the poverty line.

At the same time, the country has some 1.5 million millionaires. Here one finds the 800 highest-paid captains of industry, an elite group that in 1989 had an average annual income of $1.3 million and $40 million in stock holdings. In 1980, American managers earned 40 times as much as industrial workers; in 1989, they earned 93 times as much. On the other hand, the salary of the industrial worker went down. The average salary in countries such as Switzerland, Denmark, Norway, Canada, and Japan is higher than it is in the U.S.

At the same time, America allots about 48 percent of its total budget—a good seventh of the GNP—to social programs. Eight hundred billion dollars—the equivalent of nearly 70 percent of the GNP of West Germany—are earmarked for social redistribution in capitalist America. But without an effective plan, the nation is pouring a large portion of this money down the drain.

America's social policy does not have an overall structure. Instead, it has grown out of a patchwork of legislation created as the situation demanded, or by congressional representatives who sought to gain votes by giving something in return. Congressmen have passed laws on behalf of the elderly, the homeless, single mothers, and veterans. And once a program is put into effect, it is never terminated. The result: The city of New York and the nation pay up to $4,000 a month to house one family in a hotel for the homeless, where drugs and violence are rife. The rent alone is three times higher than the poverty-line income. Giving cash so that the family can move out of the city would be a better alternative.

Similar disparities exist between expenditures and results in American health care. Americans pay $600 billion a year for medical care, 50 percent more than they do for education and about twice as much as for the military. Yet compared with other countries that pay far less for their health, the U.S. gets pitifully little in return. In child mortality, life expectancy, and visits to the doctor, the U.S. occupies last place among the major industrialized countries.

The only successful assistance program is Social Security, which has provided security for working people in their retirement years. Yet the prospects for a successful life before retirement are becoming steadily worse. One important reason is that the public school system is falling apart. "If a hostile foreign power had attempted to give America the bad education that it has today," the National Commission on Excellence in Education has warned, "we would have viewed it as an act of war."

In 1989, the National Geographic Society found that 24 million adult Americans could not locate their own country on a map of the world. . . . The Council on Competitiveness has determined that 60,000 teachers of mathematics and the natural sciences are not fully qualified for their positions. Only a quarter of high-school graduates can solve a math problem that requires more than one step.

One-quarter of school-age children can neither write correctly nor read at a satisfactory level. Since 1985, every fourth student in high school has failed to earn a diploma and has dropped out of school.

According to a 1985 finding by a White House commission headed by John A. Young, chief executive of the U.S. computer company Hewlett-Packard, this is particularly bad news, because the highest dropout rate—from 40–45 percent—is found among the fastest-growing segments of the population of the U.S.: blacks and Hispanics. "It is clear that the competitiveness of American industry is threatened when many young workers lack the basic skills for productive work," he says.

EACH YEAR, THE U.S. SPENDS MORE THAN $350 billion on various school programs that, like much in the U.S., grew out of a patchwork of federal legislation. Individual school districts and their communities finance schools through property taxes. The average property tax of a rich community such as Stamford, Connecticut, amounts to $5,443 per year; that of a poor one such as Monroe, Alabama, comes to $128. Whenever the community cannot or does not want to pay, the educational system deteriorates, and the more affluent members of the community whisk their children off to private schools.

If American society is clearly divided along class lines, it is even more so within the educational system. Families from the underclass often give up any thought of getting a better education for their children, because they lack information. Blacks go into the military if they want to become something, and the middle class resorts to affordable state universities. It is mainly the children of the wealthy who attend elite colleges such as Yale, Harvard, Princeton, or Stanford. The two-tiered educational system has given rise to a superbly educated elite in positions of leadership and in the research divisions of the large corporations, but down below there gapes a dangerous abyss.

All American companies have to pay for the incompetence of their employees. "The mistakes range from the office worker who provides incorrect information to manual workers who measure things incorrectly, to the laborers who allow the machines to break down—all because they cannot read well enough," writes Leonard Lund of the Conference Board, a business-research organization.

Apart from the colossal cost of misguided social policies and the financing of the school disaster, there is another steadily rising cost factor: The U.S. leads the world in crime. There are many excuses and explanations for this: the clash of the First and Third worlds in the street; the symbiosis of poverty and poor education; the envy felt by the forgotten third of society; the collective aggression of a nation of immigrants; the drug catastrophe; and ever-present racism.

An almost erotic affection for guns, inherited from the pioneers, is responsible for the highest murder rate in all of the industrial countries. In 1989, 21,500 people were murdered in the U.S., about 60 percent by people with handguns. Over the past 15 years, more American citizens have met their death through firearms than the U.S. military lost in the second world war.

America's police forces are not lax when it comes to slapping on the handcuffs—7.3 million Americans were arrested in 1989. Some 3.7 million Americans, constituting nearly 2 percent of the adult population, are under continual supervision by prison or police authorities. The number of prisoners in federal and state penitentiaries rose from 250,000 in 1975 to 710,000 in 1989. All of this takes money, which a nation needs to maintain its productivity. The U.S. does not even have the money to maintain its infrastructure.

America's long-distance highways are dilapidated. Tens of thousands of overweight trucks and hundreds of thousands of private cars use the highways in congested metropolitan areas, yet the roads date from the Eisenhower era, when only half as many cars were on the road. Throughout the nation, some 40 percent of all river and road bridges are considered hazardous. In the San Francisco area, traffic has been hopelessly snarled since the 1989 earthquake. There is no money to rebuild.

The erosion of roads, bridges, schools, and industry in the U.S.—and of the social fabric itself—is accompanied by political decay. Thirty years ago, John F. Kennedy said, "Ask not what your country can do for you; ask what you can do for your country." Ronald Reagan, says television commentator Chancellor, "stood Kennedy on his head." The state, condemned as big government, became the enemy. . . .

For decades, America's productivity derived from its immeasurable reserves of raw materials, the speedy integration of immigrants, and the largest single market in the world. An energy policy that was maintained primarily with domestic reserves lay at the basis of postwar prosperity. Energy companies did not invest in coal, solar, or wind technology but rather bought bargain-price Arab oil. Years later, the bill arrived: Rich in raw materials, America had failed to develop energy reserves.

Likewise, in the 1960s the country lost another prerequisite of its superior productivity: Immigration policies were changed. Before this time, most immigrants were skilled Europeans who were able to work in industry right away. But farmers looking for cheap labor managed to push legislation allowing streams of uneducated Latin Americans into the country. An initiative by Sen. Edward Kennedy of Massachusetts put an end to this trend: Congress passed a bill allowing well-trained immigrants into the country.

CREATING AN INDUSTRIAL POLICY WILL BE more difficult, however. Americans have shied away from providing federal assistance for the development of new technologies. The maxims of the free-market economy and free competition are against it. But not once have the computer companies managed to raise the necessary capital. Have American business leaders learned nothing?

The learning process is obviously difficult, and the ideas for reawakening America are generally of a speculative nature. Nonetheless, a country of 250 million people, says historian Paul Kennedy, on the basis of its human resources alone, will not sink to the level of a second-class nation. . . .

For political scientist Walter Dean Burnham of the University of Texas, however, there is a great deal of cleaning up to be done before the country will shine again. Ronald Reagan waged his last campaign under the slogan, "A New Morning in America." What he had in mind was a promising beginning for a radiant future.

"Now," Burnham says, "it's the morning after."

NO

Herbert Stein

THE U.S. ECONOMY: A VISITORS' GUIDE

The most important thing for a visitor to know about the American economy is that it is very rich. The best measure of that is the gross national product [GNP]: the U.S. GNP is now running at $5,500 billion a year. This is a staggering figure. In 1940 when the GNP was first estimated, the figure was about $100 billion. It had been about the same in 1929. Of course, most of this increase was due to inflation. But in real terms after allowing for inflation, the GNP now is six times as high as it was in 1929 and three times as high per capita. Consider that in 1929 the United States was already the richest country in the world, and Americans were congratulating themselves on how well off they were.

Comparisons with other countries are difficult and possibly not very revealing. But by the best estimates, the GNP of the United States is probably two and one-half times that of Japan and five times that of Germany. On a per capita basis, GNP in America is probably one-third higher than in either of those countries.

Interestingly, Americans do not seem to *feel* rich today, and economic policy is dominated to a degree by an acceptance of the feeling that the country is poor. The main reason for that is the "twin deficits": the deficit in the budget and the deficit in international trade and payments. People think that the country must be poor if it cannot afford to pay for its expenditures outright or if the country cannot produce as much as it consumes and has to import the rest from other countries.

But the deficits are not a sign of poverty. Any government, however rich the country, can have a deficit if it chooses to spend more than it chooses to collect in taxes. The United States has budget deficits because Americans prefer them. They prefer to have the deficit rather than do the things that would eliminate the deficit. These things are easy to list and would not be very painful. For example, the United States is not a very heavily taxed country. Americans pay a smaller proportion of their GNP in taxes than any other industrial country except Japan, but they prefer to have the deficit rather than pay another 2–3 percent of the GNP in taxes.

From Herbert Stein, "The U.S. Economy: A Visitors' Guide," *The American Enterprise* (July/August 1990). Copyright © 1990 by the American Enterprise Institute. Reprinted by permission of The New York Times Special Features.

Similarly, the deficit in international trade or payments does not deny that the country is rich. In 1989, for example, Americans used about 1 percent more goods and services than they produced. That was the whole "deficit." Americans could have done without that extra 1 percent of goods and services easily. It was only about half of the increase in production over the previous year. They used the extra output because on the one hand they preferred to consume and invest a great deal, while on the other hand, savers in the rest of the world were willing and eager to invest in the United States rather than elsewhere, including their own countries.

Some people think that the United States is becoming poorer because Americans and their government borrow a good deal abroad. But actually, Americans are becoming richer; productive assets owned by Americans—at home and abroad—are increasing faster than liabilities to foreigners.

Another reason for the common feeling that America is not rich is the belief that the United States is falling behind other countries, notably Japan. But the fact of Japan's becoming richer—even if that were to happen—would not make the United States less rich in the relevant sense of its ability to meet the needs and desires of the American people. Anyway, the margin of the Japanese growth rate over the American rate is presently diminishing.

The rate of economic growth slowed worldwide after 1973. The U.S. rate recovered somewhat during the 1980s, but it is difficult to evaluate the magnitude because we cannot yet distinguish between cyclical and longer-run changes. We do not seem to be back to the growth rates of the best 15 or 20 years before 1973 and may not yet be back to the lower longer-run rate.

There is an interesting stability in America's economic growth rate over very long periods. We now have estimates of per capita GNP for the 120 years from 1869 to 1989; for this whole period, the annual rate of growth was 1.78 percent. The year 1929 divides the 120 years in half and is also a historical year during which many things changed radically. But the average growth rate of per capita GNP was 1.80 before and 1.77 after 1929, which, given the difficulties of measurement, cannot be regarded as a significant difference. This neither indicates an iron law of growth for the American economy nor suggests that the growth is accelerating or decelerating.

IMPLICATIONS OF BEING WEALTHY

So the American economy is very rich, and there is every reason to think not only that it will continue to be rich but also that it will get richer. The basic reason for our prosperity is that 120 million Americans get up in the morning and go to work to do the best they can for themselves and their families and previous millions did the same thing for more than two centuries. America has always had a legal system that assures its people that they will enjoy the fruits of their efforts—their labor, their saving, their education, and their initiatives. America's culture encourages people to benefit themselves economically and values their doing so. The country was populated by immigrants who wanted to live and work in such a legal system and culture. Moreover, the government has always been devoted to assisting and protecting people in these efforts. For

U.S. REAL GNP PER CAPITA

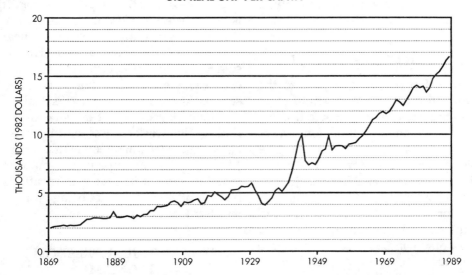

example, the government has made available large amounts of capital in the form of land and education.

Events in America have to be understood in the perspective of the size of the economy. Almost everything we see happening turns out to be small relative to the size of the economy. Also, because of its size and diversity, the system seems to be stable and immovable in the aggregate while flexible in detail.

In earlier times, an event like the change of automobile models at the Ford Motor Company or a shortage of rain in Kansas could cause a national recession. The country is much more resistant to such things now. Even the loss of about $500 billion in the value of assets when the stock market crashed in 1987 was absorbed without much effect on the economy as a whole.

Actual or proposed policy changes also have to be seen in this perspective. For example, the Reagan defense buildup, which looked so huge at the time and was expected to be so disruptive economically, made hardly a ripple in the

economy, and the same will be true of the cut in defense spending that is now under way. Similarly, a great deal of attention is now being paid to the proposed cut in the capital gains tax. But the most certain thing that can be said about it is that although the direction of its effects on the revenue and the economy is unclear, the effects will be relatively small.

For a country as rich as America is, getting richer faster is not a very important goal—or at least it is less important than it used to be and less important than it is in other countries. America's most important problems are not problems of the inadequacy of total national income but rather problems of inappropriate use of the national income the economy produces.

America's problems must also be seen in the perspective of American history. What appear to be the most critical problems now will be listed later, but first, it is useful to review some of the problems that have existed or have been alleged to exist in the past 60 years that no longer worry us. Looking back reminds us that the American society has the capacity to face its problems and deal with them.

THE STABILIZATION PROBLEM

The Great Depression gave rise to the fear that such catastrophes would recur or even that the economy would live in a state of permanent depression unless radical changes were made in the economic system. This fear is now gone, partly because that analysis was judged faulty; it underestimated the equilibrating features of the system. Changes in institutions and policies that stabilized the economy without weakening its free and efficient features dispelled those fears. Worry about the possibility of less severe, but still debilitating, recessions persisted, however. But the experience of the years since World War II has provided two lessons:

First, the only serious recessions, those of 1975 and 1982, in which unemployment rose to highs of 9 percent and 11 percent, respectively, came after fairly high inflation.

Second, even recessions of that depth turned out to be less painful than had been expected because they were short. This was because the average worker had substantial assets and was likely to be in a family with more than one worker, so that a period of unemployment was not disastrous.

What remains as the chief uncertainty about the stability of the economy is the possibility of inflation. This is seen as a political problem—whether the temptation of the short-term political advantages of inflationary policy can be resisted. The inflation rate in the United States is now about 4.5 percent. The economy is much better adapted to such a rate now than it was, for example, in 1971 when that rate caused the imposition of price controls. It is nevertheless a cause for concern.

Unemployment has been running near 5.25 percent for about a year. That is somewhat higher than used to be considered full employment, but it is not a serious figure in the aggregate. Half of the unemployed are out of work for periods of five weeks or less, and the average duration of unemployment is about 12 weeks. The unemployment problem today is serious in that it most affects black youths, who are not being brought into the work force.

THE MYTHICAL FREEDOM PROBLEM

Around the end of World War II, there was a great deal of worry in this country that although the threat of Nazism had been withstood, the threat to freedom remained serious. The threat—best described in Friedrich Hayek's book, *The Road to Serfdom*—was seen to lie in the expansion of the role of government that had been going on here under the New Deal and in England and elsewhere even longer. Although the argument was mainly about England, the author made it applicable to the United States, and the book was a best-seller here.

This worry has not since been as acute as it was in the first years after World War II, but it remains a standard part of political rhetoric and rises in pitch from time to time. There is some evidence of growing concern now. In a curious parallel to the post-Nazi era, the champions of freedom in the postcommunist era are finding the enemy at home—or are at least looking for him there.

The threat to American freedoms has never been real. Americans are more free now than they have ever been. Individual options have been increased enormously by the growth of incomes; the improvement of education, information, and mobility; the expansion of competition, including the increased exposure to the world market; and the reduction of legal and cultural discriminations of all kinds, based on race, religion, ethnicity, and gender.

The government sector in the United States has expanded in the past 60 years, but it is still small by international standards. Relative to GNP, government expenditures and receipts in the United States are at about the same level as they are in Japan and lower than in any other large industrial country.

As a fraction of GNP, government expenditures in the United States rose from 10 percent in 1929 to 34 percent in 1989. By other measures the government share is smaller and has risen less. Receipts have risen from 10.9 percent to 32 percent, government purchases of goods and services from 8.6 percent to 19.8 percent, and government output, measured by payrolls, from 4.3 percent to 10.3 percent.

But the private sector has also expanded enormously. Even if the government share is estimated to have risen from one-tenth to one-third of GNP, the nongovernment GNP is four times as large today as it was in 1929 and twice as large per capita.

The total of government expenditures however, is a poor measure of government's power to coerce individuals and limit their freedom, for several reasons. Forty percent of all government expenditures are for interest payments or transfers made according to objective formulas that do not enable the government to discriminate among individuals. The government is decentralized: the federal government makes only about 40 percent of government purchases of goods and services (less than 8 percent of GNP, three-fourths of which is for defense), the rest is made by states and localities. Moreover, the government's ability to exercise its influence in a coercive way is limited by the division of powers among the executive, legislative, and judicial branches, by the party system, and by public opinion.

U.S. GOVERNMENT AND NONGOVERNMENT GNP*

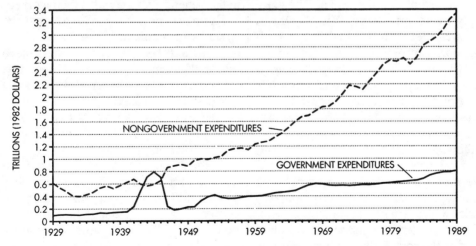

*NOTE: GOVERNMENT MEASURED BY TOTAL EXPENDITURES. EXPENDITURES ARE FOR PURCHASES OF GOODS AND SERVICES.

In one way or another, the government does regulate many U.S. industries—it regulates some of them quite a lot—but this is in fact a trivial impairment of freedom. There may be people who feel inhibited because they cannot practice brain surgery without a government license or because they cannot operate a commercial bank and an investment bank simultaneously. They are a minority. Many regulations are probably a source of economic inefficiency. It is difficult, probably impossible, to calculate the size of this effect. About ten years ago, one study concluded that the regulatory system reduced GNP by about 3 percent. This is about one year's normal growth of GNP.

OTHER WORRIES

From time to time in American history, great concern has been expressed that the economy would be dominated by giant monopolies that would smother efficiency, prevent the achievement of full employment, and concentrate excessive power in a few private hands. Such concerns were heard in the 1930s and, to a lesser extent, in the 1950s. They are hardly heard any more. The American economy is seen to be highly competitive, more competitive than ever before. Government policy has helped avert a trend to monopoly. But the main lesson is that unless government positively enforces monopoly, there are strong natural tendencies for competition to emerge. Moreover, reduced costs of transportation and communication and lowered governmental barriers to international trade have greatly widened the markets within which enterprise must compete.

Given the common notion of the United States as the country of big business, it is significant to note that most American workers are employed in fairly small enterprises. In 1985, 55 percent were employed in establishments of 99 or fewer workers and only 13 percent in establishments of over 1,000 workers. There seems to be no trend for the proportion in large establishments to increase.

Parallel to this worry about monopoly but on the other side of the political spectrum, there has been concern about the power of labor unions. This was especially notable just after World War II. Membership in unions was increasing, and so, apparently, was their economic and political power. Some thought stronger unions would stifle productivity and generate inflation. But this fear also passed. The proportion of nonfarm employees enrolled in unions peaked at about 30 percent in 1955 and has declined since to about 20 percent. Even where unions exist, they are less powerful than they were. Again, public policy, expressed in the Taft-Hartley Act of 1947, had something to do with limiting the trend to unionization. But the primary force was competition: unionized enterprises could not compete with the nonunionized—even in the benefits they provided their workers.

There was never any evidence that the spread of unionism, while it was going on, yielded benefits for workers as a whole. During the period of declining unionism, the labor share of the national income has increased from 67 percent to 74 percent. This suggests that unions were not essential to improving the condition of labor.

A third worry that has arisen from time to time is that the economy was chaotic and erratic and would stagnate because the United States had no "economic plan." This worry naturally arose when difficulties appeared, most notably in the 1930s. It recurred around the end of the 1950s, when the launching of Sputnik [the first series of artificial Earth satellites, whose launching by the Soviet Union initiated the Space Age] raised the fear that the Soviets might be outdoing the United States and when many Americans were fascinated by comprehensive British and French economic plans. There was another wave of talk in favor of planning in 1975 and 1976 after the oil shock.

But the idea that the United States should have a national economic plan never had much popular appeal. Any push to develop one has now disappeared entirely, and given recent events in Eastern Europe, none is likely to re-emerge soon.

THE ADAPTIVE SOCIETY

The American system has performed well. And it continues to do so, not because it is finished, perfect, and free of problems, on a model laid down by Adam Smith, but because it adapts to its problems and solves or at least ameliorates them. The American economic system today is a long way from the capitalism of 1929. The government has assumed responsibility for maintaining economic stability. America has become a substantial welfare state, and about 15 percent of all personal income consists of transfers from the government. The government greatly affects national saving by its fiscal policy. It regulates almost every industry a little. But still, the free market remains at the heart of the economic system.

What makes the American society so adaptable is that we have an economic system interacting with a political system, each independent and each competitive within itself. Each system disciplines the other, limits its excesses, and acts to correct its deficiencies.

AMERICA'S PROBLEMS TODAY

There is no consensus in America today about what our problems are. Three general viewpoints may be discerned:

• There are those who, despite what has been said above, give great weight to traditional aggregate economic problems: the rate of growth, competitiveness with other countries, the budget deficit, and the trade deficit.

• There are those who think that because the threat of imperial communism has diminished there are no national problems except deciding how to leave the American people alone, cut their taxes, and reduce government regulation.

• There are others who believe that the United States tolerates conditions that might be bearable in a less-rich society but that ought not to be acceptable in the United States. These include the existence of a miserable underclass; the failure for over a decade to lower the percent of the population living in poverty, after earlier years of progress; the sad state of American education; and the spread of dangerous drugs and violent crime. Moreover, the United States, as the richest, most capitalist, and most democratic country, has a role to play and obligations to assume in assisting other countries to achieve democracy, free markets, and economic development.

These viewpoints are not being explicitly debated in the United States today, but they underlie many of the specific issues that are continually being faced. Some decision about the relative weight to be given to these views of the American condition will emerge from the political process.

POSTSCRIPT

Is America's Socioeconomic System Breaking Down?

What kind of world and what kind of country are today's college graduates going into? Everyone knows that Americans are struggling economically, most marriages are troubled, drugs and crime are grave worries, jobs are hard to come by, blacks and women have legitimate complaints about discrimination, political leaders do not seem to have answers, and environmental problems may subject future generations to very adverse conditions. The one bright spot is that America's enemy has become its friend. In this swirl of problems, how should one view the future?

Many analysts agree with Meyer-Larsen that the future is likely to bring further economic decline. He presents an impressive list of failures and problems to prove his point, but are the factors that he identifies the key to America's future? Stein interprets these trends differently. He tries to show that the American economy is basically sound and therefore able to support world political leadership and the improvement of social conditions at home. Do recent changes in Eastern Europe provide an opportunity for the United States to focus on fixing its economy and becoming strong at home?

Those who see America in decline usually worry about America's debt and underinvestment, but some do not attribute these failures to overextension overseas. Walter Russell Mead urges cutbacks in American commitments in *Mortal Splendor: The American Empire in Transition* (Houghton Mifflin, 1987). Like Kennedy, Mead traces parallels with past empires and concludes that decline is inevitable, but he maintains that America can shape its postimperial future. Robert D. Hormats describes the many roots for the relative economic decline of the U.S. in "The Roots of American Power," *Foreign Affairs* (Summer 1991), but he sees imperial overstretch as only a minor contributing factor. Domestic failures such as low investment rates and broken social contracts are the paramount causes of economic decline. David Halberstam in *The Next Century* (William Morrow, 1991) describes the role of greed, shortsightedness, and class divisions in preventing the actions necessary to strengthen the economy.

Decline theory is rejected by critics who conclude that the United States has been strengthened by its commitments abroad and economic policies at home. For Norman Podhoretz, the issue is not overstretching or overspending but national will. In *The Present Danger* (Simon & Schuster, 1980) he posed the question: "Do we have the will to reverse the decline of American power?" Owen Harries rejects Kennedy's arguments in "The Rise of American Decline," *Commentary* (May 1988). Barbara W. Tuchman, in "A Nation in Decline?" *The New York Times Magazine* (September 20, 1987), blames decline on the incompetence and inefficiency that have resulted from "a deteriorating ethic." Now that the Soviet bloc is being completely transformed, the American empire will be redefined as well. A volume that looks at American decline in terms of world system theory is Terry Boswell and Albert Bergesen, *America's Changing Role in the World System* (Praeger, 1987).

Whatever our conclusions, the debate prompted by the theory of decline compels us to examine the nature and consequences of American values and goals in relation to the rest of the world. As the rest of the world changes so dramatically, the United States must redefine its values and mission in the world.

CONTRIBUTORS
TO THIS VOLUME

EDITORS

KURT FINSTERBUSCH received his bachelor's degree in history from Princeton University in 1957, and a bachelor of divinity degree from Grace Theological Seminary in 1960. His Ph.D. in sociology, from Columbia University, was conferred in 1969. He is the author of several books, including *Understanding Social Impacts* (Sage Publications, 1980) and *Social Research for Policy Decisions* (Wadsworth, 1980), with Annabelle Bender Motz. He is currently teaching at the University of Maryland, College Park, and is the academic editor for the Dushkin Publishing Group's *Annual Editions: Sociology.*

GEORGE McKENNA received his bachelor's degree from the University of Chicago in 1959, his M.A. from the University of Massachusetts in 1962, and his Ph.D. from Fordham University in 1967. He has been teaching political science at City College of New York since 1963. Among his publications are *American Populism* (Putnam, 1974) and *American Politics: Ideals and Realities* (McGraw-Hill, 1976). He has written articles in the fields of American government and political theory. He is also the author of the textbook *The Drama of Democracy: American Government and Politics* (DPG, 1990).

STAFF

Marguerite L. Egan   Program Manager
Brenda S. Filley   Production Manager
Whit Vye   Designer
Libra Ann Cusack   Typesetting Supervisor
Juliana Arbo   Typesetter
David Brackley   Copy Editor
David Dean   Administrative Assistant
Diane Barker   Editorial Assistant
David A. Filley   Graphics

AUTHORS

RICHARD APPELBAUM is the chairman of the Department of Sociology at the University of California, Santa Barbara. He is the author of *Karl Marx* (Sage Publications, 1988) and the coauthor, with John I. Gilderbloom, of *Rethinking Rental Housing* (Temple University Press, 1988).

EDWARD BANFIELD is a professor emeritus of urban studies in the Department of Faculty Arts and Sciences at Harvard University and the author of a number of articles and books on urban problems, including *The Unheavenly City Revisited: A Revision of the Unheavenly City* (Scott, Foresman, 1974).

DAVID L. BAZELON is a senior circuit judge of the United States Court of Appeals for the District of Columbia circuit and a lecturer of psychiatry at The Johns Hopkins University School of Medicine. He is the author of *Questioning Authority: Justice and Criminal Law* (Alfred A. Knopf, 1988).

ROBERT N. BELLAH is the Ford Professor of Sociology and Comparative Studies at the University of California, Berkeley.

LESTER R. BROWN is the founder, president, and senior researcher at the Worldwatch Institute in Washington, D.C., an independent think tank whose mission is to analyze world conditions and problems such as famine, overpopulation, and scarcity of natural resources. His publications include *The Twenty-ninth Day: Accommodating Human Needs and Numbers to the Earth's Resources* (W. W. Norton, 1978) and *Building a Sustainable Society* (W. W. Norton, 1981).

NOAM CHOMSKY is an institute professor in the Department of Linguistics and Philosophy at the Massachusetts Institute of Technology, where he has been teaching since 1976. He is the recipient of the 1984 American Psychological Association Distinguished Scientific Contribution Award and the author of *Necessary Illusions: Thought Control in Democratic Societies* (South End Press, 1989) and *Deterring Democracy* (Verso Publications, 1991).

ALEXANDER COCKBURN is the author of the "Beat the Devil" column in *The Nation*.

JOHN J. DiIULIO, JR., is an associate professor of politics and public affairs at Princeton University. His most recent book is *No Escape: The Future of American Corrections* (Basic Books, 1991).

PETER DREIER is the director of housing at the Boston Redevelopment Authority and a board member of the National Low-Income Housing Coalition.

DINESH D'SOUZA, a former senior domestic policy analyst at the White House during the Reagan administration, is the John M. Olin Research Fellow at the American Enterprise Institute and the editor of *Crisis*, a Catholic monthly magazine of news and opinion. He is the author of *Illiberal Education: The Politics of Race and Sex on Campus* (Vintage Books, 1991).

TROY DUSTER is a professor of sociology at the University of California, Berkeley.

THOMAS BYRNE EDSALL is a political reporter for *The Washington Post*. He is the author of *Chain Reaction: The Impact of Race, Rights, and Taxes on American Politics* (W. W. Norton, 1991).

BARBARA EHRENREICH, a writer and a contributing editor to *Ms.* magazine, is a fellow for the Institute for Policy Studies and an associate fellow for the New York Institute for the Humanities. An outspoken feminist and socialist party leader, she has authored and coauthored numerous books and articles, including *The Worst Years of Our Lives: Irreverent Notes from a Decade of Greed* (Pantheon Books, 1990).

DEIRDRE ENGLISH is a free-lance writer and lecturer. A feminist and a former executive editor of *Mother Jones*, she has collaborated with Barbara Ehrenreich on several books, including *Complaints and Disorders: The Sexual Politics of Sickness* (Feminist Press, 1973) and *For Her Own Good: 150 Years of the Experts' Advice to Women* (Doubleday, 1978).

HENRY FAIRLIE, a Londoner who has lived in the United States for many years, is a keen observer of British and American politics. His comments are frequently found in articles and books such as *The Spoiled Child of the Western World: The Miscarriage of the American Idea in Our Time* (Doubleday, 1975) and *The Seven Deadly Sins Today* (University of Notre Dame Press, 1978).

MARILYN FRENCH is a novelist, educator, and literary scholar, and she has taught at Harvard University, Hofstra University, and College of the Holy Cross. Now a full-time writer, she is the author of *The Women's Room* (Summit Books, 1977), which has become one of the major novels of the feminist movement, and *Beyond Power: On Women, Men, and Morals* (Summit Books, 1986).

MILTON FRIEDMAN, a former chairman of the president's Council of Economic Advisors, is a senior research fellow at the Hoover Institute, Stanford University, and the recipient of the 1976 Nobel Memorial Prize in Economic Science. His publications include *Free to Choose: A Personal Statement* (Harcourt Brace Jovanovich, 1980) and *Tyranny of the Status Quo* (Harcourt Brace Jovanovich, 1984), both coauthored with Rose Friedman.

GEORGE GILDER is a senior fellow of the Hudson Institute, a contributing editor for *Forbes* magazine, and the author of several books, including *Wealth and Poverty* (Bantam Books, 1982) and *Microcosm* (Simon & Schuster, 1989).

PHILIP L. HARVEY is the author of the "Forgotten Agenda: American Social Policy" column for the *Los Angeles Times*. He is the author of *Securing the Right to Employment: Social Welfare Policy and the Unemployment in the United States* (Princeton University Press, 1989).

EDWARD S. HERMAN is a professor emeritus of finance at the University of Pennsylvania Wharton School of Business. His publications include *The Terrorism Industry: The Experts and Institutions that Shape Our View of Terror* (Pantheon Books, 1989).

JOHN E. JACOB is the president and chief executive officer of the National Urban League, Inc., in New York City.

MICHAEL LEVIN is a professor of philosophy at City College, City University of New York. He has published books and articles that deal with the relation between the mind and the body, feminism, and a number of other social issues.

GLENN C. LOURY is a professor of public policy in the John F. Kennedy School of Government at Harvard University and an associate editor of the *Journal of Urban Economics*. He is the recipient of the 1987 Winner Leavy Award for Excellence in Free Enterprise Education and the author of *Achieving the Dream* (The Heritage Foundation, 1990).

THEODORE R. MARMOR is a professor of public management and political science in the Institution for Social and Policy Studies at Yale University. His research interest in the American version of the welfare state is reflected in his many publications. He is the coauthor, with Jerry L. Mashaw, of *Social Security: Beyond the Rhetoric of Crisis* (Princeton University Press, 1988).

JERRY L. MASHAW, a lawyer and educator, is the William Nelson Cromwell Professor at the Yale University School of Law and a consultant to the Center of Administration Justice. He is a former editor in chief of the *Tulane Law Review,* the author of *Due Process in the Administrative State* (Yale University Press, 1985), and the coauthor, with David L. Harfst, of *The Struggle for Auto Safety* (Harvard University Press, 1990).

WERNER MEYER-LARSEN is a journalist for the German news magazine *Der Spiegel.*

CLAUDIA MILLS is a graduate of Wellesley College and Princeton University and a doctoral student in philosophy at the University of Maryland. She is the author of *The Moral Foundations of Civil Rights* (Rowman & Littlefield, 1986).

GRETCHEN MORGENSON is a senior editor of *Forbes* magazine.

ROBERT POLLIN is an associate professor of economics at the University of California, Riverside. He is on the national steering committee of the Union for Radical Political Economics (URPE).

DAVID POPENOE is a professor of sociology and an associate dean for the social sciences at Rutgers University. He is the author of *Disturbing the Nest: Sweden and the Decline of Families in Modern Societies* (Aldine de Gruyter, 1988).

JEFFREY H. REIMAN is a professor of criminal justice at American University in Washington, D.C. He is a member of the American Society of Criminology and the American Philosophical Association. His publications include *In Defense of Political Philosophy* (Harper & Row, 1972) and *The Police in Society* (Lexington, 1974).

WILLIAM A. RUSHER, a former publisher of the *National Review*, is a senior fellow at the Claremont Institute for the Study of Statesmanship and Political Philosophy, which is a research and education institution that focuses on contemporary issues in Asian studies, American history, political philosophy, modern economics, and foreign policy.

WILLIAM RYAN is a professor in the Department of Psychology at Boston College and a consultant in the fields of mental health, community planning, and social problems. His publications include *Distress in the City* (UPB, 1969).

FELICE N. SCHWARTZ is the president and founder of Catalyst, which is a not-for-profit research and advisory organization that works with corporations to foster the career and leadership development of women.

HERMAN SCHWARTZ is a professor of law in the Washington College of Law at American University and the director of the William O. Douglas Inquiry into the State of Individual Freedom.

JULIAN L. SIMON is a professor of economics and business administration at the University of Maryland. His publications include *The Ultimate Resource* (Princeton University Press, 1982), *Population Matters: People, Resources, Environment, and Immigration* (Transaction Publishers, 1990), and *The Economic Consequences of Immigration* (Basil Blackwell, 1989).

JUDITH STACEY is a professor in the Department of Sociology at the University of California, Davis. She is a coeditor, with Susan Bereaud and Joan Daniels, of *And Jill Came Tumbling After: Sexism in American Education* (Dell Publishing, 1974) and the author of *Patriarchy and Socialist Revolution in China* (University of California Press, 1983).

SHELBY STEELE is an associate professor of English at San Jose State University in San Jose, California.

HERBERT STEIN is a senior fellow at the American Enterprise Institute for Public Policy Research and a member of the board of contributors of the *Wall Street Journal*. His publications include *Presidential Economics* (Simon & Schuster, 1985), *Governing the Five Trillion Dollar Economy: A Twentieth Century Fund Essay* (Oxford University Press, 1989), and *The Fiscal Revolution in America* (AEI Press, 1990).

CATHARINE R. STIMPSON is the dean of the graduate college at Rutgers University and a former president of the Modern Language Association. Her publications include *Where the Meanings Are* (Methuen, 1988).

WILLIAM TUCKER, a writer and social critic, is a staff writer for *Forbes* magazine. His publications include *The Excluded Americans: Homelessness and Housing Policies* (Regnery Gateway, 1989).

DAVID VOGEL is a professor of business administration in the Haas School of Business at the University of California, Berkeley. He is the author of *Fluctuating Fortunes: The Political Power of Business in America* (Basic Books, 1989).

MURRAY WEIDENBAUM is the Mallinckrodt Distinguished University Professor and the director of the Center for the Study of American Business at Washington University in St. Louis, Missouri. His publications include *Public Policy Toward Corporate Takeovers* (Transaction Publishers, 1987), coedited with Kenneth Chilton.

JAMES Q. WILSON is the James Collins Professor of Management and Public Policy at the University of California, Los Angeles, where he has been teaching since 1985. Previously he was the Henry Lee Shattuck Professor of Government at Harvard University for many years. He is the chairman of the board of directors of the Police Foundation and a member of the American Academy of Arts and Sciences. His publications include *Bureaucracy: What Government Agencies Do and Why They Do It* (Basic Books, 1989).

INDEX

abortion, 23–24

Abram, Morris, 191, 192, 194

academic standards, lowering of, multicultural education and, 13–14

achievement motivation, lack of, poverty and, 156

acid rain, 339

admissions policies, college, affirmative action and, 9, 14–15, 189

affirmative action: colleges and, 6, 8, 13, 14–15, 17; controversy over, 184–194

affordable housing, 203, 204, 208, 209

aggression, as male trait, 64

agriculture, ecology and, 341–342

Aid to Families with Dependent Children (AFDC), 201, 254, 255, 256, 257–258, 259

AIDS, 305, 359

air pollution, 339, 340, 342

alimony, 73

American Civil Liberties Union, 10

"Andrea Del Sarto" (Browning), 93, 94

apartheid, academic, 8–9

Appelbaum, Richard, on homelessness, 198–206

baby boomers, 80–81, 235, 307

Bakke, Alan, 192, 194

Banfield, Edward, 134, 135; on the future of the lower class, 150–154

Bazelon, David L., on solving the nightmare of street crime, 325–331

Bellah, Robert H., et al., on individualism and commitment in American life, 38–46

Bennett, William 300, 304

Berkman v. NYFD, 60–61, 62

Big Brotherism, 305

big business: 368; and government, controversy over, 222–244

Bill of Rights, 305

biological diversity, decline in, 340–341

blacks: and controversy over affirmative action, 184–194; crime and, 284–285; self-help by, as solution to racial inequality, controversy over, 166–180; *see also,* minorities

bracket creep, 235

Brown, Lester R., 347; on world population growth, 338–346

Browning, Robert, 93

budget deficit, federal, 356, 363

Bureau of Labor Statistics (BLS), living standard statistics of, 138–139

Burger, Warren, 192, 193, 325

Bush, George, 25, 26, 101, 198, 356; housing policy of, 202–203, 204, 205

Business Roundtable, 237

Campaign Reform Act of 1971, 238

Capital gains, tax on, 242

capitalism, 369; controversy over success of, 264–276; and distribution of wealth, 124, 131–132, 135, 140; women's movement and, 73–74

career-and-family working women on the "Mommy track," 81–84, 86, 87

carrying capacity, of the Earth, 339–340, 343

central planning, 348, 349; socialism and, 269–270

Chamber of Commerce, 237

Chancellor, John, 356, 361

Chapter One remedial education, 175, 178

Chavez, Linda, 191, 194

chemicals, health and, 294

child care, working women and, 79, 84, 115

child support, 73, 250

children, effect of family breakup on, 109, 110, 111

Chomsky, Noam, on liberal bias in the media, 28–33

Churchill, Winston, 179–180

civil freedom, 264

civil rights, 10, 168, 169, 170, 174, 231, 305

Civil Rights Act, 60, 70, 97, 98, 101

Clancey, Maura, 25–26

class and status, discrepancy between, 162

Clean Air Act, 243

Cockburn, Alexander, 23; on success of capitalism, 268–276

cohabitation, 113, 249

Cold War, end of, 338, 339

Common Cause, 225, 229–230

community, feudal idea of, 52

community action groups, 153

Community Mental Health Act of 1963, 200

compassion, argument for, and legalization of drugs, 303–304

compensatory education, 157

consistency, argument from, and legalization of drugs, 301–302

Consumer Product Safety Commission, 237

consumerism, individualism and, 45, 46, 50

convertibility, currency, capitalism and, 267

coopting the experts, 32

crime, 361, 369; controversy over incapacitation as solution to, 318–331; drugs and, 300, 301, 307; street vs. white-collar, controversy over impact of, 282–295

culture of poverty, controversy over, 150–162

custom, release from, individualism and, 50–51

death penalty, 327
defense spending, 365
deforestation, 338, 339, 340, 342, 344, 345, 347
deindustrialization, 283
deinstitutionalization: of marriage, 108; of the mentally ill, 200
Democracy in America (de Tocqueville), 39
dependency, welfare and, 256–259
Derian, Jean-Claude, 358–359
desertification, 338, 339, 340, 344
de Tocqueville, Alexis, 39, 45
Di Iulio, John J., on the impact of inner-city crime, 282–287
diminishing return, law of, 350
distribution of wealth: capitalism and, 124–135, 265, 271, 359; controversy over inequality of, 222–224
diversity, affirmative action and, 185, 186
divorce, 66, 67, 72, 73, 108, 113, 114, 115; welfare and, 249, 250
domination, sexuality and, 93, 95
Dreier, Peter, on homelessness, 198–206
dropouts, high school, 174, 176, 177
drugs, controversy over legalization of, 300–314
D'Souza, Dinesh, on multicultural education, 4–11
Du Bois, W. E. B., 169, 170
Duster, Troy, on multicultural education, 12–18

earning capacity utilization rates, 133
Earth Day, 338, 339
economic freedom, 264
economic inequality, controversy over benefits of, 124–146
economics, ecology and, 339–340
Edsall, Thomas Byrne, on government and big business, 222–232
education, 360; blacks and, 169–170; controversy over multicultural, 4–18; controversy over sexual harassment and, 92–101; decline of American, 360–361; poverty and, 150, 155, 157, 250
Efron, Edith, 24–25
Ehrenreich, Barbara, 251; on the "mommy track" for working women, 85–88
English, Deirdre, 114; on the "mommy track" for working women, 85–88
enterprise zones, 204
entitlements, 248
entrepreneurs, 126, 127–129, 130
environmental issues, and controversy over global population growth, 338–346
Environmental Protection Agency (EPA), 237, 241, 243, 340
environmental sexual harassment, 97, 100
Equal Employment Opportunity Commission (EEOC), 60, 61, 94, 97, 98, 99, 185, 191

Equal Pay Act, 70
equal protection, 70, 191
Equal Rights Amendment, 61, 114
equality, "Fair Play" vs. "Fair Shares" viewpoints on, 136–146
ethnic studies, 7
exclusionary zoning, 209
extended families, 113
externally caused poverty, 152
extinction, species, 339, 341

faculty, radical multicultural education and, 16
"Fair Play" vs. "Fair Shares" viewpoints, on equality, 136–146
Fairlie, Henry, on the fiction of "mass man," 47–54
family: controversy over breakdown of, 106–117, 134, 172; feminism and, 66–67
fathers, absent, 109, 115, 134, 156, 250
Federal Reserve Bank, 206
Federal Trade Commission, 237
Feminine Mystique, The (Friedan), 70
feminism, 92, 167; controversy over, 60–74; and family policy, 112–117
Ferraro, Geraldine, 25–26
fictive kin support networks, 113
Five Thousand American Families (Morgan), 143
flexibility, need for, working women and, 83–84
food stamps, 248, 249, 254, 259
Fordism, 273
Foster-Carter, Aiden, 272
Fourteenth Amendment, 70, 193
Fourth Amendment, 313
free market system: controversy over success of, 264–278; feminism and, 65–66
freedom: feminism and, 60–67; individualism and, 38, 43
French, Marilyn, on feminism, 68–74
Friedman, Milton, on success of capitalism, 264–267
"friendly visitor" system, 152
Fullilove v. Klutznick, 190, 192, 194
Fullinwider, Robert, 301, 304
future, lower class lack of orientation to, 134
Future Shock (Toffler), 356

gay rights, 167
Genovese, Eugene, 10–11
gentrification, 200, 202
Gilder, George, on economic inequality, 124–135
glass ceiling, for working women, 80, 87
Gordon, Diana, 328, 330
government: and big business, controversy over, 222–244; family policy and, 110–111; interventionism of, capitalism and, 270–273
grass-roots lobbying, 225, 226–227, 228, 229, 230

Great Depression, 282, 366
Great Society, 167, 174, 243, 259
Great U-Turn, The (Bennett and Bluestone), 201
greenhouse effect, 339
gross national product (GNP), growth of U.S., 363–369

habits of the heart, American character and, 39
"hard-core" poor, 151
Harvey, Philip L., on welfare, 253–259
Head Start, 175, 178
Herman, Edward S., on liberal bias in the media, 28–33
Hill, Anita, 97
Hoch, Charles, 212–213
homelessness, 175, 178, 359, 360; controversy over, 198–215
homogenization of the masses, individualism and, 47–54
housing regulations, homelessness and, 207–215
Humphrey, Hubert, 24, 25, 27
Hunter, Robert, 151
hyperinflation, 272

I, Rigoberta Menchu, 7–8
illegitimate births, welfare and, 250, 257, 258
immigrants, economic inequality and, 125, 126–127, 132
incapacitation, controversy over, as solution to crime problem, 318–331
individualism: controversy over excessive, 38–54; and breakup of family, 108–109, 111
inequality, racial, black self-help as solution to, controversy over, 166–180
infant mortality, black, 190
inflation, 126, 222, 235, 239, 268, 363, 366
information, social control of, 275–276
inner-city crime vs. street crime, controversy over impact of, 282–295
internally caused poverty, 152
International Monetary Fund, 268
investment, social control of, 275

Jacklin, Carol N., 64
Jacob, John E., on the future of black America, 173–180
Jaggar, Alison, 10
Japan, and America, 357–358, 364
Jarvis, Howard, 212
Jefferson, Thomas, 136
Jencks, Christopher, 126, 135
Jim Crow, 172, 193
Job Corps, 175
Johnson, Andrew, 193
Johnson, Lyndon, 228, 243, 248, 359
Jordan, Vernon, 326

junk bonds, 358

Kagan, Donald, 5
Kann, Mark, 213
Kaplan, John, 302–303, 309
Karsarda, John, 200
Kearns, David, 177
Kelley, Nick, 127–129
Kemp, Jack, 203, 204
Kennedy, Donald, 8
Kennedy, Edward, 362
Kennedy, John, 248, 361
Kennedy, Joseph, 205
Kennedy, Paul, 362
Kerner Commission, 177
King, Martin Luther, 191, 193, 194
King, William 7–8
King v. Smith, 249
kinship, feminization of, 115
Klein, Frieda, 100, 101
Koch, Edward, 130, 190, 327
"Kramer versus Kramer," 115
Kristol, Irving, 124, 135

labor market, social control of, 275
Larry, R. Heath, 224
Law Enforcement Assistance Administration, 324
Lederman, Leon, 348
legalization of drugs, controversy over, 300–314
Lentricchia, Frank, 4
Lesser Life, A (Hewlett), 85
Levin, Michael, on feminism, 60–67
Levinson, Andrew, 139
Lewis, Bernard, 9
Lewis, Hylan, 160
Lewis, Oscar, 151
liberal arts education, controversy over multiculturalism in, 4–18
liberal bias, in the media, controversy over, 22–33
Lichter, S. Robert, 23–24
life expectancy, black, 190
Light, Ivan, 135
Lindbeck, Assa, 211–212
living standards, of Bureau of Labor Statistics, 138–139
Livy, 46
lobbying, 225, 226–227, 228, 229, 230, 237, 240
Losing Ground (Murray), 256–258
Loury, Glenn C., on black self-help as solution to racial inequality, 166–172
lower class, controversy over culture of poverty in, 150–162
Luce, Henry, 356, 359
Lund, Leonard, 361

Maccoby, Eleanor E., 64
Makal, Mahmut, 51–52
Male and Female (Mead), 64
male dominance, universality of, 64
Malthus, Thomas Robert, 343, 344, 349, 350
Marmor, Theodore R., on welfare, 253
marriage, traditional, 106; changes in, 107, 114; work and, 133–134
Marshall, Thurgood, 191, 193
Marvell, Andrew, 92–93
Marx, Karl, 243
masculine principle, 68
Mashaw, Jerry L., on welfare, 253–259
"mass man," fiction of, 47–54
maternity leave, 78–79, 80, 83, 85
matrilineal families, 113
McCarthy, Joseph, 5
McGovern, George, 227
McKissick, Floyd, 169
McKnight, John L., 168
me decade, 1980s as, 198
me generation, 45
Mead, George Herbert, 53
Mead, Margaret, 64
media, controversy over liberal bias in, 22–33
Medicaid, 129, 175, 259
Medicare, 223
Mendel, Gregor, 343
mentally ill, deinstitutionalization of, 200
meritocracy: colleges as, 15–16; equality and, 136, 138
Meritor Savings Bank v. Vinson, 92, 98
Meyer-Larsen, Werner, on the breakdown of America's socioeconomic system, 356–362
Mickey Leland Housing Assistance Act, 205
middle class, housing crisis and, 199–200
Middle Class Radicalism in Santa Monica (Kann), 212
Milken, Michael, 358
Miller, Walter, 161
Mills, C. Wright, 49
Mills, Claudia, on the legalization of drugs, 300–306
Minarek, Joseph, 126
minorities: and controversy over multicultural education, 4–18; family structures of, 113, 114; *see also,* blacks
Mitchell, John, 290
"mommy track" for working women, controversy over, 78–88
Mondale, Walter, 25–26
monetary system, stable, capitalism and, 265, 266–267
monopolies, 368
Montreal Accord, 345
Morgan, James, 143
Morgensen, Gretchen, on sexual harassment, 97–101
Moynihan, Daniel Patrick, 113, 249

multicultural education, controversy over, 4–18
multiproblem poor, 155, 156
Murray, Charles, 256–258

Nadelman, Ethan A., 301
Nader, Ralph, 225, 294
National Association for the Advancement of Colored People, 169
National Comprehensive Housing Act, 205
National Environmental Policy Act, 238
National Federation of Independent Business, 237
National Labor Relations Board, 230, 238
National Organization for Women, 70
National Safety Council, 293
National Traffic and Motor Vehicle Safety Act, 237
"Natural Resources" (Rich), 96
New Consensus on Family and Welfare, The, 250
New Deal, 233, 366
New Homeless and Old: Community and the Skid Row Hotel (Hoch and Slayton), 212–213
New Jersey Welfare Rights Organization v. Cahill, 249
News Twisters, The (Efron), 24–25
Nisbet, Robert, 52
Nitze, Paul, 272
Nixon, Richard, 24, 25, 27, 226, 227, 243
nuclear family, 106–107, 109–110

occupational health and safety, 288–295
Occupational Safety and Health Administration (OSHA), 227, 230, 238
O'Connor, Sandra Day, 191–192
Organization for Economic Cooperation and Development (OECD), 254
organized crime, 326
Ostrowski, James, 304
ozone, atmospheric, hole in, 339, 345

parent deficit, 109
parental leave, 84
Parini, Jay, 9
parole, 322, 329
part-time employment, for working women, 83
paternalism, argument against, and legalization of drugs, 302–303
patriarchy, 64, 66, 69, 70, 110, 112
peace dividend, 206
peacekeeper, United Nations as, 345
Pendleton, Clarence, 191, 193
Persian Gulf, war in, 206, 345, 356
Person, Ethel Spector, 93
personal freedom, 264
Peter Principle, 184

Pierce, Samuel, 204
Piven, Francis Fox, 251
plateauing, career, working women and, 78
Plessy v. Ferguson, 191, 193
pluralism, affirmative action and, 185
political action committees (PACs), 229, 230, 231, 236, 241
political freedom, 264
political parties, collapse of, 224, 225–227
politics, local, individualism and, 39
Pollin, Robert, on success of capitalism, 268–276
Pope John Paul II, plot to assassinate, 30, 32
Popenoe, David, on the breakup of the family, 106–111
population growth, global, controversy over, 338–352
pork-barrel lobbying, 225
postmodern families, 112–117
poverty, 360, 361, 369; blacks and, 166, 174, 175, 176, 190, 282, 283; children and, 201, 357; controversy over culture of, 150n162; crime and, 320, 321, 331; feminization of, 71–72; health and, 294–295; nature of, 132–135; welfare and, 248, 249, 250, 257, 258
Powell, Lewis, 32
Pratt, Edmund, 79
preferential treatment, affirmative action as, 184–188
present-oriented, culture of poverty as, 134, 150, 151
prison, controversy over, as solution to crime, 318–331
private property, captitalism and, 265, 266
Progressive Era, 233
Prohibition, 301, 305
proportional representation, in college admissions policies, 8, 14–15
Proposition 13, California's, 212
Public Interest Health Research Group, 294

quid pro quo sexual harassment, 97
quotas: gender, 61, 66; racial, 185, 186, 192

racial inequality, black self-help as solution to, controversy over, 166–180
racism, 170, 174, 331, 361; affirmative action and, 184, 189, 193; education and, 5, 8, 9, 10, 12–18
"rational man" theory of crime, 328
Rayburn, Sam, 228
Reagan, Ronald, 25, 26, 27, 32, 33, 62, 114, 178, 238, 239, 241, 243, 248, 271, 357, 362, 365; affirmative action and 189, 190, 192; government, big business, and, 222, 223, 232; housing policy of, 202, 204, 207
recession, 235, 239, 240, 339, 365, 366
recidivism, 323

recycling, 339, 346
Rehnquist, William, 192
Reich, Robert, 201
Reiman, Jeffrey H., on white-collar crime, 288–295
religious leadership, black, 171
religious traditions, individualism and, 39, 51
rental housing, lack of, 200, 202, 205, 209, 210, 211
resident-controlled housing, 204
Revenue Act of 1981, 239, 242
reverse discrimination, affirmative action as, 185
Ricardo, David, 124
Rich, Adrienne, 96
Richards, David A. J., 302
Road to Serfdom, The (Hayek), 366
Robinson, Michael, 25–26
Rockefeller drug law, New York's, 328
Rodman, Hyman, 159–160
Roosevelt, Franklin, 230, 248
Rothman, Stanley, 23–24
Rudin, Lewis, 359
Rusche, Sue, 301
Rusher, William, on liberal bias in the media, 22–27
Ryan, William: on blaming the victims of poverty, 155–162; on economic inequality, 136–146

safety, worker, 288–295
Samuelson, Paul, 140
saving, definition of, 126
savings and loan industry, bailout of, 198, 203, 206, 358
Schmoke, Kurt, 300, 304–305
Schwartz, Felice N., on the "mommy track" for working women, 78–84; reaction to views of, 85–88
Schwartz, Herman, on affirmative action, 189–194
Schweiker, Richard, 292
search and seizure, unreasonable, 313
Sedgwick, Eve, 10
self-consciousness, individualism and, 52–53
self-help, black, as solution to racial inequality, controversy over, 166–180
serial families, 108
service economy, U.S., 200, 201
Sex, Drugs, Death, and the Law (Richards), 302
sex discrimination, 60–61, 62
sexism, 82, 83; education and, 5, 8, 9
sexual harassment, controversy over, 92–101
Seymour, Whitney North, 327
Shaiken, Harley, 273
Shalala, Donna, 5
Shevchenko, Arkady, 32
Shinnar, Schlomo and Reuel, 319–320

Sifton, Charles, 60
Silberman, Charles, 326
single-parent families, 108, 175, 285–286, 322
single-room occupancy hotels (SROs), 212–213
Slayton, Robert, 212–213
Slovenko, Ralph, 328
Smith, Adam, 124, 268, 369
Smith, Peter, 213
Smithey, Wayne, 228
snob zoning, 203
Snyder, Mitch, 198
social mobility, equal opportunity and, 141–143
Social Security, 129, 143, 223, 227, 257, 360
socialism, 124, 276
socioeconomic system, controversy over breakdown of America's, 356–369
soil erosion, 339, 340, 341, 347
spatial ability, gender differences in, 65
Sprague, Peter, 130–131
Stacey, Judith, on the postmodern family, 112–117
status and class, discrepancy between, 162
Steele, Shelby, on affirmative action, 184–188
Stein, Herbert, on the U.S. economy, 363–369
stepfamilies, 108
Stephen, James Fitzjames, 321
Sterling, Claire, 32
Stockman, David, 239
street crime, 326; vs. inner-city crime, controversy over impact of, 282–295
streetcar suburb, 213–214
Stimpson, Catharine R., on sexual harassment, 92–96
supermarkets, "mass man" and, 48–50
superpower, America as, 356, 357
Supplemental Security Income (SSI), 227, 259
Supreme Court, 63, 70, 115, 226, 249; affirmative action and, 190, 191, 192; sexual harassment and, 92, 98
surgery, unnecessary, 294
sustainable development, 339, 341, 343, 344

Taft-Hartley Act of 1947, 368
Tax Reform Act of 1986, 242
tax subsidy, for homeowners, 203, 205
Tawney, R. H., 145
teflon coating, Ronald Reagan's, 26, 27
Thernstrom, Stephan, 5–6
Thomas, Clarence, 97, 191
Thompson, Becky, 5
Thurow, Lester, 129, 223; on world population growth, 338–346
Tiger, Lionel, 135

Title VII of the Civil Rights Act of 1964, 60, 70, 97, 98, 101
Toffler, Alvin, 356
totalitarianism, 348; controversy over collapse of, 264–276
trade deficit, U.S., 357–358, 359, 363
training programs, employment, 251
transfer payments, 143, 248, 256, 369
tribalism, multicultural education and, 13
Truly Disadvantaged: The Inner City, the Underclass, and Public Policy, The (Wilson), 283–284
Truman, Harry, 248
Tucker, William, 207–215
turnover, working women and, 78

unaffordable, myth of welfare as, 254–255
underclass, inner-city, 283, 286, 326, 361, 369
unearned income, 129–130
unemployment, 174, 175, 177, 178, 222, 320, 323; inner-city, 283, 285, 286; welfare and, 249, 257, 258–259
Unheavenly City, The (Banfield), 134, 150–154
unions, labor, 368
United Jewish Organizations v. Carey, 192
United Nations, 345
United Steelworkers of America v. Weber, 192
Urban League, 173–180, 326
urban renewal, 213
U.S. government, control of media by, 28–33
USDA v. Moreno, 249

value system, individualism and, 39–42
victim-focused identity, of blacks, affirmative action and, 187–188
Vietnam War, 227, 300, 359
village life, romantic idealization of, 51–52
Vogel, David, on government and big business, 233–244
Von Leiberg, Justus, 343
vouchers, housing, 204, 205, 208

Walker, Charles E., 228
Wallace, George, 24, 27
War on Poverty, 258
water pollution, 340, 341, 342
Watergate scandal, 224, 227, 241
wealth, distribution of: capitalism and, 124–135, 265, 271, 359; controversy over inequality of, 222–224
Wealth of Nations, The (Smith), 124
Webb, Susan, 98
Weber v. Aetna Casualty and Surety Company, 249
Weidenbaum, Murray, on welfare, 248–252
Weitzman, Lenore, 73
welfare, 126, 143, 150, 152, 154, 170, 172, 283, 284; controversy over, 248–259

Wertheimer, Fred, 230
Where Do We Go From Here: Chaos or Community? (King), 171
White, Robert, 32
white-collar crime, 326; vs. street crime, controversy over, 282–295
Whyte, William, 228
Wicker, Tom, 330
Wiesendanger, Hans, 357
Wilkins, Roy, 191, 193
Will, George, 180
Wilson, James Q., 327–328; on incapacitation as the solution to crime, 318–324; on the legalization of drugs, 307–314
Wilson, William Julius, 283–284
Winthrop, John, 44
Wisotsky, Steven, 302
Wolfe, Alan, 117
Wolfe, Sidney, 294
Wolfgang, Marvin, 318, 319

Woods, Robert A., 153
Woodson, Robert, 170
Wooster, Martin Morse, 207
worker safety, 288–295
workfare, 251
Working Class Majority, The (Levinson), 139
Working Seminar on Family and American Welfare Policy, 251
working women: controversy over "mommy track" for, 78–88; family breakup and, 109, 111, 115
workplace, sexual harassment in, 97–101
World Bank, 268
Wright, Quincy, 352

Zabian, Michael, 126–127, 129, 130
Zen Buddhism, 46
Zimbalist, Andrew, 269–270
zoning laws, homelessness and, 203, 209, 213, 214
Zuk, Gary, 352